THE WARS OF RECONSTRUCTION

*Year of Meteors: Stephen Douglas, Abraham Lincoln, and the
Election That Brought on the Civil War*

Death or Liberty: African Americans and Revolutionary America

*Rebels, Reformers, and Revolutionaries: Collected Essays
and Second Thoughts*

He Shall Go Out Free: The Lives of Denmark Vesey

*Gabriel's Rebellion: The Virginia Slave Conspiracies
of 1800 and 1802*

Charles Fenton Mercer and the Trial of National Conservatism

The Atlantic World: A History, 1400–1888 (with Alison Games,
Kris Lane, and Donald R. Wright)

THE WARS OF RECONSTRUCTION

*The Brief, Violent History of America's
Most Progressive Era*

DOUGLAS R. EGERTON

BLOOMSBURY PRESS
New York   London   New Delhi   Sydney

Published by Bloomsbury Press, New York

All papers used by Bloomsbury Press are natural, recyclable products made from wood grown in well-managed forests. The manufacturing processes conform to the environmental regulations of the country of origin.

LIBRARY OF CONGRESS CATALOGING-IN-PUBLICATION DATA

Egerton, Douglas R.
The wars of Reconstruction : the brief, violent history of America's most progressive era / Douglas R. Egerton. —First U.S. edition.
    pages cm
Includes bibliographical references and index.
ISBN 978-1-60819-566-4 (alk. paper)
1. Reconstruction (U.S. history, 1865-1877)   2. United States—Politics and government—1865-1877.   3. United States—Race relations—History—19th century.   I. Title.
E668.E35 2013
973.8—dc23
2013009595

First U.S. Edition 2014

1 3 5 7 9 10 8 6 4 2

Typeset by Westchester Book Group
Printed in the U.S.A. by Thomson-Shore, Inc. Dexter, Michigan

For Leigh

CONTENTS

Robert Vesey's Charleston

"A CITY OF RUINS, of desolation, of vacant houses, of widowed women, of rotting wharves, of deserted warehouses, of acres of pitiful and voiceful barrenness" was how one visitor described Charleston at the close of the Civil War. But in view of the fact that the fighting had begun there, when shore batteries opened fire on Fort Sumter at four thirty A.M. on April 12, 1861, the president thought the bloody conflict should conclude there as well. Abraham Lincoln wished to stage a symbolic pageant of liberty in the state that had been home to roughly four hundred thousand enslaved Americans and in what remained a predominantly black city. In late March 1865, Secretary of War Edwin M. Stanton cabled the president regarding "suitable military arrangements for the occasion." Stanton suggested inviting abolitionists Wendell Phillips and Henry Ward Beecher. Stanton also thought it appropriate to have now—major general Robert Anderson unfurl over Fort Sumter the same banner he had been forced to lower exactly four years earlier. Lincoln agreed and encouraged Stanton also to invite William Lloyd Garrison, the editor of Boston's uncompromising antislavery newspaper, *The Liberator*; Lieutenant George Thompson Garrison was furloughed so that he might join his father in their first-ever trip to Charleston. Because the War Department wished to include black activists and soldiers, Major Martin R. Delany, the Virginia-born freeman who was the army's first African American field officer, was invited, as was Lieutenant Robert Smalls, the former Carolina slave and ship's pilot who had sailed a stolen Confederate transport craft, the *Planter*, out of Charleston Harbor. Then somebody remembered to invite African American carpenter Robert Vesey Sr., the son of black abolitionist Denmark Vesey, who had been hanged by city authorities in the summer of 1822.[1]

The city had been captured just one month earlier, on February 18. Fittingly, the first soldiers into the city were black troops, who filed into what had been the bastion of secession and proslavery militancy singing John Brown's "truth goes marching on." Anxious white residents remained indoors, but Charleston's blacks poured into Meeting and King streets to greet their liberators. One elderly woman threw down her crutch, joyfully shouting that she no longer needed it because the day of jubilee had arrived at last. Major Delany promptly set about filling his depleted ranks with former bondmen, telling potential recruits that as Confederate president Jefferson Davis still remained in control of Richmond, a freedman could yet "vindicate his manhood by becoming a soldier, and with his own stout arm battle for the emancipation of his race." So many young men stepped forward, one journalist marveled, that "the recruiting officers in Charleston are head over heels in business." Enough black Charlestonians "flock[ed] to the United States flag" that Delany was able to restructure his battered 103rd and 104th regiments and start organization of the 105th Regiment of United States Colored Troops (USCT).[2]

On March 29, black Charlestonians took to the streets again in the largest parade the city had seen since, ironically, the 1850 death of proslavery politician John C. Calhoun. Journalists placed the number of marchers at above four thousand, while another ten thousand spectators cheered them on. Soldiers from the Twenty-first Regiment of USCT led the way, followed by black artisans and tradesmen—one of them presumably Robert Vesey—who snaked through the city's streets in a procession of several miles. Observers wept openly as a mule-drawn cart passed by, carrying two women on the way to a mock slave auction and trailed by a slave coffle of sixty chained men. Behind the last came a caisson containing a coffin, draped in black and flying a banner announcing SLAVERY IS DEAD. At that juncture the parade grew festive. A "Car of Liberty" transporting thirteen girls dressed in white was followed by hundreds of children recently enrolled in schools established by the Freedmen's Bureau. Some carried signs emblazoned with THE HEROES OF THE WAR: GRANT, SHERMAN, SHERIDAN while others bore placards that read WE KNOW NO CASTE OR COLOR. As before, few whites ventured out to watch the demonstration of freedom and racial pride, and those who did, thought one reporter, looked surly but "had sense enough to keep their thoughts to themselves."[3]

The Fort Sumter rededication ceremony was set for April 14, the anniversary of Anderson's capitulation. By then Davis had abandoned Richmond, pledging to return once Lincoln's government gave up the "impossible task of making slaves of a people resolved to be free." But General Robert E. Lee had surrendered the previous week, and those Carolinians who truly knew what it meant to be enslaved prepared to celebrate the restoration of the stars and stripes atop Sumter's massive flagpole. On the night before the event, General John Porter Hatch hosted a grand ball. To drive home the point that the war had brought the nation full circle, Hatch not only chose the same hall where P. G. T. Beauregard had staged his celebratory gala for southern independence four years earlier; he hired the same caterer and ordered the same dishes served.[4]

The next morning dawned clear, the winds soft. As visitors to the city strolled toward the docks, they could not help noticing how forlorn Charleston appeared. A fire in December 1861 had destroyed a number of homes, which had yet to be repaired; one recently liberated slave assured one dignitary that the arsonist "was de good Jesus hisself." Finally, at eleven, a small flotilla of ships began their passage to the fort. Among them was the *Planter*, once again piloted by Lieutenant Smalls but this time ferrying Major Delany and Robert Vesey, and its deck, one newspaper reported, "black with the colored population of Charleston." To the north of the harbor, those crowding the rails gazed at Sullivan's Island, once the foremost entrepôt for Africans sold into the southern colonies. To the south, they could see Morris Island and what remained of Fort Wagner, where so many soldiers from the black Fifty-fourth

Massachusetts Volunteer Infantry had died. Sumter itself was nearly as shattered. Several years of shelling had reduced three of its five walls to rubble, which desperate Confederate defenders had reshaped into high barriers of debris. The guests scrambled onto a wharf recently constructed on the fort's west angle, and a flight of steps led them down to the parade ground. An honor guard of soldiers, white and black, "the survivors of the assault on Sumter," formed neat lines on either side of the flagstaff.[5]

In the center of the fort, carpenters had constructed a large, diamond-shaped platform festooned with myrtle, evergreens, and flowers. Above that sat a canopy, draped with American flags and tied back with garlands. Just after noon, Major General Anderson and his daughter stepped to the platform, their arrival "the signal for loud and prolonged cheers." After Anderson restored the flag that—as one unforgiving Philadelphia reporter scribbled—"he had lowered at the demand of traitors," the speeches began. Beecher delivered a fiery oration that placed blame for the conflict on a "wholly unprincipled ruling aristocracy who wanted to keep power." Massachusetts senator Henry Wilson earned the cheers of blacks in the audience by reminding white dignitaries that Carolina slaves had "always been loyal to the old flag of the country." African Americans had "proved themselves worthy [of] the great situation in which [they] were placed by the Slaveholders' Rebellion." They had protected American soldiers, and when possible, had joined their ranks. "You know what the old flag means," Wilson shouted, "it means liberty to every man and woman in the country."[6]

That evening, General Quincy Adams Gillmore hosted another dinner. Major General Anderson offered a toast, which was answered by Joseph Holt, judge advocate general of the army. The war was won but the struggle was far from over, Holt warned. If "the knife is to be stayed while there remains a single root of that cancer of slavery which has been eating into the national vitals," he cautioned, "then in vain shall we have expended thousands of millions of treasure, and in vain will the country have offered on the red altars of war the bravest of its sons." Those in attendance cheered, and outside fireworks lit the sky. But just around that hour, at ten fifteen P.M., on that Good Friday evening in Washington, D.C., in an event that was to dramatically alter the nation's increasingly

*The arrival of U.S. troops under General William T. Sherman forced
Confederates to abandon Charleston and Fort Sumter on February 17, 1865.
As the war had begun in the city, President Abraham Lincoln judged
it fitting that a ceremony mark both the fourth anniversary of the fort's 1861
surrender, as well as the dawn of the nation's coming reconstruction.
Courtesy Library of Congress.*

progressive course, an actor and fervent Confederate sympathizer, John
Wilkes Booth, entered the president's box at Ford's Theatre and, with a
single bullet from his derringer, assassinated President Lincoln.[7]

Word of that tragic event arrived in Charleston only the next morning, casting a pall over the festivities. As the city's blacks mourned the
loss of the president, Delany pressed ahead with a planned political rally
designed to bring Carolina's freedmen into the republican fold, inviting
Garrison and Senator Wilson to speak. On their way Garrison, Beecher,
and George Thompson Garrison stopped at St. Philip's Churchyard to
visit Calhoun's grave. The abolitionist stared down at the simple oblong

brick tomb, and placing his hand on its marble top, as if to make sure that his great foe was truly dead, quietly said, "Down into a deeper grave than this slavery has gone, and for it there is no resurrection." The group stood silently for a moment and then strode toward the open-air rally at Citadel Square. There Garrison, who had once been burned in effigy by the city's white residents, found a crowd of black citizens so large that he could not approach the platform. "The pressure and rejoicing was so great that Mr. Garrison was literally borne on the shoulders of those present to the speaker's stand," wrote one observer. Despite the grim news from Washington, the men and women who lifted Garrison toward the podium had reason to believe that their nation was at long last on the right path and, as the martyred president had promised at Gettysburg, was about to witness a new birth of freedom.[8]

To honor those soldiers who had sacrificed their lives so that their country might live, Charleston's black community sought to transform what had been a Confederate prison into a proper cemetery. In the last year of the conflict, white Carolinians had used the Washington Race Course and Jockey Club, which stood just outside of the city boundaries, as a camp for captured Union soldiers. Herded into pens without shelter or adequate food, and despite the efforts of local "negroes and Irish" to "befriend them," the prisoners had perished by the scores, their coffin-less, naked bodies dumped into shallow graves marked only with numbered wooden posts. The first post was marked simply as "No. 1"; the last "257." Shortly after the Fort Sumter ceremony, black churchmen volunteered to clear weeds from the grounds, erect a high fence, and cover the markers with whitewash. Above the old entrance to the club, they wrote in large letters MARTYRS OF THE RACE-COURSE. At nine A.M. on May 1, some ten thousand black Charlestonians visited the graveyard with bouquets of flowers. So many residents attended what in essence was the nation's first Memorial Day, a Manhattan journalist noted, that "there were very few colored adults left in the city." Members of the Twenty-fifth and 104th Colored Troops marched around the graves in double columns, and black children sang the "Star-Spangled Banner." Several officers addressed the crowd, and as the reporter caustically observed, the speakers were "from the recently enslaved and ostracized race," there being an "absolute dearth of white men who truly adopt the doctrines of the Declaration of Independence." Among the few whites in attendance was an elderly mother, clad all in black, who had traveled from Boston in hopes of recovering her son's body.[9]

Just two weeks later, a troubling crack appeared in the facade of black unity, a fissure that was to cause political difficulties over the next decade. Supreme Court Chief Justice Salmon P. Chase became the latest Republican dignitary to visit the city, and black members of Mount Zion Presbyterian Church invited him to speak. As was now typical, so many people turned out that nearly two thousand could not squeeze into the building. Several local leaders were also invited to introduce the chief justice. The first to do so denounced "the old ruling class, who profaned their ballots and showed themselves unfit to be entrusted with the rights of suffrage four or five years ago, and who now seek to resent any attempt to invest with the political franchise the only class here who are loyal alike to the flag and the principles it represents." But Martin Delany adopted a different approach.[10]

Charleston, unlike Delany's native Virginia, was home to a large caste of mixed-race freedmen, who for decades had styled themselves "browns" so as to draw a distinction between themselves and the enslaved black majority. According to one startled journalist, Delany's speech "sought to show that the ill-feeling between the blacks and mulattoes arose out of the betrayal of Denmark Vesey by a mulatto." Vesey's 1822 conspiracy to liberate the city's slaves before sailing for Haiti had in fact been betrayed by two mixed-race Charlestonians, and perhaps the dark-skinned soldier had recently become aware of this crippling division. Quite possibly, the sons of those two men, William B. Penceel and John C. Desverney, who in 1860 had assured seceding planters of the loyalty of their caste, sat in the audience. Not without cause, recently liberated bondmen feared that prosperous freemen like Desverney expected to speak for all African Americans, and they worried that the brown elite might decline to embrace their radical agenda of land reform. But the spring of 1865 was a time for racial healing and empowerment, and Delany's inopportune rant was cut short by the timely arrival of Chase. "Instantly, the vast multitude arose, and cheer after cheer of the most heartfelt enthusiasm showed how well they knew or how deeply grateful they were to their illustrious visitor for his lifelong services to their cause."[11]

Solidarity among *all* African Americans—and not merely those who lived in what had been the Confederacy—was to be critical as the reconstruction of the republic commenced, and as the white resentment witnessed around the city balanced precariously between submission and defiance. Southern whites were painfully aware that they had failed in their bid to create what the *Charleston Mercury* once described as a "slave republic," and many stoically prepared to accept whatever terms Washington intended to demand of them. Few, though, were ready to forgive, making the first moments of Reconstruction critical. When the federal commander in Columbia, South Carolina, instructed Reverend Peter J. Shand, the white pastor of the Trinity Episcopal Church, to lead a prayer for President Andrew Johnson from the Episcopalian Book of Common Prayer, Shand at first refused. When warned that an officer would visit the church that Sunday to see it done, Shand reluctantly agreed. But when the time came, the minister "hurried through it as if the words choked him." When Shand concluded, the annoyed officer reported, "not one *amen* was heard throughout the church." In Charleston, the rector at St. Paul's Episcopal flatly declined to say the prayer, so the local commander ordered the church closed. Ironically, the same devout Christians who could not find it in their hearts to bless Lincoln's successor were soon to discover that the new president was their most powerful ally and supporter.[12]

A very different sort of service took place three months later, when three thousand black Charlestonians gathered to lay the cornerstone for the new African Methodist Episcopal Church. Reverend Benjamin F. Randolph, a black military chaplain, read the opening prayer, while "the choir rendered an appropriate chant." Reverend Richard H. Cain, a Virginia-born freeman known to his followers as "Daddy" Cain, spoke next. The church's new minister, Reverend E. J. Adams, described by a black Philadelphia reporter as "looking truly like an African prince," lectured from the Book of Kings and assured his brethren that the promise of the Old Testament had at long last been fulfilled. "If thou wilt walk in my statutes and execute my judgments," Adams read, "then I will perform my word with thee." The modest structure of yellow pine stood on Calhoun between Elizabeth and Meeting streets, not far from the location of the original "African Church," which had been razed by city authorities four decades earlier. Every man "who is working on it is a colored man," boasted a black Carolinian. "Robert Vesey, son of Denmark Vesey, is the architect." White passersby scowled, but for the elderly black carpenter and his fellow parishioners, there was cause to hope that a new day had dawned in their country, and that most Americans were finally ready to live up to the promise that all men were created equal.[13]

Such hopes were premature. What had constituted the state's white leadership before the war soon attempted to reclaim its old position and deny political rights to the liberated Carolinians. That November, the city's black activists fired back with what one dubbed "an extraordinary meeting," extraordinary in that just months earlier such a gathering would have been met with military force. Since the AME building remained under construction, the group convened in the Mount Zion Church, still draped in black in honor of the fallen president. Delany spoke, as did "Daddy" Cain, soon to be the first black clergyman to serve in the House of Representatives. Francis L. Cardozo also took the pulpit. Born in Charleston to a freed slave and a Portuguese-Jewish father, Cardozo had attended the University of Glasgow and trained in London as a Presbyterian minister. The meeting was remarkable in "the history of South Carolina," Cardozo marveled, given "*who* composed it and for what *purposes* it was *allowed* to assemble." Those in attendance voted to condemn the state's political establishment for denying them those basic rights afforded to the "meanest [white] profligate in the country" and demanded that the federal government employ "the strong arm of the law over the entire population of the state." Other resolutions called for "equal suffrage" and urged Washington to repay them for "their unquestioned loyalty" during the "rebellion" by refusing to accept any new state constitution that failed to treat all citizens equally "without distinction of color."[14]

Although the meeting reflected new resolve on the part of black Carolinians, the protest meeting at Zion was possible only because federal troops still occupied the city. For Robert Vesey, whose very name had once relegated him to the shadows, the presence of soldiers meant that although an old man—at roughly sixty-five, he had surpassed average life expectancy for black males by several decades—he could begin life anew. Born around 1800 to a bondwoman known only as Beck, he and his mother were first owned by John Barker, who then sold "the Negro Wench named Beck," together with "her son Robert" to James Evans in 1808 for the paltry sum of four hundred dollars. Although he continued to eke out a living as a carpenter in the years after the 1822 execution of his father, Vesey and his wife Patsey vanished from sight. No census taker or city directory recorded his existence. Nor did Vesey ever answer his door to pay the free-black tax his state imposed upon former slaves in hopes of driving them north. But in the months after the Sumter ceremony, Vesey attended virtually every public function organized by black activists. As would be the case with other black urbanites across the South, Vesey's sudden reappearance into public activism personified a collective rising to political involvement, a group movement out of the back-alley shadows into political sunlight. His role in rebuilding his father's church brought him new fame, and he was soon seen at the weekly meetings of the city's Mechanics' Association. There he served, no doubt uneasily, on the Committee on Charity with the group's president, John C. Desverney, the son of the informer who had caused his father's death.[15]

The need to live away from the prying eyes of hostile authorities had damaged the Vesey family's financial and social status. Denmark Vesey had been fluent in several languages, but Robert's son, also named Robert and born in 1832, neither learned to write nor acquired a skill. Another son, Michael, had died young, but two of Robert's daughters, Susan and Martha, had both married and survived the war. Even so, Robert Jr., and his wife, Anna Crate, put aside money enough to open an account at the Charleston branch of the Freedman's Savings and Trust Company. He signed only with "his mark" and identified his occupation as a simple "laborer," but four daughters completed his household on East Bay Street, and like the other depositors who opened accounts, the thirty-nine-year-old Robert Vesey Jr. supposed that black Americans might now join their white neighbors in bettering their lives and governing the nation they shared.[16]

For African Americans long denied access to education and literacy, that also meant enrolling their children in the hundreds of new schools sponsored by the federal Freedmen's Bureau. Northern teachers had

ventured south beside Union troops, and as portions of the Confederacy had fallen under Union control, the Bureau had established day
schools for freed children. At first, they taught only reading and spelling; although few southern states had flatly banned the education of
enslaved children—South Carolina was one of the four that had—no
system of public education existed for free blacks in the years before the
war, and society frowned on masters who bestowed literacy on slaves
beyond a few trusted domestics and drivers. Within two months of the
celebration at Fort Sumter, the Bureau founded four schools in Richmond, Virginia, educating two thousand children. By the summer of
1866, more than nine hundred academies and fourteen hundred teachers
taught ninety thousand pupils. Supporters of Bureau schools observed
that white children might also attend if they wished, and one Republican journalist thought it in his party's interest to have undereducated
white farmers learn to "read the general news [and] form opinions for
themselves" without having to turn to the "rich masters" for political information. Basic public education came at a cost, of course, and southern
Democrats complained about the higher taxes necessary for Bureau
schools. Before 1867, a black Louisianan replied, free people of color in
New Orleans paid property taxes yet "never was this tax used but to the
exclusive benefit of white children."[17]

    To blacks, joining the republic as equals also meant putting their ed-
ucation to good use, particularly when it came to political involvement.
Within five years of the war's end, republican officials in Mississippi
reported that eighty-five percent of black jurors could read and write.
Black activists demanded integrated police forces, and to show they
harbored no racial bias, black policemen in Mobile, Alabama, arrested a
greater proportion of African American suspects than had their white
predecessors. With the passage of the 1866 Civil Rights Act, an editor
of the black-run *New Orleans Tribune* commented, "there is not a right
that a white man can enjoy, to which the colored man is not also entitled."
By 1868, African American men constituted a majority of registered
voters in South Carolina and Mississippi, and armed with those numbers, blacks began to run for state and national office. After the 1872
elections, African Americans held fifteen percent of the offices in the
South (a larger percentage than in 1990). Just seven years earlier, a

majority of these voters and jurors and police officers had been the property of white Americans. Little wonder that Robert Vesey Sr. thought it
safe to emerge from the shadows and take his rightful place among
Charleston's businessmen.[18]

For communities emerging out of slavery, political rights required
social equality, and most blacks argued that the Thirteenth Amendment
constitutionally erased all legal distinctions between themselves and
their former masters. When, in March 1867, black Charlestonians gathered on the Citadel Green to organize a branch of the Republican Party,
speaker after speaker encouraged those in attendance to return home on
the city's horse-drawn streetcars. (Although not mandated to do so by
any city ordinance, the Charleston Railway Company had long prohibited blacks from boarding its cars.) Families traveling from the Republican rally did just that and were arrested by local police. But when large
numbers of freedmen and freedwomen boarded the cars again on April
1, the president of the company gave in and integrated the system. In
New Orleans, a "perfectly intoxicated" white woman informed a streetcar driver that she would board only if there were no "negro women
there." The driver had her arrested by two policemen. Pinckney B. S.
Pinchback, a Virginia-born freeman and army captain who had arrived
in Louisiana with federal troops, took the principle one step farther.
Having purchased a first-class ticket for a sleeping car on a New Orleans railroad, the light-skinned Pinchback was denied the seat upon
boarding and ordered to sit in a second-class car. By then a state senator,
Pinchback sued the company for twenty-five thousand dollars. Accustomed to submissive, deferential behavior from their black populace,
whites began to understand that they lived in startling, revolutionary
times.[19]

Like the Charleston congregants, such assertive young men as Pinchback were free to challenge southern customs due largely to the continued presence of federal troops. "We understand very well that we must,
for a time, keep a strong army, and hold our military grip upon the
Southern states," editorialized the *Cincinnati Commercial*. It was not
merely that soldiers provided a shield against white retribution. As those
who listened to Major Delany's fiery speeches understood, the military
provided a platform for later political service. The army taught black

privates to read and black corporals to command and to sway others
with their words and through the strength of their personalities. Camp-
fire discussions became political tutorials. Soldiers who had survived
the bloody assaults on Fort Wagner or Port Hudson were little inclined
to vacate a streetcar to appease white sensibilities. By the end of the conflict, more than 178,000 African Americans served in the nation's army;
in Louisiana, parts of which fell under Union control as early as 1862,
thirty-one percent of black men of military age donned a blue uniform.
Especially when those soldiers had been chaplains, their appeal to black
voters was greater still, since the African American community on both
sides of the Mason-Dixon had long regarded religious figures as civic
leaders. Organized into political clubs through the Union League, a
Republican-affiliated group formed in Philadelphia during the darkest
days of the war, black veterans first became voters, then county activists, then state assemblymen, and finally federal congressmen and senators. In a century that equated manhood and military service with
citizenship, a proud freedman wearing a tattered uniform proved a formidable candidate. The story of their service, and the saga of their transformation from soldiers into political actors, opens this volume.[20]

To those conversant with the modern civil rights struggle, stories of
the integration of public transportation, determined soldiers returning
home from combat, courageous ministers, and battles over decent public schools sound all too familiar. If so, why did this period of progressive reform end? Why did similar battles have to be waged anew by a
later generation of activists one hundred years later? There is no simple
answer, and the theories explaining the end of Reconstruction are as
numerous as the politicians, writers, journalists, and historians who
have advanced them. One school of thought holds that southern whites,
even as they recognized the futility of fighting on, remained loyal to the
Confederacy, hostile to the government in Washington, D.C., and
united in the cause of white supremacy. Seen this way, whites of all
classes and both genders waged a relentless guerrilla war on black republicans and their carpetbagger allies. Faithful to a lost cause, even
those white southerners who stood to benefit from Republican economic programs ultimately decided that race trumped self-interest and
resolutely worked to set back the political clock. Although true in

part—and virtually every theory purporting to explain the demise of Reconstruction has some merit—this view underestimates the amount of middle- and working-class disaffection with the Confederacy during its final years and overplays the extent of white unity and resistance in the immediate aftermath of the war.[21]

Delany's impolitic denunciation of Charleston's already-free browns provides other scholars with a different clue. Some historians note that a small number of mixed-race Carolinians assumed a large role in Reconstruction and observe that those liberated *before* the war—the so-called freemen (as opposed to the *freed*men, those liberated during the war and at its end)—disproportionately held seats in the South Carolina assembly. These historians argue that these middling African American politicians failed to endorse the more sweeping program of land redistribution favored by the rural freedmen. By failing to advance a truly progressive platform, this theory suggests, light-skinned urbanites played into the hands of white conservatives and moderate southern Republicans—often derided as scalawags—and so lost the support of their agrarian constituents. But only Charleston and New Orleans were home to large numbers of browns who had won their freedom by emphasizing their white patronage and then drawing linguistic distinctions between themselves and those black laborers liberated by the war. Critics of this theory add that even in South Carolina and Louisiana black freedmen—and particularly veterans, artisans, and ministers—promptly challenged the old colored elite, just as they questioned whether most Charleston browns could rightly be characterized as bourgeois, given their relative lack of wealth and economic autonomy.[22]

An even more recent theory holds that the determination of millions of suddenly liberated people to achieve an independent cultural life played into the desire of racist whites to maintain a separate political identity even as they laid the basis for future civil rights struggles. Historians of the antebellum era continue to debate how much autonomy enslaved blacks were able to maintain while locked into a legal and economic arrangement that tied them to their white masters. Some hypothesize that the black community was something bondmen and bondwomen forged in the quarters *after* long days of labor, away from white supervision, while others respond that even while entangled in an

oppressive system, enslaved southerners laid the groundwork for a separate black society that allowed slaves to psychologically resist their legal degradation. Since even a period as revolutionary as Reconstruction
was constructed on prewar foundations, this theory implies that post-
1865 black autonomy, ironically, contributed to the end of America's
short-lived experiment in interracial democracy. This is not to imply
that black activists such as Delany or "Daddy" Cain were to blame for
the demise of the era, but simply to recognize that the roots of black
agency predated Appomattox, and that old racial wounds were slow to
heal.[23]

Other "revisionist" scholars—the not terribly accurate term imposed
on modern historians who believe, as did that era's progressives, that
Reconstruction was a noble attempt to create a more democratic
America—look to the failures of the North, and particularly the inherent conservatism of the Republican business class. In this interpreta-
tion, the growth of industrialization, already under way in pockets of
the North, accelerated during the war and led to the first meaningful
stirrings of working-class organization as early as 1866 with the National Labor Union. Faced with new labor militancy, Republican mag-
nates were increasingly sensitive to desires of southern Redeemers—the
indigenous white business class—and what remained of the old planter
class to control *their* laborers, and so influential northerners gradually
turned a blind eye to all but the most egregious civil rights abuses. The
victory of the same Republican free-labor ideology that proved so dangerous to proslavery beliefs, ironically, ultimately failed to serve the
needs of southern freedmen. Tragically, these early attempts by northern workingmen to unite against their industrial bosses hindered the
ability of black southerners to do so as well.[24]

A second criticism of the North is lodged against the voting public,
rather than its industrial or political elites. Rightly recognizing that
northern racism varied from its southern variety only by degree, a
number of writers emphasize white attitudes toward African Americans
and find it unsurprising that northern voters, even Republicans, failed
to stand by far-reaching racial policies. Critical of what they perceived
to be special-interest legislation designed to assist southern freedmen,
these middle-class voters believed they had fulfilled their obligation to

former slaves by fighting for the Union. Flattering themselves that their economic success was based upon their private industry, rather than on the happy accident of race, gender, and region, they used their embrace of individualism to excuse their failure to maintain support of meaningful social change in the South. Since most northern legislatures (outside of New England) only grudgingly endorsed black voting rights and shied away from legislation that promoted social or gender equality, skittish Republicans in Washington had to be careful not to get too far out in front of their constituents. When southern whites continued to resist democratization into the 1870s, often through murder and mayhem, weary northern voters simply gave way in pressing for a progressive social agenda they rarely supported in their own communities.[25]

Few of these many theories are mutually exclusive. Some complement other schools of thought or provide a different view of the same thorny issue. All add to the larger picture. Yet in seeking to explain why the progressive crusade of the late 1860s ground to a halt, historians invariably focus on the later years of the era, those terrible moments that came well after the reformist legislation of the late 1860s, as it became clear that political momentum was fading. Working from an understanding that Reconstruction collapsed in much of the South during the mid-1870s, scholars are naturally inclined to look *there* in search of the problem, supposing that critical events in the former Confederacy or political missteps in Washington toward the end of the era brought the nation's first meaningful campaign for racial equality to a halt. Too often the central question becomes why Reconstruction *failed*, as opposed to *ended*, which hints that the process itself was somehow flawed and contributed to its own passing.

Nor is there any scholarly consensus on precisely *when* Reconstruction ended. Many writers point to the contentious presidential election of 1876, which resulted in victor Rutherford B. Hayes withdrawing what remained of federal troops from the South. As important as military protection of the freedmen and freedwomen was, the number of soldiers had steadily declined over the 1870s, and, even when relatively numerous, soldiers tended to be stationed in urban areas and not in the rural districts where white violence was most pronounced. But to identify specific dates for the era's beginning or end is to define the period by Washington-based political contests and Congressional acts. Many of those laws, demanded as they were by black veterans and determined abolitionists, *were* crucial. Yet for black activists across America, military service and claims of citizenship in 1863 merely marked a quickening of old demands. Nor did all advocates of civil rights and social justice cease their struggle in 1877. Black congressmen represented southern districts until 1901, and African American voters in Illinois and New York who gained the franchise during Reconstruction never lost that right. Reconstruction neither failed nor ended in all parts of the republic, and even in those states where activists were murdered and voters were denied their political rights, the crusade for democracy carried on.

This book looks *forward* from the dawn of Reconstruction and situates the roots of its demise in its inception. Although white southerners would eventually unify across class lines in the name of racial supremacy and romanticize the government of Jefferson Davis—an administration many of them despised during the war—this intra-racial accord grew only slowly. True it was that a number of former planters and Confederate veterans never accepted defeat or acknowledged the equality of black Americans. Yet in the spring of 1865, as exhausted and starving soldiers came straggling home—and sadly, 258,000 southern men never returned to their farms and families—a majority were prepared to accept whatever terms Lincoln's government planned to impose. "I must do the Southerners justice to say," reformer Charles Stearns admitted, "that at that time the great masses were evidently more intent on repairing their pecuniary fortunes, than their political ones." A journalist from Vermont agreed. "The work of reconstruction went on swimmingly for several months," he observed in 1866. "The rebellious States seemed to 'wheel into line' with remarkable alacrity." No less a figure than Confederate general James Longstreet published an editorial calling for "moderation, forbearance, and submission." White southerners were "a conquered people," Longstreet counseled, and must face that hard truth "fairly and squarely." There was "but one course left for wise men to pursue, and that is to accept the terms that are now offered by the conquerors." If prospects for enlightened reform were promising in the months after the Confederate surrender, if the

celebrants at Fort Sumter were not naïve in believing that the rededication heralded a fresh start in American race relations, what "inflamed
the Southern mind," as Stearns phrased it? What "re-instilled the evil
genius of rebellion into the hearts of those who were sick of the war and
would have liked to remain quiet?" The nation was presented with a
window of enormous opportunity, however brief; but that moment was
soon lost.[26]

The window began to close as early as Good Friday of 1865, not so
much, perhaps, because Lincoln was the only person capable of restoring the nation, but rather because Andrew Johnson proved to be utterly
the wrong man for the job. From his first moments in office, the Tennessean Johnson signaled his fellow white southerners that he would demand almost nothing of them. Always hostile to black Americans and a
slave owner himself until midway through the war, Johnson initially
demanded only ratification of the Thirteenth Amendment as the price
of southern readmittance to Congress. For this accidental president,
black liberation was the end of the process, not the first step in a march
toward political and social equality, and he had no desire to employ the
army to ensure constitutional rights for freedmen. Writing to Illinois
senator Lyman Trumbull in the summer of 1866, one Alabama Republican complained that the "reconstruction policy of President Johnson
and his extreme favoritism to open Enemys of the Government here has
made and is fast bringing back a state of anarchy." A Maryland journalist added that although he once had feared that Lincoln would be "too
vindictive" in making "treason odious," Lincoln's successor was instead
"making loyalty odious" to the point that a white or black Republican was
"no longer safe with his life and property in the rebellious states." Realizing that the president only drew a line at the formal re-enslavement of
liberated blacks, a small but determined cadre of aggressive reactionaries seized control of events and elected former Confederate officials, including Confederate vice president Alexander H. Stephens, to state and
national office. Southern moderates fell silent or were intimidated into
acquiescence as Mississippi and Texas refused to ratify the Thirteenth
Amendment, and as most defeated states, including South Carolina,
enacted a set of laws dubbed the Black Codes, which severely restricted

the political rights of African Americans. It was Carolina's Black Code that led to the November protest meeting at the Mount Zion Church.[27]

With a dwindling number of federal soldiers available to protect black Americans, and aware that Johnson thought their actions justified, the handful of white southerners who had never accepted defeat responded to black activists and white reformers with a campaign of targeted violence. Although scholars have recently chronicled the series of deadly riots that followed the election of 1872, particularly the massacre in Colfax, Louisiana, in April 1873, small-scale but highly lethal violence began as early as 1866. By that year Confederate veterans grasped that the White House would not crack down on their retribution. Rather than continue to engage in the sort of wholesale, public savagery that attracted the wrath of northern journalists and politicians, dogmatic southerners quietly but methodically attacked the rising generation of Republican Party functionaries. Among those assassinated in 1868 was Reverend Benjamin F. Randolph, who had read a prayer at the dedication ceremony of Charleston's black church.[28]

As black activists paid for their convictions with their lives, terrified carpetbaggers—northern politicians, missionaries, and teachers—fled the South. Reformers who might have taken their places often opted instead for survival, unhappily aware that the price of abandoning the work of Reconstruction meant that a future generation of activists would have to risk *their* lives in the cause of voting rights and integration. As these men and women well knew, Reconstruction did not fail; in regions where it collapsed it was violently overthrown by men who had fought for slavery during the Civil War and continued that battle as guerrilla partisans over the next decade. Democratic movements can be halted through violence.

White vigilantes not only assaulted black people, they targeted the institutions that permitted social advancement and carried freedmen and freedwomen away from the plantations into a different life. All too typical was the report submitted in early 1866 to General Oliver O. Howard, the head of the Freedmen's Bureau, by a colonel stationed in North Carolina. "A serious disturbance occurred at Elizabeth City," he reported, "during which an old church which was being prepared for a freedmen's school was burnt, and some discharged negro soldiers cruelly beaten." The colonel ordered more troops into the area, but that meant they had to be withdrawn from other parts of the state where they were also needed. By the time soldiers arrived in hope of "arresting the assailants," the perpetrators had vanished. Yet another school was gone, and a church, the focal point for Elizabeth City's black community, was reduced to ashes, black veterans had been brutalized and disarmed, and the county had been taught the deadly price of hope.[29]

Those courageous enough to continue the struggle understood the cost of democracy, and many of them were willing to gamble their lives in the cause. "We will have a big meeting, certain our circulars are out & we will have a grand rallying" in Macon, Mississippi, reported Republican scalawag James L. Alcorn. It was no coincidence, Alcorn added, that local authorities sentenced "3 negroes [to] be hung on Friday & our meeting [was to] take place on the next day." For the timid, such blunt warnings rarely had to be repeated. For the resolute, strange fruit swung from the poplar trees as party activists vanished one by one during the dark of night. "I voted in town on de Republican ticket," recalled John Davenport of South Carolina. "None of my friends held office, but I remember some of dem. Old Lee Nance was one, and he was killed by a white man" after being elected to the legislature in 1868. Soon even those who wished merely to cast a ballot faced Election Day mobs armed with shotguns and bludgeons.[30]

Among those who fell silent was Robert Vesey Jr. By the time he opened his account with the Freedman's Savings Bank in 1871, his father, Robert Sr., had passed away, as had his mother. The bank failed in 1874, a victim of the global depression of the previous year. At its peak, the Washington, D.C.–based institution held assets of 3.3 million dollars for 61,131 depositors; no record indicates how much money Robert and Anna Vesey lost in the panic. In January of that year they lost a far more valuable treasure, when their newborn son, named Robert A. Vesey after his father, died of "spasms." Reflecting the family's return to poverty, the child was interred in the City Burial Grounds, a paupers' field. Although the grieving father was but forty-two, the Veseys vanished yet again from the public record, their short-lived prosperity and optimism a tragic mirror to the shattered promise of the era.[31]

Today tourists in horse-drawn surreys clop past the dilapidated Charleston city jail and the Old Exchange building, in whose vault Denmark Vesey spent the last moments of his life. Like so many Americans, the city's tour guides, all of whom are required to undergo training for their job, are not quite sure what to make of Reconstruction. On one recent tour, the white guide pointed toward Fort Sumter and explained that "radical Reconstruction was the most undemocratic period in South Carolina history." To the contrary, Reconstruction, which was in fact far from radical, constituted the *most democratic* decades of the nineteenth century, South *or* North, so much so that it amounted to the first progressive era in the nation's history. Just ten years after Supreme Court Chief Justice Roger B. Taney endorsed the expansion of slavery into the western territories and announced that black Americans, even if free born, could not be citizens of the republic, blacks were fighting for the franchise in northern states; battling to integrate streetcars in Charleston, New Orleans, and San Francisco; funding integrated public schools; and voting and standing for office in the erstwhile Confederacy. How black veterans, activists, ministers, assemblymen, registrars, poll workers, editors, *and* a handful of dedicated white allies risked their lives in this cause, nearly brought down a racist president, but ultimately lost their fight because of white violence is the subject of this book.[32]

CHAPTER ONE

"An Eagle on His Button"

Black Men Fight for the Union

T HEY CAME FROM ALL OVER. During the first days of 1863, Governor John A. Andrew announced the formation of the Fifty-fourth Massachusetts Volunteer Infantry, the first regiment to be mostly comprised of northern freemen, and black men from across the republic answered the call. George Dugan of Concord was a forty-four-year-old farmer and widower. Jefferson Ellis was just nineteen, working as a boatman in Poughkeepsie. With at least one African American ancestor, the blue-eyed, "sandy"-haired youth was regarded as "colored" by his neighbors, so he joined, too. Robert Jones was a twenty-year-old farmer from Hamilton, Ohio; at five feet seven inches, he was of normal height in a century when poor diets robbed working-class children of necessary nutrition. His fellows, Daniel Kelley and Louis Kelsey, farmers from Burbank, New York, and Detroit, Michigan, were shorter by four inches. Some came from the South. Samuel Kinney was a thirty-nine-year-old blacksmith from Rockbridge County, Virginia, who abandoned his forge to fight for black freedom. Joseph Barge was a North Carolina freeman who, thinking himself "a yankee by cultivation and thinking principles," had left the Confederacy for Boston. Eighteen-year-old George Alexander was a farmer from Charleston, South Carolina, a state that was home to very few freemen, and most of them the mixed-race "browns" Martin R. Delany was so suspicious of. The army's "descriptive book" listed Private Alexander as "dark," and five feet four inches tall.[1]

In time, some of these young men would become teachers, ministers, community activists, Republican Party functionaries, state assemblymen, and members of Congress. Of the 1,510 identifiable men of color who held office during Reconstruction, at least 130 first served in the nation's military. They included men such as Landon S. Langley, who would take part in the South Carolina constitutional convention of 1868, and Martin F. Becker, a South American–born barber from Fitchburg, Massachusetts, who was to become a southern election official. But in the winter of 1863, some were simple "laborers," the occupation listed by young Henry Kirk, who journeyed east from Hannibal, Missouri. So too was Enos Smith of Easton, Pennsylvania. John Simmons of Kentucky told recruiters he was a "foundryman." The army was to be their home, for many, their school, and for most, their political club. Their courage and service and rank would recommend them to voters in the decade after Appomattox.[2]

First they had to survive the war. Farmers Kelley and Dugan died at Fort Wagner, South Carolina, that July. Robert Jones endured the assault on Wagner but was "killed in action" near Jacksonville, Florida, in early 1864. Ellis and Kelsey suffered wounds at Wagner; Kelsey was discharged, and the blue-eyed Ellis, captured by Confederates after the attack, was "paroled & exchanged" after being imprisoned for seventeen months. Ellis returned to service and was promoted to corporal. Enos Smith and Samuel Kinney were less lucky. Captured after the July battle on James Island, South Carolina, the Pennsylvania laborer "died of starvation in prison pen at Florence" on February 20, 1865. Kinney, the Virginia blacksmith, lost much of his kneecap at Wagner but resolutely refused discharge. Promoted to corporal in early 1865, he was killed in a skirmish on April 18, nine days after Robert E. Lee surrendered at Appomattox.

A good number of older black activists encouraged their young relations to join the regiment. Abolitionist and women's rights activist Sojourner Truth sent a grandson. Antislavery editor and orator Frederick Douglass, then living in Rochester, New York, signed two sons into the unit. Delany's son, Toussaint Louverture Delany, also served with the Fifty-fourth. Then, at the age of fifty-one, Delany himself joined the army. Born in 1812 in western Virginia to a slave father but a freed mother, and so free himself, Delany was raised in what his white neighbors found most curious, a black family with dreams of a better life. Delany's mother, Pati, was determined that her children learn how to read and purchased the *New York Primer and Spelling Book* from a traveling peddler. When the hostility of their neighbors became clear, and after slave catchers attempted to seize Martin and one of his siblings, Pati moved the family to Chambersburg, Pennsylvania; after purchasing his own freedom a year later, Martin's father, Samuel Delany, reunited with his family. At nineteen, Martin relocated to Pittsburgh, where he joined the Bethel AME Church and studied the classics at Jefferson College. A young man of ambition, Delany apprenticed himself to Dr. Andrew McDowell, who taught him the bloodletting art of cupping and leeching. At about that time, Delany married Catherine Richards, the daughter of a prosperous food provisioner, who bore six children, all of them named after black heroes or nations. The couple decided to move again, this time to Boston, so that Martin might study medicine at Harvard University. Armed with seventeen letters of recommendation, Delany began classes, only to be asked to leave after several white students petitioned the university to dismiss him and two other black students. Undeterred, Delany removed to Detroit and opened a practice. When in 1854 the city was devastated with cholera, he was one of the few doctors to remain behind to care for the sick.[3]

A man of many parts, Delany took up his pen later in the decade to respond to what he regarded as the too-passive depiction of slave behavior in Harriet Beecher Stowe's *Uncle Tom's Cabin*. His rejoinder, *Blake: Or, the Huts of America*, appeared in serial form in 1859 in the *Anglo-African* newspaper. *Blake* told the story of an Afro-Cuban runaway who traveled the South in hopes of sparking a slave revolt. But the novel also betrayed a sense of hopelessness increasingly common in the free black community in the wake of the Dred Scott decision, which denied federal citizenship to freemen like Delany. In May 1859 he visited Liberia. Few black Americans showed any interest in emigrating to the now-independent republic founded forty-odd years earlier by the white-run

American Colonization Society, but as early as 1852, Delany suspected that his nation would forever deny African Americans basic rights. Even his sometime collaborator Frederick Douglass, long a foe of emigration, began to consider the prospect of a mass exodus to Haiti. As he continued to craft chapters for *Blake*, Delany started to raise funds for his venture and gather a group of potential settlers. Then came the war.[4]

When at long last, in 1863, the federal government agreed to enlist black freemen, the middle-aged Delany eagerly stepped forward. Influential white friends from Illinois peppered President Abraham Lincoln with testimonials for "Doctor Martin R. Delany." Republican Charles Dyer assured the president that Delany was a man of "energy and intelligence." Chicago businessman Peter Page played upon the president's well-known advocacy of black expatriation, evidently missing the irony of promoting the domestic career of a black American who had wished to emigrate. Based upon what he knew of Delany's "explorations in Africa" and support for the "colonization of the free colored people of this country," Page thought him "eminently qualified" for any position Lincoln might think suitable.[5]

In large part because in Dred Scott the Supreme Court formally articulated a position privately held by most whites, Delany was anxious to demonstrate his loyalty to the land of his birth. "If we establish our right of equal claims of citizenship with other American people, we shall have done all that is desirable in this view of our position in the country," he assured one audience. Although initially employed as a recruiter of northern free blacks, Delany longed to personally carry the fight into his native South. Writing to Secretary of War Edwin M. Stanton, Delany asked to be given command of "Colored Troops in any of the Southern or seceded states," as that service was "one of the measures in which the claims of the Black Man may be officially recognized." A good many activists shared Delany's hope that once large numbers of blacks joined the army, white Americans could no longer deny them a political voice. Delany was aware, however, that although Crispus Attucks had been "the first victim in the revolutionary tragedy" of the Boston Massacre, his death had done little over the decades to foster integration. The fact that Delany was especially anxious to lead black troops into Charleston, a hotbed of secession that "from earliest

Born free in western Virginia, Martin R. Delany came to believe that African Americans had no future in the United States after he was forced out of Harvard University's medical school. In 1859, he journeyed to Liberia, and he returned home with intentions of starting a new settlement on the West Coast of Africa. By 1863, he abandoned those plans and began to recruit soldiers for the new black regiments. Delany was finally commissioned a major, becoming the highest ranking African American during the Civil War era. With the collapse of the Confederacy, he transferred to the Freedmen's Bureau and served in Hilton Head, South Carolina. Courtesy Moreland-Springarn Library, Howard University.

childhood" he had "learned to contemplate with feelings of the utmost abhorrence," suggests that he and other black abolitionists were as anxious to destroy slavery and "attack the already crushed and fallen enemy" as they were to establish a bid for citizenship.[6]

Citizenship indeed came slowly. In the first moments after the 1861 surrender of Fort Sumter, Lincoln called on loyal governors to raise seventy-five thousand volunteers for what he hoped would be a brief, ninety-day campaign against the seven seceded states. Missouri and Kentucky balked, and when faced with the prospect of federal soldiers tramping across the slave-heavy counties of the tidewater, Virginia and three other states seceded and attached their fates to the Confederate cause. Black men across the North stepped forward, only to be rebuffed by a War Department that hoped to define the conflict as a simple war for Union. Allowing for the enlistment of black soldiers, the administration feared, would drive Kentucky, Maryland, and perhaps even Delaware into the Confederacy. Lecturing across the North, Delany condemned the exclusion of blacks from the military and pressed for enlistments on the grounds that service remained the best way to bring "forward the claims of his race." Frederick Douglass, who regarded his youthful fistfight with overseer Edward Covey as his initiation into manhood, promised audiences that "nothing would please [him] more, and bring the race into favor, than to see Southern chivalry well whipped by an equal number of black men." The policy of a whites-only soldiery sacrificing their lives merely to save a racist Union, Douglass complained, was as much a violation of American pretensions to liberty as it was strategically foolish, for it meant fighting "the rebels with only one hand" while keeping "the black hand chained and helpless behind them."[7]

Enslaved southerners chose not to wait for Washington officials to agree. In May, just one month into the conflict, three bondmen whom the Confederate military used to construct fortifications escaped and reached the gates of Fort Monroe, an instillation at the southern tip of the Virginia peninsula that remained under federal control. In command of the fort was Major General Benjamin F. Butler, a Massachusetts Democrat who during the previous year had endorsed proslavery candidate John C. Breckinridge for the presidency. Dozens more runaways followed. By late July, an overwhelmed Butler reported to his superiors, roughly nine hundred refugees were living under his protection. Only three hundred were "able-bodied men." The rest were women, children, and aged slaves "substantially past hard labor," with "many more coming in" daily. Butler requested clarity from the War Department: "Are these men, women, and children, slaves? Are they free?" Since the state of Virginia had behaved "traitorously," had "all property relation ceased?" Since the first runaways to reach the fort had been put to work digging Confederate trenches, Butler, an attorney and politician before the war, thought it best to consider them liberated "contraband of war." Butler's position accorded with traditional war-power theory, and on August 6, 1861, just one week after the receipt of Butler's inquiry, the president signed the Confiscation Act, which effectively ratified the general's suggestion by allowing for the seizure of all property, including bondmen, being used to support the Confederate military. Among those who escaped to Monroe was Harry Jarvis, a thirty-one-year-old Eastern Shore slave who stole a canoe and paddled the thirty-five miles across the Chesapeake Bay. Being freed as contraband was not enough for Jarvis, who informed Butler that he wished to enlist. The general demurred, saying *"it warn't a black man's war."* Jarvis thought otherwise. "It *would* be a black man's war 'fore dey got through," he predicted.[8]

A few hard-pressed generals agreed. Near Port Hudson, Louisiana, General Nathaniel P. Banks battled to open the Mississippi to federal gunboats. Like Butler, Banks hailed from Massachusetts, but this former Democrat had quit his party in disgust after the 1854 Kansas-Nebraska Act allowed for the expansion of slavery into the Midwest, and he supported Republican candidate John C. Frémont in 1856. Running short of healthy troops, Banks recruited African Americans, some of them runaways and others light-skinned free people of color. Whatever "doubt may have existed heretofore as to the efficiency of Negro regiments, the history of the day proves conclusively," Banks reported in May 1862, "that the Government will find in the class of troops effective supporters and defenders." Despite Banks's success and an array of military setbacks elsewhere, the administration remained reluctant to deploy black troops. Yet offers of service continued to pile up in the War Department. Garland H. White, a former slave of Confederate secretary of state Robert Toombs, assured Secretary of War Stanton that he had traveled about the South with his master, and now he was "quite willing to spend [his] life in preaching against sin & fighting against the same." Then living in Canada and serving as minister to a congregation of runaways, White told Stanton he was "called upon" by his flock to lead them "as soldiers in the southern parts." Stanton filed the missive away without comment, but as Union casualties mounted, the administration could continue to ignore such offers only at some risk to military success.[9]

While Banks and White showered Washington with requests, a voice with far more clout weighed in. Major General David Hunter, a career soldier, had been stationed at Fort Leavenworth, Kansas, during the election season of 1860. While in the West he had corresponded so frequently with candidate Lincoln that the president-elect invited him to accompany him as he traveled from Springfield to Washington. Later, as the commander of the Department of the South, the New York–born abolitionist found himself on the South Carolina coast, and in April 1862 he requested fifty thousand muskets and an equal number of "scarlet pantaloons" with which to arm and clothe "such loyal men as [he] could find in the country." Although he did not say so directly, Hunter meant to free and enlist Carolina slaves. When Stanton and Lincoln failed to reply, perhaps thinking it prudent to let the general quietly proceed with his plans, Hunter did just that, sending Union troops into the Sea Islands to round up black recruits.[10]

Despite the large numbers of bondmen in the area, the process of enlistment went slowly. Hunter's white junior officers and enlisted troops made no effort to hide their disdain for the experiment, while white Carolinians hastened to caution their laborers that the Yankees intended to sell them to Cuba. Hunter was unable to promise them pay or assure them that their families would be freed as well; wisely, many slaves chose to watch and wait. To encourage enlistments, on May 9, finally Hunter declared free all slaves in Florida, Georgia, and South Carolina, motivating Robert Smalls to steal the *Planter* several days later and pilot it out of Charleston harbor into the Union blockade. By midsummer, enough men had gathered to form the First South Carolina Volunteer Regiment. Laura M. Towne, a northern schoolteacher traveling with the army, thought the men "looked splendidly" and "did great credit to their commander." The public response was less effusive. Fearing the regiment was the first step toward race war, the *New York Times* warned that the venture was "laden with possible dangers to humanity." Democrats in Congress angrily demanded to know whether Stanton had approved the regiment. Ironically, Lincoln was then in the process of drafting his Preliminary Emancipation Proclamation, but even Treasury Secretary Salmon P. Chase, who privately applauded Hunter's actions, publicly agreed that only the commander in chief had the authority to liberate so many bondmen. In August, Lincoln over-ruled Hunter's edict and approved his request for reassignment. Although he did not disband Hunter's black regiment, the move infuriated the president's liberal critics, who correctly charged that the administration was "at sea on the subject" and had failed to formulate a clear policy.[11]

Slaves lucky enough to reside near Union lines continued to flood toward federal soldiers, however, and their numbers, together with the persistent and forceful urging by so-called Radical Republicans in Washington, finally forced the issue. On July 17, just weeks before the president countermanded Hunter's decree, Congress passed two inter-connected laws, the Second Confiscation Act and the Militia Act. The latter empowered Lincoln to request the states to collectively call up an-other three hundred thousand men for a nine-month enlistment, based on each state's population. The law allowed blacks to serve as part of each state's quota, but only as free men, and it stipulated that their de-pendents should also be free, which provided blacks with an additional incentive to enroll. The new Confiscation Act went beyond the previous year's law by stating that all bondmen and bondwomen owned by Con-federate officials would be freed if their masters did not surrender within sixty days. The act authorized Lincoln to "employ as many persons of African descent as he may deem necessary and proper for the suppres-sion of this rebellion" and to emancipate any slaves who enlisted, pro-vided their owners were known Confederate sympathizers. Both laws passed Congress by comfortable margins, if perhaps for less than noble reasons. Black soldiers might dig latrines and haul lumber and do other sorts of "Negro work," Iowa's governor informed General Henry Hal-leck. When the fighting was over, he added, "I shall not have any re-grets if it is found that a part of the dead are *niggers* and that *all* are not white men."[12]

Despite this apparent gulf between the slow-acting president and more progressive members of Congress, Lincoln increasingly sup-ported the use of southern blacks, provided federal commanders did not exceed their authority with wholesale emancipations. Even as Hunter was requesting a new command, Washington was searching for a suitable replacement to lead the South Carolina Volunteers. General Rufus Saxton, whose abolitionist father had gained fame on the lyceum circuit as both a feminist and a transcendentalist, recommended fellow abolitionist Thomas Wentworth Higginson, a minister tough enough to be a veteran of the fighting in Bleeding Kansas yet gentle enough to serve as friend and mentor to poet Emily Dickinson. Higginson was serving as captain in the Massachusetts infantry and had just drafted an essay for the *Atlantic Monthly* on Denmark Vesey when Saxton's missive arrived. He eagerly accepted. He "had been an abolitionist too long, and had known and loved John Brown too well," he remarked, "not to feel a thrill of joy at last on finding [himself] in the position where [Brown] wished to be." Higginson, then training in Worcester, called on Governor Andrew and resigned his old commission. Without waiting for his colonelcy, he sailed for the Carolina coast and cast his lot "altogether with the black troops" for the remainder of the war.[13]

Like most white abolitionists, Higginson had never set foot in the South. While exhilarated with his new command, he was unsure of what he would find upon landing in Union-occupied Beaufort, South Carolina. As expected, he spied a scoffing officer, "whose curled lip and upturned nose told the whole story of *his* patriotism." But Colonel Higginson was impressed by the "stalwart band" of soldiers he was to command. They were "all as dark as printer's ink" and "proudly shouldering their guns, as they stood in their red pants, blue coats, and caps." The new colonel had known too many runaways to be surprised by the political sophistication of black Americans. Even so, he was saddened by the drummer boy who told him that while a slave near Georgetown, he had been whipped for singing "We'll soon be free" upon hearing of Lincoln's election. Despite their general illiteracy, his soldiers knew what had brought on the war, and they knew what they were fighting for. Speaking to the troops one night (in a language recorded, dialect and all, by a white observer), regimental Chaplain Thomas Long reiterated that their service had forced reluctant Republicans in Washington to support black freedom. "If we hadn't become sojers, all might have gone back as it was before," Long lectured, and "our freedom might have slipped through de two houses of Congress & President Linkum's four years might have passed by." But because Carolina freedmen had "showed our courage & our naturally manhood," the country could "never go back" on the promise of liberty. White Americans doubted that bondmen would serve with distinction, Long added, slamming his hand down on the camp table for emphasis, but "Tanks to dis regiment, [they] never can say dat any more, because we first showed dem we could fight by dere side."[14]

Higginson found enormous inspiration in the devout Unionism of his men. "I believe de United States is fighting for me," insisted one recruit with more faith than accuracy, "and for my people." Since no enlistment bounty existed and pay was slow to arrive, none had joined for the money. Few, rather to Higginson's surprise, signed on for revenge. One soldier who enlisted under Hunter confessed that he would not mind if on Judgment Day the Lord briefly shook his cruel master "over the brink of hell," yet he prayed that God ultimately would not drop him into the pit. But the Massachusetts abolitionist also witnessed the hard realities of military service. Most of his recruits left loved ones behind when they fled toward federal lines. One private lamented that he had left his "wife in de land ob bondage," and another almost thought he heard his "little ones dey say ebry night, where is my fader?" Many knew they would not live to return home as liberators. One Carolina freedman later recalled his "daddy go 'long with other niggers to fight for 'Uncle Abe' and we never see him no more."[15]

Lincoln continued to fret about the political impact of black regiments in the lower North and the loyal slave states, and with good reason. The Preliminary Emancipation Proclamation of September 22 initially dampened the enthusiasm of potential white recruits, who wished to restrict the conflict to reunion, forcing the president to concede that he ought to "take some benefit from it" by enlisting more black soldiers, and not just southern runaways. Vice President Hannibal Hamlin ushered a delegation of young officers into the White House, one of them his own son and all of them ready to lead northern freemen into battle. The governor of Rhode Island wrote to request permission to allow the state's black men to enlist, noting that "Rhode Island has a historic right to this regiment," as its earlier "colored regiment in the war of independence gained for itself an enduring fame." With his armies faring badly in the bloody months following Antietam and conservative Democrats campaigning against his Proclamation, the president resolved to move beyond arming runaways along the Carolina coast. "I suppose the time has come," he informed Hamlin's delegation.[16]

The growing use of black troops terrified the Confederate government. By the late fall, Higginson's regiment was joined by similar units in Louisiana led by General John W. Phelps and a still-reluctant Benjamin Butler, who had been reassigned from Fort Monroe to recently captured New Orleans. Confederate General Samuel Cooper declared Phelps and Hunter "outlaws"—not knowing that the latter had been replaced—which meant that if captured they would not be exchanged but rather "held in close confinement for execution." That November, Confederate soldiers captured six black troops on the Georgia coast. "They are slaves taken with arms in hand against their masters and wearing the abolition uniform," wrote their captor. Confederate Secretary of War James A. Seddon ordered one of the men "executed as an example" to other runaways. Black soldiers, Seddon added, "will not be regarded as prisoners of war." In Richmond, President Jefferson Davis expanded the policy, declaring federal officers who commanded black soldiers were little better than "robbers and criminals deserving death." On December 23, in a ghastly preview of the fate former Confederates intended for black activists and white progressives during the Reconstruction era, Davis decreed that all white officers and "negro slaves captured in arms" be turned over to local courts "to be dealt with according to the laws of said States." That meant their execution as insurrectionists.[17]

Although never formally rescinded, Davis's decree was not put into effect. Even northern newspapers and politicians hostile to the use of black troops condemned the Confederate policy. Hannah Johnson, a resident of Buffalo, New York, whose father had escaped from slavery years earlier, wrote to the president regarding her son. "I thought of this thing before I let my boy go," she wrote, confident that the government would "never let them sell our colored soldiers for slaves." Should they do so, she counseled, "You must put the rebels to work in State prisons to making shoes and things." In fact, Lincoln had already reached that conclusion. During the previous July, the two governments had agreed to prisoner exchanges, but Lincoln denounced the enslavement of black soldiers as "a relapse into barbarism" and threatened to discontinue repatriation unless the Confederates treated alike all prisoners in uniform. A Confederate commissioner ultimately agreed to exchange all soldiers born free, such as Johnson's son, but vowed to "die in the last ditch" before surrendering "the right to send slaves back as property recaptured." Secretary of War Stanton retorted that if that was Davis's policy, he had doomed the twenty-six thousand Confederate prisoners to long months in federal prison camps. "Uncle Sam is firm," reported a journalist who spoke with the president about the Union policy, "and will not give up his protection of his soldiers."[18]

As New Year's Day of 1863 approached, and with it the signing of Lincoln's final Emancipation Proclamation, black Americans and white abolitionists prepared to celebrate "the day of jubilee." A few feared that at the last moment the warring nations might forge a compromise that would result in the president rescinding his decree. They watched nervously as New Jersey Democrats advanced a series of "peace propositions" that offered the state's services as "mediator." But the Massachusetts Anti-Slavery Society gathered in Boston to rally "in favor of that godlike object," asserting that as long as "four millions of the inhabitants of the land" remained enslaved, their crusade remained unfinished. Nearby at the Tremont Temple, a combination museum and Baptist Church, congregants met to pray and sing. A rousing "Blow Ye the Trumpet Blow" was followed by a solemn prayer of thanksgiving, and by cheers "for the President and for the Proclamation." In Manhattan, blacks braved howling winds to celebrate a "Watch Night of Freedom" at the Shiloh Church. New York Democrats were less enthusiastic. The Proclamation "will be the opening of Pandora's box of evils upon the country," warned one editor. The consequence, he feared, was "the employment of negroes as soldiers in the service of the government" and the resulting "war to the savage extremities of mutual extermination."[19]

Having at long last elevated the conflict from one of simple reunification to the more exalted grounds of liberty and freedom, the administration moved to replenish a military devastated by the previous December's disaster at Fredericksburg, Virginia. "After the Proclamation of Emancipation and the enrollment of colored soldiers in defense

of their country," observed one black Republican, "universal emancipation was inevitable." Nobody in the War Department believed that
black civilians would be ready for front-line duty anytime soon, but
Stanton assured Massachusetts senator Charles Sumner that the president hoped to have "200,000 negroes under arms before June." Those
fresh recruits could hold the already captured points along the Mississippi and coastal Carolina while seasoned "white soldiers" redeployed
to the front until the newer troops received a rush training, Sumner
enthused. "Let the music sound, & the day be celebrated."[20]

Sumner did not speak for all white Unionists. Conservatives had campaigned against the Proclamation during the fall elections, and unhappiness with the shift in Lincoln's goals, together with anger at high
wartime taxes, cost the Republicans twenty-two seats in the House.
Since Lincoln issued his decree in his guise as commander in chief, it
was not a legislative act and did not affect those slave states that remained with the republic. Andrew Johnson, a loyal Democrat then serving as military governor of Tennessee, cautioned the White House that
raising black troops in his state would only motivate defeated whites to
fight on. Since Johnson as yet owned slaves and was appalled by the notion of black citizenship, his views on the matter were obviously biased.
But Lincoln received similar advice from General Ambrose Burnside
regarding Kentucky. Enlisting either freemen or liberated slaves "would
not add materially to our strength," he warned, but "would cause much
trouble." Free blacks in the nation's capital clamored to enlist, however,
and "a colored regiment will easily be raised in this city," reported one
journalist. Writing from southern Illinois, Major General Ulysses S.
Grant was as enthusiastic as Johnson was hostile. By "arming the negro
we have added a powerful ally," he advised Lincoln. "They will make
good soldiers and taking them from the enemy weakens him in the same
proportion they strengthen us."[21]

Whether antagonistic or supportive of the policy, whites assumed
that blacks were anxious to serve. For the most part, that was true, and
a good many of the freemen in Washington who were ready to enlist
still had cousins, friends, and loved ones who remained enslaved in
neighboring Maryland and Virginia. Black men in New England enjoyed the right to vote, but the same white New Yorkers who had flocked

to the polls to support Lincoln had chosen to maintain a $250 property qualification on blacks not imposed on white voters. Nor could blacks vote in Chase's Ohio or Lincoln's Illinois. Black activist Joseph Stanley published a letter in the *Chicago Tribune* charging that the state had no right to ask for black service so long as its discriminatory laws remained in effect. A few blacks dubbed the war a "white man's quarrel," and most recognized that the desperate need for fresh troops drove this new recruitment strategy every bit as much as any northern hatred of slavery. As soon as the country had "any real fighting to be done—any Bunker Hill battles to win," one abolitionist sourly observed, reluctant politicians "would doubtless be willing enough to have [black soldiers] shot or bayonetted."[22]

Although hardly naïve as to the correlation between national need and black service, more abolitionists and African Americans thought as did Douglass, who believed that black sacrifice would help stake a claim to political equality. As a Maryland runaway, Douglass harbored deep hatred for southern slaveholders and welcomed the chance for younger men to "go down and kill white rebels." Yet if a thirst for vengeance played a role, most of Douglass's public statements that winter followed a nobler path. "To fight for the Government in this tremendous war," Douglass assured a black Philadelphia audience, was "to fight for nationality and a place with all other classes of our fellow citizens." This apocalyptic war was sure to be followed by a countrywide reassessment, a new political order. Once a black man got "an eagle on his button, and a musket on his shoulder, and a bullet in his pocket," Douglass reasoned, there was "no power on earth" that could "deny that he has earned the right of citizenship in the United States." Supreme Court decisions might be overturned by future courts or amendments, especially once black troops' service forced whites to acknowledge the African American contribution to the saga of American democracy. "Remember Denmark Vesey, of Charleston," Douglass exhorted in his "appeal to arms" published widely in the North. "Remember Nathaniel Turner, of South Hampton!"[23]

Massachusetts, a state with an extensive history of antislavery activism, was the first to heed the call. Just days after the Emancipation Proclamation, Republican governor John A. Andrew requested authorization to raise two black regiments for three years' service, the Massachusetts Fifty-fourth and Fifty-fifth. On January 6, after Republicans beat back a last-ditch effort by a Kentucky senator to deny black soldiers *any* pay, Stanton granted the request, making these units, unlike those irregulars raised by Hunter and Saxton, the first formally authorized black regiments. Andrew regarded the Fifty-fourth "as perhaps the most important corps to be organized during the whole war." To lead it he turned to twenty-five-year-old Captain Robert Gould Shaw, a veteran of Antietam and the son of prominent Boston abolitionists. As it was "the first colored regiment to be raised in the free States," the governor informed Shaw's father, "its success or its failure will go far to elevate or depress" the future prospects of black Americans. Although unconvinced of the unit's potential success, Shaw agreed and gained promotion to the rank of colonel. Norwood P. Hallowell, also the son of abolitionists, signed on as Shaw's lieutenant, and Dr. John DeGrasse, a black doctor from Boston, served as the company's surgeon. "I [am] a Nigger Col," Shaw laughed, cheerfully embracing that epithet to ease the sting of his new role, and possibly unaware that a good many white teachers and activists were soon to apply the same hated word to their professional titles as they readied to move south.[24]

Because the state was home to but a small number of black men of military age, Andrew looked beyond Massachusetts's borders to fill his ranks. Douglass promptly put down his editor's pen in Rochester and took to the hustings to encourage enlistment. Traveling nearly two thousand miles as he crisscrossed the North, the forty-five-year-old Douglass first recruited abolitionists, including Delany, to act as agents for the unit. Then, speaking from western New York to Manhattan's Cooper Union to Philadelphia, he appealed to young men to sign up. Twenty-five listeners in Syracuse agreed, although in each community he also met with resistance and concern over whether the War Department would make good on its promise of equal pay and treatment for black soldiers. Douglass privately expressed some "hesitation" over Stanton's refusal to allow African Americans to serve as commissioned officers, but publicly he exhorted audience after audience to become part "of the glorious band who shall carry liberty to your enslaved people."[25]

Too old for active service himself, Douglass proudly announced that his two sons, Charles and Lewis, "were the first two in the State of New York to enlist." The elder of the two, Lewis, was twenty-two and a printer. Charles was nineteen on the day of his enlistment. Neither possessed their father's impressive height, but both had his surname, and possibly because of that Charles was promoted to lieutenant corporal shortly after arriving at Camp Meigs in Readville. There they were joined by Sojourner Truth's grandson James, who boasted that it was "our time [to] prove that we are men." Among those who agreed was runaway Stephen Ennis, a light-skinned musician from southern Pennsylvania, who swore he was legally free prior to the attack on Sumter, and Peter Smith, a twenty-four-year-old sailor born in Central America. Another Smith, named Thomas, crossed, or perhaps recrossed, the border from Montreal to enlist. Private Robert J. Simmons was a hazel-eyed clerk from Bermuda but still dark enough to pass for African American.[26]

Orders to ship out arrived in late May. Charles Douglass remained behind, too ill to travel, but Lewis, recently promoted to sergeant major, boarded the train for Boston, where Governor Andrew staged a parade down Beacon Street. Thousands turned out to wave the ten companies off as they boarded the *DeMolay* for the Carolina coast. William Lloyd Garrison, gazing down from the second floor of Wendell Phillips's home, wept quietly as he leaned against a bust of John Brown. Douglass remained on the wharf until the ship carrying his eldest son had sailed out of the harbor. The voyage south, Lewis reported, took "six sea-sick days" on water so choppy that some of the men "wish[ed] they never had gone for a soldier." Upon landing at Beaufort, Douglass met escaped pilot Smalls, who provided the navy with information about the Confederates' harbor defenses, and family friend Harriet Tubman, who at the age of forty-three was an unofficial "captain of a gang of men who pilot the Union forces into the enemy's country." Just days before, Tubman had helped steer three steamboats past Confederate mines as Union forces raided up the Combahee River and liberated hundreds of slaves.[27]

Only a few soldiers serving in the regiment hailed from the deep South, and in a preview of another fissure that was to plague the black community during the Reconstruction era, some in the unit thought

The moment the fighting began at Fort Sumter, black activists lobbied the federal government to allow free black men to serve. Among the first to join the pioneering Fifty-Fourth Massachusetts Infantry was New Bedford–born Lewis Douglass. Promoted to sergeant major shortly before the July 1863 attack on Fort Wagner, Douglass promised his fiancée that "should I fall in the next fight killed or wounded I hope to fall with my face to the foe." Courtesy Moreland-Springarn Library, Howard University.

black Carolinians—many of them the children and grandchildren of Africans—strange and foreign. Although himself the son of two Maryland-born African Americans, Lewis Douglass had been raised in Lynn, Massachusetts, and Rochester, New York, and he found those newly liberated to be almost quaint. "The natives seem to enjoy themselves very much here," he informed his fiancée. "I can hear them singing and praying nearly every night in their prayer meetings. They are a happy people." Harvard-educated Colonel Shaw had even less regard for a speech delivered to the camp by a freed minister, telling his mother that it "was very bad." But July 4 arrived and with it a grand celebration. A black boy read the Declaration of Independence, and a group of children stood below the flag and sang "My Country." "Can you imagine anything more wonderful than a coloured-Abolitionist meeting on a South Carolina plantation," Shaw enthused. "Here were collected all the freed slaves on the Island listening to the most ultra-abolition speeches, that could be made," while just months before, "their masters were still here, the lords of the soil & of them."[28]

Fourteen days later on July 18, hoping to capitalize on the recent victories at Gettysburg and Vicksburg, the regiment prepared for an assault on Fort Wagner, a fortified battery on Morris Island that guarded the southern entrance to Charleston Harbor. Days earlier, Confederate defenders had repelled an attack, and General Quincy Adams Gillmore, the Union officer who now ordered the assault, knew that casualties would be high. Lewis Douglass posted what he feared might be his final letter to his fiancée, Amelia Loguen, the daughter of Tennessee runaway and Syracuse activist Jermain W. Loguen. "Remember if I die I die in a good cause," he wrote. "What a day of rejoicing it will be the day that heralds the downfall of [Charleston] from whose halls and streets rang first that treason and disloyalty which has overturned the nation." Around six P.M., Shaw gave the order to march up the beach. The regiment approached within a mile of the fort, then lay with fixed bayonets and waited for darkness to descend. At length, Shaw stood, unsheathed his sword, and pointed it toward Wagner. "I want you to prove yourselves," he shouted. "The eyes of thousands will look on what you do tonight."[29]

Northern critics of black deployments had scoffed that African Americans would flee at the first sound of cannon. Yet racing behind Shaw, the regiment splashed through the waist-deep moat and clambered up the sandy rampart. One hundred soldiers reached the parapet, among them Lewis Douglass. "Our men fought like tigers," Douglass assured his worried parents, but they were badly outnumbered. The Confederates raked the parapet with "grape and canister," and the "splendid 54th is cut to pieces." Shaw was shot through the heart as he crested the rampart, and Hallowell was "wounded in three places." Sojourner Truth's grandson was taken captive, as were Jefferson Ellis, the sandy-haired boatman from Poughkeepsie, and Robert Simmons, the Bermuda-born clerk. Daniel Kelley, the young farmer from New York, died in the assault, one of 1,515 federal casualties lost before Gillmore finally called retreat. Although Douglass told his parents only that his "sword sheath [was] blown away," he was badly wounded as well. The next morning, Confederate defenders dug a ditch and buried the dead in the sand below the fort. When asked by a captured surgeon what had become of Shaw's body, the fort's commander smirked: "We have buried him in the trench with his niggers."[30]

To care for the wounded, "the irrepressible Harriet Tubman" ceased her scouting activities long enough to organize the freedwomen of Beaufort into a nursing corps. Douglass hoped to return to his regiment, but within weeks his wounds festered into gangrene. Shipped to Manhattan, Douglass was "seriously ill," and Dr. James McCune Smith, a Glasgow-trained black surgeon and abolitionist, judged him several months away from "even the lightest military duty." By then, his brother Charles had recovered enough to return to active service, and in the spring of 1864 Charles was discharged from the Fifty-fourth so that he might join the Fifth Massachusetts Cavalry as a first sergeant. Joining Charles's old regiment at about the same time was Nathan Sprague, a handsome former Maryland slave and gardener at the Douglass household in Rochester. Having caught the eye of Frederick Douglass's daughter Rosetta, Sprague enlisted in September and was married while on leave at Christmas; his papers indicated he was "volunteered by Frederick Douglass," and most likely his betrothal to the great abolitionist's daughter was contingent on military service.[31]

The survivors of the assault on Wagner understood that their struggle had only just begun. James Allen made it out of the fort alive but was captured in a skirmish days later. Not yet thirty, he languished in a prison camp near Florence, South Carolina, for seventeen months before starving to death a few days before Christmas in 1864. Henry Gardner, a laborer from New York, was wounded in action at Ocean Ponds, Florida, and died of his wounds while held captive in the infamous "Rebel Prison" at Andersonville, Georgia. Another laborer, the mysterious six-fingered Samuel Turner, who was born in 1842 in Southampton County, Virginia, signed on when Union forces established a base on nearby Mason's Island. He too was killed in action in his native Virginia as his regiment tried to fight its way into Richmond.[32]

Nor was Shaw the only white officer to fall at the head of his African American troops. Other reformers stepped forward in the days after the news of the attack on Wagner filled northern newspapers. Edward P. Adams, a graduate of Hamilton College and a schoolteacher before the war, was recommended for service as a lieutenant by family friend Samuel Gridley Howe, a physician and abolitionist from Boston. Known for his "courage, intellectual strength and sagacity," Adams did not live to witness the successes of Reconstruction. Edward L. Stevens left Harvard College during his senior year to enlist as a private in an all-white regiment. After Shaw fell in battle, Stevens requested a transfer to the Fifty-fourth as a lieutenant. While leading his regiment at Boykin's Mill, South Carolina, Stevens was shot and killed so close to Confederate fortifications that senior officers judged it too dangerous to retrieve his body. But his men, one reported, "promptly presented themselves for that duty." They recovered his body and buried Stevens just behind their lines; he was twenty-one.[33]

Even during the hardest campaigns, the black soldiers enjoyed lulls in fighting, and they put the quiet moments to good use. Many northern soldiers—the vast majority of whom hailed from working-class backgrounds and whose parents had been enslaved—found reading a chore. The fact that so many privates and noncommissioned black officers were illiterate in many instances hindered the carrying out of routine tasks of army life, and this forced white officers to undertake responsibilities that in all-white regiments were typically carried out by underlings. Literate black soldiers, who understood that their regiments were being closely monitored by suspicious white civilians, were embarrassed that so many privates scratched their "marks rather than their signatures on the payroll." James Jones of the Fourteenth Rhode Island Heavy Artillery admitted that his "face burned with shame" upon learning that only two hundred fifty of the nine hundred men in his regiment were functionally literate, and these were men born free in New York, Ohio, "and even in the very cradle of literature and learning[,] Massachusetts." As the nation invariably linked learning with the privileges of citizenship and voting, simply serving in the country's military would not be claim enough for political inclusion, Jones believed. His comrades would have to prove to their white neighbors that they were educated enough to help guide the republic as it emerged from the war.[34]

The soldiers required no prodding. Determined that their service would signal not only a finer day for their country but opportunities for themselves, the men were anxious to better their condition. A few ambitious black corporals already anticipated public careers should they survive the fighting. "Every camp had a teacher," Joseph T. Wilson of Massachusetts reported, and "in fact every company had some one to instruct the soldiers in reading." Many of the northern freemen had parents or grandparents who had resided in slave communities where the literate few had regarded it as their duty to assist the nonliterate majority, at least when away from the prying eye of the master. Blacks regarded book learning as a treasure consciously withheld from them, and so Thomas Wentworth Higginson was not surprised that his men's "love of the spelling-book [was] perfectly inexhaustible." Sometimes it was "the blind leading the blind," the Harvard-educated Higginson admitted. But many of the young troops who later became ministers and politicians, Wilson remembered, learned their "first letters" in camp, and battle-hardened soldiers thought it no dishonor to sit by the fire at night and receive "their first lessons from some manly officer." One female abolitionist applauded the desire of black soldiers to "*educate themselves*," if necessary, and in "the absence of teachers, they are determined to be self-taught." Some soldiers learned to march and read at the same time, she added, and "everywhere some elementary book may be seen in the hands of negroes."[35]

Even after the government embraced the use of black soldiers, the War Department failed to develop a comprehensive program of education for working-class troops of either race. As military law prohibited senior officers from issuing arbitrary orders, some colonels believed that they lacked the authority to demand that their recruits learn to read. Others, especially chaplains, stepped forward willingly. One minister insisted that the "cartridge box and spelling book" be "attached to the same belt." In particular the white officers who were the products of antislavery communities established informal schools within their regiments, and they knew whom to contact back home for assistance. As early as 1862, the Freedmen's Aid Society of Syracuse funded schools and supplied books to soldiers under Hunter's and Higginson's commands. By the dawn of 1863, the American Missionary Association provided teachers for units in the South, teaching 1,044 soldiers in informal camp schools. "I never witnessed greater eagerness for study," reported the chaplain of a regiment stationed in Louisiana. "The attendance of the men has been as regular as was consistent with the performance of their military duties."[36]

When no outside funding was available, black soldiers pooled their meager pay to hire civilian teachers. Since soldiers moved often, especially as Confederate-held territory began to shrink after the summer of 1863, they used their largest tent as a traveling school. One soldier in the Twenty-second Colored Infantry marveled that the unit's commander supplied them with "a big tent almost as long as a meeting house." When stationed in one locale for any length of time, soldiers foraged for materials and constructed a rude building they employed as both a schoolhouse and a camp chapel. Even during the final year of the conflict, when the soldiers found few quiet moments for study, most made enormous academic progress. One chaplain asserted that a totally illiterate corporal could sign his name after only two days, and after five months he could not only read the Bible and a tactical manual but maintain the company's reports. Another minister, who taught classes in a unit comprised of Pennsylvania freemen and former slaves from Maryland and Kentucky, cursed "the miserable institution of Slavery" for keeping his men "unacquainted with the alphabet." Yet once supplied with materials from the American Tract Society of Boston, his pupils made "surprisingly rapid progress."[37]

Nightly firesides became political schools as well. Soldiers practiced their newfound literacy on the era's highly partisan newspapers and debated policy and leadership. For those considering public service at war's end, the fact that black noncommissioned officers were blocked from advancing into commissioned ranks became a subject of bitter complaint. Each previous war had catapulted an entire generation of white veterans into political office, and by 1864, black soldiers had seen service enough to demonstrate their courage and management skills. Proven leaders remained sergeants and corporals while white recruits with less experience received preferential treatment when it came time for promotion. Black recruiters complained that the most effective way to spur enlistment was to assure African American recruits that they would be led by men of their own race. "I but ask for Justice regardless of my Colour," Private William D. Matthews insisted, "as we are all fighting for the same great and glorious Cause of Union and Liberty." Black soldiers wanted it understood that they asked for no special treatment, and they saw no contradiction in fighting for their country while serving their own ambitions. There were "hundreds of non-commissioned officers in colored regiments" who were amply qualified for advancement based on "education and experience," Lewis Douglass assured Stanton, careful in his missive to first emphasize black literacy. Simply instruct "the Board at Washington" to consider promotion without regard to race, another soldier contended, "and I have no fear for the result."[38]

Nor was it merely the promotions board in Washington that sought to keep black soldiers in subordinate positions. More than a few white officers who initially volunteered to lead black regiments found neither the men nor the cause to be what they expected. Some ambitious white captains had volunteered only to secure the promotion that had eluded them in white regiments. Even upper-class officers whose ideology tended toward abolitionism could be patronizing toward the working-class men they led. Colonel John F. Bartholf thought his men too tough on southern whites and protested that military policy was "no longer 'Conciliation' or 'Compromise' but 'Confiscation' & 'Emancipation.'" He requested a transfer. Unfortunately, Bartholf spoke for many northern conservatives who objected to Lincoln's evolving war aims. When black soldiers boarded a train in Philadelphia, residents of the City of Brotherly Love stoned the troops' cars. Black soldiers from New York, fretted one recruiter, "were abused worse than any negroes had been on the plantations, and they were abused by men who wore the uniform of the Army of the United States."[39]

As the stoning of black soldiers in Pennsylvania indicated, racial animosity was not a commodity reserved for Carolina planters. Streetcar lines across the North remained either segregated or simply off-limits to black passengers. Outside of Camp William, Pennsylvania, black women trod beside clanging streetcars as they journeyed to say a final farewell to their departing husbands and sons. "Our colored population promptly responded to the call for men to drive back the rebel invaders of Pennsylvania" following the Gettysburg campaign, observed a furious member of the Female Anti-Slavery Society, but black women had to hire expensive carriages to visit sick or dying relations. In most cases, state or local law did not require segregated cars, yet wounded black soldiers often waited in the rain or snow for black-only cars. After army surgeon Alexander Augusta was refused a seat on a Washington streetcar, Charles Sumner denounced the policy as a "disgrace to this city." When told that the Washington and Georgetown Railroad Company planned to purchase additional special cars for black riders, Salmon P. Chase exploded. "Who volunteers now a'days except colored men?" he demanded of the company's director. "Let all decent people ride in any car convenient when they get in." As a cabinet official and a stockholder in the company, Chase was in a position to have his way in the capital, but advocates of integration made less headway against popular prejudice elsewhere. When Private John Lee returned home to Manhattan on a fifteen-day furlough to bury two of his children, several toughs assaulted him and broke two of his ribs as he stepped off a streetcar on Broadway.[40]

Although Jefferson Davis never enforced his order to enslave captured black soldiers, some of his senior officers committed atrocities against black troops in violation of the code of war. When Confederates under the command of former slave trader Nathan Bedford Forrest overran Tennessee's Fort Pillow on April 12, 1864, soldiers shouting "No quarter" shot and bayoneted nearly three hundred black troops after they surrendered. Even more common was violence committed against individual black soldiers in captured areas of the South. In Morehead City, North Carolina, whites murdered a black soldier for taking "rather more liberty than an Anglo-Saxon [man] likes to submit to." Soldiers expected danger from uniformed opponents, and northern blacks were raised to be wary of white neighbors, but few were prepared for the threat of assassination in the dead of night; for those who moved into public service in the years after the war, such treatment provided early lessons in caution.[41]

Faced with endemic harassment from white southerners, black soldiers occasionally lashed out at those who fell under Union control. Alfred Lee, a young farmer from Pennsylvania, was wounded at Fort Wagner but returned to his regiment in time to serve as "guard" along the Carolina coast. One night, having endured one insult too many, Lee got into "a state of beastly intoxication" and prowled the streets, aiming his "loaded musket at a number of Citizens." Short on able-bodied men and weary of southern inhospitality themselves, Lee's superiors merely ordered him back to his tent until sober. In New Orleans, three black soldiers walking along Perdido Street were "insulted by a citizen." The three returned to their barracks, loaded their muskets, and combed the streets for their tormentor "with the intention of shooting him." A white officer arrived in time to order them to "go back to their quarters, which they did." Yet such brushes with violence between soldiers and civilians served as a reminder that the days in which haughty whites were able to freely abuse cowering blacks were long past.[42]

For the handful of black soldiers in northern regiments who hailed from the South, returning to the land of their birth could be a painful experience. Twenty-three-year-old Grimm Z. Smith signed on with the Massachusetts Fifty-fourth in September 1863, a self-described "artist" who provided neither honest nor consistent stories about his past. Smith assured one Boston recruiter that he had been born in "Calcutta," yet his company account book gave his birthplace as "Tahoe Arizona Terr[itory]," a curious fiction given that that lake sat on the border of the new states of California and Nevada. Shortly after the capture of Charleston, the light-skinned Smith burst into the Glebe Street home of Margaret Smith, waving a loaded pistol and shouting, "You damned bitch, I will kill you." Ordered to return to his quarters, Smith instead deserted and forever vanished from the public record. Because both victim and assailant bore a common surname, it remains possible that Private Smith joined the regiment in hopes of delivering a most personal message to a hated former owner, and having done so, disappeared.[43]

Far and away the biggest grievance for black soldiers was inequality in pay. Under the Militia Act of 1862, white enlistees received a salary of sixteen dollars each month, with an additional clothing allowance of three dollars and fifty cents. Black soldiers received ten dollars and faced a clothing deduction of three dollars. Because most black northerners came from working-class homes, the families they left behind faced financial hardships due to their absences, and the soldiers' meager pay only impoverished their wives further. "If the white man cannot support his family on seven dollars per month," grumbled John H. B. Payne, an Ohio schoolteacher, "I cannot support mine on the same amount." Many soldiers decided to serve without pay rather than accept an inferior salary, although their protests, as they well knew, imposed even greater privations on loved ones back home. Faced with a unified wall of opposition from Democrats regarding black military service, the War Department hoped a segregated pay schedule might dampen northern criticism, but all the policy did was provoke disharmony in the ranks. A soldier from a Rhode Island regiment warned one paymaster that "the boys will not take it." Just before the attack on Fort Wagner, Shaw complained about the policy, and despite the fact that the Massachusetts Assembly offered to pay the difference, the entire regiment voted to boycott each payday. Since even the least skilled soldier could earn seven dollars on the home front, the issue was ultimately about racial pride and self-respect. As one of Higginson's men explained to a reporter, "we won't 'spise ourselves so much for take de seben dollar." Some regiments, such as the Fifty-fourth, served for as long as eighteen months without pay in protest over their wages.[44]

More infuriating still for civilian progressives was that border-state masters received compensation for their bondmen who enlisted in the military. James Mathews, a self-professed "loyal citizen" of Maryland, donated his eighteen-year-old slave Frank Tyler for service and then filed a claim for compensation. The practice grew particularly common following the 1863 draft law, which allowed northern men to provide substitutes or buy their way out of combat. John J. Cooke, whose wealthy father owned the segregated Washington and Georgetown Railroad Company, hired James H. Adair, a young freeman, as his substitute. One former master, John W. Helsby of Talbot County, Maryland, demanded the standard three hundred dollars compensation for Private Levin Barrett, whom he had purchased in 1842 at the age of seven for far less. Evidently Helsby expected Barrett to serve him after the war, and when the soldier instead died of pneumonia in a Florida military hospital, Helsby thought himself ill-used. Black Americans actually serving in combat believed otherwise, and wondered how an antislavery administration could pay them so little while handing out generous bonuses to loyal slaveholders. In this cause, as in similar campaigns during Reconstruction, black activists discovered they enjoyed a handful of white allies. Maryland judge Hugh L. Bond, a former Whig who had voted Constitutional Union in 1860 but was increasingly radicalized by the war, protested the policy to Stanton. "The Government makes no such allowance to a poor [white] father whose son is enlisted," he fumed, "nor to the mechanic whose apprentice is drafted." Just a few years earlier, a group of "ultra pro-slavery" legislators had tried to drive free blacks from the state by proposing a law that threatened to sell them to the highest bidder, and now that war had come, those same legislators opted to purchase substitutes for their sons while receiving taxpayer monies for donating slaves to the military before they might be emancipated.[45]

Some carried their complaints to the highest levels of government. In late July 1863, Francis George Shaw wrote to the president regarding his "only son," who had died earlier that month at Fort Wagner "& now lies buried in its ditch." The late colonel's men had served without pay, Shaw observed, yet they had proven "their valor & devotion in the field." Now their government must respect "their rights" and fight for them. Massachusetts governor Andrew also lobbied the president, noting that during the War of 1812, the federal government had paid black soldiers from New England the same wage as white men. "Thus half a century ago," Andrew lectured, the government saw no reason to "deny the wages of a soldier" to anyone who served, "not even though he was black." Why, the governor wondered, did a Republican administration now pay greater attention to race than had President James Madison, a Virginia slaveholder? One month later, on August 10, Frederick Douglass paid a call on the president to push for equal salaries. Douglass found Lincoln affable and "kindly," if noncommittal. Lincoln believed that as conservative Democrats "despised" the use of black troops, a segregated pay scale "helped smooth the way." Although impressed with the president's honesty and lack of "vain pomp and ceremony," Douglass demurred, speaking for the "trustworthy and Patriotic Colored men" under arms. Abolitionists thought him slow to act, Lincoln conceded, but once he had "taken a position," he promised, he never "retreated from it."[46]

In the House of Representatives, seventy-one-year-old congressman Thaddeus Stevens of Pennsylvania was not inclined to be patient. On December 14, 1863, he introduced legislation to equalize pay, and for good measure, he also drafted a bill to repeal the hated Fugitive Slave Act of 1850. On June 11, 1864, both chambers passed the first bill, which not only placed black soldiers "on a footing of equality" with white troops but also provided back pay to cover past discrimination. Yet even at that late date, Congress retained the enlistment bounty promised to loyal masters, although it reduced the award to one hundred dollars.[47]

On the front lines, where common soldiers of both races were thrown together in ways unimaginable to all but the most progressive Republican in Washington, competence in battle eroded entrenched northern racism. "I have been one of those men, who never had much confidence in colored troops," one soldier admitted, "but these doubts are now all removed, for they fought as bravely as any." Respect for combat prowess did not necessarily translate into support for black social equality, but most African American soldiers were willing to settle for political gain, and that was more easily accomplished. It was far "safer to trust 4,000,000 loyal negroes than 8,000,000 disloyal whites," a white Illinoisan mused, for "the faithful & patriotic negro soldiers have richly earned the boon of suffrage." Moderate Republicans were reluctant to push for black voting rights for fear of alienating their constituents. But following the courageous assault on Petersburg, Virginia, led by African American troops, one black chaplain crowed that the attack would be remembered as the moment "when prejudice died in the entire Army." As white soldiers grew accustomed to seeing black men in camp, and as anger and frustration toward southern planters grew in the bloody war of attrition that ensued after Gettysburg, more than a few officers endorsed all manner of equality. "A few more fights like" Petersburg, one effused, "and our Col[ore]d boys will have established their manhood if not their Brotherhood to the satisfaction of even the most prejudiced."[48]

Newspaper accounts of battlefield valor on the part of black soldiers quickly reached the home front, and activists believed the time had come to advance long-held demands. John Jones, a black abolitionist based in Chicago, successfully lobbied the Illinois legislature "morning, noon, and evening" for the removal of the state's discriminatory statutes. Boston's John S. Rock became the first black attorney to present a case to the Supreme Court, an act one magazine regarded as an "indication of the revolution which is going on in the sentiments of a great people." To celebrate Lincoln's fifty-sixth birthday, Reverend Henry Highland Garnet, born a slave in Maryland, delivered a sermon in the hall of the national House of Representatives, an occasion he used to press for black citizenship. Governor Andrew continued to urge the administration to reward combat initiative. In March 1864, Andrew promoted Stephen A. Swails of the Fifty-fourth to second lieutenant upon the recommendation of a white colonel, although it took Secretary Stanton ten months to approve the appointment. Andrew advanced the names of several other men as well, including C. L. Mitchell, who was instead mustered out after a cannonball shaved off his foot the following November. In February 1865, Lincoln approved a commission for Martin Delany, who became a major of infantry and the highest ranking African American officer during the war.[49]

For Douglass, who had high ambitions for his sons, citizenship was only the first step. Just months earlier, thoughts of black veterans serving in the nation's counsels would have struck even the most optimistic reformer as absurd, but with black lawyers appearing before the Supreme Court, could political or judicial service be far behind? "You and I know that the mission of this war is National regeneration," Douglass told an audience at New York City's Cooper Union, the same venue where Lincoln had made his reputation in early 1860. Douglass envisioned the "black man a soldier in war; a laborer in peace; a voter at the South as well as at the North." Within a year of the formation of the Fifty-fourth, talented and ambitious black northerners were demonstrating leadership capacity, inspiring others with their courage, leading troops in battle after the death of white officers, and learning to inspire fellow soldiers with their words and deeds. If anything, Douglass underestimated the value of African American service under arms. No fewer than forty-one black delegates to the postwar southern conventions that would draft new state constitutions were veterans. Sixty-four future state legislators had once donned Union blue, as had three lieutenant governors (including Captain Pinckney B. S. Pinchback, who also briefly served as acting governor of Louisiana). Military service opened doors for four congressmen, one of whom, army chaplain Hiram R. Revels, went on to the U.S. Senate. Many others, including Major Delany, held lower offices, such as jury commissioner. As former Virginia slave Lewis Lindsay put it upon being elected to his state's constitutional convention in 1867, "thank God that the negroes had learned to use guns, pistols, and ram-rods."[50]

As Lindsay's career suggests, by late 1863, large numbers of southern blacks joined with Union forces as northern generals aggressively pushed south in the months after Gettysburg and Vicksburg. Initially, only Massachusetts's New England neighbors followed the Bay State in raising black regiments, but other northern states soon followed. In May 1863, the War Department officially organized the Bureau of Colored Troops, and that October, Lincoln authorized the recruitment of men still enslaved in Delaware, Maryland, Missouri, and Tennessee. Since it appeared "that all of the colored people South of Washington were struggling to get to Massachusetts," a migration of young men that served only "to take recruits [away] from Virginia," Lincoln decided it made better sense to enlist bondmen in the upper South. Compensation for their masters eased criticism from the border states, but white resistance in Kentucky was so great that Stanton delayed placing a recruiting post there until early 1864. Even then, Governor Thomas E. Bramlette groused that any officer who encouraged bondmen to leave their masters and enlist should be prosecuted under state law. Nonetheless, almost twenty-four thousand black Kentuckians served in the nation's military. Since Lincoln had captured only 1,364 votes in Kentucky in 1860, the notion that black veterans deserved the ballot began to strike even moderate Republicans as sound politics. More progressive Republicans, such as Sumner, feared that Lincoln might lose in 1864, or that the Republican convention would abandon the president in favor of his increasingly conservative secretary of state, William H.

Seward, and so he wished to arm as many southern blacks as possible as quickly as possible.[51]

"It has been understood that our troops carried liberty with them wherever they bore their conquering eagles," one Albany editor enthused, "that all the shackles of despotism were removed." For those yet enslaved, the chance to earn their freedom was the most obvious incentive. For soldiers fresh out of bondage, the opportunity to extend that liberty to loved ones meant more than winning the right of citizenship. Nat Gadsden, who carried the surname of prominent white Carolinians, fled Charleston and signed on as a cook with General William Tecumseh Sherman's invading army. In some cases the slaves' motives were sophisticated. Most white officers assumed that southern runaways understood little of wartime politics beyond a quest for their freedom and so the officers were surprised when soldiers such as Charles W. Singer, a sergeant from Kentucky, expounded on the larger dimensions of the conflict. Evidently aware that Lee's invading army had enslaved free black Pennsylvanians during the Gettysburg campaign, Singer grasped the implications of a Union victory and Lincoln's reelection for all black Americans. "We should not forget the fact that the free colored man's elevation is at issue, as well as the slave's," Singer observed. "Suppose the rebel army was as far North as the Union army is South; what would be the result? Our homes would have been burned to the ground, and our aged and defenseless parents barbarously treated." Fighting for freedom at a time when British and French forces had invaded Mexico, and after the second French republic had collapsed in a coup d'état, Singer understood that the "eyes of the world" were upon black men. Like Lincoln, he believed that "the stability of this Government [was] a source of strength to other nations." By war's end, of the 178,000 blacks who served, 140,313 were former bondmen recruited from the slave states.[52]

As had their northern brethren, southern blacks signed on with the Union army for a variety of reasons. If military service meant hard times for their families, liberation meant little, and savvy bondmen pressed northern officers about pay and bonuses. There was never any chance that blacks might be loyal to the Confederacy, one abolitionist reported, but early in the conflict, slaves simply scattered "to the woods" as federal soldiers approached, opting for a safe neutrality in a war waged by white men over reunion. The presence of black soldiers from the North, together with "large bounties, have induced many to enlist," so that "nearly every able-bodied man is now in uniform." Prudent soldiers, having while enslaved been allowed no property beyond a rude chair or table, tucked their salaries safely away in hopes of a better life after the fighting ended. William R. Jervay, a domestic slave of South Carolina's Gabriel Manigault, ran off to join the 128th USCT; at the age of eighteen, he was promoted to commissary sergeant. By 1865, he had put aside capital enough to open a small store in Charleston. Within five years, the future state senator was able to buy a farm of 257 acres worth nine hundred fifty dollars. Living in a society that placed great emphasis on land—and as former property themselves who knew how to tend crops—most southern black soldiers aspired to become farmers. On occasion, siblings pooled their income, and officers reported instances of entire regiments organizing building associations. "Every colored man will be a slave," Sergeant Prince Rivers explained, "and feel himself a slave, until he can *raise him own bale of cotton* and *put him own mark upon it* and say *Dis is mine!*"[53]

For men whom life had literally beaten down, banding together with passing armies was a way to demonstrate racial pride. Union officers, understanding that, played upon it. The commander of the Fifty-ninth Colored Infantry staged ceremonies in which runaways stripped off their tattered clothes. The rags were then burned, and the newly freed men were handed fresh uniforms. "This was the biggest thing that ever happened in my life," remembered one former slave. "I felt like a man with a uniform on and a gun in my hand." For runaways, new clothing was no mere matter of fresh apparel. To don a uniform worn by thousands of other free men, and to hold a weapon banned by southern law, constituted physical evidence of freedom and membership in a national cause to bring freedom to those still enslaved. As one white soldier who witnessed the transformation observed, "Put a United States uniform on his back and the *chattel* is a *man*." As slaves, they could not legally leave their masters' estate without a pass, and some took special pleasure in walking "fearlessly and boldly" down the streets of captured

New Orleans, Atlanta, and Charleston. Other black men, remembering how proslavery polemicists defended their way of life by infantilizing African Americans and describing adult blacks as children, took pains to emphasize their manhood. "Now we sogers are men—for the first time in our lives," a black Carolina sergeant insisted. "Now we can look our old masters in de face. They used to sell and whip us, and we did not dare say one word," but should he now come across his previous masters, he would not hesitate "to run the bayonet through them."[54]

Since soldiers routinely charged with fixed bayonets, the sergeant's words were more than simply bravado. Knowing that blacks they once had brutalized—and aggressive young men with little prejudice against violence, at that—now possessed the weapons and training to do them harm, terrified whites. That terror, which the whites had previously hidden from the slave community and perhaps even from themselves, in turn emboldened blacks yet held in bondage. Few black soldiers were openly vengeful, but neither were veterans of tough campaigns willing to accept verbal abuse from white Confederates who fell under Union control. In New Orleans, black soldiers boarded streetcars, refused to yield the sidewalk, and talked back to whites who insulted them, "while hundreds of idle negroes," one southerner complained, "stood around, laughing and applauding." Abram, a Carolina recruit, confided that he had always feared whites until he saw how fearful they were of black soldiers. "Diabolical savages" such as Abram, planter Henry Ravenel complained, turned his "quiet, contented, & happy people" into "dissatisfied, unruly, madmen." Rather than admit that their slaves had always been "intoxicated with the fumes" of liberty, southern whites instead assured themselves that their laborers were being led astray by abolitionists and Republican officers.[55]

By the day in November 1864 when Lincoln was reelected, the old South was shattered beyond repair. In seceding and precipitating a civil war, ironically, planter-politicians had eventually forced reluctant Republicans in Washington to arm black Americans and elevate the conflict into a revolutionary struggle that challenged racism in all sections of the republic. As black activists meeting in a convention in Syracuse, New York, observed, "after nearly two centuries of sufferings unparalleled in the world's history," black Americans had "come to the rescue of the country." That more than eighty percent of those armed saviors had been chattel at the time of secession indicates how sudden and stunning this revolution was. Many northern whites who had denounced the Emancipation Proclamation and sworn they would never fight beside black soldiers grew to respect the courage of black regiments, even if they resisted resulting claims of political or social equality. Typical in this was William M. Dickson, a Midwestern Republican. Although Dickson thought it unfair to "place the bravery of negro soldiers above that of the white," he conceded that "but for the opposition of the entire negro population to the rebel cause, we could scarcely have succeeded."[56]

As Union generals prepared for a final march toward Richmond, and as black soldiers readied for a conclusive assault on the remnants of slavery, the administration prepared to send out invitations for the spring 1865 inaugural. One of them was mailed to Frederick Douglass, who had often been the president's fiercest critic. Believing his sons' service earned him the honor, every bit as much as had his own crusade against slavery, Douglass accepted. When the president could "no longer withstand the current," Douglass remarked, "he swam with it." Shortly thereafter, when Major Delany returned to Manhattan, the *New York Herald* reported that he and his men were met by "a large crowd of friends and relatives, who cheered the gallant soldiers enthusiastically." That night, Delany was feted and toasted at the elegant Astor House, as any successful white officer would have been, and glasses were raised to Sherman's increasingly black army of liberation. The last moments of the war were at hand, and with them, slavery's end.[57]

CHAPTER TWO

"To Forget and Forgive Old Scores"

War's End, Activism's Beginning

A T THE AGE OF FOURTEEN, Dolly was put up for sale at auction. In later years, her son William told of Dolly boldly marching up to a man she hoped was kind and asking him to buy her, saying she "liked his looks." The prospective buyer was thirty-four-year-old Andrew Johnson, then a Tennessee state senator. Born into poverty in North Carolina, Johnson was apprenticed to a tailor, but while still young he ran away to Tennessee, where he opened what became a very successful tailor shop in the front room of his home. At the age of eighteen, he married sixteen-year-old Eliza McCardle, the daughter of a shoemaker. Eliza taught her young husband to read and write, skills he mastered so inelegantly that he later required the aid of co-authors and editors in composing his state papers. Johnson's growing prosperity as a tradesman earned him no respect at the hands of his landowning neighbors, and so in 1842 he bought Dolly and became a slaveholder. Shortly thereafter, he purchased her half brother Sam as well.[1]

Over the next several decades, Johnson rose in the political world, first as a congressman, then as Tennessee's governor. In 1857 he became a U.S. senator; in 1860 his renown was such that some Democrats thought of putting his name forward for the presidency, and Johnson himself hoped that he might be named as Stephen Douglas's running mate. As his political fortunes grew, so too did his ownership of black Americans. According to the 1850 census he owned four, and six appeared in the 1860 listing, but as he rented some to other whites—on occasion he hired Sam out to chop wood for his neighbors—that was probably an undercount. In various speeches just before and during the war, he boasted ownership of as many as ten slaves. (Prudently, he later assured Frederick Douglass that he had never *sold* a single slave.) But given that Johnson was a city dweller and a politician who was often away in Washington, his purchases reflected his desire to impress his state's planter politicians far more than they filled any economic purpose. Some of his slaves helped Eliza with her household duties, but his income would have enabled him to hire domestics rather than purchase them had he wished to do so. At least in part because Johnson petitioned the president to exempt Tennessee, Lincoln's Emancipation Proclamation did not apply there or to the loyal border states of Missouri, Kentucky, Maryland, and Delaware, or to portions of the Confederate theater then under Union control; so Johnson's slaves were not among those liberated on January 1, 1863. But as the appointed governor of Tennessee and a man of ambition, Johnson thought it politically expedient to free his slaves later that year. Their liberation came just in time for Johnson to be tapped as Lincoln's running mate in 1864, replacing the reliably antislavery Republican Hannibal Hamlin, whose Maine residence rendered him a less credible symbol of unionism than the Tennessee tailor.[2]

Johnson's relationship with Dolly and Sam remained complicated, or at least typical of the more multifaceted interactions common to whites and domestics in urban or small farm settings. By the time Sam was thirty, Johnson's son Charles encouraged his father to sell the slave into the country, complaining in a semiliterate letter that Johnson's "kindness" had turned the bondman into one who did not "know [his] place." When ordered to cut wood for a neighbor, evidently without compensation, Sam replied that he would "be damned" if he would, and when threatened by Charles with sale, Sam laughed that Johnson might do as he "pleased, he did not care a *dam*." Later, upon becoming free, Sam adopted the surname of his former owner and took a position as commissioner with the Bureau of Refugees, Freedmen, and Abandoned

Lands, more commonly known as the Freedmen's Bureau, an agency established in March 1865 to assist former slaves and impoverished whites with food, education, and labor contracts. In a letter written in 1867 to then-president Andrew Johnson, which revealed previously hidden intellectual gifts superior to those on display in Charles's clumsy missive, Samuel Johnson inquired about a parcel of land "on which to build a School House for the education of the Coloured children of Greeneville." Should Johnson be willing to part with one of his tracts west of town, the freedman promised to send him "the money." Although employed by a federal agency despised by southern Democrats, Samuel promised his old master that he had "not changed any in Politics still being for you as much as ever." Despite his public hostility to the Bureau and its endeavors, Johnson, perhaps flattered by Samuel's professed desire to call on him when possible, agreed to the sale.[3]

The vice president's relationship with Dolly was more curious still. As an adult, Dolly gave birth to three children: Liz, Florence, and William. Although described by census takers as "black," her light-skinned children were listed as "mulattoes." Their father might have been anybody in Greeneville, yet Johnson's gentleness toward her children, together with the fact that William was given the same forename as Johnson's brother, led Tennessee whites to speculate that Andrew Johnson maintained a "colored concubine." Characteristic was Johnson's 1854 letter to his son Robert, in which he promised small gifts for Robert and Andrew Jr., together with "a little chair for Liz and Florence." But as the war turned into an antislavery crusade, Eliza Johnson, aware of what needed to be done to advance her husband's career, called the slaves together and, according to William, "said we were free now. She said we were free to go, or we could stay if we wanted. We all stayed." (Slavery remained legal in Tennessee as late as February 22, 1865, when Unionists finally ratified an amendment to the state constitution banning the institution.) William Johnson lived long enough to meet President Franklin D. Roosevelt and writer Ernie Pyle. The president gave the freedman a cane, but Pyle wondered "if he [hadn't been] better off when Andrew Johnson owned him than since then." To that, the seventy-nine-year-old William replied, "Yes, we were mighty well off then. But any man would rather be free than be a slave."[4]

Two years after he bought Dolly (middle), then-congressman Andrew Johnson denounced abolitionist petitions in the House of Representatives. "If you liberate the negro, what will be the next step?" Johnson wondered. "It would place every splay-footed, bandy-shanked, humpbacked negro in the country upon an equality with the poor white man." Yet William (bottom) and Sam Johnson (top), who later worked for the Freedmen's Bureau, remembered Johnson as a lenient master who allowed him to hire his own time and keep a portion of his wages. Courtesy National Park Service.

By the final year of the war, as unfree labor collapsed along the border, Sam and Dolly had to make a number of choices, as did millions of black Americans across the dying Confederacy. Many of the questions they had to wrestle with were unavoidable, yet they offered up few easy solutions. Like thousands of bondmen and bondwomen across the South, Sam and Dolly had no surnames as late as 1863. Sam adopted the name of his owner rather than his biological father, possibly being unsure as to that man's identity. Dolly's choice was less obvious; if she too took the vice president's surname for herself and her children, that might reinforce local rumors as to their paternity. Now that they were free, should they stay or leave, and if they chose to quit Eliza's home, where would they go? As a male, Samuel Johnson had the option of public service with a federal agency, a profession not open to the possibly illiterate Dolly. As did young William, they desired freedom, but like all Americans trying to survive a ghastly civil conflict, they also wondered how the final moments of the war would unfold, and how those last days, together with their own actions, would shape the national Reconstruction that was next to come.

White policymakers in Washington and Richmond faced hard choices as well. In the months after the successful summer campaigns of 1863, Lincoln began to draft plans for the restoration of the Confederate South, and especially for those sections that had already fallen to federal troops. As he prepared his December message to Congress, Lincoln consulted with party leaders about how to gather southern Unionists back into the national fold. Senator Charles Sumner of Massachusetts was dismayed to discover that Lincoln tended to think of Unionists as whites, as Sumner suspected that African Americans were the only men in the Confederacy loyal to the United States. Lincoln finally chose to split the difference, informing Congress that he was prepared to offer surrendering rebels a "full pardon" complete with "restoration of all rights of property, except as to slaves," as soon as ten percent of the population of voting age took an oath of allegiance. Roughly eleven thousand Louisianans promptly accepted his terms, agreed to black liberty, and elected a governor and state legislature. The president quietly lobbied the new governor to confer the vote on "the very intelligent

[blacks] and especially those who have fought gallantly in our ranks."
Not only did the "loyal" assembly refuse to do so, but sixteen members
stubbornly cast their votes against emancipation. As ever, the president
found himself wedged between party moderates and frustrated progressives. He conceded that the emerging political order in Louisiana was
what "the egg is to the fowl," but he thought it wiser to "have the fowl
by hatching the egg than by smashing it." Southern blacks were less
confident. One complained to Sumner that it was "better [to] smash the
egg than permit it to produce a viper." Even so, Lincoln's growing support for black voting rights reflected a new phase in his thinking, and
his ten-percent plan, he insisted, was a wartime measure meant to encourage Confederate defections rather than constitute a final Reconstruction program.[5]

Republicans in Congress countered with a bill crafted by Ohio senator Benjamin F. Wade and Congressman Henry Winter Davis of Maryland. The act made restoration contingent on the capitulation of a
majority of southern whites in each state, instead of Lincoln's far smaller
percentage, and that majority would then have to swear an "ironclad
oath" testifying they had never "voluntarily borne arms" in support of
the Confederacy (a carefully crafted phrase that exempted southern
draftees). But the bill, like Lincoln's message to Congress, was silent on
black voting rights, and even then four Republicans, including Lyman
Trumbull of Illinois, voted against the measure. The fact that Davis was
a moderate and a cousin to David Davis, Lincoln's longtime friend and
1860 campaign manager, indicated that the bill was designed as much to
maintain a Congressional role in the process as it was to impose tougher
requirements on white southerners. Primarily for that reason, the president, who wished to retain control of Reconstruction, pocket vetoed the
law in July 1864.[6]

The intra-party squabbles in Washington, as well as the yawning
gulf that separated the president and his party from Democrats when it
came to issues of race and slavery, meant little to black southerners, who
continued to force the question by voting with their feet. As Union
forces carved into the Confederacy in the fall of 1864, slaves took the
opportunity to flee in increasingly large numbers. In the years before
the war, young bondmen typically ran away by themselves, or with a

friend, and usually from border South counties adjacent to free soil. Now entire families and even plantations took advantage of moving Union lines and federal gunboats on the Mississippi. As Douglass assured Lincoln, "every slave who escapes from the Rebel states is a loss to the Rebellion and a gain to the Loyal Cause," for flight withdrew thousands of productive field hands. White soldiers who expected to find cowering slaves in conquered territory were often surprised by the warmth of their welcome. Iowa soldier John Shepherd heard the "shouting" long before his unit stumbled upon the blacks who "came out to meet us." One elderly woman "was jumping up and down and Shouting Glory to God and the Yankees," since now her ten children were "all free haliluyah." Another soldier came across a single woman near camp. She offered to help prepare dinner for his men, asked about directions toward safety, and, perhaps intending to disguise herself as a soldier, exchanged her services as cook for "pants, coat & cap of one of the boys." She asked for a gun, too, which a surprised soldier handed over.[7]

In northern Virginia, where word of mouth and the so-called slave grapevine were quick to spread word of affairs in Washington and Richmond, self-emancipated slaves engaged in a veritable "stampede" toward federal lines. Especially after the state of Virginia tried to "impress" free blacks and up to twenty thousand slaves into the Confederate army for the limited purposes of "erecting batteries [and] entrenchments," African Americans "scattered in every direction," a disgruntled Virginia justice of the peace admitted, with "some leaving the Country." Even in the months after Union general Benjamin F. Butler adopted a policy of liberating contraband, Virginia slaves had wisely chosen to watch events, fearing Union lines were too far to reach or dreading the cost of failure. But after Confederate general Robert E. Lee called upon the War Department to commandeer "52 negroes to work on fortifications" and labor for the dangerous "Nitre and Mining Bureau," both slaves and free blacks had no choice but to risk everything by making their way toward Washington.[8]

A number of high-ranking Confederates and influential whites lost slaves in the mass exodus. After John A. Washington, the late president's great-grandnephew, rode south to join the Confederate army, the slaves at his Mount Vernon estate took advantage of his absence to liberate themselves. Some marched down the Potomac for the capital. Others waited nearby until they deemed it safe, moved back into their old cabins, and began to support themselves as free farmers and hired hands. Closer still to Lincoln's White House were the sixty-three bondmen and bondwomen owned by Mary Custis Lee at Arlington plantation. When Mary's father, George Washington Parke Custis, died in 1857, he stipulated in his will that his slaves were all to be freed within five years, a promise to which he alerted his slaves. But Mary's husband and her father's executor, then-colonel Robert E. Lee, believed that unfree labor was crucial to improving Arlington House's financial status. He rented eleven of them away to nearby whites and sent others to the family's Pamunkey River estates. When bondman Wesley Norris and his cousin Mary tried to escape in 1859, Lee instructed his overseer to give them fifty and twenty lashes, respectively; on leave from the military, Lee watched to ensure that the stripes were laid "on well." In accordance with his father-in-law's instructions, Lee officially freed Mary's slaves on December 29, 1862, but by that date her plantation had been seized by federal troops and her slaves had found freedom across the river in Washington.[9]

Elsewhere in Virginia, black refugees congregated in towns and ports under Union control. In Norfolk, five thousand free blacks and runaways gathered to celebrate the Emancipation Proclamation at the charred ruins of a makeshift school torched by local whites. Former slave Harriet Jacobs reported that literate freedmen in Alexandria had set up a school for eighty "little contrabands." The presence of soldiers "[had taken] all fear out of their hearts, and inspired them with hope and confidence," Jacobs observed, and in exchange recently liberated women, despite having little themselves, had "fed the soldiers at their own tables." The cheers and support of black southerners, together with their growing anger at "disloyal" civilians, further eroded the already diminishing racial animosity of white officers. Lieutenant Hiram Allen, for instance, directed his men in November 1863 that all black Virginians, regardless of gender or age, "who may quit the plantations, and join your train, are not to be driven back, but are to be protected by you." Should they arrive bearing "any of their masters' property," he added, "you are to protect that also," as soldiers were under no obligation "to restore any such property" to slaveholders. The longer the war lasted, the more radicalized officers such as Allen became, as they witnessed scenes of white cruelty and black daring. As 1864 dawned, the Army of the Potomac had become a machine of liberation, an army that was inspired by black activism and in turn stimulated black autonomy. Typical was Cyrus, a Virginia bondman who informed his former owner there was "goin' terbe no more Master and Mistress, [as] All is equal." Cyrus was also done working in the fields and preferred to cook. "Besides," he reasoned in a succinct accounting of past labor due, "de kitchen ob de big house is my share. I help built hit."[10]

Farther south, as General William T. Sherman's army sliced across Georgia and began its march into South Carolina, African Americans far from what once had been the front lines experienced their first taste of freedom. For planters, Sherman was the cruel enemy, but for the black men and women owned by southern politicians, federal troops were an angry God's sword. "Us looked for the Yankees," recalled Savilla Burrell, as if they were "de host of angels at de second comin'." Again and again, soldiers and recruiters on the march commented on the Biblical terminology employed by liberated slaves. James M. Simms, a future Georgia assemblyman who had been publicly whipped the year before for teaching other slaves to read, wrote of slaves greeting the army, shouting, "Glory be to God, we are free." Cotton Belt slaves who had learned from childhood not to trust even friendly whites marveled at the increasingly interracial army, as thousands of black soldiers and recently liberated recruits marched behind Sherman's advance troops. As soldiers filed into Savannah, blacks poured into the streets, hugging the troops and reaching out to touch the sleeves of nearby officers. "Shout the glad tidings o'er Egypt's dark sea," rejoiced an aged Georgian. "Jehovah has triumphed, his people are free."[11]

If liberated blacks along the Carolina coast saw the hand of providence in Sherman's army, that meant their former owners were cast in the role of pharaoh's people, as a few perceptive masters understood. Bondage had been particularly harsh in the cotton and rice fields of the low country, and some young men who had fled to join Sherman returned to wreak vengeance. In Beaufort, a gang of workers remained on the estate only long enough to administer "a beating" to their owner.

Black soldiers who had witnessed the sale of loved ones broke open the family vault at William Middleton's plantation and scattered his ancestors' bones before putting Middleton on trial for his life. Soldiers and slaves at Chicora Wood, the estate of Robert Allston, burned the plantation records and helped themselves to provisions from the storehouse. They "*think it right* to steal from us," Allston fumed, "as the Israelites did the Egyptians." Even when runaways did not tarry to exact retribution, masters who flattered themselves as benevolent were stunned when entire communities simply vanished overnight. While dining in his Charleston townhome, William Grimball received news that all eighty of his laborers, "men, women & children," had quit his estate. His overseer had heard rumors of a nearby federal ship, and he had hurried to the fields to usher the slaves "to a place of safety but found them already gone." Such mass escapes required extensive planning and leadership, and masters were particularly aggrieved to discover that trusted drivers—enslaved foremen who answered only to white overseers and owners—often guided entire plantations toward Union lines. "Mr. Grimball is quite unstrung by it," his wife admitted.[12]

Similar scenes played out in the great plantation districts along the Mississippi. Here too, soldiers were welcomed by throngs of "Negro men & women waving their hats and wight hankerchieves." Before war's end, nearly one hundred thousand enslaved Mississippians—about one fourth of all African Americans in the state—came within advancing Union lines. Desperate slaveholders tried a number of tactics to dissuade their laborers from fleeing. Some warned their slaves that federal officers would work them to death "on de big forts" along the river. When asked why blacks crowded into federal camps despite such cautions, one runaway laughed at the foolishness of the question. "Oh, we knowed massa lied," he chuckled. Other masters resorted to more draconian measures. Soldiers reported women arriving in camp bloodied from having had their ears carved off as lessons to other potential runaways. Hardly dissuaded, Archy Vaughn ran for Union lines, but failed. Having caught up to him, his master tied him up, castrated him, and shaved off the lobe of his left ear. Taking no chances, one group of Mississippi runaways slit their overseer's throat before quitting the plantation.[13]

Most escaping slaves, however much they might have been mis-treated, did not seek to abuse their former masters. But more than a few settled old scores with a brutal farewell to the owners' property. Black soldiers with the Thirty-fifth discovered Carolina mansions scarred "by hatchets and axes, the doors and windows broken out, [and] the fruit trees cut down." In Mississippi, slaves torched fourteen homes and set fire to a county courthouse, the local symbol of Confederate author-ity. As such acts of arson revealed, slaves took special pleasure in de-stroying those structures associated with plantation discipline. Bells that had rung slaves into the fields in early mornings were pulled down, and "task houses" where defiant bondmen had been confined or whipped were burned. A number of officers observed just how much runaways hated and feared plantation dogs. Several soldiers approached one estate owned by a minister, who assured them that the dogs would not "bite, cep'n yo' is niggers," as the animals were "nigger dogs." Carolina bond-men warned Major Henry Hitchcock, one of Sherman's officers, that most dogs they encountered were trained to "catch nigga, Sah, and catch de soldiers dat run away." When his men shot one of the large hounds, the refugees "were in great glee over" its death. "[N]o wonder," Hitch-cock mused.[14]

As Hitchcock's sympathy indicated, by the last year of the war Union soldiers and southern bondmen often became partners in liberation. That was particularly true when the soldiers in question were black. In Louisiana, diarist Kate Stone grumbled, slaves from four plantations fled as a group for a nearby encampment. They returned "with a squad of soldiers and wagons and moved off every portable thing—furniture, provisions, etc." With the assistance of the Union cavalry, other Louisi-ana bondmen made off with "hogs and cattle and sheep" belonging to Governor Thomas Moore. In South Carolina, the arrival of federal troops, one planter complained, resulted in armed blacks "taking pos-session of and patrolling this village night and day, threatening the lives of men." Whites regarded such behavior as "insubordination & inso-lence," if only because the sight of African Americans protecting their families and assuming law enforcement responsibilities—scenes the white South as to witness again and again in coming years—turned their antebellum world upside down. Yet such improbable spectacles, one white complained, happened "everywhere officers of Colored troops have had jurisdiction any length of time."[15]

What whites considered theft and the wanton destruction of property, blacks instead regarded as payment for years of uncompensated labor. Before liberation, enslaved women tended the animals and prepared the food they were not allowed to sample, yet their masters were shocked when the arrival of troops was accompanied by the emptying of smokehouses and the drinking of fine wines. Confederates "take all our labor, and steal our chil'ren," one liberated slave explained, "and we only take dare chicken." Now that freedom had arrived, African Americans expected not only back pay but also assets with which to begin their new lives. At war's end, whites returned home to find desks torn open, trunk linings slashed, and easily traded silverware and jewelry taken. When Peggy, the slave of Carolina rice planter Charles Manigault, heard that soldiers were in the area, she compensated herself with a "handsome Mahogany Bedstead & Mattrass" for her cabin and "some *Pink Ribands*" for her daughter. Manigault and a former overseer tried to reclaim the bed, but Peggy stood in her doorway and threatened to contact a Union officer if he continued his efforts to steal her "property." In some instances, former slaves even refused to destroy property on the instructions of Confederate authorities, on the grounds that the materials now belonged to them. As planters fled the Carolina low country, Jefferson Davis ordered all cotton burned. "Why for we burn de cotton," wondered Will Capers, a literate slave who had been reading local newspapers. "Where we get money then for buy clo' and shoe and salt?" After whites abandoned the area, the freedmen and freedwomen guarded the cotton around the clock, with the women keeping watch and the men ready to defend it if the alarm was sounded.[16]

Enslaved women, who worked long hours in the fields beside their husbands, never conformed to southern ideals of domesticity. Even so, whites were stunned by the suddenness with which women such as Peggy tore off the old mask of subservience and asserted their rights. In the same way that planters felt especially distraught when trusted drivers ushered entire communities toward Union lines, white women were shaken when favored domestics quit their households to be with their own families. Before the war, planters' wives often bragged that they spoiled their household staff, but the coming of freedom revealed just who had been pampered. One young woman discovered that she could not comb her own hair, while another former mistress broke into tears as she had no one to wash her feet at night. Whites had believed their domestic servants to be devoted to their interests, but given that slaves within the big house enjoyed the greatest access to information and tended to be among the few literate blacks on any estate, it surprised only their masters that they were the first to leave when soldiers arrived. Even before troops reached one Louisiana plantation, slaves approached the overseer and demanded wages. When the overseer refused on orders from his employer, the slaves erected a gallows on the estate so that they might "hang their master [and] be free." The prudent overseer paid in full and fled the plantation.[17]

Almost from the cradle, slaves had learned how to behave around whites. Sensible parents advised their children to be courteous to the master race, for a submissive demeanor was a valuable survival skill in the slave community. But the presence of black troops erased the pretense of servility, and even children could rarely resist boasting of their new condition. One irritated Savannah woman woke one morning to the song of a black girl, who "amused herself by jumping up and down under my window, and singing at the top of her voice: 'All de rebel gone to h___ Now Par Sherman come.'" Nervous whites regarded newly revealed boldness as evidence of servile unrest, as in previous years proud bondmen who deported themselves as capable adults had often been punished as potential conspirators. Julia LeGrand, a white resident of New Orleans, feared that liberated slaves planned to revolt on January 1, 1863. Why recently freed blacks might feel the need to engage in insurrection was unclear, but LeGrand and her friends armed themselves with hatchets "and a vial of some kind of spirits" with which "to blind all invaders." What whites described as revolutionary was in reality collective resistance channeled into military form, as when twenty-seven Kentucky slaves elected one of their own, Elijah Marrs, as their captain and strode to the Union recruiting office in Louisville to volunteer for service. For former masters, even to overhear slaves boast of freedom was insurrectionary. As one black soldier laughed when seeing his former master taken prisoner, "Lay low, white man, the bottom rail is now on top."[18]

Having persuaded themselves that their slaves were loyal not merely to them but to the Confederacy, planters responded badly when they realized how severely they had been misled, or perhaps at how severely they had deceived themselves. During the first months of the conflict, Carolina diarist Mary Boykin Chesnut wondered why, if slavery was as "disagreeable" as Republicans claimed, slaves didn't "all march over the border where they would be received with open arms." By war's end, they had done just that, and Chesnut witnessed the removal of what she aptly described as her servants' "black masks." Her friend Varina Howell Davis, the Confederacy's first lady, also lost several domestics in 1864. James Dennison and his wife, Betsey, who worked as Davis's maid, financed their escape by seizing eighty gold dollars of back pay, and Henry, a butler, vanished one night, but not before building a fire in the mansion's basement. Even as slavery collapsed around them, one furious master threatened to "teach" his laborers not to "disobey" his orders by selling every "last one of them," as if any traffic in humans remained. Catherine Edmondston, a North Carolina mistress, lost a beloved maid who once had nursed her through a long illness, and she could not fathom why a house slave preferred freedom to her own companionship, as the maid "left in the night and that too without the slightest noise." A few former masters swore that they were better off without their disloyal servants. "I lost sixteen niggers," one Charlestonian insisted, "but I don't mind it, for they were always a nuisance."[19]

As the army advanced, some masters tried to flee with their slaves, and the noun "refugee" became a new verb—"refugeeing"—during the last moments of the war. One Florida planter drove his laborers across a river into a swamp and warned them that "if any of them turned" and tried to escape "they would be shot." Mississippi governor John J. Pettus, understanding as well as Douglass that every bondman who reached Union lines was "a laborer lost to the country," urged state action empowering the Confederate military to relocate slaves in the name of "the public good." South Carolina went so far as to pass legislation authorizing officers to reposition slaves even over the protests of their masters.

Among those who tried to force his slaves to leave with him was Joseph Davis, co-owner with his younger brother, the Confederate president, of a pair of plantations just below Vicksburg known as Davis Bend. In Richmond, Jefferson Davis received telegrams informing him that the slaves were "in a state of insubordination." When told to ready themselves for movement away from the river, an appointed spokesman informed Joseph "that on no conditions would they agree to leave the place." As was the case elsewhere, as Union gunboats approached, entire families quietly disappeared, and "their departure," Joseph informed his brother, "was sudden and in the night." Increasingly, however, there was no geography left for dogmatic Confederates to hide within.[20]

As desperate masters retreated into the ever-shrinking hinterlands, self-liberated blacks flocked to urban centers. Plantation artisans had always been the type of bondmen to run for free soil, figuring their skills might earn them decent wages in northern towns. Now blacksmiths, carpenters, and mechanics remained within the South and headed to Atlanta and Savannah. Williamsburg waiter Beverly Tucker, who bore two names of a prominent white Virginian, escaped to Washington, where he briefly practiced his trade before enlisting in the infantry. Tucker was joined by seamstresses and laundresses, a new development, as very few women had risked flight before the war. The exodus into cities also reversed the antebellum trend of declining numbers of African Americans in urban areas, just as it laid the basis for black activism in the years after 1865. Atlanta, which was only twenty percent black in 1850, more than doubled that figure to forty-six percent by 1870, while Montgomery's black population rose from twenty-five percent to forty-nine percent in the same period. New Orleans, which fell to the U.S. Army in April 1862, proved especially popular for refugees from both Louisiana and Mississippi. For decades, the city had been home to a large population of mixed-race freemen. Just before the war, one Louisiana slave confided to a traveler that he "would rather live in New Orleans" than any other place he had seen, as it was "gayer there" and had "more society." Even before Lee's surrender, Louis Charles Roudanez, a forty-one-year-old native of St. James Parish, began to publish the *New Orleans Tribune*, the region's first black-owned newspaper and one destined to become the voice of black Republicanism across the South.[21]

Even in cities under Union control, black migrants found life in the urban South precarious at best. Never blessed with plentiful food or the modest sanitation facilities enjoyed in Boston and Philadelphia, southern cities grew so rapidly that recent arrivals from the countryside were unable to locate decent housing or employment. Where soldiers were stationed, black women obtained work as cooks and washerwomen, and officers in Vicksburg and Natchez quickly constructed crude barracks for this informal supply corps. On occasion, families replicated their previous lives within the safety of tent cities. Provided she "washed for [her husband] during his entire service in the army," Elizabeth Kane was permitted to "live in a tent" with her spouse. Yet so poor were the conditions in most urban areas that the editor of Nashville's *Colored Tennessean* urged those new to the city to "go back to the country where employment exists for manual laborers." In Washington, a relief association reported that black "destitution and suffering" exceeded anything that had existed when the capital was a slave city. Refugees around Fort Monroe, Virginia, grew numerous enough that General John A. Dix encouraged Massachusetts governor Andrew to provide asylum for two thousand women and children. Despite the Bay State's long support of antislavery and Andrew's well-known endorsement of black regiments, the governor believed it wiser for the federal government to assist blacks in the South rather than ship them as "paupers and sufferers into a strange land and a climate trying" even for Massachusetts natives.[22]

For those who left loved ones behind, or had "abroad" spouses and relations on nearby plantations, freedom meant not only potential hardships but also fears for those still in bondage. Some refugees became soldiers primarily so that they might return to the countryside and retrieve family members. Women approached officers in hopes of hearing news of shifting battle lines, or of Confederates who had failed in their efforts to relocate black communities to the interior. One man arrived at the gates of Fort Monroe, having walked more than two hundred miles. When asked why he had left his wife and children behind Confederate lines, the unnamed freedman announced that he planned on "going back again" after his spouse, once he had "earned a little money." Private Calvin Smith was hardly alone among black soldiers in leaving his company without permission during the early days of 1865 to search for his dependents. Less concerned with his family than in finishing the war, a military court sentenced Smith to "hard labor for the period of six months, with Ball and chain for three months of that time."[23]

The few African American women unaccustomed to fieldwork found the absence of their husbands particularly trying. Victoria Randle Lawson served as a domestic in a small Mississippi town, but after most of the field hands had absconded to join the army, her master put a hoe in her hands, and "den, I didn't know nothing 'cept go out dar and chop dat corn and cotton." A number of domestics told of the same experience during the last months of the war, one recalling that on a plantation near Athens, Mississippi, "de women and boys had to finish de crop dat year." Some masters sought revenge on those left behind. In southern Missouri, ostensibly a slave state loyal to the Union, but also one that provided forty thousand troops to the Confederate cause, owners of small farms and modest plantations not only herded domestics into their fields but continued to abuse them after sundown in calculated acts of retaliation. Life grew so grim for one enslaved woman that she wrote to her husband, a soldier, begging him to return. "I have had nothing but trouble since you left," she sighed. "They abuse me because you went" away and "beat me scandalously." Despite such pleas, few runaways returned, knowing that the quickest way to end their families' plight was to finish the job on the battlefield. A few enterprising soldiers, however, found ways to smuggle clothing and supplies to those on the home front. Colonel John Foley complained that the men in his black regiment routinely stole "clothes for their families to wear and dispose of," and shortly after the fighting ended, one government inspector reported that "a great many [black] people are found to wear more or less parts of the Uniform prescribed by the U.S. Army."[24]

Aware that the end was in sight and mindful that their service meant not only freedom but civil rights, soldiers urged their loved ones to hold fast. John Boston, a Maryland runaway, wrote to tell his wife that he had signed on with a New York regiment fighting in neighboring Virginia. On "this Day i can Adress you thank god as a free man," Boston observed, hoping that the white family his wife and son worked for "[would]Continue kindness to you." He fought, he wanted his spouse to understand, not merely to escape "the Slavers Lash" but to make the nation "a land Whare fredom shall rain." A missive from a Connecticut soldier revealed similar grasp of what the war meant. Private Meunomennie Maimi, also fighting in Virginia, warned his wife that if "the Southern Confederacy succeeds, then you may bid farewell to all liberty thereafter." Maimi knew that his service imposed new hardships on his family. But slaveholders, he swore, "are my enemies, my flag's enemies, and [enemies to the] flag I was born under." By fighting for a country that previously had scorned its black citizens, African American soldiers could forge a new order, a "starry banner this is to be the emblem of freedom to all, whether black or white."[25]

Enough fugitive women arrived with their husbands to force a change in federal policy toward black families. The army continued to employ some wives as cooks or washerwomen, but in late 1862, even before his victory at Vicksburg turned the trickle of black refugees along the Mississippi into a flood, Ulysses S. Grant appointed John Eaton Jr., a chaplain from Ohio, to organize refugees into camps on abandoned plantations on the river. As Superintendent of Contrabands, Eaton was to report to the president on his handling of what soon was tens of thousands of former slaves. Sherman endorsed the policy, more from military practicality than from reasons of humanity. If black soldiers worried about wives yet enslaved, he argued, they would make poor soldiers. But if there was a method of getting a runaway's "family to a place of safety, then afford him the means of providing for his family" through a decent salary, former slaves were "lost to their masters [and] the cause of war is gone." Shortly after the fall of Vicksburg, Adjutant General Lorenzo Thomas formalized the policy. All "children and females of negro descent" who sought refuge within federal lines, he instructed in Special Order No. 45, should "be advised to remain on the plantations" where they previously had labored. Black families were "to receive the protection of this government," and those liberated slaves "incapacitated by old age, [or] ill-health" would "be duly cared for." Thomas explained to the secretary of war that his order was designed also to alleviate the overcrowding and disease at Union camps along the Mississippi River. Left unstated in this and other orders from commanders in the field was precisely who would own the abandoned estates with the coming of peace.[26]

The refugee camps were never designed to be permanent, and as Freedmen's Bureau head General Oliver O. Howard insisted, it was his agency's desire to "do away with all camps, colonies or homes" as quickly "as possible," especially in areas that had been exempted from the Emancipation Proclamation and so did not fall under Bureau auspices. Yet it was precisely those areas that had first come under federal control that saw the greatest number of emigrants. Freed people in camps near Fort Monroe, Virginia, and along the Carolina coast began "clearing up their little acre of land," one Bureau official reported, "preparing it for their rude loghouse." Black men and women established camps and tilled the soil on estates once owned by Jefferson Davis and the recently deceased John Tyler, who had left his plantation to serve in the Confederate Congress. A number of villages dotted the Potomac, with the largest settlement appearing on the Arlington estate of Mary Custis Lee. Soon known as Freedmen's Village, the camp consisted of nearly fifty buildings, neatly arranged in semicircular rows behind the big house. The government had seized the plantation for nonpayment of federal taxes and as early as 1864 began to use the front two hundred acres as a Union cemetery. The Bureau ran the village, considering it an intermediate step toward self-sufficiency; after residing briefly in the camp and reuniting with their husband soldiers, black women and their families were expected to relocate across the river into Washington, making way for a new wave of freed people. The village contained a hospital, a home for the poor and indigent, a school, a chapel, and a variety of craft shops, where former slaves might practice their skills or learn "the use of the needle & of the sewing machine." As was the case at other large manors, elderly blacks who had helped manage the estates in their masters' absence remained on to assist with new arrivals and function as estate spokesmen with the agency. One of the "old patriarchs," who had run a portion of Arlington House for fifty years, had kind things to say about his former owners; but, like William Johnson of Tennessee, he wanted reporters to understand that he preferred being free.[27]

Having learned early on not to trust even those whites who appeared

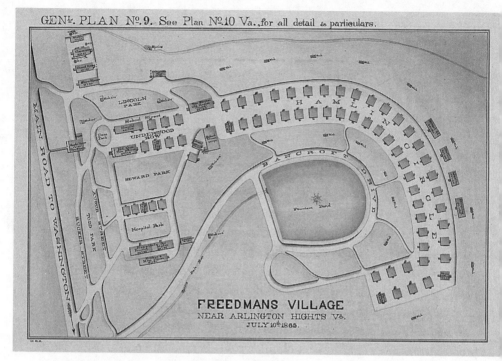

GEN⅃. PLAN N⁰.9. See Plan N⁰.10 Va.,for all detail & particulars.

FREEDMANS VILLAGE
NEAR ARLINGTON HIGHTS VA.
JULY 10⅏ 1865.

Established in May 1863 as a camp for escaped slaves and black refugees, Freedmen's Village was located on Arlington plantation, the confiscated estate of Mary Custis (the wife of Confederate general Robert E. Lee). One of many "contraband camps" established during the war, Freedmen's Village was home to eleven hundred African Americans, who paid between one dollars' and three dollars' rent each week. With its spectacular view of the nation's capital and the Potomac River, the site attracted the attention of developers. Over the objections of its residents, the federal government paid its inhabitants seventy-five thousand dollars for the land and demolished the village in 1900. Courtesy National Park Service.

friendly, and sensitive to the patronizing air of some Bureau officials, camp dwellers preferred to serve under black supervisors. Particularly those freemen and freewomen who remained on lands they had worked for years or even decades as uncompensated laborers hoped that small portions of those estates might become theirs. Too many white soldiers and agents simply wished to run efficient camps, and they rarely hid the fact that their main mission was to return home following Lee's defeat, rather than to serve as advocates of land reform. Robert Cromwell, a Virginia-born freeman who had practiced medicine in Wisconsin before the war, worked with refugees in New Orleans and discovered that they complained about camp regimen almost as much as they complained about their former masters. The Bureau provided but two meals each day, one of them a meager breakfast at eleven. "That is too long for Children to wate or old Persons *either*," Cromwell snapped. "My People want a *Black man* among *them* a *man* who has the good of his *Race* at heart," adding that he was just the person to run the city's hospital. Cromwell settled in New Orleans, and in peacetime moved into politics as well. In Louisiana, he was to help pull freedmen into the Republican Party, and he later openly challenged the Unionist governor on the question of voting rights and land confiscation. After serving in the state's constitutional convention in 1868, Cromwell journeyed west to Texas, where he was lynched in 1880.[28]

The camps also served to draw refugees north, beginning a black migration out of the South that over the years was to transform and enrich American society. One camp, constructed in an old hospital in Cincinnati, attracted African Americans drifting up from the gulf, rather than those from nearby Kentucky. By the spring of 1864, Reverend W. F. Nelson reported, "more than nine hundred [blacks] from Louisiana" were living in his camp, with their numbers "steadily increasing" by the day. Most were women, their husbands having enlisted in the army. Having fled the countryside for Cincinnati, a city of 160,000 people, black women labored for wages, usually as domestics or cooks or laundresses. Although they remained tied to the same menial tasks they had performed in slavery, they did so now for compensation. They "work like Turks" marveled one white soldier, whose birth into a free labor society made it hard for him to fathom how astonishing it felt for former chattel to earn even a small wage. Despite this, a few Bureau agents were exasperated by their charges' stubborn determination to behave as they saw fit. Expecting unquestioning gratitude, white officials were taken aback when challenged by black women about the wages they earned when employed by the military, or concerning the quality of camp schools and hospitals, or regarding their relationships with their husbands.[29]

Anxious to keep young soldiers content and marching south, even as their relations fled northward, the army began to hand out certificates to "families of colored soldiers." The documents granted black families "protection and benefits" to relieve the "suffering" of refugees. To ensure that the army would care for their spouses, soldiers were careful to formalize long-standing relationships with Union chaplains. "My husband and I have lived together fifteen years," announced the mother of several children, "and we want to be married over again now." During the antebellum era, masters typically wished their slaves to marry, if only because stable relationships gave them a measure of control over unruly bondmen and provided the next generation of unpaid labor. But no southern state legally sanctified slave marriages, which would have afforded human chattel too many rights and inhibited the ability of slaveholders to sell their slaves. Mildred Graves, like most bondwomen of her age, had been granted a brief, informal ceremony in which she wore a ragged dress given to her by her white mistress. But understanding that a legal relationship was something that had been denied her under slavery, Graves wished to hold "a real sho' nuff weddin' with a preacher." A ceremony conducted by an army chaplain, and preferably a black minister, signified that old bonds were broken and that a new and permanent bond was forged between black men and women. "The marriage law gives a general satisfaction among the Freedmen and their wives," reported one agency official. For soldiers departing for the front, repeating the ritual and putting their marks to a certificate meant their wives could legally file for claims should the men not return, and it legitimized children once owned by other adults. For the women who remained on abandoned plantations as their husbands enlisted, a license meant they might share in the estates they had tilled for years, and which now were rumored to be slated for division at war's end.[30]

As border slave states limped toward emancipation or as portions of Confederate states were reconstructed, white legislators struggled to codify domestic relationships. Kentucky, Maryland, and Louisiana simply required that black couples file paperwork with a county clerk. Tennessee and West Virginia—the latter created in 1861 after Virginia's western counties voted to remain loyal to the United States—instead opted to recognize all preexisting "customary marriages" as legal, while

Missouri required remarriage before a judge or minister. Complicating matters was the fact that many freedmen and freedwomen had been separated from a spouse by sale, and while some had taken a new partner, many preferred, if possible, to be united with their first wife or husband. As a result, when states attempted to clarify matters, as Mississippi was to do, by passing legislation announcing that "all persons who have not been married, but are now living together, cohabiting as man and wife, shall be taken and held, for all purposes in law, as married," more than a few former slaves chose to defy white lawmakers and restructure their families in their own way.[31]

Coming as so many of them did from upper-class, northern families, Freedmen's Bureau officials could be every bit as patronizing as southern legislators, as if freedmen and freedwomen had to be prodded to formalize long-cherished relationships. Unnecessarily worried that liberation might result in moral wreckage, one Louisiana-based agent drafted a lengthy circular elucidating "the plainest rules" on marriages. Boys could not marry until the age of fourteen, and girls must be at least twelve. Marriages were "prohibited between brother and sister," he felt obligated to add, as were those "between parent and child, [and] also between uncle and niece." Because many older freed people had former spouses who were still living somewhere in the South—a situation less common among whites, for whom divorce was difficult and expensive to obtain—the Bureau recognized "legally obtained" divorces. But a black "woman [was] not at liberty to contract another marriage until ten months after the dissolution of her preceding marriage." Another well-intentioned agent, stationed in Virginia, thought it only fair to insist that former masters be held responsible for "all illegitimate children by a colored woman," since prewar legislators had held white fathers accountable for children they produced with unmarried white women. But for the most part, since blacks in any section of the republic had never had much use for laws crafted by white assemblymen and slaveholders, few were now much inclined to accept their rules and standards.[32]

For those freed people seeking loved ones lost to them, the emotional moments of reunion were as passionate as they were rare. Since the 1790s, the Chesapeake region had been infamous for exporting young slaves to the fresh lands of the lower South, and while slave traders kept strict accounts of their profits and losses, no company or state maintained records of the names of those marched in coffles across the South to the pens of New Orleans. In cities already under Union occupation, blacks placed countless advertisements in black-run newspapers, hoping to find news of lost family members. The *New Orleans Tribune* and the *Black Republican* both featured lengthy "information wanted" sections. Nathan Malony of South Carolina joined the army "when Sherman was marching through," and he sought his wife, Eve, who resided on a neighboring plantation. Robert West hoped to find his wife, two married sisters, and two brothers, one of whom went by the different surname of Williams. In New Orleans, the Bureau maintained lists of the "familiar names" and "locations of all colored persons on the plantations" to assist black troops in finding loved ones. For the lucky few, finding a spouse torn away by the slave trade was both exhilarating and heartbreaking, if only due to an awareness of lost time. Betty and Ben Dodson had once begged their master to sell them together, but to no avail. When he spotted Betty in a refugee camp twenty years later, Ben scarcely knew whether to embrace his wife or step back to see that it was truly her. "I foun' you at las'," he shouted. "I's hunted an' hunted till I track you up here. I boun' to hunt till I fin' you if you's alive." In other cases, reunited families were shocked at how badly a loved one had aged, or had been mistreated during the intervening years, while a few remarked that the years apart had transformed a partner into someone they no longer knew.[33]

If government agents could be patronizing, they well understood the importance of family, especially since they were so far from home themselves. Eunice Knapp, a northern teacher who arrived on the Carolina coast with Thomas Wentworth Higginson, was approached by a boy who wanted to learn to write so that he could contact his mother in Florida. Knapp expressed surprise, since she had seen the boy with an older woman, but he explained that the woman was his "father's wife." He had lived with both parents in Florida, but "the white folks [had] parted [his] father and mother" around 1855. "I thank God that what he joins together now, no man can put asunder," she rejoiced. From his Washington office, General Howard instructed "all colored preachers" employed by the military as chaplains to gather information on divided families. Once data was collected, the Bureau transported refugees about the South at the government's expense. Despite his enormous workload, typical was Howard's order to procure transportation for a black family living in Gordonsville, Virginia, to Annapolis, Maryland, where their father had been located.[34]

When nuclear families could not be rebuilt, many freed people turned instead to their larger kinship networks. Due to the interstate traffic in humans, the black community had long relied on fictive families, with elderly slaves essentially adopting the children of other parents after the sale of one or both adults. Such kinship arrangements had served as survival mechanisms for the antebellum black community, and with the coming of freedom, extended families became a means through which to limit dependence on a Bureau they did not completely trust and a bulwark against the hostility of their former masters. In the wake of a horrific civil conflict, locating distant relatives was as difficult as finding a long-lost spouse. David Williams, formerly owned by A. M. Huger, found a house to rent on Charleston's Bull Street, just blocks from where Denmark Vesey once resided. His wife was deceased, but he had a daughter and a sister who lived in Beaufort. His brother Benjamin, however, had been "sold away [a] long time." Ann Jackson and Margaret Haler both found themselves in Manhattan at the war's end. Born on Maryland's Eastern Shore, Haler's mother had been "sold away" when she was still young, and her only sister, Angelina, had then been "sold away after [her] mother." Haler worked as a chambermaid, a profession that paid little enough, and so the need to locate her sister and reestablish that family tie was critical to her survival, as were any extended kin for Jackson, who was from Savannah and "never knew her mother or father." Her sole sibling, a brother named Charles, was deceased, and she had been "raised by her mistress."[35]

A number of black soldiers were mustered out in Philadelphia or New York, and other bondmen simply wandered north in hopes of putting their old life behind them. John Henry Neal, born in Washington, discovered that reestablishing his extended family was nearly impossible from his new home in Manhattan. His father, he hoped, was yet alive, but since his father had been "sold away when John was a young boy," he was hardly sure. A stepfather was buried in Washington, as were two of his stepbrothers. John Walker Rutledge, who made his living in New York City as a messenger, had been born in South Carolina, where his father had died. His mother had been sold into Georgia, and he feared that his brother Boysy had been "killed in [the] war." The light-skinned Louisa Emily Trusty was unusual in that she had relocated to Manhattan as a child with her godmother. Her mother had died in New Orleans when Louisa was a child, and she identified her father only as "white (don't know)." She believed she still had siblings in Louisiana, as well as aunts and uncles on her mother's side, but with six children of her own, Trusty, like all but the wealthiest of Americans, required the assistance of an extended family.[36]

Rebuilding families shattered in bondage was often complicated by the fact that black soldiers had spouses who belonged to different masters from themselves, which meant that their children also belonged to another. Slavery had denied the traditional status of breadwinner to black males, and so had conferred upon black women a measure of equality within the family, to the extent that both genders were powerless to raise their children without white interference. The Freedmen's Bureau, however, officially recognized males as heads of black households and even endorsed labor contracts that paid women less than men for similar plantation labor. Yet where families had been separated by sale and now decided to remain separated, Bureau agents refused to grant black fathers the same rights that state courts afforded white fathers. Especially when women were able to provide for themselves and their children, the agency sided with the mother. Eliza Banyon "had raised the boy at her own expense and had always had him with her," so when her son's father demanded custody, the Bureau agent, impressed by Banyon's ability to survive without the financial support of either former husband or former master, decided the case in her favor.[37]

More common was the trouble faced by black parents who sought to retrieve their children from a former master or from slaveholders in loyal regions. A number of planters believed that, having paid for the upkeep of children who had yet to reach their most productive years, they were owed compensation by the black families; and southern apprenticeship laws often supported those claims. Bureau agents filed "frequent complaints" registered by black parents who could not obtain "the custody of their children." In one Mississippi case, a freedman named Nolan went to collect his wife and four children, but their former owner refused, saying "that he had raised them and they belonged to him." Complicating matters was the lack of marriage licenses, birth certificates, or other documents demanded as proof of paternity by state courts. So sure were they that the law was on their side that some planters complained to the Bureau, assuming white authorities would take their part. A. L. Lazar complained to an unsympathetic General Alvan C. Gillem that the "two collard boys apprenticed" to him had left with "some of [his] enemies." Harvest time had arrived, and Lazar asked Gillem "to send me an order that I may get them immediately as now is the pushing time in my crop." One emigrating master kidnapped "three colored children" before sailing to Cuba, where slavery remained legal.[38]

Having faced Confederate rifles, black soldiers on leave were in no mood to permit white men to dominate and abuse their children. One Kentucky soldier returned home to discover that his child "had been apprenticed to its former master" while he "was in the United States service." In most cases, armed veterans and Bureau agents carried the day. In Maryland, where as many as four thousand children were apprenticed to white employers, dozens of parents took former masters to court; and in Baltimore, the increasingly radicalized Judge Hugh L. Bond—already famous for denouncing government bonuses to owners of young bondmen who volunteered to serve—became more beloved still by the black community by consistently finding against white masters. When one husband visited a Louisiana plantation that had fallen to federal forces in search of his wife and children, the new manager denounced the father as "a d[amne]d scoundrel" and refused to release them. The former bondman returned the next day with a Bureau agent, who renewed the request to "release the wife and children of the Negro." The overseer again refused, so the agent and the husband simply rounded up his family and left. If the agent was confident in enjoying Washington's support, it was because General Howard continued to sign orders designed to reunite children with their parents. When Clara James Lewis approached the Bureau about her child in Richmond, Howard not only directed "that steps be taken to find the child" but contributed three dollars "to pay her fare from Richmond to Washington."[39]

As Union chaplains reunited families and solemnized nonlegal relationships, former slaves had to undertake a task unknown to free-born Americans. They had to adopt a surname. Although slaves often adopted family names for use among themselves, few masters wished to bestow upon their chattel the sense of dignity a surname implied. In the kinship-conscious South, family connections conferred respect and social rank, and for black men in blue uniforms, a surname also meant manhood, every bit as much as did the stripe on their shoulder. For black fathers, the adoption of a surname meant an acceptance of patrilineal authority in a society that defined the status of black children by the legal condition of their mother. One former bondman insisted that adoption of a surname was a way to get "clean of slavery." In choosing, a small percentage simply adopted the family name of their master, either as a tie to an ancestral birthplace, or perhaps so that relatives might find them at war's end. David, a South Carolina runaway, was liberated in the spring of 1862 by Major General David Hunter. Upon enlisting in the Thirty-third infantry, he became David Blake, the former property of Walter Blake.[40]

Far more freed persons chose to put as much linguistic distance as possible between themselves and their former masters. The adoption of an owner's surname also implied a biological kinship that did not exist; should hundreds of liberated slaves on a large estate adopt the same name, that might suggest a family tie many neither recognized nor desired. Yet in older parts of the South, such as Virginia, African Americans often worked the same land as their parents and grandparents. The plantation legally belonged to the white family in the big house, but it might also be the burial place for hundreds of deceased slaves. Some adopted a surname that was unique to them, yet also tied them to a past family heritage. One black Kentuckian, the former bondman of Jesse Sinclair, enlisted under the name of Sinclair Cupit. George Augustus became Private Augustus Brown. Complicating matters was the fact that a good many company clerks were former slaves and were themselves new to literacy. Lucas, the slave of Renben Barrow, told recruiters to put his name down as Lucas Barrow, but the clerk instead spelled it as "Bond," so he "served under that name." Yet it never meant much to Lucas, and at war's end he changed it again, to Lucas Creech.[41]

Denied the usual trappings of class status before the war, enslaved artisans instead took pride in their craft skills rather than in visible wealth or an elegant home. As a result, some adopted what they dubbed the "titles" that identified them with their trades, as had people emerging from various forms of bondage in earlier societies. Barber, Cooper, Smith, Carpenter, and Taylor all graced military reports or marriage licenses. Others took patriotic names, and while Jeffersons and Jacksons were not uncommon, bondmen preferred names identified with the struggle against slavery. Hannah, the South Carolina daughter of Diane Macy and a father she could not identify, became Hannah Grant. New York was home to Secretary of State William Henry Seward, but also to relocated freedman William Henry Barager. Samuel Simmons, also a resident of Manhattan, was one of thousands to christen his son Abraham. A smaller number of former slaves opted instead for names that reached into their past and connected their lives to those Africans sold into the colonies. Over sixty years of age, Robert Mustafa of Charleston was old enough to have been sold into the city prior to the federal ban on human importations in 1807.[42]

By adopting family names that proclaimed a new status, many veterans staked their claim as heads of their households, for freedom allowed them to fulfill their Victorian responsibility to care for their families. Andrew Jackson Free, born in South Carolina and a veteran whose father called himself Andrew Aldridge, combined a patriotic forename with a statement of liberty. Another veteran and the son of a slave named Allen styled himself Freeman Pew. Others, such as John Freeman, preferred that moniker as a surname, assuring one lieutenant that it "suits me a heap." But John's wife was less sure that she wished to go by the masculine "Mrs. Freeman," as she had just achieved her liberty but now found herself again defined in masculine terms. But the officer instructed John to "give your wife the same name," and all his "children too." When first called by that name, she hardly knew "what to do." So invisible was "Mrs. Freeman" outside of the marriage relation, that the lieutenant never bothered to ask for her forename.[43]

Even as the assertive behavior of John Freeman or Hannah Grant demonstrated that slavery and the Confederacy created to protect it were all but moribund, Richmond officials made one final, extraordinary attempt to salvage both. As southern soldiers fell in combat or quit the cause and began to straggle home, the Confederate high command began to consider the use of black troops. General Patrick Cleburne of the Army of Tennessee was the first to draft a detailed plan for the use of slaves as soldiers. His proposal, dated January 2, 1864, discussed the use of galley slaves at the 1571 Battle of Lepanto, and the Irish-born Cleburne believed Confederates could replicate that moment, liberating enslaved soldiers just as they marched into battle. For eleven months, Davis suppressed Cleburne's plan and instead endorsed a new draft law that conscripted all white males between the ages of seventeen and fifty for the duration of the war. No matter how pressing manpower needs were, Davis worried, even to discuss emancipation undermined the very "right" for which they had seceded. But finally, on November 7, with few options left to him, Davis endorsed a variation of the plan in his message to the Confederate Congress. The southern government, he urged, should purchase forty thousand young males who would become free at the war's successful conclusion. Since his Constitution flatly prohibited all antislavery legislation, the offer to manumit only those bondmen purchased from their masters was designed to soothe any legal scruples his critics might have. In what was a "radical modification" of southern theories, Davis admitted, if the time had arrived to either arm slaves or accept defeat, "there seems to be no doubt what should then be our decision."[44]

Davis's message was accompanied by the endorsement of Robert E. Lee, who reasoned that since thousands of African Americans were already fighting for Lincoln's government, the Confederacy might as well pursue a similar policy and "obtain all the benefits that accrue to our cause." But no advocate of the policy ever hinted that antislavery sentiments inspired the change. If the government emancipated only young bondmen, "[the South's] independence [would be] secured," John H. Stringfellow counseled the president, while "the white man only [would] have any, and all political rights" and so could continue to "make the laws to controll the free negro, who having no land, must labor for the land owner." South Carolina general Samuel McGowan agreed. His fellow planters might support limited emancipation, "with one condition in return—that we are hereafter left political masters in this State." Unlike the federal government, the Confederacy was silent on the fate of potential soldiers' wives and children and parents, and Davis hoped to liberate just enough young bondmen to save his nation, while also preserving some variety of unfree labor and maintaining civil authority over the few who would be freed.[45]

Even more than Davis feared, the response was brutal. Three years earlier, advocates of secession had spoken plainly. Southern planters had embraced secession to protect and expand slavery, but now, in the name of saving their government, the president was asking them to bargain away what Vice President Alexander Stephens once described as its "cornerstone." Perceptive critics scoffed that once thousands of young black men were trained and armed, holding their loved ones in bondage would hardly be possible. The *Charleston Mercury*, long the region's most proslavery journal and one that in 1860 championed the creation of a southern "slave republic," was the most caustic. "The African is an inferior race," editor Robert Barnwell Rhett Sr. insisted. "But if the slavery of the Confederate States be not the best condition for the negroes amongst us—if they are fit for freedom and manumission" even in "reward for service—then the justification heretofore set up for holding them as slaves is false and unfounded." Howell Cobb of Georgia, a Confederate officer and one of the delegates to the 1861 Montgomery convention that created the new country, denounced the proposal in nearly the same terms. "The day you make soldiers of them is the beginning of the end of the revolution. If slaves will make good soldiers," he conceded, "our whole theory of slavery is wrong—but they won't make good soldiers."[46]

On the day Cobb uttered those words, well over one hundred thousand black soldiers in the Union's service were proving him wrong. There were "now nearly one hundred and fifty regiments of negroes," noted Louis Charles Roudanez, editor of the *New Orleans Tribune*, "but now the rebel leaders are using [northern] arguments in colored troops." Roudanez guessed that Davis's plan was unlikely to pass, but even so he argued that Sherman should not only recruit more black troops, he should spark "servile insurrection" among those still enslaved to put a quick end to the fighting. Those still in bondage, Roudanez understood, merely had to bide their time. Catherine Edmondston of North Carolina discovered just what her slaves thought about Davis's plan when she made the mistake of discussing the idea in front of several domestics. The next morning, her entire plantation was deserted. Less naïve was diarist Mary Chesnut. Just a year earlier, the plantation's black drivers had assured her husband of their desire to serve. "Now they say coolly that they don't want freedom if they have to fight for it." Chesnut understood why. "That means they are pretty sure of having it anyway."[47]

Asking wealthy whites to abandon the single most defining feature of their new country was too much. Following an angry debate, the Confederate Congress voted to arm selected bondmen but not to free them. Understanding the absurdity of that position, on March 23, 1865, Davis overruled the legislature with General Orders No. 14, granting any recruit "the rights of a freedman." Instructed to raise a company of black troops, majors J. W. Pegram and Thomas P. Turner placed a notice in the Richmond newspapers, urging those masters who had "freely given their sons and brothers, their money and their property" to the Confederacy now to donate their slaves as well. Rhett continued to argue that the time had not yet arrived for such desperate measures. "It was on account of encroachments upon the institution of *slavery*," he wrote, that South Carolina had seceded. "*We want no Confederate Government without our institutions*." Ironically, General Cleburne was not alive to see his proposal endorsed, having died in battle the previous November. But there were no takers, and seventeen days later Robert E. Lee surrendered.[48]

When it became clear that Richmond was doomed to fall, Davis and his cabinet fled south on the last secure rail line. The sounds of panic were clear to blacks in the city. One young slave, Mittie, remembered cannons "booming, it seems like everywhere." Mittie's father, who was to adopt the surname Freeman, began to cheer. "It's victory!" he kept shouting. "It's freedom. Now we's gonna be free!" Richmond had served as a major center for reselling slaves into the lower South, with twenty-eight residents advertising their skills as "auctioneers" and "commission agents," and a few blacks, such as Louis Hughes, awaited sale. But "as the market was dull" due to the shrinking Confederate geography, Hughes remained captive in the pens and heard the nearby guns. Richard Forrester, a seventeen-year-old freeman, scrambled to the top of the capitol to raise the American flag. As a boy who formerly had run errands for the legislature, the light-skinned Forrester had hidden the twenty-five-foot flag following secession, and he wanted approaching troops to see the old banner. Fittingly, the first soldiers to do so were black cavalrymen from companies E and H of the Fifth Massachusetts, and the Thirty-sixth USCT were not far behind. Thousands of African Americans filled the streets. Men waved their hats, and women shouted, "You have come our way at last, Glory, Hallelujah!"[49]

Understanding that some of the hardest battles lay ahead, as the conflict moved from the battlefield into Congress and the state assemblies, black activists stepped up their efforts to prod white Republicans into embracing black political and social equality. When Lincoln had crossed the Potomac to visit Freedmen's Village in November 1864, Sojourner Truth waited in line behind other black women to speak with the president. The two discussed abolition, and Lincoln showed the deeply spiritual former slave the ornate, expensive Bible presented to him by black Baltimoreans (at a cost of $580.75). He urged her to call on him again, and Truth agreed to; after all, she mused, "by the grace of God" he would be president "for four more years." A black delegation arrived in Washington from New Orleans led by Jean Baptiste Roudanez, the elder brother of the publisher, to encourage Lincoln to publicly endorse black voting rights. For the first time in American history, African Americans marched in the 1865 inaugural parade, and that evening, Frederick Douglass attended the White House reception. Speaking loudly enough so that "all around could hear," the abolitionist noted, the president announced the arrival of his "friend Douglass" and wondered what his guest thought of the inaugural address. "[T]here is no man in the country whose opinion I value more than yours," Lincoln added, a piece of flattery that had the virtue of being true, as Douglass was known for his oratorical skills. If such pleasantries, judged trifling by later standards but nearly revolutionary for that era, signaled a better future for the nation, more ominous was the expression of "bitter contempt and aversion" that Douglass saw flash across Andrew Johnson's face when the new vice president spotted him in the crowd.[50]

By the morning of April 10, the nation's capital began to celebrate. Secretary of War Edwin M. Stanton ordered five hundred cannon fired, a roar that shattered windows across Washington. At Freedmen's Village, blacks gathered on Mary Custis Lee's front lawn to sing "The Year of Jubilee." Speaking at a White House victory celebration the next evening, Lincoln revealed not only a further evolution of thought regarding the franchise, but also a willingness to compromise with his radical critics in Congress. Illuminated by candlelight as he read his prepared text to the crowd gathered below, Lincoln defended the new Unionist government in Louisiana but assured his listeners that he did not believe the job of Reconstruction lay wholly with the executive branch. He had "distinctly stated" from the outset that his December 1863 proposal was just "*a* plan of re-construction (as the phrase goes)," one of many formulas that "might possibly be acceptable." Only the legislature, moreover, enjoyed the right to say "when, or whether members should be admitted to seats in Congress from [southern] States." Repeating words previously expressed only in private correspondence, Lincoln admitted that he too was unhappy with Louisiana's decision to deny blacks the right to vote. "I would myself prefer that it were now conferred on the very intelligent, and on those who serve in our cause as soldiers." Although the president promised also to reconsider his support for the Louisiana regime, editor Louis Charles Roudanez pronounced the speech "a mixture of good and not very good sense." Salmon Chase, recently elevated onto the Supreme Court, privately urged Lincoln to go further still and endorse voting rights for all "colored loyalists." The April 11 speech, however, was to be the president's last public address.[51]

Across the nation, Americans struggled to come to terms with their strange new world. Blacks in southwestern Georgia and portions of Texas did not yet know they were free, and more than a few masters far removed from Union lines believed that slavery might yet be saved. On May 4, nearly a month after Lee's surrender, a woman in Lawrenceville, Georgia, purchased a slave girl for fifty dollars in gold. "Seems affectionate and well disposed," the woman claimed, "and if she remains with me I will do my duty towards her." In Richmond, a black soldier, in a reversal of antebellum plantation discipline, demanded to see a white traveler's pass. When the matron huffed that he was "as ill-bred as old Lincoln himself," the soldier "cursed" at her, shouting, "You haven't got things here no longer as you did. Don't you know that?" As Susan

Warfield, a white Marylander, confided to her diary, "Country life is not what it used to be during the halcyon days of slavery. Emancipation has crazed everybody blacks, and whites," and "the world is turned upside down."[52]

Among those trying to negotiate the rapidly changing racial currents were Colonel Patrick H. Anderson of Tennessee, and his former slave Jourdon, who had escaped to Ohio. The forty-year-old Jourdon, a former coachman and butler, regarded the colonel as a kind enough master, so in freedom he took the surname of Anderson. His former master somehow tracked him down and wrote to ask him to return to Tennessee, promising decent wages and freedom. As to the latter, Anderson observed, he had received his "free-papers in 1864 from the Provost-Marshall," so there was "nothing to be gained on that score." Anderson also wished the colonel to be more precise as to wages, and his wife, Amanda, questioned the quality of schools for their children in Tennessee. As a goodwill gesture, Anderson suggested that his former master first send him his back pay. "I served you faithfully for thirty-two years and Mandy [for] twenty years," Anderson calculated. "At $25 a month for me, and $2 a week for Mandy, our earnings would amount to $11,680," plus interest, and minus "our clothing and three doctor's visits for me, and pulling a tooth for Mandy." Should the colonel send the wages along, he and his wife—"the folks here call her Mrs. Anderson"—could "forget and forgive old scores." Either way, Anderson concluded, he asked the colonel to say "howdy to George Carter, and thank him for taking the pistol from you when you were shooting at me."[53]

Euphoria quickly vanished, however, as word spread of President Lincoln's assassination. On the gray, rainy morning following the Good Friday tragedy at Ford's Theatre, blacks gathered outside the White House to mourn the fallen president. Secretary of the Navy Gideon Welles pushed through a crowd of hundreds of newly freed slaves, "weeping and wailing their loss." Veterans John Eubanks and William Lattimore, like other black soldiers, hung "wreaths on their guns" and wore a "black band around their arms." Major Delany, stationed in Charleston, published an open letter to African Americans, urging them to contribute toward a memorial for "the Father of American Liberty." In Rochester, New York, Douglass and other activists met at the city hall, where he was asked to say a few words. "What are sweet dreams of peace," he wondered, "what are visions of the future?" Douglass had delivered many speeches in the city, but for the first time, he and the entire nation "shared in a terrible calamity," and this "crime" committed against "our country and our government," he thought, "made us more than countrymen, it made us kin."[54]

The division of a vast estate, sadly, often sends the closest of kin into bitter squabbles, and even Republicans in Washington were unsure of what the next step should be in Reconstruction. Although the U.S. Congress had passed the Thirteenth Amendment on January 31, 1865, forever banning slavery, it had yet to be ratified by the states. Nor had Congress passed a comprehensive Reconstruction law, and all of Washington was unsure where the new president stood on the great questions of the day. A number of white progressives and black activists hoped to transform sporadic wartime experiments in abandoned lands into permanent federal policy, a goal shared by virtually all freed people. In a predominantly agricultural society, the ownership of land was the truest gauge of a person's worth. As one freedman explained, "What's de use of being free if you don't own land enough to be buried in? Might just as well stay slave all yo' days." For black Americans, land ownership conferred real liberty. It provided for independence from old masters, lifted African Americans up as a people, and allowed individuals to pass prosperity on to the next generation. Such dreams were hardly naïve. Just over 140,000 black southerners had served with the Union army, and most expected to use their salaries to purchase lands. In South Carolina alone, forty thousand freed people had been settled on four hundred thousand acres of abandoned lands, and not by insignificant federal bureaucrats, but on the orders of Secretary of War Stanton and General Sherman. For a weary nation, the wars of Reconstruction were just beginning, and it was to be a struggle complicated, if not rendered impossible, by the rise to power of a racist, accidental president.[55]

CHAPTER THREE

"*All De Land Belongs to De Yankees Now*"

The Freedmen's Bureau

Born in Middlebrook, New Jersey, in 1812, only eight years after the state became the last in the North to pass legislation for gradual emancipation, Tunis Campbell was the eighth of ten children of a respected blacksmith. Only an unusually bright child could stand out under such circumstances, yet Tunis did. When he was five, a white neighbor offered to provide funds for him to attend an Episcopal school on Long Island. Campbell spent the next thirteen years at the school, and despite being the only black child enrolled, he remembered that the "principal and assistants were very kind" to him. The fact that he failed to mention in his 1877 autobiography the treatment afforded him by the other pupils perhaps hints that they were not as welcoming. Either way, Campbell excelled in school and learned to deal with whites as his equals rather than his superiors, marking his background as nearly unique even in the North and quite different from southern freemen, let alone former bondmen.[1]

His Episcopalian tutors hoped to groom him for a ministry in Liberia, the quasi-American colony for freed people that enjoyed the support of the governments of presidents James Monroe and John Quincy Adams. Instead, upon returning to New Jersey, he formed "an anti-colonization society" and pledged himself to never abandon his country "until every slave was free." In 1849, he spoke elegantly against emigration at a Manhattan rally, as he did again in a Rochester conference in 1853, saying "that as for the American Colonization Society, we have no sympathy with it, having long since determined to plant our trees on American soil." But anti-colonization oratory paid few bills, and so the indefatigable Campbell also taught school, became an AME minister, worked as a hotel steward, and in 1848 published the *Hotel Keepers, Head Waiters, and Housekeepers' Guide*, a widely reprinted manual on hotel management. When the South seceded, Campbell was also a partner in a New York bakery.[2]

After the War Department finally began to allow for black enlistments, Campbell said his farewells to his wife and three children and signed on. Still fit at the age of fifty, Campbell was ordered to report to General Rufus Saxton to assist with the resettlement of freed people along the Carolina coast. Carrying three thousand dollars of his own money with him, Campbell set out for the Sea Islands "to organize civil government, to improve the colored people in the South," and to "instruct and elevate the colored race." After Congress created the Freedmen's Bureau on March 3, 1865, Campbell won an appointment to oversee land claims and supervise resettlement on the five Georgia islands of Ossabaw, Delaware, Colonels, Sapelo, and St. Catherines.[3]

With the course of Reconstruction still undecided in Washington, Campbell, insisting that "order is Heaven's first law," devised a new government for the roughly six hundred residents of St. Catherines. The system featured an eight-member senate and a twenty-man house, with a supreme court and himself as governor. Understanding the need of the island's people to defend themselves and their new property from its original white owners, Campbell organized a militia of 275 men, many of them former soldiers. Campbell's actions clearly exceeded his instructions from Saxton and the Bureau, but as a man who had owned property enough to vote in New York, he believed it his duty to teach the freed people the basic tenets of democratic government. One Macon editor denounced him as "our Brigham Young, who persists in having a little government of his own," although the same Democratic publisher conceded that the "able bodied freeman" was up to the task. What Georgia whites disliked the most, however, was that Campbell supported the former slaves' vision of a better future as educated farmers. By war's end, he had asked the Bureau to send him ninety-eight basic primers, forty spelling books, clothing, blank marriage licenses, and plows.[4]

The eighth of ten children born to free parents in New Jersey, Tunis Campbell, like many black activists, was forced to combine reform activities with a reliable income. While speaking against slavery and working to establish decent schools for black children, Campbell labored as a hotel steward in Manhattan and Boston. In 1848, he published a manual to supervising a first-class guesthouse, Hotel Keepers, Head Waiters, and Housekeepers' Guide. *(This image was the frontispiece to the guide.) Although primarily meant to assist in the supervision of a hotel, the book also demanded that managers recognize the dignity of labor and pay workers a living wage, just as it also urged workers to educate themselves and be prompt and clean. As recently as 1973, the book was republished as* Never Let People Be Kept Waiting: A Textbook on Hotel Management. *Courtesy Moreland-Springarn Library, Howard University.*

After it became increasingly clear that President Andrew Johnson instead sided with the former masters of St. Catherines and Sapelo, Campbell was forced out of his Bureau post in December 1866. Rather than return home to New York, he invested one thousand dollars of his savings to purchase the Belleville plantation near Darien from a cash-poor planter. As a minister, Campbell preached of the righteousness of his people's cause. As a justice of the peace, the 160-pound, six-foot-tall Campbell enforced it. Whites complained that his courts "destroy[ed] the efficiency of labor in this section and inaugurate[d] a reign of terror," but freed people left the fields "en mass" to attend his hearings and political rallies. When a new (and white) Bureau agent arrived, he discovered that blacks refused to sign labor contracts until they consulted Campbell, and they ignored the agent's orders to cease "fishing, hunting, &c—and laboring under no guiding head," as Campbell encouraged them to provide for their families as they saw fit, and not in the way that former masters or government bureaucrats desired. Conservative whites fought back, as they did elsewhere in the republic, by burning Campbell's house and even trying to poison him. Undaunted, Campbell served in the state's constitutional convention and won election to the state senate, where he advocated integrated juries, integration of public facilities, equal education, fair elections, and most of all, the retention of confiscated property by Georgia freedmen. Campbell's struggle was played out again and again across the South, but by the time he was sentenced to a chain gang in 1876 for incarcerating a white man, there was no clear resolution to this new war over southern soil.[5]

The policy of settling freed people on the same plantations they had labored on as slaves had no single parent, nor was the idea forged in a single region. Saxton began the policy as a commonsense solution to his refugee problem almost from the first moment he arrived in the Carolina low country, and General Benjamin Butler established a program for leasing abandoned estates shortly after the capture of New Orleans in 1862. Writing that February from Hilton Head, South Carolina, General William T. Sherman, irritably noting the lack of "proper legislation on the subject," believed it the military's responsibility to assist "the Blacks to support and govern themselves in the absence and abandonment of their disloyal guardians." By that date, Sherman estimated,

at least nine thousand black Carolinians had fallen under Union jurisdiction, and he emphasized to General Lorenzo Thomas the "impera-
tive necessity of putting the blacks in the way of avoiding starvation."
At almost the same moment, a Treasury Department agent stationed in
nearby Port Royal informed Secretary Salmon P. Chase that the former
slaves wished "to remain on the Plantations where they were raised, if
they can receive something for their labor." General Quincy Adams
Gillmore continued the policy, and acting on his orders, Colonel
Thomas Wentworth Higginson relocated the dependents of the black
soldiers under his command to abandoned plantations in the Sea Islands.
Long before Thomas formalized the strategy after the fall of Vicksburg
in Special Order No. 45, senior officers in three states had taken steps to
elevate freedmen into economically independent citizens.[6]

Although designed primarily to damage the Confederate cause by
liberating bondmen and bondwomen owned by known rebels, the Second Confiscation Act of July 17, 1862, also allowed for the seizure of all
"property" under federal revenue laws, including "real estate." Complicating this legislation's emancipatory objectives was the clause requiring new titles to be secured in federal courts, as well as the condition
that the proceeds from all confiscations be used to prosecute the war,
rather than to serve as back pay to impoverished blacks. But the angry
debates in Congress reveal that conservative critics of confiscation feared
that it would end in just that way. John Law, a Democrat from Indiana,
warned the House that the bill could result in the seizure of "the whole
property of eleven states and six millions of people." Republican Thaddeus Stevens fired back in a speech that defended the revolutionary potential of land redistribution. "I would seize every foot of land, and
every dollar of their property as our armies go along," he snapped. To
pay off the mushrooming national debt, Stevens proposed selling the
confiscated estates to veterans. "Send those soldiers there with arms
in their hands to occupy the heritage of traitors, and build up there a
land of free men and of freedom." If Stevens's words initially gave little
solace to the blacks listening in the gallery, within months, many would
themselves be soldiers.[7]

One of the most successful examples of black autonomy was also one
of the most discussed in Washington. When Joseph Davis galloped

away from the Mississippi plantation he owned with his brother, the Confederate president, slaves smashed open the mansion's door and divided up the clothes and furniture. General Ulysses S. Grant advocated turning the vast estate into a "negro paradise" and turned the undertaking over to Chaplain John Eaton Jr. Together with a group of Philadelphia Quakers, Eaton raised ten thousand dollars for tools, mules, and rations. Liberated blacks were responsible for repaying the capital investment. Under the leadership of Benjamin Montgomery, the former black driver on the estate, the laborers fashioned the very model of black entrepreneurship, bagging two thousand bales of cotton for a profit of $160,000. Blacks at Davis Bend and on the nearby plantation of the late John A. Quitman, one chaplain assured Lincoln, "bought and paid for their gin houses, machinery [and] have built for themselves and their teachers, comfortable log houses," which they used "as a church and school house," a hospital, and "an Infirmary where the aged and decrepit and young orphan children are furnished a home." Black women planted gardens and sold produce to passing steamboats. If doubting moderates required evidence that former slaves would work long hours if provided with incentives and given the chance to purchase lands, the Davis Bend success provided the proof they needed, just as it demonstrated that freedmen also made good party members. In 1867, Thornton Montgomery, Benjamin's son, was to become the state's first black postmaster.[8]

In a concession to northern critics of emancipation and land appropriation, both the Second Confiscation Act and the Preliminary Emancipation Proclamation contained windows of sixty and one hundred days, respectively, during which repentant Confederates might surrender and retain their human property. When the former, as Republicans fully anticipated, went into effect on January 1, 1863, federal tax commissioners began to auction off confiscated estates in South Carolina. In some cases, black families had saved enough cash to bid against white speculators. In six of the first forty-seven sales, African Americans pooled their earnings, outbid whites, and obtained 2,600 acres at roughly one dollar an acre. More commonly, individual freedmen bought animals and impounded equipment. One man bought his former owner's horse, laughing that the steed now had to "call him massa." Saxton complained to Secretary of War Edwin M. Stanton that the law made "no provision for the negroes, who have been for so many years regarded as a portion of the live stock for the plantation." Several freedmen wrote to the president regarding one speculator, who promised to sell them the land they had worked for one dollar per acre, and when Lincoln did not promptly reply, they warned the investor "that the land was theirs & they would shoot the first man coming onto it to dispossess them." In fact, Lincoln also wished to give former slaves "an interest in the soil." After consulting with Chase, the president issued an order during December 1863 allowing single men above age twenty-one to choose and occupy twenty acres, while families might claim up to forty, as could wives of absent black soldiers. Thus from the president's pen, and not from an officer in the field, came the first mention of forty acres. The price of land was to be fixed at $1.25 per acre, forty percent of which was due at the time the claim was filed with tax commissioners. That meant that for as little as twenty dollars, black families might obtain a plot of land; and as Congress equalized the pay of black soldiers in 1864 at sixteen dollars each month, that sum was hardly out of reach. As with Lincoln's evolving views on black suffrage, his December edict revealed an increasingly flexible politician willing to reconsider old positions as new contingencies arose.[9]

Chase was ready to do far more. The treasury secretary argued that under the March 1863 Captured and Abandoned Property Act, he already possessed the power to lease land to former slaves. Stanton's War Department required investors who purchased large estates to pay their workers on a yearly or twice-yearly basis, but Chase instead lobbied for a weekly or monthly wage. He also advocated the division of plantations into smaller parcels of twenty to eighty acres, since freedmen could afford to bid on those lots. Chase was especially open to advice from activists in the field. As Mansfield French, an educator and cofounder of the National Freedmen's Relief Association, recommended from Beaufort, blacks should be permitted to "*purchase every plantation at tax rates*" only. "None need, none deserve these lands," French added, "so much as the negroes themselves." As the politically ambitious Chase understood, black economic independence was necessary not merely for the creation of a free wage-labor capitalist South, a dynamic, expansive society built on the dignity of individual industry , but also for a viable Republican Party to take hold in the region.[10]

To better coordinate the increasingly vast effort, in early January 1865 Stanton sailed south to meet with Sherman in Savannah. Although combat operations were nearly at an end, Sherman's army had arrived on the coast accompanied by twenty thousand liberated slaves. Stanton "agreed perfectly" that young black men "should be enlisted as soldiers" or employed by the quartermaster. The secretary wanted also to meet with "a large number of the old negroes, mostly preachers," as Sherman later explained, and in a January 12 meeting with the general and Garrison Frazier, a black minister, Stanton took copious notes while they spoke. The "way we can best take care of ourselves is to have land," Frazier insisted, "and turn it and till it by our own labor." The Ohio-born Stanton was new to the low country but knew enough about plantation agriculture to understand that the black workers who had created southern wealth were hardly an idle or incapable people. After the lengthy meeting, Stanton "was satisfied that the negroes could, with some little aid from us, by means of the abandoned plantations on the sea islands, take care of themselves." Stanton tasked the general with "draw[ing] up a plan that would be uniform and practicable." Sherman did so that night, and before Stanton returned to the capital, he reviewed the proposal and suggested a few changes.[11]

Three days later, on January 15, Sherman issued Special Field Order No. 15. The order set aside a four-hundred-thousand-acre strip of land along the Carolina and Georgia coast for the use of black refugees. In accordance with his commander in chief's December 1862 directive, Sherman recommended that the land be divided into forty-acre parcels; the freedmen might also have the use of worn-out army mules. As a warrior desirous of putting a quick end to the conflict, Sherman was less interested in radical reform than in ridding himself of women and children who slowed his campaign, but forty thousand blacks rushed to take advantage of his offer. His edict, the general admitted, lacked the authority to convey actual title to the land and instead gave the claimants only "possessory titles" to work the soil and benefit from their labor. But as Sherman explained to Stanton several days later, it was up to Congress and the president, and not the military, to resolve such matters. All of the local whites Sherman spoke to "realize[d] the truth that Slavery as an institution is defunct, and the only question that remains are what disposition shall be made of the negroes themselves."[12]

Congress, in fact, had been debating just such legislation since the previous year's session, and just before midnight on March 3, 1865, Republicans in Washington legalized Sherman's order by crafting legislation to create the Bureau of Refugees, Freedmen, and Abandoned Lands, soon known simply as the Freedmen's Bureau, as an agency of the War Department. The Bureau's mandate was to provide food, clothing, and medical supplies to destitute southerners, as well as to settle freed people on abandoned estates. By this date, the federal government controlled more than 850,000 acres. In addition to the 400,000 acres accounted for by Sherman's Special Field Order No. 45, the Bureau was given 65,000 acres in Tennessee and 60,000 in Louisiana, including the plantation owned by the Confederate son of former president Zachary Taylor. The bill's chief author, Massachusetts Republican Thomas D. Eliot, framed the law after reading the reports of the American Freedmen's Inquiry Commission, and especially Sherman's Order, as it stipulated that "every male citizen, whether refugee or freeman," was to be allowed to lease forty acres of abandoned land for three years, and then to purchase that land from the federal government "with such titles as it can convey." The Bureau was to be run by a commissioner and ten assistants, all of them named by the president with the advice of the War Department. Lincoln chose General Oliver O. Howard, who had lost an arm in combat but was called "the Christian general" for his advocacy of northern benevolence, and tapped Rufus Saxton as his assistant. White planters, Saxton believed, had forfeited their right to land ownership due to treason, while loyal blacks and African American soldiers "and their ancestors [had] passed two hundred years of unrequited toil."[13]

For black southerners and their Republican allies, the act was a promising beginning. The bill, as well as the ideology of the northern, middle-class politicians that informed it, contained several imperfections. Since federal courts were not yet functioning in the collapsing Confederacy, most lands captured by the army were legally categorized as "seized" or "abandoned" rather than owned by the government. The assumption of those who supported the bill was that with peace, treasury agents and tax commissioners would have leisure to institute formal confiscation procedures while blacks leased their small parcels, and that after three years, the estates would be properly obtained by the federal government and freedmen would have had time enough to put aside the down payment. But the law contained no provision for those refugees who had moved into southern towns, and clearly the idea of turning the land over to black veterans who had tilled it as slaves meant the exclusion of black women. Of the 110 self-described "colored planters of Davis Bend" who petitioned Congress for the right to retain those acres, only two were women. In the North, the ownership of farms by soldiers' widows and affluent women was not unheard of, yet clearly Republicans instinctively thought of *men* when they envisioned black yeo*men*.[14]

Staffed as it was by northern officers, the Bureau and its ranks of white agents were infused with middle-class concerns regarding charity and dependence. Even when the commissioners hailed from antislavery backgrounds and demonstrated no obvious racial animus, they carried with them paternalistic attitudes about the working poor and the responsibilities of the recently liberated to help themselves. As Massachusetts senator Henry Wilson cautioned at the Sumter rededication ceremony, "Remember that you are to be industrious. Freedom does not mean that you are not to work." Whereas black men desired land, some Bureau agents were content to have former slaves contract for wages. In an advertisement posted in the black-run *New Orleans Tribune*, the Bureau assured freedmen that they could "work for whom they pleased," but the Bureau also counseled that once a yearly contract was signed, neither party could dissolve the agreement without proper cause. The handful of black agents, such as Major Martin R. Delany and John Mercer Langston, a Virginia-born attorney and army recruiter, understood the limited opportunities facing former slaves, most of whom were illiterate and resided in isolated rural areas. General Howard might believe that his free wage-labor edicts were liberating, but the Cincinnati *Colored Citizen* denounced wage scales as evidence that "serfdom" yet lived in the South. White agents were stunned by this seeming lack of gratitude. "A man who can work has no right to a support by government or by charity," one fumed.[15]

Black veterans who recollected decades of uncompensated labor hardly needed to be reminded of the importance of hard work. Nor did they believe that the opportunity to save toward purchasing a parcel of land on the estates where they had been born constituted government charity. As New Orleans editor Louis Charles Roudanez argued, whites were "no longer needed in the character of masters," but they were still required "as capitalists." For some time, blacks had advocated a national lending institution to "strike a mortal blow upon the remnants of slavery." In Washington, John W. Alvord, an abolitionist minister and army chaplain, armed with supporting letters from generals Rufus Saxton and Nathaniel P. Banks, lobbied for a series of "Negro savings banks." The idea resonated with those congressmen who hoped to mold freedmen into middle-class citizens, and with tens of thousands of southern soldiers and veterans drawing wages in a region that never had housed many banks, the need for secure places of deposit was obvious. On March 3, 1865, just hours before creating the Freedmen's Bureau, Congress chartered the Freedman's Savings and Trust Company. "This bank is just what the freedmen need," Lincoln remarked at the bill's signing. Presided over by Alvord, the board of trustees included Howard, financier Henry Cooke, and New York industrialist and philanthropist Peter Cooper.[16]

Six weeks later, Lincoln lay dead, and the new president was a states' rights Democrat who shared the racial attitudes of his white Tennessee constituents and denigrated blacks as an inferior people forever unsuited for citizenship. If Andrew Johnson had been willing to finally part with his slaves midway through the war, as late as 1862 he had assured the voters of Davidson County that he "believe[d] that slaves should be in subordination, and [would] live and die so believing." Tragically, as Congress was out of session from April through November, Johnson was on his own for months following Lincoln's assassination. Without consulting leading members of either chamber, Johnson issued two proclamations on May 29. The first recognized the newly formed government of Virginia. In the second, Johnson appointed a provisional governor for North Carolina—who was authorized to call new elections—and granted amnesty for all rebels except those with taxable property valued at or above twenty thousand dollars. Neither of these proclamations made any mention of black suffrage or civil rights for the freed people, and the former tailor, who had never been accepted by his planter brethren, promised that clemency for the wealthiest southerners would be "liberally extended" to those willing to apply in person, which was to say those disposed to grovel. Although Johnson also hinted at the restoration of lands to their former owners, most Democrats understood that Reconstruction was far from over. "We are but at the beginning of the war," fretted a white North Carolinian.[17]

It was a war Johnson had no reason to instigate, and not merely because Republicans and African Americans across the nation were unwilling to abandoned their hard-won political gains. All but the most obstinate Confederates understood that their power was utterly shattered, and most were prepared to accept whatever terms the victorious North saw fit to impose. Johnson's supporters back in Tennessee had been farmers and artisans, the sort of hardworking laborers who, as one Charleston mechanic wrote, believed that the "land here ought to be forfeited to the US." Even those planters who had never supported Johnson, as one mistress cautioned her husband, had to learn to live under "the new order of things." Virginian George Munford wondered "whether the Yankees will permit us to have any rights or property." Following an initial moment of Confederate nationalism, southern yeomen had increasingly turned against Davis's government, alienated by a series of inequitable draft laws and increasingly confiscatory tax policies. As one southerner argued *during* the conflict, the war was one "of class—the planters against the people North and South [but] *especially against those of the South.*" Another disenchanted veteran learned that "the Yankees [were] not his enemies" when they offered "to feed us when they camped near us." Republican policies of land reform and public education, which had rarely enjoyed the support of wealthy planters who hired private tutors, could benefit poor white families as well as blacks. "A colored man will help us a heap more than a rich man," the veteran added. "They don't care for poor people. You [northerners] have free schools [but] we can't get them." For weary farmers straggling home, the mood was not simply defeatism but anger. "There are thousands of unprincipled white men amongst us," worried South Carolina's Benjamin F. Perry, "who will unite their destiny with the negro." Having survived a war waged by planters, common veterans "[would] easily be persuaded that it is right and proper that the lands should be divided out equally amongst all of her citizens."[18]

If official Washington was not in session, influential Republicans were nonetheless paying close attention. Now seventy-five years old and in increasingly poor health, Thaddeus Stevens roused himself to deliver a series of speeches in Pennsylvania designed to remind the president and those planters emboldened by his proclamations that the death of more than half a million soldiers could only be justified by altering "the whole fabric of southern society." In an appeal designed to strike a chord with hard-pressed middle-class Americans everywhere, Stevens wondered how "republican institutions, free schools, [and] free churches" could exist so long as a small number of "nabobs" residing in "lordly palaces" governed a populace it derided as "low white trash." It was not vengeance that inspired land reform, he insisted, but the democratic virtues of teaching the sons of planters "to enter the workshop or handle the plough." Speaking in Lancaster, Stevens advocated the seizure of property belonging to those landlords not covered by Johnson's offer of amnesty. He placed their number at roughly seventy thousand, and their lands at 394 million acres. If those acres were sold at auction at a minimum of ten dollars per acre, the federal treasury would grow by $3.54 billion, which could pay off the nation's war debt and provide for loyal blacks and veterans of both races. Stevens's math was off, as he placed the black population in the defeated Confederacy at six million—too high by nearly two million—but he estimated that nine tenths of land owned by white southerners would remain untouched by this policy. Justice required "that the poor, the ignorant, and the coerced should be forgiven," but since slaveholders had seceded, "the wicked enemy [must] pay the expenses of this unjust war."[19]

Other progressives agreed. The Reverend Justin D. Fulton, a self-described New England "radical," assured his flock that the "Confiscation Act, if enforced, will save us." Should the large antebellum estates remain in the hands of their former owners, Fulton warned, the planters would also retain their "monopoly of labor [and] the blacks and poor whites [would] not be in much better condition than before." A belief in the sanctity of property, which was a critical element in Republican free

wage labor ideology, did not preclude redistribution in the name of economic efficiency. "The land belongs to the industry of the country,"
another Republican insisted, and in the South the industrious were "the
laboring men." Even General Banks agreed that the Bureau's emphasis
on wage labor for the freedmen was but a temporary expedient. The real
"question should be," he wrote in 1864, "in what manner and how soon
can he become an owner of the land himself?" Conservative southern
whites feared that Banks's hopes would become reality. "If the Radical
party is victorious," predicted Louisiana's Charles Delery, "confiscation shall be decreed against the whites, and [blacks] shall become the
owners of this soil."[20]

Consequently, Bureau agents were stunned by the president's May
proclamations. Although Johnson's edicts did not explicitly restore rebel
property, they indicated that he believed that the end of combat required a quick return to prewar conditions. Yet only two months into
the agency's life, the department was making enormous strides. Near
St. Augustine, Florida, one agent informed Saxton that "98 Acres of
public land have been cultivated by the Freedmen for their own benefit,"
and that the land, about half of which had been purchased by tax sales,
housed "4 teachers & about 150 Children." Forced to follow orders from
his commander in chief, Howard issued Circular No. 13 on July 28,
which established procedures for returning the land to its original owners. He chose, however, to interpret Johnson's proclamations as exempt-
ing those estates already being worked by the freedmen. Howard also
moved to bring all confiscated lands under his authority, writing to a
sympathetic Secretary Stanton that the act of March 3 had effectively
granted the Bureau jurisdiction. The general also noted that their efforts at transferring forty-acre parcels to former slaves was in keeping
with the explicit mandate of that law, which, he delicately declined to
add, had been signed by Lincoln and was not subject to repeal by future
presidential edicts. Only those lands that had not been sold by tax commissioners or reserved by Sherman, Howard argued, might be returned,
and only then after their owners took an oath of allegiance and obtained
the president's pardon.[21]

As enormous as that concession was, it failed to please the new president. In the first step down the road that would culminate in his impeach-

ment, Johnson issued a direct order on August 16 that countermanded Howard's Circular No. 13 and implicitly negated an act of Congress. Provided they obtained pardon and paid their taxes, he insisted, all southern whites could recover their estates. Less than a month later, a delegation of white politicians from nine southern states called upon Johnson, who by then was issuing an average of one hundred pardons each day. They expressed their "sincere respect" for his determination "to sustain Southern rights in the Union," neglecting the fact that millions of black and white southerners disagreed with Johnson's policies. In South Carolina, a furious Saxton raged about the president's bias. "Could a just government drive out these loyal men who have been firm and loyal in her cause in all her darkest days?"[22]

With that, the battle left the nation's capital and moved to the countryside, at least for a time. For southern blacks, as numerous runaways had explained to officers during the conflict, their claims to the land they worked were not made as a demand to be released from labor, but instead as the exercising of a fundamental right born of decades of uncompensated toil. Since northern free wage-labor ideology was based on the rights of working people to benefit from the fruits of their labor, the freedmen's desire to obtain land as back pay resonated more with middle-class Republican voters than it did with their wealthier leadership in Washington. And if Bureau leaders such as Saxton dragged their feet in carrying out Johnson's conservative policies, black field agents like Delany absolutely refused to carry them out. On July 23, five hundred freed people on St. Helena, South Carolina, crowded into the island's black church to hear the major speak. To a growing chorus of "yes," "yes," "yes," Delany reminded his audience that southern whites owed their prosperity to the unwaged labor of blacks, just as the nation owed its military victory to black soldiers. "We have now two hundred thousand of our men well drilled in arms and used to warfare," he shouted, "and I tell you it is with you and them that slavery shall not come back again." Delany assured the crowd that Saxton was on their side, and "this matter [would] be settled," so that freedmen could "plant and work [their] own farms." The question of land reform "is in your hands," Delany warned.[23]

White planters, or what was left of their class in late 1865, saw it differently and believed that the president was on their side, even if Congress and the law were not. "If there is one thing that the former slaveholders of this State dislike more than another," observed Francis L. Cardozo, a South Carolina–born freeman and teacher for the American Missionary Association, "it is to see their former slaves become the owners of land, and thereby independent." Traveling through Maryland, Lewis Douglass made a similar observation. "There seems to be a combination among the white people to keep the blacks from buying land," he warned his father. "Large tracts of woods that the whites will neither use nor sell to the blacks lie idle, and wasting." A good number of planters had been bankrupted by the war, and some tried to hold on to part of their estate by selling small parcels. But as one Alabaman admitted, the "feeling against any ownership of land by the negroes is so strong, that the man who should sell small tracts to them would be in actual personal danger." For southern blacks, who knew little of Washington affairs beyond the fact that Lincoln was dead, the very fact that Confederates had lost their struggle for independence meant that African Americans had won. When the absentee planter of South Carolina's Keithfield plantation, a Confederate widow, instructed her former overseer to restore ownership, freed people and black veterans drove him off, and the 150 African Americans continued to live on and cultivate the plantation. As one former slave explained it to his old mistress, "All de land belongs to de Yankees now, and dey gwine to divide it out 'mong de colored people."[24]

The battle over land was especially intense and bitter in the South Carolina and Georgia low country, in part because so many acres had been set aside by Sherman, but also because the black majority population had long enjoyed a good deal of labor autonomy. Tax commissioners had auctioned off small parcels to black veterans during the war, and trusted Bureau officials such as Delany urged them to stand fast. Although some historians have patronized unlettered freedmen for foolishly believing that land redistribution was to continue and even increase in scope, from their perspective, this was a war they were winning. Near Georgetown, South Carolina, William Bull discovered that his former slaves had moved from their cabins into his mansion. After being ordered to leave, they returned to their huts and fields only after burning his home to the ground. In Colleton County, South Carolina, black Carolinians beat up the driver, scared off the previous owner, and swore that no white man would ever again pass through the plantation gates. Former slaves did more than merely fight to hold their land. On Friend-field plantation, in Georgetown County, South Carolina, seventy blacks subdivided the former rice estate into strips, on which families then planted cereal crops. The people there, one officer observed, were "un-willing to do anything except cultivate their own little lots." Bureau agents reported that on many of the sea islands, such as those managed by Tunis Campbell, "the freedmen have established civil government, with constitutions and laws for the regulation of internal affairs, with all the different departments for schools [and] churches." Disinclined to wait for a reconstituted state or distant president to restore order, blacks along the coast sensibly proceeded to govern themselves.[25]

"What's the use of giving us freedom," one Carolinian remarked to a northern traveler, "if we can't stay where we were raised and own our houses where we were born?" For a time, Andrew Johnson's furious backtracking notwithstanding, it appeared that federal policy was about to enable the birth of a black landowning class. Politically astute veter-ans argued not only that their prewar labors had enriched individual planters, but that enslaved Americans collectively had built the nation. "Didn't dem large cities in de North grow up on de cotton and de sugars and de rice dat we made?" wondered one freedman. Since 1789, slavery and the traffic in humans had been protected by the Constitution and enabled by a series of federal laws, so freedmen believed that the gov-ernment in Washington had a responsibility to return the soil to those who, as another argued, had "made these lands what they are." Conse-quently, former slaves were unwilling to countenance the demands of their old masters, or to endure the coming of northern investors who proposed to purchase abandoned estates. When four Pennsylvania busi-nessmen visited St. John's Island, South Carolina, they were set upon by black yeomen, a journalist reported, and "narrowly escaped with their lives." Another party of investors arrived at Edisto Island, where they encountered a black soldier named Elias Jenkins, who warned them that Bureau agents had promised him that his people would "never be driven from the coast." Congress had passed a bill "giving [the freed people] the land for three years," he reminded the businessmen, and advised that the men "had better go back to Charleston and go to work there" as the island "was already theirs."[26]

As freedmen took stock of what their sweat had achieved for others, some were willing to accept an equitable division of the manor. In Tennessee, Sidney, a former driver, announced himself to be the "joint heir" of the estate; and the astonished former owner complained that Sidney had moved his own family into "the rooms of my house." So sure was Sidney "of his rights," that he dug up part of an apple orchard and planted the trees on what he claimed was his side of the estate. A black Virginian informed his old master that he was "entitled to a part of the farm after all the work he had done on it." The stunned master failed to grasp that the freedmen thought this a more than reasonable partition, as it left part of the estate to its original owner. Along South Carolina's Waccamaw River, a landlord returned to discover sixty blacks, most of them his former human property, tilling the soil and "claiming the right to remain on the place." Having had the Freedmen's Bureau Act explained to them, they vowed only to "work in their own way & at such times as they think fit, without the supervision of an agent or any white man & insist upon renting the lands, they to fix the amount to be paid us according to their notions of justice." For Confederates accustomed to giving orders and responding with the whip if those commands were not obeyed, the idea that those who had produced the region's wealth should now benefit from it was baffling and revolutionary. As a band of freedmen responded when told of the president's disregard of the Freedmen's Act, "have we broken any laws of these United States?' After laboring "nearly all our lives as slaves," they petitioned, "this is our home, we have made These lands what they are." While their masters had been away fighting against the republic, "We were the only true and Loyal people that were found in possession of these Lands."[27]

Although southern whites rarely conceded the point, this sense of a right to part of the land stretched back to the antebellum period, when masters permitted slaves, and especially bondwomen, to maintain small garden plots near their cabins. On these small parcels, black women grew extra food for their families and vegetables to sell in nearby markets. Masters had sanctioned the practice, if only because it reduced the cost of providing for their laborers. To an extent, postwar demands for portions of the entire plantation were simply an expansion of these old privileges—and as a result, black women were as inclined as their husbands to claim their fair share. During the war, when Union soldiers landed on the Carolina coast, one officer found it "a very common thing for each woman to secrete a few handfuls of the cotton she had picked when she left the field." Bureau agents reported that while black veterans were "tolerably civil" to their former masters, their wives, "especially those advanced in age, [were] abusive" and hurled "threatening language" at offending whites. Louisa Smythe grumbled that the women on her Carolina plantation were "venomous and spiteful and disposed to make trouble." During the war, the women had begun to market potatoes, which they now claimed "belonged to them—they had worked for them and Mr. Smythe didn't hab nuttin to do wid 'em anyhow." Louisa denounced their claims as "stupid" and "nonsense," but the women stood their ground and threatened to destroy the potato hills rather than allow their former owners to profit from their hard work.[28]

On occasion, whites resorted to the sort of brutality common in earlier decades in hopes of restoring the lost world of the old South. Ironically, one drawback to the partition of estates into remote parcels of land was that it made blacks less physically secure. Before the war, slaves resided in sections of a property organized into quarters, in which cabins often stood in neat rows close beside other cabins. As freed people carved up the plantations, they scattered their homes across large estates, their isolation rendering them more vulnerable to sporadic violence. Near Mobile, Alabama, Oscar Evans was murdered when an employer, Dennis Moses, tried to wake him for work early one Sunday morning. Evans refused to get up on what was traditionally the slaves' day of rest, and Moses pulled a gun and shot him. In rural Louisiana, ex-Confederates attacked remote cabins in the dead of night. "Colored men who left those counties to enter the service cannot now return to see their families," Louis Charles Roudanez testified, "except at risk of being shot down by returned rebel soldiers and guerrillas." Elsewhere in the state, a small band of heavily armed whites murdered "four discharged colored soldiers." Since hardened veterans were the most likely to insist on a share of the land, guerrillas targeted black soldiers in hopes of eliminating "Union men" and potential activists.[29]

By year's end, tensions were such that blacks took to practicing military drills in their off hours. In the Barnwell District of South Carolina, where units of the Massachusetts Fifty-fourth and Thirty-fifth were stationed, groups of "forty men, women, and children" gathered each day to muster at sundown. "Some shouldered sticks, some had gunstocks, some gun barrels, some guns, and some were empty handed," reported Ralph Ely, a white officer. "They marched and countermarched and halted, and marched again in straight lines and curves for nearly an hour." Those who had served taught others, either as a precaution against growing white violence, or to prepare for the dawn of 1866, when rumor had it that the federal government planned to formalize prior rental agreements into actual land ownership. "The impression has got abroad among the negroes that some thing very important is going to happen about Christmas," General Carl Schurz warned President Johnson. "A great many of them firmly believe that the Government will divide among them the lands belonging to their former masters." Nervous whites dubbed this "the Christmas insurrection," but for former slaves it was merely the first day of the first year after the war, and so a new start in race relations. As December 25 approached, both sides grew resolute. Planter Jack Lassiter, emboldened by the president's leniency, informed his laborers "that all Negroes were ordered to return to their former masters." One of his former slaves, Jack, refused to do so, and Lassiter pumped "three slugs [into] his body, inflicting severe wounds." In Richmond, a gunfight broke out between black soldiers and "white military police." The soldiers got the better of the policemen, wounding two, although not mortally. The "truth is there is a great deal more danger of 'Cuffee,' " that is, of freedmen, "than 'Thad Stevens' taking our lands," former South Carolina governor Benjamin F. Perry fretted.[30]

Uneasy planters blamed the unrest on the "incendiary teachings of the Coloured Troops and white abolitionists." Writing from St. Johns Berkeley Parish, South Carolina, Sanford Barber complained that black soldiers had assured freed people "that the whole property of the country, land included, is theirs—and soon to be divided among them." A few of his former slaves warned him "that any use of it by the whites is an usurpation of their rights—and some have accordingly declared their purpose to resist any division of the crop by force of arms." Since federal troops had confiscated his weapons, Barber worried, his only "defence against personal Violence [was his] own Cutlery." Slaveholders had long regarded any act of self-assurance on the part of their laborers, or the discovery of any antislavery book or pamphlet from the North, as evidence of black aggression, and eight short months of general emancipation was hardly time enough to alter decades of white suspicions. Yet reports of African American "lawlessness and insolence" were voiced by numerous state officials. Former governor John L. Manning, who had lost his twenty-five slaves to federal forces, alerted Perry to "the danger of insurrection among the freedmen" around the town of Manchester, adding that he had few doubts "that things are by no means quiet among that unfortunate class."[31]

The fears of a Christmas revolt were not limited to the Carolina coast. Prior to leaving office on November 29, Governor Perry received an avalanche of letters on the topic, all of them blaming "the incendiary teachings of the colored troops and white abolitionists"; and authorities across the South heard similar warnings. A terrified Mississippi planter urged the governor to arm whites against the widespread view "that by the first of January next the lands [were] to be divided." In Florida, Governor William Marvin agreed that "everyone" in his state feared "that the niggers are going to clean us out." As both Perry's and Johnson's correspondents revealed, southern whites attributed the African American faith in land redistribution to "the intermeddling of [Bureau] agents" and the presence of "negro regiments," just as they had previously accused northern abolitionists for inspiring antebellum slave revolts. Southern blacks, of course, hardly required outsiders to tell them what they desired, but former slave owners were right enough in suspecting that Bureau agents and black soldiers were encouraging freedpeople not to back down in their demands. Determined to "disturb the peace of society," one white editor charged, "some" Bureau officials persisted in the belief that "the lands belonging to the whites who had been slaveholders were to be divided among the colored people [and that] the 'bottom rail' was to be on top."[32]

So nervous were authorities that in Louisiana, General Edward R. Canby took the unusual—and fateful—step of disarming black soldiers about to be mustered out. In Washington, the Johnson administration urged Howard to "denounce" potential black violence, and to the disgust of the *New Orleans Tribune*, he was "weak enough to do so." Christmas and New Year's passed without general unrest, but not without bloodshed. In the town of Portsmouth, Virginia, fighting in the streets broke out "between a lot of white boys and the colored people," with one white man and another black killed. Just across the Potomac from Washington in Alexandria, rioting began early on Christmas morning when both white and black revelers stumbled out of taverns "well armed." Four whites were killed, one of them shot in the head when he tried to enter an all-black party at Chapel Hall. By one o'clock the melee was so chaotic that General Winfield Scott Hancock called out three regiments to suppress it. Nearly one hundred rioters of both races were arrested, so many that the town was forced to incarcerate them in the old slave pens built in the 1830s by the Franklin and Armfield Company.[33]

In other parts of the South, three white policemen were "severely wounded" in New Orleans after being confronted by a large group of armed blacks on Christmas Day. In Clarksville, Tennessee, a brawl ensued between "some drunken negro soldiers" and equally inebriated whites. A white policeman attempted to resolve the dispute by clubbing a black soldier, who fought back with his bayonet. Nick Carney, "formerly a notorious [Confederate] guerrilla," then shot at the soldiers, who in turn fired into the crowd, missing Carney but wounding two whites. A similar disturbance erupted in Wilmington, North Carolina, when white policemen attempted to arrest a group of black mariners for being "drunk and disorderly." The seamen drew pistols and fired more than a dozen shots, wounding the policemen. And a "serious riot" occurred in Charleston when black soldiers from the Thirty-third USCT tried to enter a ball without paying their entrance fees. Refused entrance, they returned "armed with revolvers," and as in Alexandria, peace was only restored when more soldiers were called out to disperse the crowd. Although brawls between soldiers, sailors, and citizens were hardly uncommon in antebellum ports, the fact that black veterans were so quick to resort to weapons reflected a new determination to assert rights both large and small.[34]

"Christmas has come and is over," observed Roudanez, and no "terrific revolution" occurred. No laborers armed themselves "to kill the planters." Pinckney B. S. Pinchback, a former captain in the Seventy-fourth USCT who had settled in Louisiana, agreed. "No sane man can fear an Insurrection unless some of those mad caps attempt to revive the Scenes of the Past [and] disregard all civil rights." But the first days of 1866 did mark a crucial change in Bureau policy, whether black Americans perceived that or not. With Republicans in Washington yet hoping to maintain cordial relations with the president they had accidentally placed in power, General Howard understood that chances of meaningful land reform were slipping away. As another planting season was already under way and ever more black soldiers were returning to civilian life, Bureau officials increasingly saw their role as mediator between pardoned landlords and freed slaves. Fearing that another season of contested land claims could only result in widespread hunger, agents reluctantly urged freedmen to sign labor contracts. Some Bureau officials were inclined to regard *all* workers as indolent and had little patience for what they regarded as naïve black hopes of financial independence. But more progressive agents and black Bureau officials sided against the former Confederates and supported ongoing demands for the division of land. Few Republicans in the nation's capital openly condemned Johnson's disregard for the Freedmen's Bureau Act, yet in the field, agents tacitly supported those freedmen who gathered in Greensboro, Alabama, and called for "land or blood"; and they helped black Carolinians draft petitions to Congress demanding Washington honor past "pledges of government to us concerning the land question."[35]

Bureau officials who warned planters that the penalty for not paying their workers fair wages—and regional salary scales were invariably set by the agency—was to have their lands confiscated undoubtedly saw themselves as advocates of social reform. Some former slaves thought so, too. "Dat one time Massa Charley can't open he mouth," marveled Sally Ford, "'cause de captain tell him to shut up, dat he'd do de talkin'." General Saxton reported that freedmen in South Carolina were prepared to sign contracts "where they are sure of receiving their pay," but he noted that their obvious lack of "confidence in their former masters," together with their hopes of obtaining their own land, made them slow to do so. Other blacks objected to the Bureau's emphasis on yearly contracts, which they regarded as a federal concession to planter demands and frighteningly similar to previous labor relations. Agricultural contracts in northern states, Roudanez charged, were for shorter periods, and free state workers could quit and seek new employment. Why did southern whites "need the binding of the laborer to the plantation?" Even Bureau agent Samuel Thomas noted that the department also sought to assist white yeomen whose lives had been destroyed by the war, yet these "homeless, poor wandering, idle white men" were not counseled to sign twelve-month contracts or quit urban areas for the countryside. The racially based emphasis on yearly contracts gave the lie to the Bureau's promise of equal treatment to both landlords and laborers.[36]

Despite a series of Bureau-created courts to help negotiate and adjudicate contracts, the process of forging equitable agreements proved easier outside of the large plantation districts that once had produced staple crops for export. Agents in Mississippi reported that the 1866 cotton crop would not constitute half of the prewar harvest. In western Texas, small "farmers and freedmen" signed contracts "for the next year satisfactory to both parties." But on the old sugar and cotton estates along the Brazos and Colorado rivers, African Americans either hoped to obtain their own farms or balked at signing lengthy agreements, and so General Edgar Gregory toured the region in hopes of persuading them "to make contracts for labor next year." In the Carolina low country, only those freedmen who had not already obtained parcels of land were willing to hire out to nearby plantations, and that scarcity of labor allowed for what one editor denounced as "rather too liberal contracts."[37]

Nor were all the difficulties due to the unwillingness of former slaves to sign long-term agreements that limited their autonomy and mobility. Federal officials quickly discovered that whites expected the Bureau to negotiate contracts that effectively restored their prewar authority. In Alabama, planters conceded that slavery was "a dead letter," the Thirteenth Amendment having been ratified the previous December. But a delegation of whites lobbied the Bureau to push for labor contracts that bound "their late slaves" for an unspecified "number of years." Planters also hoped to force black workers into antebellum-style work gangs, and to write wage-withholding penalties for tardiness or insubordination into the contracts. One Vicksburg planter informed an agent that while he was willing to pay his workers, it was also "absolutely necessary to have some mode of punishment" for them. Well into 1866, Bureau officials reported finding freed people residing in their former huts, called to labor each morning by whip-wielding overseers. A South Carolina woman confided that she now dubbed her black drivers "captains, out of complement to the changed times," but that otherwise she expected blacks to labor according to prewar routines. Since planters recognized that some white Bureau agents shared their suspicions of black indolence, they expected the agents to negotiate contracts that reinstated the planters' power. "Upon this point turns the entire question," a Carolina editor maintained, "and as that is decided, so is the safety or ruin of this country."[38]

Even when they were reluctantly willing to sign contracts, African Americans had very different expectations from their employers. In the pages of his *New Orleans Tribune*, Roudanez advocated a profit sharing plan, in which blacks would first draw modest wages to see them through the season, but then later receive one third of the plantation's final profits. The virtue of that arrangement, the editor suggested, was that it would motivate blacks to labor diligently and also provide them with the capital necessary to become landowners themselves. Assisted by literate veterans and Bureau agents, others quickly became conversant in the language of negotiation. Chosen by ten other freedmen to represent their interests, Louisiana's Virgil Loyd complained that their employer had committed a "gross violation of the rights of said Freedmen" by intimidating them into signing a second "Substituted Contract" that "robed [them] of their labor." Women especially insisted upon short-term employment, which was easier to obtain in domestic service than in agricultural labor. In part, the desire for temporary employment stemmed from the fact that household work reminded some black women of their enslavement. But in a period of general poverty and in a region short on hard currency, freed people were prudent to be watchful of economic betterment. Although one frustrated Bureau agent complained that black women refused to "set a due value on their labor, and [were] ever dissatisfied with their wages," they were merely demonstrating the virtues of free wage-labor mobility that Republicans professed to admire.[39]

Given the vast gulf between white assertions and black aspirations, it was hardly surprising that a new war ensued in the countryside—a battle over wages. In regions close to urban areas, freedmen took advantage of labor shortages to bargain for both higher wages and shorter periods of employment. Near Lexington, Kentucky, agents reported that black men refused "to engage for a longer period than a week or month *at a time*." Planters across the South, in an act that betrayed a good deal of collusion, offered fifteen dollars "per month and rations," but laborers in Terrebonne Parish, Louisiana, struck for forty-five dollars instead. In Texas, "thousands" refused to contract unless they received "one-third of the crop"; and when denied that, they preferred not to work or relocated their families to the nearest town. In heavily black areas, where labor solidarity was easier to maintain, and where black Bureau agents supported workers' claims, wages remained well above what landlords wished to pay. Along the Georgia coast, a Republican editor enthused, Tunis Campbell found so many decent jobs for black refugees that he was "unable to supply the demand for [hired] labor made at his office." If Bureau agents could not reverse the reactionary policies pursued by a distant president, they could at least set wage scales high enough to provide a living for his constituents. "High wages offered by *asses* has turned their heads," groused one landlord, and a South Carolina rice planter added that the blacks on his land "laugh at threats of dismissal as there are any number of places where they can go and do as they please."[40]

Former slaves also fought with landlords over plantation routines, and especially over estate personnel. Blacks resisted attempts by planters to reassert order by rehiring the same overseers they had employed before the war. One Louisiana woman hired her former manager in hopes of setting her workers "straight," but they anticipated his arrival. As he rode toward his cabin, they surrounded his horse. One man "seized the bridle and told him he should not step foot in that house, that the quarter belong to them and no d[amned] white man should live there." The overseer shouted that he was in charge, but the freed people "told him they did not want to hear a word from him" and that if he returned, they "would burn powder and lead" around his home. Since they regarded the home as their domain, black women were particularly incensed when overseers searched their cabins in attempts to reclaim their employers' property. When an overseer named Hazel tried to do so, black women armed themselves with "Axes hatchets hoes and poles" and threatened to kill him. Hazel returned with the planters' son, but the women rained stones and bricks down on them, while Sukey and Becky, newcomers to the fight, attacked the men with clubs. The son called on black men watching the affray to stop "the maddened women," but one husband laconically replied that the two "had no business over there anyhow—that no white man could control them now they were free."[41]

One of the factors that allowed for the growing chaos across the South was the rapidly diminishing number of soldiers stationed in the former Confederacy. Although images of countless overbearing occupiers routinely graced popular literature (and eventually also film) in the years after the war, the government demobilized rapidly after 1865, leaving but a skeleton force in place by the first months of 1866. White farm boys clamored to return home, and black regiments were either disbanded or ordered west to confront the perceived Indian menace. Within a year of Lee's surrender, just two black regiments remained in Alabama, with one each in Georgia, South Carolina, and Florida. Regiments were stationed in urban areas and patrolled the countryside infrequently. In towns and cities, however, few soldiers had much patience with unreconstructed Confederates. In Vicksburg, John Cormick attempted to purchase a small plot of land from Mary Miller, a freedwoman and soldier's wife. Miller, he complained, demanded too much money and was "insolent, obstinate, and unreasonable." Assuming the local Bureau agent would take the side of a fellow white man, Cormick filed a grievance, only to discover that the agent merely handed the paperwork to Miller, who denounced Cormick as a "grand rascal scoundrel." Furious at being spoken of in that manner by a black woman, Cormick struck her with a switch, only to find himself arrested for assault. A similar saga unfolded in Yazoo City, Mississippi, when a dispute between former master and slave ended with the young black man throwing a hatchet at the planter. When the planter complained to the Bureau, they simply gave the youth a "lecture" after they heard his side of the quarrel: "He never done nufin all his d[am]n life but beat me and kick me and knock me down."[42]

The countryside was a far different matter, and there clashes over wages and contracts often turned violent. In Mississippi, Amos Dorsey refused to sign a second contract with his former employer and master, who then shot him while he was "attempting to Escape," as if Dorsey were a runaway slave. Nearby in Gallatin, planter John Reynolds reneged on his agreement to grant his employees one third of the cotton crop, keeping "*all* the Cotton and all the Cotton seed." When two freedmen seized their portion and announced they would work for Reynolds no longer, he had them arrested for theft. Unable to post bond, the two "were suffering for bread." Bureau agents in Seguin, Texas, reported that an aged freedman, too sick to pick cotton, had been beaten with a strap fastened with a two-inch iron buckle. The same agent testified that Henry Jones had been murdered by his employer after filing suit for seven dollars, and that another black man, named Oliver, had been shot after reporting his employer's abuse to the Bureau. Hagar Barnwell, who had signed a contract to work in the fields, refused her employer's demand to work in the kitchen. Swearing that he would kill her had he not a crop to bring in, the landlord pulled a pistol, dragged Barnwell to a shed, and tied her up by her thumbs so that her toes barely touched the ground.[43]

The idea that the Thirteenth Amendment marked a fundamental change in race relations took hold only slowly with some Confederates. Yet another disagreement over the division of "some property" led Mississippi's J. F. Ford to "hang up a negro." Elsewhere in the state, landlord Isaac Smith employed Sam and Jim Neal to plant fifty acres of corn and cotton and split rails for a fence. After three months, Smith ordered them to plant a different field from the one they were cultivating. When they refused, the white man "commenced beating Jim," and Sam intervened with a large stake. White policemen arrested the two black men and charged them with battery; for being assaulted, Jim received sixty days in the county jail, and Sam was sent to the state penitentiary for one year. Reactionary whites even attacked other whites who accepted the new order of things. In Tennessee, thirty armed "guerrillas" attacked a planter named Ransom, who "had made himself obnoxious by renting portions of his land to negroes." The commander in Nashville dispatched a company of troops to the county, but not before the rebels had "succeeded in driving the negroes off the place." If landlords such as Ransom indicated the possibilities for a new society in the aftermath of war, the guerrillas served as a grim reminder of the folly of Andrew Johnson's program of unreciprocated conciliation.[44]

Unable to stem the tide of violence, some Bureau officials instead tried to move freed people out of harm's way by helping them to relocate north. Thanks to the Homestead Act of 1862, thousands of white farmers and immigrants had pushed west during the closing months of the war, and nearly two thousand black men and women found employment in Iowa working as field hands, day laborers, domestics, and laundresses. Freedwoman Rebecca Rakes, who earned enough to purchase a ticket to Des Moines, rented a room with other blacks. "We all kept house together," she later wrote, and hired themselves out each morning "by days work." Bureau agents in Washington discovered that refugees from Virginia refused to "go to any of the southern States," no matter how attractive the wages. Freed people desired decent "treatment and schooling for children," and while neither were found in large supply in Washington nor in most cities to its north, the relative lack of violence drew thousands of former slaves to the North. Sojourner Truth placed employment requests in the Rochester *Express* and received numerous requests for black girls "to assist in tak[ing] care of young [white] children." So anxious was Josephine S. Griffing, an agent and Garrisonian abolitionist, to get blacks out of the South, complained General Howard, that she simply packed them onto trains "without providing homes beforehand." Even Howard, however, occasionally signed orders "for freedpeople to go to Chicago" and instructed the Bureau to pay "for their transportation." By comparison to the millions of slaves freed by the war, the migration North was small enough, yet it continued a process that had begun during the war and was to accelerate by the end of the century.[45]

Because Bureau agents in the field could neither overrule Johnson's policies nor bring themselves to abandon their campaign to improve the lives of the freed people, they often found themselves trapped in a cross-fire, hated by planters and distrusted by their constituents. As one visitor to the region observed, landlords "were quite willing for the Bureau to punish their refractory hands, but utterly unwilling to be placed in the same category with their former slaves." Another traveler assured an unsurprised Secretary of State William H. Seward that the "Southern [white] people is very much opposed to these Freedmen's Bureau's." But as agents routinely expelled blacks from promised lands on the orders of the president, freedmen like Richard Parker regarded them as suspect. "We don't care for the President nor the Freedmen's Bureau," he told a Nashville reporter. "We have suffered long enough; let the white man suffer now." Parker noted that whites had herded southern Indians west into Oklahoma, so he thought it only just that the government should "drive" defeated Confederates "away." Although forcible emigration for planters was not on anybody's political agenda in Washington, Parker was right enough in wondering why the president's policy was based on appeasing slaveholders who had seceded from the American republic. As Colonel Charles Whittlesey reported from the South, the "Bureau is hated as a representation of Federal *rule* but is respected as a representative of Federal *power.*" Had Johnson chosen to share his predecessor's goal of using the government's authority to usher in a new birth of freedom, the tools were at his disposal.[46]

Anxious to achieve in peacetime what they had failed to accomplish in war, former Confederates maintained a steady fire against the Bureau. Previously willing to expend federal dollars in catching and returning runaway slaves, Virginia Democrats charged that the agency cost twelve million dollars each year simply to please "Southern haters, negro fanatics, and greedy adventurers." The North Carolina legislature went so far as to promise a "Freedmen's bill of rights," provided the state would be "relieved from the operations of the Freedmen's Bureau," although the argument that the federal government was "preventing the negroes from obtaining civil rights" in the state convinced few African Americans. Georgia Unionists tried a different tactic and encouraged their more bellicose neighbors to cease their assaults on black bodies. "Prove that the negro is safe in all his rights," editorialized the Macon

Daily Telegraph, "and we shall soon get rid of the institution." So widely did southern whites blame the Bureau for a variety of ills that when a black actor took to the stage in Owensboro, Kentucky, two young men left the theater in disgust, grumbling that "niggers and whites on the same stage is what people git by having a Freedmen's Bureau in Owensboro." Yet this disdain was not limited to southern planters. James Gordon Bennett's staunchly Democratic *New York Herald* denounced the agency for assisting "broad-shouldered, gigantic Sambos" while ignoring white poverty. General Howard, Bennett wrote, maintained "the bureau for the support of big, fat buck niggers" and their "greasy wenches and pickaninnies." Why not create a Woman's Bureau, he wondered?[47]

Critics were correct in noting the high cost of the agency, but in the wake of a bloody civil war, the number of relief recipients was staggering. By August 1865, the Bureau provided food rations to 148,120 people—both black and white—each day. With an uncountable number of wounded Confederates returning home, medical supplies cost almost as much as rations. Many of the blacks who applied for aid were the widows of Union soldiers. Mrs. Motin Ramsel, the wife of a soldier and the mother of three, appealed for assistance as a "respectful colored woman" who eked out a marginal living "by taking in washing." Howard reported that during the Bureau's first full year of operations, the agency dispensed thirteen million food rations across the South, four million of them to impoverished whites. As agent C. E. Lippincott assured Republican senator Lyman Trumbull, when he was stationed in Alabama, "there were largely more whites than blacks supported by Gov't charity." Very few of the African Americans who asked for food were "able bodied Negroes," he insisted, but "it made the work of five or six hours *daily* for a Staff officer to Examine the applications of crowds of white people." Since state authorities rarely assisted freed people, Howard argued, his agency had little choice but to assist blacks. When asked if the Stafford County, Virginia, overseers of the poor would aid former slaves, its president snapped that "not a *dam bite* will I give them. I would choose *hell* first." Since Democratic critics of agency relief offered only widespread poverty as an alternative, Republicans believed themselves justified in continuing to fund the Bureau.[48]

So convinced were they of the Bureau's success, Republicans in the capital hoped to extend the agency's life and extend its powers. On January 1, 1866, Howard announced that the Bureau had 92,752 acres of abandoned and confiscated land in Virginia under cultivation, and former slaves working Maryland farms had stored 1,200 bushels of corn and filled six barns with tobacco. Howard and Saxton were anxious to validate Sherman's land titles, or at least what remained in the hands of freedmen. Trumbull began work on a new bill, largely modeled on the

Formally known as the Bureau of Refugees, Freedmen, and Abandoned Lands, but commonly dubbed the Freedmen's Bureau, the federal agency was initiated by President Abraham Lincoln in early 1865 to assist former slaves in their transition to freedom. As this 1866 poster for Pennsylvania gubernatorial candidate Hiester Clymer reveals, conservative Democrats around the country charged the Bureau made freedmen idle while forcing hardworking whites to pay for the agency. Despite his racist campaign, Clymer lost the election to Major General John Geary. Courtesy Library of Congress.

previous act and interconnected with pending civil rights legislation (a battle discussed in Chapter 6). The bill allocated an additional $594,450 to the Bureau under the army payroll (since the agency had never enjoyed a separate budget). As had the previous law signed by Lincoln, the 1866 extension empowered tax commissioners to lease "not more than forty acres" of land to "loyal refugees and freedmen" for terms of "three years, at an annual rent not exceeding six per centum" of the land's value in 1860. Renters could purchase their lots at "the end of said term, or at any time during" that period. Trumbull called on the president to discuss the bill's provisions and was pleased to find that Johnson voiced no objections. Agents Laura Towne and Cornelia Hancock, who also journeyed to Washington to speak with Johnson and Secretary Stanton on behalf of the Carolina freed people, were less sanguine. "I know how they stand," Hancock lamented, "the President has the power but not the will to do for the colored people. Stanton has the will and not the power to help."[49]

When the bill came up for debate, Democrats trotted out all of their earlier objections to the Bureau. Indiana's Thomas A. Hendricks denounced the agency as "clearly an unconstitutional institution," adding that while it might have been necessary during wartime, it now constituted "Federal interference" in state matters. Others argued that it was "bad policy even as regards the negro" on the rather hazy grounds that as the Bureau had jurisdiction "over so wide an extent of the country," its authority led to unspecified "collusions and troubles." Republicans responded with testimony from the field that gave indirect voice to the aspirations and hopes of millions of African Americans. Justin Smith Morrill of Vermont, a founder of the Republican Party and an advocate of public education, presented a memorial from the National Freedmen's Relief Association of the District of Columbia, asking that "authority be given to the Secretary of War to place under the control of the Freedmen's Bureau such buildings belonging to the government as are not required for public service." Sumner presented a petition from "colored citizens of the State of Mississippi, assembled in convention at Vicksburg, in that State, November 22, 1865, praying that they may be protected in all the rights of freemen, and that the Freedmen's Bureau may be rendered more efficient." Although Democrats charged that stories of white atrocities were largely fabricated to justify federal intervention, progressive Republicans presented enough stories of southern violence to convince even their most moderate members. In the end, every Republican cast his vote in favor.[50]

Although few Republicans imagined that Johnson supported the Bureau's larger goals, almost everybody in Washington expected the president to continue his predecessor's policies and sign the bill. In addition to Trumbull, moderate Republicans William P. Fessenden of Maine and James W. Grimes of Iowa had met with Johnson and had left the conferences convinced of his support. Lincoln had written only two regular veto messages, his rebuff of the Wade-Davis Bill having come in the form of a pocket veto. "A veto at that time," Republican congressman Shelby Cullom agreed, "was almost unheard of." Despite his ascension to power as Lincoln's running mate, Johnson remained a Democrat, and apart from his distaste for civil rights, he had come to believe that his future lay with his old party, or at least with a coalition of Democrats and moderate Republicans. "Words amount to nothing unless verified by deeds," one Democrat warned during the debates over the bill. For Johnson, ever the ambitious politician, the worst scenario would be to alienate Democrats by signing the law, only to watch Republicans nominate a party regular three years thence.[51]

On February 19, Johnson returned the bill accompanied by an abrasive, confrontational veto message. Drafted in consultation with a number of advisors, chiefly Navy Secretary Gideon Welles and William H. Seward—whose steady retreat from his progressive stance of the early 1850s baffled and stunned party leaders—the message opened with the assurance that he shared "the strongest desire to secure the freedmen the full enjoyment of their freedom and property." But as the act of March 3, 1865, was still in force, he saw no logic in extending the powers of the Bureau, particularly now that war had ended. During cabinet discussions, Seward had argued for a message that held out the hope of compromise on a more moderate bill. Johnson, however, adopted the position that any federal control of the former Confederacy marked an unconstitutional extension of Washington's power. The president also raised the objection that a more effective Bureau could only antagonize white southerners at a time when eleven states remained excluded from representation in Congress, yet nothing in his lengthy remarks suggested that the readmission of southern states to the Union would alter his views on the bill's legality. For dismayed Republicans, hardest to credit was the president's insistence that the Bureau was unnecessary because freed people could adequately care for themselves, and that state courts afforded black Americans adequate protection—two theories clearly at odds with the memorials and petitions presented to Congress by southern blacks.[52]

Democrats showered praise on the message. "Great victory for the white man," crowed one editor. A southern newspaper, previously hostile to the Tennessee Unionist, now judged him "All right on the negro question." Trumbull tried to rouse the Senate for its first-ever veto override but failed to achieve the necessary two thirds by 30 to 18, with ten moderate Republicans who still hoped to work with Johnson reaching across the aisle. Eager to achieve compromise, House Republicans forged a second version of the bill on May 29, which they believed addressed some of the president's concerns; the Senate concurred on June 26. Determined to end what he regarded as federal meddling in southern race relations, Johnson vetoed this as well on July 16. If Johnson's earlier message was met with dismay by the Senate majority, his second veto earned only scorn. An angry Senate voted to override that same afternoon by a vote of 33 to 12, and this time only three moderate Republicans stood with the president. Despite this historic rebuke—an override of the president's veto of the Civil Rights Act of 1866 came at nearly the same moment—a resolute Johnson continued in his course, granting wholesale pardons to Confederates and overturning tax sales. By the spring of 1866, he had returned 414,652 acres of land to planters, including fifteen thousand acres previously turned over to freedmen. Johnson also sought to nullify the law's force by replacing Republican officers in the field with conservative Democratic soldiers less enamored of social reform. The president "musters out all my officers," Howard complained. "Measures are on foot [that] are doubtless intended to utterly defeat Reconstruction." When Congressional Republicans passed legislation, even over the president's veto, Johnson's response was to use his constitutional authority as commander in chief to invalidate federal law by refusing to enforce it. "Thus Johnson defeats

Congress at every point," Howard protested. "While Congress is passing acts to reconstruct the South, the President is driving a carriage and six through them."[53]

To more effectively nullify the law, Johnson decided that Saxton had to go. On January 1, 1866, the president fired Saxton, saying he could no longer endure his subordinate's obstructionism. As his replacement, Johnson chose General David Tillson, a conservative Democrat from Maine. During the war, Lincoln had removed a number of generals, but always for competence, never for politics. Tillson promptly visited the Sherman reserve, and he was surprised to find the freedmen on the islands under the control of Tunis Campbell to be "armed" and still refusing to "allow any white person to land." Tillson fired Campbell and ordered him off the islands. "Rebels, who before had appeared humble and repentant," Campbell observed, "now insisted that all colored men and women should sign [labor] contracts; and when they refused, they would waylay them and beat them, telling them that they would have them back when the Yankees left the State." Instead of returning north, Campbell moved to the mainland, helped to organize a lobbying organization dedicated to black instruction, the Georgia Education Association, purchased an estate called Belleville, and began to prepare for a run for the state senate.[54]

Although unenthusiastic about its mission, Johnson was less hostile toward the federally chartered Freedman's Savings and Trust Company. Like the Bureau, the system of banks was designed to encourage diligence and thriftiness and elevate freedmen out of both charity and poverty. Also like the Bureau, which remained a subdivision of the army, the Freedman's Bank was chartered by the federal government but was not a sector of the Treasury Department. Massachusetts senator Henry Wilson bragged that depositors' money was "just as safe there as if it were in the Treasury of the United States," and as it had been created on the same March day as the similarly named Bureau, unlettered investors might be forgiven for believing it a part of the government. Its main branch, run by director Alvord, sat on the corner of Pennsylvania Avenue and Madison Place; its interior, gracefully finished with black walnut and marble counters, was designed to reflect the new prosperity and capabilities of black Americans. Frederick Douglass marveled that he could not pass it without glancing "into its spacious windows, and

Located at 710 Madison Place in Washington, D.C., the Freedman's Savings Bank symbolized the potential for African American economic advancement in the years after the war. Although not part of the Freedmen's Bureau—as many blacks assumed it to be—the bank was chartered by Congress in 1865 in hopes of helping black veterans, immigrants, and working-class whites to build their savings and fund community organizations. Courtesy Library of Congress.

look[ing] down the row of its gentlemanly and elegantly dressed colored clerks, with their pens behind their ears and buttonhole bouquets in their coat-fronts." The bank opened branches across the South and in Manhattan and Philadelphia. Although its director and most of its trustees were white, each branch hired black clerks so as to attract black veterans and freed people. Most investors opened accounts with less than fifty dollars, and parents opened accounts for their children with as little as a few pennies. [55]

To demonstrate that he supported the cause, Solomon Brown, the curator of the Smithsonian Institution, opened an account in late August of

1865. Rather more typical was depositor Edward King, the former slave of William Russell of nearby Loudoun County, Virginia. King was a veteran of the Twenty-third USCT who had lost a leg outside of Petersburg, Virginia, during the summer of 1864. His army savings amounted to sixty dollars. Catherine Smith, a former Maryland slave and the widow of Nathaniel Smith, who died at Petersburg, deposited three hundred. On occasion, entire regiments opened accounts with the Washington branch as they were mustered out. Private Morris Barber and Corporal Monroe Tabok, both Kentucky runaways, marched twenty-two fellow members of the 114th through the bank's doors.[56]

At the Charleston office, located at 9 State Street, the first investor in line that December morning was George S. Holmes, a fisherman who signed his account with "his mark." Hundreds of freedmen, Alvord observed during a tour of the southern branches, drew on accounts as they purchased small farms, generally for ten dollars an acre. Fifteen industrious former slaves, he added, "clubbed together with the proceeds of their crop and bought a whole Sea Island plantation of seven hundred acres." The Charleston Home Association opened an account to assist in the "Purchase of Homesteads for [its] members," as did John Cook, a Bavarian-born Union soldier. Major Delany became depositor number 7,638. Faith in the bank and confidence in a better future papered over some of the old scars that Delany himself commented on that summer at the Mount Zion Church. William B. Penceel, the son of the mixed-race freeman who had helped betray Denmark Vesey, opened an account for his two young children, as did Robert Vesey Jr. Malcolm M. Brown, a thirty-six-year-old contractor and the son of the Reverend Morris Brown, who had been exiled to Philadelphia in late 1822 for his alleged complicity in the plot, did too. Waiter Charles Nesbitt, whose father had decided not to join his old friend Vesey in revolution, trusted his money to the bank, as did Susan Drayton, whose father had been transported outside the country for his part in the plot.[57]

The Philadelphia branch never attracted many investors, perhaps because a thriving free black community there had already constructed the foundation necessary for financial solvency. Most of the Pennsylvania accounts held donations for black charitable organizations, such as the "Thaddeus Stevens Lodge" or the "Independent Sons and Daughters of Richard Allen." Manhattan's office, tucked inside the American Exchange Bank Building at 87 Cedar Street, drew large numbers of black depositors, particularly those freed people who had recently relocated from the South. But the branch also held accounts for large numbers of working-class and immigrant whites, who, like black investors, regarded the Freedman's Bank as the safest place to keep their meager earnings. Liverpool-born Annie Louisa Broadfoot, who had lost a brother during the Atlantic crossing, maintained an account, as did eight-year-old Christopher Bradley, who had arrived from Ireland the previous year. Joseph Taylor from Huddersfield, England, opened an account with his wife, Ella. Since the bank had to maintain records for depositors who lacked identification, clerks scribbled down defining features. Taylor, once a factory worker, had "lost all fingers on right hand."[58]

By late 1873, the bank boasted thirty-four branches that held deposits of $3,299,201 for 61,131 depositors. But John W. Alvord, the bank's founder, was a minister and abolitionist rather than a financier, and his institution could not afford the nearly three-hundred-dollar monthly salary expected by "model bankers." Alvord instead relied on black cashiers, paying them $60 to $125 each month, and most of the clerks had been soldiers and Bureau workers; they too had little financial experience. Due to the unfortunate influence of board member Henry Cooke, the president of the First National Bank of Washington, the bank made a number of risky loans, including one to Henry's brother's firm, Jay Cooke and Company; another to Henry's own bank; and a third to the Union Pacific railroad. With the onset of a serious depression in 1874, new board member John Mercer Langston decided that the aged Alvord needed to step down. Having removed a white abolitionist with no business acumen as president, the board made the mistake of replacing him with a black abolitionist of limited financial experience. Most likely, however, there was nothing that Frederick Douglass could have done to save the institution, especially given the global nature of the economic crisis. After only two months as president, Douglass admitted that he was "in a hard place" with the bank. In desperation, he lent the bank ten thousand dollars of his own money, but on July 1, 1874, he voted with the other trustees to close the bank. Neither Douglass nor the working-class depositors—only three thousand of whom had accounts worth more than two hundred dollars—ever saw their money again.[59]

By that date, thanks to President Johnson's resolve to roll back the gains of the war years, most of those depositors had abandoned their hope of becoming landowning farmers and agreed to work for wages. Increasingly, young, strong freedmen, and particularly those whose skills allowed them to hire their labor in the rare off hours, instead opted for sharecropping agreements, as an arrangement that rewarded diligence and expertise allowed blacks to earn more than if they drew a standard wage. For blacks who preferred to work their own land, share-cropping was the best available option. By working a section of a plantation as if it were theirs, they controlled their own work schedules and family arrangements. Their children were allowed time to attend schools, and unlike under slavery, their wives largely withdrew from the fields except during intense periods of planting and harvest. Primarily for that reason, most landlords detested sharecropping. "When the negro becomes a copartner in the plantation the employer sacrifices intelligence to ignorance, judgment to vanity, and self-respect to race and color," grumbled former South Carolina assemblyman D. Wyatt Aiken. "Wages," agreed another, were "the only successful system of controlling hands," who stubbornly insisted on being "masters of their own time." Some farsighted landlords, however, recognized that the arrangement introduced labor incentives into a system that had lacked them in the antebellum years—apart from the overseer's whip. One North Carolina planter hired a number of freedmen and "sold some of them horses and mules." By spring, the estate was "the busiest farm and finest prospect [he] had ever seen." White neighbors arrived at his door to warn "that no nigger should straddle his own horse." Instead of backing down, the planter called on the nearest federal officer, who gave him "as many old guns as [he] wanted" to defend himself. The colonel "is a good fellow and a gentleman, if he is a Yankee," the planter mused.[60]

As with most momentous issues in history, there is no precise benchmark with which to evaluate the relative successes or failures of land reform. Although the president's obdurate policies hindered the emergence of a black middle class, and with it, regional prosperity in what had been the Confederate states, a good number of freedmen prospered in the years just after the war. Prior to the collapse of the Freedman's Bank, two brothers saved toward the purchase of fifteen hundred acres of Georgia cotton land, while another black, Peter Walker, was able to acquire the same amount of land. Congressman Richard "Daddy" Cain, the minister who had spoken at the rededication of Charleston's AME Church, bought two thousand acres in South Carolina, which he re-named Lincolnville and subdivided into smaller parcels for resale to his black constituents. At the time of secession, virtually no southern blacks owned land, but by 1880, twenty percent of black agriculturalists held the deeds to their parcels. By 1920, that figure had risen to twenty-five percent, while at the same time, the percentage of whites who owned southern land dropped from eighty to sixty percent. One of those black landowners was Georgia assemblyman William A. Golding, the former slave of planter Charles Colcock Jones. Employed by the Bureau, he put aside enough money to buy a portion of his former master's estate. When Jones's son called on the assemblyman in early 1874, Golding politely showed him his farm. "Ah, sir," Golding observed, "things is mightily changed since you and your father lived down here. Almost all the big plantations have been cut into small lots by the owners, who couldn't any longer work or fence them, and *sold* out to the colored peo-ple." A Macon editor bemoaned the fact that once "noble mansions" were now "occupied by the ignorant [former] slaves," but for Golding and the industrious freedmen, Reconstruction was anything but a failure.[61]

CHAPTER FOUR

"The Lord Has Sent Us Books and Teachers"

Missionaries and Community Formation

BORN IN 1828 into a well-to-do Baltimore family, Hugh Lennox Bond was raised to value moderation. He graduated from the University of the City of New York by age twenty and returned to Maryland to read law with an established firm. Typical of wealthy white men from the Chesapeake, Bond was attracted to the Whigs, a party that stood for sobriety, commerce, and firm stewardship of the nation's financial well-being. Following the collapse of the Whigs, Bond followed his friend Congressman Henry Winter Davis into the short-lived American Party. Four years later, he cast his ballot for John Bell and the Constitutional Unionists, thinking Lincoln too radical. As Bond had argued in 1856, there was always a third choice besides "a union Democrat and a [R]epublican demagogue." Bond's equability and legal abilities won him a seat on Baltimore's Criminal Court, a position he was to hold until 1867.[1]

The war changed everything for Bond, as it did for so many white men and women. A devout Methodist and never sympathetic to slavery, the judge was furious at the pro-Confederate sympathies demonstrated by most of his state's Democrats. Bond announced himself a Republican. He protested the policy of federal bonuses to white masters who enlisted their bondmen in the military, used his judicial perch to return apprenticed black children to their parents, and championed the state constitution of 1864 that banned slavery and manumitted more than eighty thousand black Marylanders. Most of all, Judge Bond so treasured literacy that he joined his city's Association for the Moral and Educational Improvement of the Colored People and endorsed the freedmen's schools that began to appear in 1865. The increasingly radicalized Bond made himself unwelcome in Methodist circles by publicly lamenting that "every colored Methodist" from Maryland who sought higher education had to rely on northern philanthropy. "No Methodist congregation in Maryland has yet contributed one cent toward the education of colored Methodists," he groused. Bond's labors earned him the reputation "as a judicious friend of the colored man" among Boston evangelicals and reformers. But no accolade meant as much to him as did an overheard conversation in which a former bondman told a black girl that he planned to attend a night school being opened by the Freedmen's Bureau. "You know," the former slave insisted, "all we've got to do is work hard days, and get larning nights."[2]

Although a bookish man, Bond did not believe in education for its own sake. As a progressive Republican, the judge believed that knowledge was inextricably linked to citizenship, and as an upper-class moralist, he hoped education might cure working-class freed people of their "degradation" and "viciousness." Typical of many affluent whites, Bond also regarded schools as essential not merely for black financial advancement but for statewide prosperity. "Educated labor," he lectured Baltimore businessmen, "produces more than uneducated labor," and so whatever doubts conservative whites might have of black literacy, it was in "the interest of the State that all labor should be instructed." His close friend Henry Winter Davis, who had become a congressman in 1863, died too young in 1865. But thanks to Henry's cousin David Davis, Lincoln's 1860 campaign manager and now an associate justice on the Supreme Court, Bond remained politically well connected in both Baltimore and Washington. He routinely funneled correspondence, queries, and advice to Oliver O. Howard at the Freedmen's Bureau, and together with the general's brother, Bureau assistant commissioner Charles H. Howard, Bond spent the summer of 1867 touring freedmen's schools in southern Maryland. Rather to the surprise of an accompanying reporter

for the *Baltimore Sun*, Bond's speeches at Leonardtown and Port Tobacco were well received by both blacks and whites, "and everything
passed off pleasantly."[3]

Justifiably concerned that Bureau academies would not long survive
President Andrew Johnson's veto pen, Bond endorsed publicly funded,
integrated state schools. That earned him the enmity of Democrats,
who already complained that the judge never heard a dispute between
black families and former masters without finding for the former. By
late 1866, Maryland governor Thomas Swann, a supporter of the president's policies, urged the state legislature to impeach the judge. The
drive stalled, but angry whites posted threatening letters. "Look out
you black hearted nigger loving son of a bitch," wrote one. "Why don't
you leave Maryland[;] its no place for you. We are white men here.
Leave go to Massachusetts and be a nigger. You above all other men we
hate, so damn you." Bond calmly filed the missives away, content that
his God and his state's black population were on his side. "They say,
Presi't Johnson doesn't dare to visit Baltimore," chuckled a Boston correspondent, "for fear that you will lock him up."[4]

Bond's enemies only succeeded in shoving him into ever more radical
positions. In the fall of 1866, he spoke at Baltimore's Front Street Theater, sharing the stage with such Republican luminaries as Chief Justice
Salmon P. Chase, General Howard, and Reverend Henry Ward Beecher.
Noting that a banner displayed in the back of the hall denounced him "as
a negro-worshipper"—Bond surely sanitized the sign's wording in his
remarks—he replied that he paid no heed to "any person on God's earth
[who] trample[d] upon the man who has followed the flag." He then tore
into those ministers "who have said nothing about negro education."
Why did his state persist in denying blacks the right to education? he
wondered. As a judge, "there was no place to which he could send any
erring colored person under eighteen years of age except to the penitentiary." He did not intend to rest, he assured the audience, until "every
negro shall have the right to go to school." Democrats jeered, but by the
time General Ulysses Grant paid a visit to the city in November and
was hosted by the judge, Bond's crusade was more overtly political and
he headed the state's "universal suffrage party." Three years later, then-
president Grant elevated Bond to the fourth federal circuit court. Senate

Republicans confirmed the appointment, and Bond continued to hand down progressive decisions until his death in 1893.[5]

Although forgotten today, Bond was typical of the tens of thousands of white activists and progressive evangelicals who were radicalized by the war and its immediate aftermath. Reviled in older scholarship and popular mythology as selfish, insincere carpetbaggers, these earnest militants labored beside black ministers and veterans to build churches and schools. Serene in the conviction that God favored their cause, young men and women cheerfully accepted low pay, selflessly endangered their health, and bravely risked their lives so that recently freed Americans might enjoy better lives. For their part, blacks, determined to build, or, in some cases, rebuild communities and institutions either neglected under slavery or shattered by the war, erected rustic sanctuaries and schools—and then assembled them again after innumerable acts of arson. Freedmen who hoped to put aside hard-earned cash for their own farms donated money for books and pews. The efforts of these men and women—and the endless stream of enlightened decisions from Judge Bond's bench—serve as a reminder that the Reconstruction era neither reached a precise conclusion nor failed to achieve all of its goals. Less than two years after Appomattox, Howard reported that the Bureau was running 1,207 southern schools that employed 1,430 teachers, instructing 77,998 pupils. By 1869, that number had doubled to 3,000 schools and 150,000 students. In Texas alone, one agent observed, "many small schools in obscure places are scattered throughout the State, taught mostly by colored people." That number, impressive though it was, did not include those adults who attended informal night schools in nearby churches, or acquired basic literacy from their children each evening. "It is supposed that at least ten thousand colored persons, old and young, have learned to spell and read in Texas within the year," the agent testified.[6]

For Bureau agents dispersed across the South, for young teachers from Boston, or even for established public servants such as Hugh L. Bond, the task of assisting black community formation was formidable. Freed blacks combed the countryside for loved ones sold away during the antebellum era. As one Norfolk woman explained to a young teacher, her beloved aunt had been "sold as far as wind and water could carry her." The war liberated roughly four million enslaved Americans, but in the process bloody battles buried thousands of black soldiers and reduced their wives and children to widows and orphans, fueled population shifts to Washington and nearly every other southern city, and drove refugees and rural survivors into the urban North. New York and Philadelphia had long sustained black churches and fraternal orders, but their meager resources were ill-equipped to accommodate the rising tide of southern emigrants. Baltimore already supported several AME congregations, lodges, and African American debating societies, but even so, black leaders struggled to raise the sixteen thousand dollars necessary to build the Douglass Institute, a community center named for the former Maryland slave and housed at 11 East Lexington Street. Lower South cities had proven even more hostile to the institutions that supported black communities, and following the razing of Charleston's AME church in 1822, black churches had struggled to survive. Yet even the South Carolina port had grown thanks to the war. While many blacks fled north, veteran William Hord, a black Canadian raised in Indianapolis, saw only opportunity in the partially burned city. He opened a restaurant on Church Street and brought his wife south to join him.[7]

For black refugees raised in southern states, adjusting to life in Manhattan meant learning to survive in a sprawling, bustling seaport of nearly one million people. Twenty-six-year-old Martha Augusta Wilson was from Maryland's Eastern Shore. Her brother remained in Maryland, where her only other sibling was buried. Like so many black and immigrant women, she took in laundry as a "Washer & Ironer." Charlotte Ann Clark, also born in Maryland, had lost both husband and mother, and relocating to New York could not erase her time in bondage. Clark's hair was "*scraped* up on side of head," a bank teller noted, and she had a "Scar on upper lip." Stephen Green, who had been born and raised in Washington, found employment as a porter, but in other ways he was alone in the city and required all of the assistance churches and black lodges could provide. Green's father had either moved to or been sold into Richmond. His mother had died twelve years earlier, when he was thirteen; a sister remained in Washington, and his brother was deceased.[8]

These emigrants from the Confederate states were hardly isolated cases. Only twelve at war's end, Davis Laws had recently lost his brother; his father, a free black mariner, "died at Sea when son was 6 mo[nth]s old." Alexander Bridgeford was also freshly arrived from Virginia, where his father had died "just after surrender." Bridgeford perhaps hoped to find work and then bring his mother north as well, as she remained in Petersburg. Charles Friday Roberson relocated from Alexandria to seek employment as a waiter while his parents stayed in Virginia, where his three siblings lay interred. Richmond-born Cornelius Fletcher was also a waiter. His father, Phil, had been "sold [away] when he was a little boy," and although his mother was alive, she had gone to Mississippi to search for her husband. "Bro[ther] Gus dead," recorded a Freedman's Bank clerk.[9]

For both emigrants and the black majority who remained in the South, religion was the most immediate source of solace. Philadelphia's black congregations stretched back to the 1790s, with Manhattan not far behind. But southern whites regarded AME churches as centers of black resistance; routinely raided and closed by authorities, most survived only in urban areas in the upper South. In the southern countryside, African Americans who embraced Christianity inclined toward the Methodist or Baptist denominations, which allowed blacks the flexibility necessary to practice the traditions of their ancestors while adopting aspects of their region's dominant faith. Nashville's First Colored Christian Church had existed for four decades; competently run by freemen, the institution was a monument to black capabilities. As the city grew during the war, so too did the church, which by 1866 boasted more than three hundred members. In Richmond, blacks opened the doors to the Fifth Colored Baptist Church in December 1865, but the congregation had met clandestinely at various locations throughout the conflict. As the Richmond story suggests, black congregations within the former Confederacy tended to become visible only following federal occupation. Teachers accompanying Saxton's forces observed that blacks flocking to Port Royal immediately constructed buildings for services. The "deacons and preachers," one added, were long recognized as such by the slave community but only now were free to summon their flocks, "three evenings in the week, and thrice again on Sundays."[10]

Like their parishioners, most of these churches had humble origins. The Fifth Colored Baptist Church in Richmond, perhaps fittingly, was housed in an adapted stable. Atlanta's First Colored Baptist Church, founded in 1868 by twenty-five members, was a railroad boxcar. In the countryside, brush arbors served as chapels, as did larger slave cabins. One Louisiana cottage, built to house two families, was subdivided into a church and a home for the minister. "As you entered," remembered one congregant, "you had your choice—you could visit the family or go to church." Maine-born Adelbert Ames, a major general who remained in Mississippi as a Republican activist, reported that the church he visited was "not half built." There were no windows, and the roof was so shoddy that "the stars shone through the cracks." But for a recently liberated people desperate to rebuild a shattered community, a place to gather and pray and organize came first. Money for food, books, and a down payment on a farm took precedence over the construction of more elaborate churches. The freed people Ames encountered prayed and sang and "probably enjoy[ed] the meeting more than meetings are enjoyed even when the audiences sit on velvet cushions."[11]

In urban areas, at least, churches grew quickly and most flourished. After fourteen years in their converted boxcar, the First Colored Baptist Church's fifteen hundred members raised thirty-five thousand dollars for the construction of a handsome wooden building. In Columbus, Georgia, a new AME church lasted only four years before its membership had "increased to such an extent that a new church building [had] become a necessity." The elders planned to buy nearby Temperance Hall, a Macon newspaper reported. The simple pine Charleston church on Calhoun Street designed by Robert Vesey almost immediately proved too cramped for its congregation. Led by "Daddy" Cain and Moses Brown, an illiterate farmer from Edisto Island, the congregation purchased a dilapidated Lutheran structure on Morris Street as a second home, which was named for Morris Brown, the minister exiled to Philadelphia decades earlier. In 1872, the Calhoun Street church was replaced with a larger building. Once the second largest AME congregation next to Philadelphia's original church, the city's thriving postbellum black community quickly reestablished itself; by the early 1880s, Charleston's African Methodism boasted five thousand members. As one journalist observed, black southerners contributed far more to their churches than did whites "in proportion to their property and earnings."[12]

Southern migrants who wandered north were especially in need of spiritual nourishment. Manhattan's black community supported the African Methodist Episcopal Zion Church, St. Philip's, and the First Colored Presbyterian Church. John Johnson, a black Virginian whose mother had "died in Albemarle County during [the] War," found employment as a sexton at the Shiloh Presbyterian Church. Black refugees who followed veterans of the Fifty-fourth back to Massachusetts found solace at black churches in Boston and Worcester. Particularly in less established congregations, freedwomen played critical roles in sustaining the fledgling churches. One year after the war's end, black women in Davenport, Iowa, formed an AME sewing circle and raised sixty-four dollars toward the building of a new sanctuary. Churchwomen in Oskaloosa collected $177 for furnishings for their new sanctuary, and women in Des Moines hosted an Emancipation Day fund-raising dinner. Always accustomed to hard toil, if usually for others, freedwomen put in long hours in behalf of their congregations, understanding that they were not constructing houses of worship as much as they were crucial community resources.[13]

In few corners of the postwar republic did white Christians welcome these visible symbols of black autonomy. Since independent black congregations had been habitually harassed by antebellum authorities— and flatly banned in Charleston between 1822 and 1834—most southern blacks had previously attended white-run churches. Yet all predominantly white congregations exhibited the hated segregated pews that had driven blacks out of Philadelphia churches seven decades earlier. When Private Benjamin Bond of the Fifty-fourth visited Charleston's First Methodist Church during the summer of 1865, he discovered "separate seats" for black worshippers, an arrangement "unworthy of the name of Christian." Even white evangelicals from northern churches could be obtuse when it came to understanding black spirituality. Bureau agent and schoolteacher Laura Towne, who arrived in the Sea Islands with federal troops, was shocked to witness a black prayer group, which she denounced as "the remains of some old idol worship." Rather than sit quietly through a proper Presbyterian sermon, Carolina freed people gathered in a circle to pray and shout, walking and "stamping so that the whole floor" shook. "I never saw anything so savage," she confided to her diary. Former slaves, of course, could endure the patronizing stares of well-intentioned Boston reformers. Rather more serious were the objections of white southern ministers, who objected to the loss of their flocks—and the loss of their black congregants' donations—to independent black churches. Since black donations had helped fund white-controlled churches before the war, many freed people were as determined to take with them a portion of those congregations' possessions just as they confiscated material goods from their former masters' estates. "We claim all such property as our own," one Georgia freedman put it in 1866, as well as "the right to unite in brotherhood with any [C]hristian body that may, in its teachings and sympathies, accord with our feelings." White churches were "rebel" institutions, "Democratic" congregations, and "old Slavery Church[es]." Few blacks wanted anything to do with them.[14]

Once established, black churches performed the same functions as did black congregations in the North, albeit also duties thitherto refused by white clergymen. The same freed people who wanted to solemnify long-held relationships with a black minister typically wanted to do so before a black congregation. As one Bureau official reported in 1865, the African Americans in his jurisdiction "all manifest[ed] a disposition to marry in the church, and prefer[red] a minister of the Gospel to unite them." Wishing to bestow the same solemnity on their unions as they had witnessed in their masters' families, blacks preferred to marry within a building, no matter how small or makeshift. From the state, freed people desired a license to prove that they were legally married, and as a hedge against re-enslavement and sale, but from their God, they begged the sanction of an African American church. Bureau officials in the Sea Islands noticed that even on large plantations, couples held the actual ceremony in tiny cabins until more spacious buildings could be erected.[15]

Far more than their white counterparts, black churches everywhere also performed a variety of nontraditional roles. At least initially, impoverished freed people could rarely afford to construct and endow churches and schools together, and they frequently used the same building for both purposes. In Macon alone, the Second Baptist, First Baptist, and Colored Presbyterian churches all held daily classes, often as early as eight o'clock in the morning. Some congregations raised funds to support schools and teachers, but in the immediate aftermath of the war, most churches sponsored night classes and conducted lessons in basic literacy on Sunday afternoons. As entire families pitched in to save for a down payment on a small parcel of land, few families could spare their children for daily Bureau schools. During one of his many tours of the South, Alvord noticed that "Sabbath schools among freedmen have opened throughout the entire South; all of them giving elementary instruction, and reaching thousands who cannot attend the week-day teaching." Missionary Sarah Jane Foster observed much the same thing. Few southern blacks had ever seen a book apart from a Bible, and although every black parent desired a decent education for his or her children, for most of them, "Sunday school affords their only chance to read."[16]

If black postbellum churches blurred the lines between theology and education, their involvement in the political realm was even more overt. For those ministers who had been enslaved before the war and remembered the difficulty of holding public services, merely defending their right to worship as they saw fit was a political act. In the lower South, congregants understood that their continued existence required influential contacts and friends in Washington. As Florida AME minister Charles H. Pearce later explained to a Congressional committee, he thought it "impossible" to separate religion and government. "A man in this State cannot do his whole duty as a minister except he looks out for the political interests of his people." As respected community leaders in a region that had not permitted freemen to enter into those other professions that denoted status in the nineteenth century, ministers were called upon to read labor contracts, explain stories in newspapers, and assist their nonliterate parishioners in understanding legal documents. Not surprisingly, as African Americans won the right to vote, they often elevated their ministers to elective office. At least 243 black ministers served in various official capacities during Reconstruction, advancing their numbers ahead of black soldiers to mark them as the top profession among postbellum officeholders. (Since many ministers had served as Union chaplains during the war, however, there was considerable overlap with the 130 black veterans who held office during the era.) A majority were Baptist, with African Methodist clergymen capturing the second most offices. Reverend Pearce was among their number. Born a slave in Maryland, Pearce was ordained as a minister during the 1850s, moved to Florida as a missionary, and was elected to the state constitutional convention in 1868. For the next six years, he represented his district in the Florida senate. Always believing that his life's work was to help his flock in every way, he also served as superintendent of education and helped to raise funds for the Brown Theological Institute.[17]

This fusion of spiritual fervor, educational advancement, and political ambition attracted the ire of former Confederates. If white southerners were grudgingly willing to accept independent black congregations, that acceptance diminished as ministers and congregants turned their churches into schools and joined the battle over land and voting rights. Whites torched a black Methodist church in Anne Arundel County, Maryland, one member insisted, "for no other cause only for the teaching of a Sunday School." Mobs burned churches in nearby Montgomery, Kent, and Somerset counties for conducting night schools. William Mallet, an Arkansas freedman, wrote to Congressman Thaddeus Stevens in hopes that "something [could be] done" to prevent "the Rebbels" from further violence. They "Burned Down a fine African Church which Cost the Freed Man about $5000," he reported, and left "24 Negro Men Woman and Children" hanging from "trees all round the Cabbins."[18]

For a people emerging into freedom, no need was as great as basic education. As with land reform, it was also an issue that spoke to class as much as to race in the South, which meant that if pitched properly by Republicans in Washington, public education had the potential of appealing to a good many southern yeomen. Freed people rightly complained that masters had sought to deny them access to information. "De white folks didn' never help none of we black people to read en write no time," remembered Sylvia Cannon of South Carolina. "[I]f dey catch we black chillum wid a book, dey nearly bout kill us." Neither had southern states wished to educate free blacks, since many of them retained kinship ties with the slave community and might teach cousins and nephews to read. Even in Tennessee, only 152 of the 160,000 students who attended state schools in 1860 were African Americans. Yet the situation was not much better for middle- and working-class white children. Planters tended to educate their sons and daughters with private tutors. Generally poor by comparison to the North, the South also lacked the tax base necessary to fund systems of public education. In the Confederacy, only Texas and Louisiana provided for tax-supported public schools. Regional suspicion also worked against educational reform; through the 1850s, citizen groups passed a series of resolutions urging that "no teacher should be employed who was not born South." As a result, illiteracy for adult white males, while nearly unknown in New England, approached twenty percent in most southern states.[19]

Outside of New England, where black voting rights translated into effective demands for public education, black children faced a variety of obstacles. In Michigan, the state legislature required segregated schools, but the growth of the black community in Detroit by 1860 meant that the single school set aside for blacks in the city was both inadequate and staffed only by white teachers. Finally, with the war over and ever more blacks migrating north, the state assembly began to debate the virtues of integration and hired the first black teacher, Virginia-born Fannie Richards. Pennsylvania required districts with more than twenty black students to construct separate black schools, and where those existed, black children were denied the right to attend the more rigorous white academies. New York had created a series of taxpayer-supported schools in 1842, but the state struggled to maintain quality in the face of rising industrial poverty and immigration. Even in upstate New York, celebrated by reformers as the Burned-Over District for its fiery revivalism, only Syracuse and Rochester offered integrated schools, and the latter only as of 1857. Even in Lincoln's Illinois, as activist Joseph Stanley lamented, racism denied most black youths educational opportunity, and as late as 1865 "less than one hundred of our colored children [were] in public schools."[20]

In the South, as was the case with reemerging black churches, schools arrived with federal troops. Northern teachers initially sailed south with regiments destined for New Orleans or captured coastal regions. Shortly after Benjamin Butler began to liberate "contraband" in Virginia, white educators inaugurated schools near Fort Monroe, in Norfolk, and even on the plantation of slaveholding president John Tyler. Teachers converted slave cabins into one-room schoolhouses at Port Royal. Jefferson Davis's mansion at Davis Bend was put to good use, housing three teachers and two hundred children. A number of white soldiers had been teachers during their civilian days, and as Massachusetts chaplain Horace James remarked, those men coming "from a part of the country where free schools are an essential and very powerful element of its civilization, we naturally desired to establish similar institutions here." James found a number of former teachers, particularly the most devout, eager to conduct classes each evening, "so that they may study their own bibles, and find out for themselves the will of God." No sooner had Sherman marched out of Savannah than the city's black clergy founded the Savannah Education Association, and virtually the moment that Charleston fell, the association hired fifteen instructors and purchased abandoned buildings to be used as schools, including the city's slave mart on Chalmers Street. Louis B. Toomer, who had secretly taught classes before the conflict, became the new system's "principal teacher."[21]

The first wave of teachers who arrived in the collapsing Confederacy did not draw a governmental salary. Most were funded by the American Missionary Association, an evangelical abolitionist organization founded two decades earlier in Albany. The association paid missionaries—a majority of whom were young Protestant women—and purchased books and Bibles for southern children and black soldiers. "Any church, by the payment of about $200," the group announced in a widely circulated pamphlet, "may select their own missionary or teacher, to be sent by the Association, and report directly to the churches." Typical of those who stepped forward was Chloe Merrick of Syracuse, who journeyed south to establish schools in St. Augustine and Fernandina. Helen Pitts, a graduate of Mount Holyoke Female Seminary and the future wife of Frederick Douglass, taught in Norfolk, Virginia. Other missionaries arrived in such large numbers that by the first day of May 1865, less than one month after Lee's surrender, the AMA and a handful of black clergymen were instructing more than one thousand black children in Richmond, the former Confederate capital. Although their efforts were often coordinated by the military, their salaries were based on private philanthropy. As peace returned to the nation and state and local governments recovered sufficiently to create tax-supported systems, the association's directors hoped the teachers might find employment in those schools.[22]

When Congress created the Freedmen's Bureau in the spring of 1865, the agency was tasked with taking over and coordinating the various missionary endeavors. Some reformers believed the undertaking to be so enormous that only a cabinet-level position would do. "[L]et there be a new Executive Bureau established," declared the Reverend William J. Potter, "with a new Cabinet officer, whose duties shall be to care for and protect, and educate these four millions of new born freedmen." Although Congress failed to elevate the Bureau into the president's advisory circle and the agency remained under military auspices, General Howard was empowered to select a superintendent of Bureau schools. He tapped Chaplain John W. Alvord, future head of the Freedman's Bank. By July, Alvord and his assistant commissioners dispatched one agent to each southern state to act as regional supervisors. When Republicans passed the second Bureau bill over Johnson's veto in July 1866, they allocated $521,000 for the coming year's educational activities and salaries, so that the Bureau could begin to take responsibility for the missionary teachers' salaries. Many of the soldiers who staffed the Bureau came from religious backgrounds, and they shared a common vision with the young evangelical women who sought to impress upon African Americans their duties as both citizens and free wage laborers in a post-slavery world. Teachers needed to "[e]ducate them for the country's sake," one New York missionary asserted, "for the laborer is productive and valuable just in proportion to his intelligence."[23]

For recently liberated adults, demands for basic education were born of pragmatism. As the struggle over land continued across the South, blacks required literacy to understand deeds and to read labor contracts. Those men who aspired "to be farmers on their own hook," Bureau agent Alvan Gillem noticed, would only sign contracts that contained "stipulations that will enable them to secure Educational advantages." A number of recently freed Charlestonians understood the historic link between the state's denial of educational opportunity for blacks and its determination to hold them as propertyless chattel. In early 1865, blacks gathered at the city's Mount Zion Church to draft a resolution condemning their "forced ignorance and degradation in the past" and request that new legislation not only create public schools but require that black children be "kept in regular attendance at same." In nearby Georgia, Tunis Campbell was of a similar mind, advocating free and integrated schools as the first step toward black prosperity and land ownership.[24]

Nearly as closely associated with literacy were political rights, which were tied to the struggle over land. Black veterans insisted they had earned the right to the ballot, but even those African Americans who were too old for military service regarded the franchise as the key to land reform, and literacy as the guarantee of electing those who had their interests in mind. "They say they want to know themselves, what name they put into the ballot box," teacher Harriet Greely reported from Florida. Former planters derided black aspirations to education and ridiculed as mindless their attachment to the Republican Party precisely because they feared that an educated and politically astute black community might well use that power to obtain their own farms. Unlettered freedmen knew little of global affairs, but they grasped the fact "that many conservatives hope to reduce them again to some form of peonage," as one Tennessee Republican explained. For decades, Democratic planter-politicians had ignored the educational needs of their constituents, which now allowed Republicans to position themselves as the spokesmen for all "working-men" regardless of color. The "poor whites of this State, the laboring classes," editorialized the *Columbia Daily Union*, had "no other hope for the education of their children but in the continuing success of [the Republican] party."[25]

Reformers hoped that reconstructed states might soon establish taxpayer-supported public schools, and northern Bureau agents such as Cornelia Hancock believed that the division of large plantations into "thrifty little farms" could provide lawmakers with the financial basis to do so. Black parents, however, placed little faith in state authorities and saw no reason to wait. "I haven't any education myself but I intend my children shall have," one Virginian freedwoman assured Cynthia Everett, a teacher from Remsen, New York. In the upper South, home to larger and more established free black communities, African Americans pooled what little resources they had to construct schools. A Bureau agent in Maryland reported that black farmhands found it hard to "make ends meet," yet when it came to schools for their children, they furnished "all the money they can, anywhere from $50 to $150." In Little Rock, another agent marveled that black parents raised funds enough by late 1865 to finance "the first free schools in Arkansas—whether for whites or blacks." Nearly three hundred African American adults crowded into a small Richmond school, many of them spilling out into the lawn "for want of room," and vowed to each contribute at least sixty cents "toward providing fuel" for the Bureau schools. During their first summer of freedom, parents in Mobile and Montgomery "contributed $4000 for educational purposes."[26]

Black communities everywhere emphasized cooperation. Freedmen in Charleston purchased a handful of books and organized the Historical Library Association, a "library for the Improvement of the Colored People." Former slaves in San Antonio each provided a local Bureau agent with "fifty cents to one dollar" toward the purchase of two schoolhouses. When black clergyman William Hillery announced that he had to close his AMA-sponsored school in October 1865 for lack of heat, fathers and sons turned out to chop firewood and haul it to the Virginia schoolhouse; girls brought chunks of "fat pine," a resin-rich wood, to use for light. In Georgia, Bureau agents witnessed "grey-headed old men" attending classes "after the day's work with the children, each bringing his candle to light the shanty, and paying a penny for his lesson." As the state superintendent from South Carolina explained to Howard, there was "no place of any size where such a school was not attempted by the colored people." The educator was amazed. "We have just emerged from a terrific war—peace is not yet declared, there is scarcely a beginning of reorganized society at the South," yet a people "long imbruted by slavery" were transforming cabins into schools. "What other people have shown such a passion for education?"[27]

By the time Alvord toured the South in early 1866, he estimated "that half a million of these poor people are now studying the spelling-book, or advanced readers" and the Bible. Bureau agents and devout teachers undoubtedly viewed these efforts through the lens of true believers who posted few negative reports to their superiors in Washington. Yet enough of them repeatedly commented upon the "desire" of freed people to read to support claims that the "whole race wanted to go to school; none were too old, few too young." While teaching in Norfolk, Cynthia Everett wrote to her family of those "adults who passed through the bitterness of slavery," yet after a long day's toil put in "earnest application in the night-schools." As had been the case during the antebellum era, those in the countryside who could read taught one another, and in southern cities, a Boston journalist observed, children who attended classes during the day taught their parents by night. "Thank God I have a book now," gushed one black pupil. "The Lord has sent us books and teachers. We must not hesitate a moment, but go on and learn all we can."[28]

If black students appeared delighted at the prospect of working under Yankee schoolmarms, some modern scholars have been less than enthusiastic about them as a group. Coming from middle-class, evangelical backgrounds, these educators routinely revealed patronizing and condescending attitudes toward their recently liberated charges. They prayed that education might assist in racial uplift, but less so that former slaves could better themselves economically than in becoming a more Christian and proper people. Teachers rarely advocated social equality, in part because in their northern communities they rarely associated with immigrants or the laboring poor. Unlike many northern soldiers, they demonstrated no racial animus, but that did not mean they were not keenly aware of race itself, and they frequently expressed this awareness in supercilious ways. As one of Cynthia Everett's New York friends wrote, "it was something to get those little darkies tamed and to have them love the schools." Everett herself reported from Charleston that she "had to rise at cock-crowing in order that her mind might combat those of the dull African." Even after teaching in South Carolina for two years, Laura M. Towne congratulated herself for dining with two African American teachers. "I actually forget these people are black," she confided to her diary, "and it is only when I see them at a distance and cannot recognize their features that I remember it." Towne flattered herself that the "conversation at dinner flowed just as naturally as if we were Northern whites," but such an imperceptive remark hints that her companions were all too mindful of her whiteness.[29]

While Towne's companions occasionally thought her cloying and

Prior to 1865, no southern state featured a system of universal, state-financed public education, even for white children. Although freedmen and black activists demanded a variety of reforms, from voting rights to land redistribution, decent schools for their children invariably topped their list of demands. The emerging schools, funded in part by the American Missionary Association as well as by the federal government (through the Bureau) and by black parents, gave northern women the opportunity to transform the South. Despite widespread poverty and the requirements of labor, attendance rates during the first years of Reconstruction ranged from seventy-nine to eighty-two percent. Courtesy of the Schomburg Center for Research in Black Culture.

superior, they surely also found her and her cohorts dedicated, resolutely cheerful, devout, and, as events were to necessitate, courageous. Ohio-born Albion Tourgée, a soldier and radical attorney who settled in North Carolina after the war, shared some of the missionaries' conformist sensibilities, yet he aptly described the seven women who taught in Greensboro as "pure-hearted Northern girls" who were secure in the knowledge that "they were doing God's service." Outnumbered both by their pupils and by hostile white southerners, these teachers—who

rarely totaled thirteen hundred in any given year for the entire South—
gave up an easier life in the North in hopes of dramatically altering the
educational landscape in the South. As had a good many white soldiers,
these women—and a few men, such as Austin Love of Boston—slowly
rid themselves of their inherent racial prejudice and sometimes even
their old notions of domesticity as they battled white hostility and con-
ventional attitudes regarding their proper place in Victorian society. Like
the late Colonel Robert Gould Shaw, who had laughingly embraced a
hated racial epithet when describing his leadership of a black regiment,
Everett similarly sought to ease the sting of the label hurled at her by
former Confederates. She and the other educators in Charleston were
"Nig[g]er teachers," she proudly assured her brother.[30]

Most of the women were daughters of antislavery activists, and some
of the older teachers had been militants themselves during the 1850s.
Well educated for their day, a large number had attended Oberlin College in Ohio, the first school to graduate an African American woman.
Typical was Sallie Holley of central New York, whose father, Myron,
was an officer in the American Anti-Slavery Society and active in the
Liberty Party. Despite her brother's pleas not to attend that "nigger
school," she enrolled at Oberlin, where she successfully nominated a
black student to be president of the college's Ladies' Literary Society.
With the onset of Reconstruction, Holley opened a school in Lotts-
burgh, Virginia, where she remained until her death in 1893. While in
Virginia, she became acquainted with John Blevens, who had served
sixteen years in the Virginia Penitentiary for helping a runaway and had
been liberated only when Richmond fell. Although sixty years of age,
Blevens stayed on in Richmond and taught school. Despite this history
of antislavery work, however, few teachers exhibited any enmity toward
white southerners; imbued as they were with humanitarian instincts and
religious zeal, they did not much dwell on anger. One teacher at Atlanta's Storrs School even taught to atone for perceived past sins. Although
as a woman she was unable to vote, she felt "ever guilty" for previously
having endorsed the Democrats, and she daily "ask[ed] God [to] forgive
[her] for ever having sympathy, in the least, with them who would keep
these people in slavery."[31]

The teachers required every ounce of devotion they could muster. Black parents toiled long hours in raising funds for school and constructing rudimentary buildings, but Bureau dollars went toward salaries and administrative costs, not to structures, and teachers rarely thought the rooms conducive to learning. In Alabama, the Bureau's superintendent of education reported that Huntsville "school buildings are in a *miserable condition*" and were so small that "one half of the pupils are taught in the forenoon & the other half in the afternoon." Esther Douglass, who taught on the Wild Horn plantation near Savannah, faced the same issue. Douglass converted the largest room in the "great house" into her school, but even so it was often "*packed* [with] ninety five pupils of various sizes; for lack of seats about a score stand *huddled* up in one corner." In Memphis, freed people erected a schoolhouse that was one hundred feet long and forty feet wide, but it had to accommodate five hundred students. Annie Wilkins, whose school in Darien, Georgia, was financed by the American Missionary Association and protected by Tunis Campbell and the Bureau, fell into bed utterly exhausted each Friday evening. She taught eighty students during the day and their parents at night and then blacks of all ages each Sunday.[32]

Certainly the teachers did not endure such conditions for the financial rewards. The AMA recommended salaries of fifteen to twenty-five dollars each month, depending on experience and gender, a wage scale approved by financially strapped Bureau officials. Had they remained in the North, the same teachers could have earned monthly salaries of fifty dollars for women and sixty for men. The association did promise to cover "travelling expenses each way once a year," but those in their service were "expected to be as economical as is consistent with comfort." Despite these unaccustomed hardships, Everett promised her family that she was amply rewarded for her work in other ways. Eunice Knapp, who taught near Houston, also found gratification in the work itself. Although her tiny schoolhouse could not easily fit the ninety students she enrolled, their "parents exert themselves to the utmost to buy books for the children," she told a journalist. Knapp had taught for several years in the North, "but never had so interesting a school as present."[33]

As the daughters of abolitionists who had grown up reading antislavery tracts critical of southern folkways, the women were little surprised that their pupils' level of literacy was as imperfect as the makeshift schoolhouses. "It requires less courage to go as a missionary to Burmah than to teach colored children in Georgia," admitted one New Englander. A. C. Edler, who ran a school in Blackstock, South Carolina, discovered that the basic textbooks provided by the AMA were far above the abilities of his pupils, and so in place of the "Readers" he "used the Bible & Testament as text books extensively," as the children were more familiar with those stories. Cynthia Everett's first position was in Norfolk, and of the eleven boys in her class, only three could decrypt even a few words. None had a clear understanding of how the federal government functioned, but they knew who General Grant was. When asked "who freed them," every "dusky hands come up all over the room," and when the young evangelical queried them on "how many love him," they cheered and shouted out Lincoln's name. "[H]ow the large earnest eyes do glisten."[34]

The enthusiasm of Everett's students and their devotion to the republic was matched only by the bitterness of the whites she encountered outside of the classroom. A handful of former Confederates, either because of their own religious beliefs or due to practical considerations, endorsed the education of black children. A Macon newspaper lauded the example of the Reverend James R. Smith, a southern evangelical who obtained a teaching appointment from the Freedmen's Bureau, on the grounds that it was better to have "natives" running schools than "teachers imported into our midst from sections of [the] country where hostility to the South is proverbial." Bureau agents Alvan Gillem and John Mercer Langston reported that some Mississippi businessmen conceded that if "the abolition of Slavery is a fixed fact, the freedmen ought to be educated." But those dissenting voices found their way into newspapers precisely because they were atypical. R. D. Harper, the superintendent of education in Alabama, marveled at the progress the Bureau had made despite "the prejudice against and the opposition to the education of the freedmen." An educator in Mobile noted that local whites were "displeased that negroes should desire to improve their intellectual condition, and yet more displeased that any white person should be found, perverse enough to encourage these improper aspirations." The moment they quit their classrooms each day, northern teachers faced a steady barrage of criticism from those raised to believe that black inferiority justified and even necessitated their enslavement. "I do assure you," a white woman snapped at one teacher, "you might as well try to teach your horse or mule to read, as to teach these niggers. They *can't* learn." Just as the Confederate leadership understood that the potential recruitment of black soldiers negated their carefully constructed proslavery ideas, the notion that educated blacks might prove to be as clever as whites challenged long-held assumptions. The "country niggers are like monkeys," the woman added. "You can't *learn* them to come in when it rains."[35]

When it came to dealing with female teachers, southern whites invariably resorted to social ostracism, hoping to make the young women so miserable that they would abandon their crusade. "The teachers are mostly a tabooed class," sighed Bureau agent H. H. Moore. As they walked down the street or shopped for goods, Harriet Greeley wrote, schoolmarms were insulted, told to "go to the devil," and they watched as locals "pass by on the other side because we are associated with the Colored people." Housing was a consistent problem. Single teachers rarely wished to reside with black families, who in any case had little room to spare, and even those white women who desperately needed additional income refused to rent rooms to northern women. When Maria Waterbury of Saratoga, New York, took a position in Tennessee, she and three other young teachers were turned away from a nearly empty boardinghouse. "No you can't come into the house," the proprietress snarled. "*Nigger teachers*, indeed. As though we would disgrace ourselves having them in the house." In Tallahassee, freed people rented "an old Rebel commissary building," carved windows into the walls, and installed stoves to provide housing for teachers. But "not one in a thousand" whites had "the moral courage to brook the odium which would be visited upon them by their neighbors," lamented a Bureau agent. One "respectable Southern lady" who did have the nerve to do so found herself shunned. Her old friends refused to speak to her and a man in the street spat on her, "for the simple reason that she had rented part of her house to the lady teachers." The unnamed lady sold her home and moved north.[36]

Male teachers faced far worse. Reports from around the South told of endless attacks on men employed by Bureau schools. "When a teacher goes to some [Louisiana] village and opens a school for colored children," *Tribune* editor Louis Charles Roudanez charged, "he is turned out and not seldom beaten, stabbed or killed." Black Republicans in Texas complained that in many cases "violence has been used against both teacher and buildings." Black agent John Henry Butler, who purchased a number of Maryland lots on which to construct schools, complained to superiors that he was "often threatened with imprisonment or being shot or [attacked by] some other violent means." In Granada, Mississippi, Lieutenant J. B. Blanding, a twenty-five-year-old Bureau agent, was shot three times in the head while out for an evening stroll. The next morning, "a committee of citizens" paid a call on the dying Blanding's captain, warning him "that the teachers must leave, and that if he himself did not leave he would be killed next." How much longer, protested a Memphis editor, "[would] President Johnson shut his eyes to the fact that these Rebels are determined to restore the old state of things?"[37]

The White House remained silent, but on the ground, black activists and white educators redoubled their efforts. So many students sought an education on the Georgia islands controlled by Tunis Campbell that he used his own savings, combined with the funds provided by the Bureau, and instructed his son T. G. to transport textbooks down from Manhattan. "We cannot take anymore [pupils] at present," he informed General Saxton, "as we have not got books for them." Cynthia Everett urged her family to send her both clothing and money for her Charleston school. One of her students, Hilda, remained home "this week because her shoes and dress were not decent," and "4 or 5 of our boys [were also] particularly ragged." Student Henrietta Burtlett could not afford the single dollar the school charged for yearly tuition and had "not bin goyin to school for the lase two weeks" as she had "bin out into the country" looking for work. Despite these obstacles, Paul Mishow, who taught with Everett, cheerfully reported that his charges were "improving finally in Rhetoric." Unlettered chattel in 1865, some of his older students had not merely mastered simple mathematics but had "finished book-third" of geometry. His four brightest young men were "making rapid progress" in Greek and Latin, an advanced curriculum that inspired one angry Charlestonian to charge that "the little *nigger race*" was being readied to attend "college, whilest our poor white children are growing up in ignorance."[38]

Rather than waiting for students to knock on her door, the intrepid Everett went in search of those most in need of education. Charleston's imposing, castle-like Workhouse, a penitentiary for African Americans, stood beside the city jail, which in normal times was reserved for white detainees. Everett toured the Workhouse, which once had served as both lockup and courtroom for Denmark Vesey's men, and discovered "a long line of boys" who had been arrested for vagrancy. "They are taught nothing, have nothing to do," she complained to her sister. "Some of them could read, but they had nothing to read." Having seen something of the country beyond her sleepy hometown of Remsen, New York, Everett understood the link between poverty and crime. The warden was taken aback by her request, but after visiting her regular classroom, he agreed to allow for the establishment of a school for incarcerated children. In her rare off hours, Everett tutored thirty-five inmates, all of whom were under the age of eighteen. "Quite an effort is being made to organize a reform school," she informed her family, "which will be so much better a place to take the many like vagrants that now are taken to the jail."[39]

Yankee schoolmarms taught more than literacy and mathematics. As an evangelical, Everett saw her mission as one of moral uplift as much as imparting basic skills, and educators who instructed from the Bible hoped to "inspire the pupils with the desire to do right & to study for study's sake." The black students who flocked to the Bureau schools required no lessons in decency, yet inevitably the pious sensibilities of the teachers permeated all aspects of Bureau classrooms. In a century in which country schoolmasters rarely spared the rod, the New England Freedmen's Aid Society warned its missionaries that "corporal punishment is strongly objected to." Christian teachers, as Laura Towne observed, should never "resort to any course which brings in an appeal to the lower motives." Especially since many of the children had been abused while enslaved, the teachers were particularly sensitive on this point. "If I had to use [a whip]," Sarah Williams admitted, "I know I would cry as much as the scholars." Having rarely, if ever, encountered a white person they could trust, the students responded in kind. "Sometimes I feel much discouraged," one pupil confided to Everett, "but the best way to do is to do the best you can to day." When Everett returned north for her health, her former students wrote to assure her that they were learning their "Sabbath School lessons and [trying] to understand them." Pupil A. G. Townshend was confident that Everett "love[d] to here of all who are trying to live like Christ."[40]

Given this level of devotion on the part of both teachers and students, and with funding for the Bureau rising each year, field agents reported astonishing gains in literacy. In the first fall after the fighting, North Carolina superintendent F. A. Fiske tallied sixty-three schools created in his state, with eighty-five teachers hired. By the spring of 1866, as planting season drew students out of the classrooms and teachers returned north for the summer, agents stationed throughout the former Confederacy filed similar numbers. Alvord's tour documented a total of 975 schools, 1,405 teachers, and 90,778 students in fifteen southern states and the District of Columbia. Alvord's numbers did not include small schools constructed by freed people who had built their schools without Bureau assistance, and that, he told a journalist, "would add perhaps about one-fourth more." These accomplishments, noted Jane Grey Swisshelm, Republican editor of Washington's *Reconstructionist*, were especially impressive considering the previous lack of statewide educational systems, the impoverished and undereducated black working class, and the fierce antagonism of local whites. The American Missionary Association enrolled 1,800 students in Virginian's Shenandoah Valley alone. "The most difficulty was found in Lexington," Swisshelm reported, "where students of Mr. [Robert E.] Lee's [Washington] college combined with the populace against it."[41]

Justly pleased with the success of Bureau schools, Republicans in Washington increased the agency's educational budget when Congress reconvened in late 1866. But freed blacks, as before, contributed more than their share. Army chaplain Benjamin F. Randolph, who had said a prayer at the rededication of Charleston's AME Church, became South Carolina's assistant superintendent of education and opened new schools in Camden, Columbia, Darlington, Cheraw, and Marion. In Kentucky alone, freedmen contributed $1,101 toward the education of their children, and benevolent associations donated another $725. Nationwide, the Bureau expended $220,834 during the first six months of 1867, with black southerners raising a collective $7,332 and constructing 391 schoolhouses without federal backing. The Bureau furnished an additional 428 schools. Bookkeepers for the American Missionary Association counted 506 teachers funded by the group. In Hugh Bond's Maryland, blacks built another thirteen schools during the first three months of the year, adding 1,431 pupils for a total of 5,606 black children being educated in the state. Including night schools, Sunday schools, and industrial schools, General Howard counted 130,735 students enrolled in classes by the end of spring 1867. Tragically, only 1,348 pupils were white; despite the absence of statewide systems in most southern states that year, most parents preferred to consign their children to illiteracy rather than see them educated alongside black children.[42]

By then, what had begun as social ostracism of Yankee women and the isolated beatings of white schoolmasters escalated into a vigorous campaign of arson and murder. The violence was increased for a variety of reasons. Two years after Appomattox, the reactionary white minority had learned that almost nothing they might do could arouse the wrath of President Johnson. At the same time, black teachers began to replace those white teachers who found the work too exhausting or who, like Cynthia Everett and Helen Pitts, eventually fell victim to low-country diseases. Despite the fact that African Americans comprised only two percent of the northern population, by the end of 1867 they filled thirty-three percent of the Bureau's teaching positions, a figure that was to increase to fifty-three percent within two years. A few came from Oberlin. African Methodist congregations in Philadelphia and Manhattan supplied far more, believing their own "pious and educated colored people" were less inclined than white schoolmasters to fall victim to the "deceptive flippancy of oily-tongued slaveocrats." Still others were light-skinned African American freemen who had received modest educations in Charleston and New Orleans before the war. By April 1867, of the

144 teachers in Georgia, 45 were black; and two months later, Bureau agents in Kentucky found 79 black teachers but only 21 white educators. When Everett accompanied a white friend to a Norfolk Sabbath school in 1870, she discovered that "the officers and all of the teachers excepting Miss Jenks are colored."[43]

Although most of the black teachers were less experienced educators than their white predecessors, African American parents preferred teachers of their own race. In the decades before the war, the few brave souls willing to surreptitiously tutor their fellows were other members of the slave community, typically those artisans and craftsmen whose occupations required a modicum of literacy. Older freed people who had learned their lessons behind closed doors, an aged Texas freedman explained, were the most "disposed to distrust" white teachers. White schoolmasters were also more inclined than their female counterparts to maintain a social distance from their pupils; parents rightly resented those Nashville teachers who forbade their students from greeting them in public. The majority of black teachers were men, and primarily for that reason southern whites detested them more than women of either race, regarding them as dangerous examples of African American accomplishment. If many, such as Charles Thomas of Georgia, espoused the same homilies on moral elevation typical of white schoolmarms and encouraged their pupils to "make yourself models of industry, politeness, honesty, and [be] law abiding," their visibility in the community catapulted a good number into political office. Teachers accounted for 176 of the black officeholders during the period, ranking their occupation second to black clergymen and slightly ahead of soldiers.[44]

Tensions also escalated over the issue of integrated schools, which were rare in any corner of the republic. The Freedmen's Bureau itself was maddeningly evasive on the matter. Howard believed that southern children should learn together, but the old soldier was pragmatic enough not to demand integrated academies. Most benevolent associations advocated schools that were blind to class or color, but as many teachers discovered, white parents adamantly refused to send their children to Bureau schools. Those few who did risked the same level of ostracism from their wealthier neighbors as did impoverished landlords who rented rooms to schoolmarms. When asked why she had withdrawn her daughter from a South Carolina Bureau school, despite not having any state-supported alternative, one farmer's wife confessed: "I would not care myself, but the young men laugh at my husband. They tell him he must be pretty far gone and low down when he sends his children to a 'nigger school.'" Not for the first time in the region's history, a small but powerful cadre of landholders employed race as a weapon to divide laboring people who shared similar interests and needs.[45]

Had leading voices in Washington, from the White House to the Bureau, proved more resolute on the question, those southern whites who desperately required decent schools might have found the courage to speak up. Ironically, because blacks and whites in the South often lived and labored in closer proximity to one another than they did in the North, some prayed that federal policies might encourage both to overcome several centuries of racially based hostility. "I have been a slaveholder and had a Mammy, whom I loved better than my own mother in my childhood," Om Langhorne assured Blanche K. Bruce, a former slave and rising politician. "I long to pay off the indemnity," the native Virginian added, and "after diligent study of our Southern problem have come to the conclusion that mixed Schools are the remedy for existing evils." New York's Maria Waterbury discovered just how irrational the question could be when a respected doctor arrived at her Bureau school holding the hands of "two little beautiful white children, [both] finely dressed." When the flustered Waterbury explained that hers was "a colored school," the doctor replied that one girl was the child of his late wife. The other, he deadpanned, was the daughter of his housekeeper, a woman "as white as most people [but of] African extraction." Waterbury enrolled both girls. "[S]ometimes we didn't know who suffered the most from the mixed-up prejudices," she sighed, "the doctor's family or the teachers."[46]

Once southern states began to be reconstructed, and as state-funded systems began to replace Bureau schools, the issue could no longer be avoided. Democrats, who recognized that their yeomen-constituents desired comprehensive systems of public schools, suggested that black and white children might attend the same institutions but be educated in separate rooms. To be educated in the same chamber, conservative Arkansans insisted, created "indiscriminate social intercourse between whites and Negroes." Blacks and Republican activists, including those northern men who had attended all-white institutions in their youth, pushed for integrated schools. Segregated schools, they argued, violated the social advances brought by the war, and few doubted that black schools would receive far less funding than white academies. In South Carolina, former ship's pilot Robert Smalls, who was emerging as a leading Republican voice in the low country, called for free, integrated, and compulsory education for all state residents, as well as the creation of new state colleges. Sensitive about his own lack of education, Smalls devoted each evening to a diligent course of study, and he insisted that all children should attend classes for "at least 6 months for each year, under penalties for non-compliance." Former slave John A. Chesnut hoped that children of both races would attend prospective schools but added that "if there be a hostile disposition among the whites, an unwillingness to send their children to school, the fault is their own, not ours."[47]

Inevitably, progress in the South had implications for the North and West, as Republicans and black reformers continued to regard Reconstruction as a national crusade. Believing the time had come for a thorough review of their scheme of instruction, New York Republicans sought to centralize their haphazard state system, and with black soldiers and veterans of the antislavery movement demanding integrated academies, even conservative Democrats gave way. The bill signed by Governor Reuben Fenton on April 16, 1867, enjoyed broad bipartisan support. The battle in California took longer, but there progressives were aided by the small number of black children. "It seems absurd to say that 944 colored children, if admitted to the schools with [white pupils], will destroy our schools," lectured one state legislator. In a reminder of how far the country had advanced in just a few years, he added, even the most optimistic abolitionist in 1860 would have scoffed at the notion that blacks would soon be voters in the state, "and five years hence you will wonder how you were so prejudiced as not to see with a clear eye that you were far behind the age" on education. California fell into line in 1874. Ohio followed in 1887.[48]

Conservatives everywhere objected to the higher costs required by new tax-supported systems. Reformers responded that decent schools and teachers could not be had for free. Adopting an argument that tried irony's patience, wealthy Carolina planters pretended to speak for white yeomen, insisting that farmers could not afford the light taxes necessary to educate their own children. In Louisiana, where mixed-race freemen had long paid property taxes that went for the exclusive use of white children, black Republicans countered that it was time for "Rebels" to contribute to public schools for all and scoffed at fears that middle-class parents would send their sons and daughters to expensive private schools when they could "get them educated freely in the public schools—be it even alongside of colored children." Freed people were already contributing to Bureau schools, and agents calculated that they would have to pay little more if all citizens were taxed for public institutions. "[A]t least thirty percent of the white population are unable to read or write," Charleston agent T. J. Mackey estimated, yet "enough money is annually expended in building monuments and scattering roses over the graves of the Confederate dead" to finance public schools.[49]

For white politicians who had served their states during the antebellum years, the idea of public education for a people they regarded as inferior was nearly incomprehensible. During one of his tours of the South, Alvord was stopped by a former Louisiana assemblyman who wondered about the black children at recess. "What!" he shouted, a school "of niggers?" Raising his hands to the sky, he glared at Alvord. "I have seen many an absurdity in my lifetime, but *this is the climax of absurdities.*" Unwilling to accept the reality of a strange new order, conservative Democrats persisted in regarding postwar reforms as experimental curiosities that would soon fade away. "Hoeing, ploughing, spinning, and sewing are more necessary now to the negro [than] the study of that multiplication table and alphabet," editorialized the *Richmond Dispatch*. Black Virginians, the newspaper assumed, "will eventually find [this] out in spite of all the 'strong minded females' in Yankeedom." For African American parents, the education of their children marked a critical step toward financial security and political awareness, but what remained of the old planter class, a Vermont journalist lamented, wanted "to keep the negro in his condition of ignorance, that they may retain him as nearly as possible in his old state of slavery."[50]

At least initially, northern evangelicals were so confident in the righteousness of their work that they assumed logic and reason might win over doubting southern whites. The American Missionary Association attempted public shaming, publishing essays in friendly Unionist newspapers that denounced those "chivalrous whites" who engaged in "social ostracism and frequent mobbing of teachers [as] cowardly and despicable." G. L. Eberhart, the Bureau's superintendent of schools for Georgia, published a series of letters "refuting the slanders which certain of the pro-Slavery, negro-hating papers of the country have circulated respecting the female teachers in the Southern colored schools." But even veteran officers such as Eberhart, who had experienced combat during the war, were unprepared for the escalating violence they faced, as black teachers began to replace Yankee schoolmarms, and as struggles for integration moved into legislative chambers.[51]

Eberhart's words were no match for southern torches. As it became clear that black educators were prepared to run for office themselves, if necessary, in the cause of educational reform, whites across the South responded as had Charlestonians in 1822 when they razed the city's AME church. Especially in rural areas, where few soldiers were stationed and where federal patrols were less frequent, schools turned to ashes at a frightening rate. In less than three months in 1866, North Carolinians set fire to four schools; two more, one in Greene County and another in Chatham, burned down the following year. Similar reports flooded into Washington from across the region. An agent in Mississippi wrote of numerous "schoolhouses, including churches used as schoolhouses," being torched. Alvan Gillem, a Bureau operative also stationed in Mississippi, confirmed that arson in his district had destroyed a new building "capable of accommodating four hundred pupils." Its loss, he added, "cannot easily be over-estimated." Texas Republicans complained "that school houses were burnt nearly as fast as they could be erected," and General Thomas Swayne informed his superiors that the "people of Mobile are violently opposed to colored schools. They have burned two buildings used for that purpose, one a Presbyterian Church." Enough Alabama schools were burned to encourage Alvord to lament the declining number of federal soldiers in the South and suspect that "only military force for some time to come could prevent the frequent outbreak of every form of violence."[52]

While arsonists engaged in their almost nightly assaults on Bureau schools, leading southern Democrats provided cover for these nocturnal raids with a series of increasingly incendiary speeches. Politicians argued that the root cause of the "troubles" was northern agitators who filled the heads of southern freedmen with visions of equality and supported black activists in their demands for land and political power. "A little learning is a dangerous thing in its application to" African Americans, huffed one Democrat. As the "educated among them are the most dangerous class in the community," arsonists were merely acting defensively against those who "exercise a malign and blighting influence over the future prospects of their race." In the decades before the war, southern statesmen routinely alleged that northern abolitionists inspired literate blacks such as Denmark Vesey or Nat Turner into acts of rebellion, which in turn were used to justify white retribution. Their postwar rhetoric changed little as the 1860s wore on. From Norfolk, Cynthia Everett complained bitterly of "the influence of a powerful rebel" in the city council, and Bureau agent Edwin L. Dawes warned Howard that in Columbia, despite the state's new constitution, the "School Commissioner of the County is a Democrat, and is violently opposed to the education of Colored Children."[53]

At least for a time, activists had the law and the army on their side, and southern blacks, as Charleston-born freeman Francis L. Cardozo put it, were "determined not to submit so tamely as they did before the war." In Virginia, blacks petitioned the state in a request for safety. "[A]ll we ask is Education and lawful protection," they stated, "and with our efforts and Northern benevolence" black students "who never knew a letter prior to Lee's surrender" would continue in their efforts to improve their lives. Even white children discovered this new sense of black resolve. When a Bureau school opened in 1866 in Marianna, Florida, white students gathered to jeer and throw rocks. Perhaps as their fathers had learned to do in the army, the black children began to march to school in formation. As whites again began to taunt the freed children, the blacks responded with a fusillade of rocks before charging into the youthful mob. "There were many bruises on both sides," bragged one of the black students, "but it taught the white youngsters to leave the colored ones alone."[54]

For Republicans who wished to highlight the successes of their Reconstruction agenda, the astonishing achievements in public education around the nation stood as incontrovertible evidence. Despite endemic white hostility and weak or nonexistent statewide foundations upon which to build, a combination of private philanthropy and public expenditures accomplished near miracles in a just a few short years. (Despite President Johnson's opposition to the Bureau, Congress allocated a total of $5,262,511 for education between 1865 and 1870.) Their efforts coordinated by Washington, black parents, missionary women, and now-forgotten community activists such as Judge Hugh L. Bond transformed children kept ignorant by state law and custom into educated young citizens. Of the 256,354 pupils enrolled in Bureau schools by the late fall of 1869, 192,327 had been slaves just four years before. Sometimes at odds over long-term goals, separated by race and region, and hampered by class distinctions, these educators, veterans, Bureau agents, and freed people battled penurious legislators, hostile planters, violent arsonists, and a distant, indifferent chief executive in hopes of turning the postwar era into an era of national progressive reform. If often condescending toward their pupils and patronizing of their parents, Yankee schoolmarms quit their families and safe communities to finish a job started on the battlefields by their fathers and brothers, and their superciliousness melted away as they watched freedmen "erect schoolhouses without the aid of the bureau, and without an immediate prospect of procuring teachers." As white missionaries, fatigued and frequently ill, returned north, their positions were filled by black teachers, educated in institutions such as the 1867 normal school built for blacks in Richmond, the former capital of the Confederacy.[55]

Periods of progressive reform rarely continue unabated, and integrated schools would fall victim to southern Jim Crow legislation in the 1890s and to de facto geographic segregation in northern communities. One North Carolina study revealed that as late as 1918, seven percent of black pupils studied in log schoolhouses, compared to just one percent of white children. Even so, the spectacular gains in literacy—skills that could not easily be erased—suggest again that the Reconstruction era came to no abrupt end in 1877, or that sweeping allegations that the crusade was a failure must exclude many categories of reform. In the year the nation went to war, at least ninety percent of black Americans were illiterate. Within twenty years, that figure dropped by twenty percent, and by the end of the century it was reduced to fifty percent. Despite ferocious opposition to integrated schools, Republican rule resulted in the quadrupling of the student population in South Carolina. Compared to modern standards, these gains appear modest. But drawbacks were due as much to rural poverty as to racism; in 1880, thirty-four percent of black children nationwide attended public schools, and if that paled by comparison to the sixty-two percent of white children, that figure had increased only two percent since 1860. Put another way, black literacy increased four hundred percent in the thirty-five years after Appomattox, a triumph not witnessed by any other nineteenth-century post-slavery society. And as black parents, North and South, gathered to construct schools and hire teachers, so too did they meet in conventions to demand political rights, understanding that the two were forever linked.[56]

CHAPTER FIVE

"We Will Remember Our Friends, and Will Not Forget Our Enemies"

Black Codes and Black Conventions

S HOOTING COLORED MEN in Philadelphia seemed to be the order of the day [for] Tuesday," October 10, 1871, charged the *New National Era*, a venerable Washington antislavery newspaper then owned by Frederick Douglass and edited by his sons Charles and Lewis. "As in the South, the Democratic party North resorts to murder and intimidation of voters opposed to the villainy and treason sustained and upheld by its leaders." The editorial accompanied an essay on "the assassination of [Octavius] Catto," a thirty-one-year-old educator, militant Republican, and civil rights activist who had been shot in the back as he walked home on Election Day.[1]

Born in Charleston in 1839 to Sarah Cain, a free woman of color, Octavius was carried north to Maryland at the age of five when his father, William T. Catto, a former slave and millwright, accepted the pastorate of a small Presbyterian church in Baltimore. Within months, the family relocated again, this time to Philadelphia, where Reverend Catto preached at the African Presbyterian Church. The politically conscious minister lectured both his congregation and his son on the importance of applying one's spirituality to the secular world. "Every man, more or less, has some part to perform in the drama of life," the reverend preached, and "as individuals we must go forward and contribute our something toward the press of interest that impels forward." The boy took his father's sermons to heart. He enrolled in the Vaux Primary School and then in Lombard Grammar School, both segregated academies in the heart of the City of Brotherly Love. His abilities won him acceptance into the all-white Allentown Academy in Allentown, Pennsylvania; and although he was the only black student in the school, his entrance began the process of integrating the school. The following year, 1854, he returned to Philadelphia to join the city's Institute for Colored Youth on Bainbridge Street, as the school's curriculum promised classes in Greek, Latin, and geometry. Catto graduated from the institute in 1858, only to continue his studies in classics with a private tutor in Washington. On the eve of the war, he returned to Pennsylvania and began to teach English grammar and mathematics at the institute.[2]

When Robert E. Lee led his Confederate army into Pennsylvania during the summer of 1863, Governor Andrew Curtin issued the call for new recruits to repel the invaders, and Catto enlisted virtually all of his young charges in a black company. When they reached Harrisburg, General Darius Couch refused them induction with the excuse that Congress required soldiers to enlist for at least three years and made no exceptions for emergency militias, even in the most dire of crises. When the news reached Washington, Secretary Edwin M. Stanton cabled to overrule Couch's decision, instructing him to induct "any volunteer troops that may be offered, *without regard to color.*" By then Catto had marched his recruits back to Philadelphia. There they were invited to a mass protest meeting at Franklin Hall organized by Republican congressman William D. Kelley and black activist David E. Gipson. Although his teaching duties remained his chief responsibility, Catto was eventually appointed major and inspector of the Fifth Brigade of the Pennsylvania National Guard. As it had for so many young black men, his military service, together with President Abraham Lincoln's increasingly progressive positions, won him over to the Republican Party. When in October 1864 he traveled to Syracuse to attend the National Convention of Colored Men, he agreed with fellow delegate Frederick Douglass that black spokesmen must prod the party to embrace "the perfect enfranchisement of the entire people of the United States." At war's end, Catto spoke in front of Independence Hall in Philadelphia, presenting a ceremonial flag to the surviving members of the Twenty-fourth Colored Troops. "Let soldiers in war be citizens in peace," he shouted.[3]

In the months after Appomattox, Catto put that principle into practice. He joined the Pennsylvania State Equal Rights League—a state auxiliary to the national black convention movement—and devoted himself to what he believed were the Christian principles of social equality, educational uplift, and community integration. That meant joining the struggle for integrated transportation that had erupted in other cities across the nation. On the afternoon of May 17, 1865, he boarded a Pine Street public carriage, ignoring the driver's demands that he step off the all-white passenger car. Since a Pennsylvania judge had recently fined a teamster for turning away a black rider, the driver thought it prudent to simply unhitch his team and leave the car sitting in the street. In an early instance of what would much later be regarded as a peaceful sit-in, Catto quietly remained in the car. By the next morning, observed a reporter, "crowds of sympathizers flock[ed] around the colored man," and when the stunned driver returned to reclaim the car, he found it filled with black passengers waiting to be carried to work.[4]

Even as Philadelphia blacks engaged in peaceful protest, they also lobbied the state and federal governments to resolve the problem. Named to a three-member committee by the National Equal Rights League, Catto met with assemblymen and sympathetic congressmen, particularly Kelley and Thaddeus Stevens. Unwilling to wait for their white Republican allies to address the situation, the committee drafted a sample bill that made preventing persons from riding on public accommodations a crime punishable by fines of up to five hundred dollars and ninety days imprisonment. After the state legislature heard testimony of a disabled black veteran "forced to plod his weary way" after being denied entrance to a car, moderates banded together with progressive Republicans to forcibly integrate state streetcars on March 22, 1867. When, just three days later, Catto's fiancée, Caroline LeCount, was denied a seat by a teamster who shouted, "We don't allow niggers to ride," the two located a friendly magistrate and had the conductor arrested and fined one hundred dollars.[5]

Catto's refusal to give way to popular prejudices, together with his speaking tour on behalf of the Fourteenth Amendment, which guaranteed black Americans the right of citizenship denied them under the Dred Scott ruling, earned him angry letters and death threats. As his travels carried him into Virginia, Catto approached the police for protection, only to be told to buy a pistol and "protect [him]self." The former major finally did so on Election Day 1871, after being confronted by armed toughs on the way to the polls. The weapon did him little good. On his way home from casting his ballot, white Democrat Frank Kelly pumped three bullets into Catto's back at close range. As Catto lay dying, a streetcar filled with black and white riders pulled up beside him. Two months later, on December 16, his father too died, purportedly of a heart attack.[6]

That Friday, black and white Republicans gathered to mourn the young activist and "demand the adoption of the most vigorous measures to bring the offender to justice." For those who believed that the war had been about more than sectional reunion, his death marked "another addition to the long list of martyrs who have been assassinated for their fidelity to the principles of liberty." Students from the institute as well as the entire Fifth Brigade turned out for his funeral, marching in long ribbons through the streets in what W. E. B. Du Bois would later describe as "the most impressive [service] ever given to an American Negro."[7]

Catto's all-too-brief life serves as a reminder that the wars of Reconstruction were national. Across the South, freed people struggled for land and basic civil rights against a background of postwar laws collectively known as the Black Codes, state legislation passed by former Confederates who recognized that with Lincoln gone they now had an ally in the White House and so hoped to stymie the progressive gains of the past two years. In the North, veterans and activists, sometimes assisted by progressive Republicans, prodded moderates into embracing a host of reforms. African Americans met in a series of state and national conventions to demand the integration of streetcars, civil rights, and, increasingly, voting rights as well. Far out in front of all but a handful of so-called Radical Republicans, black activists lobbied state legislators, congressmen, senators, and even the president to reward veterans for their sacrifice by creating a more democratic republic. Many, like Catto, died in this war. Slavery might have been eradicated decades earlier in

OCTAVIUS V. CATTO.—[Photographed by Messrs. Broadbent & Phillips, Philadelphia.]

The product of segregated schools prior to attending the all-white Allentown Academy in New Jersey, Octavius Catto pressed for the integration of public transportation and public schools, as well as the hiring of black educators in all sections of the nation. "It is at least unjust to allow a blind and ignorant prejudice to so far disregard the choice of parents and the will of the colored tax-payers," he lectured one audience, "as to appoint over colored children white teachers, whose intelligence and success" could "neither obtain nor secure for them positions." Courtesy Library of Congress.

Pennsylvania and New York, but "the spirit of caste," one black editor wrote, lingered on in Philadelphia and Manhattan, and there was "but a single step from the exclusion of colored people from the horse-cars to the shooting of Major Catto."[8]

Civil rights activists and progressive Republicans had their work cut out for them. Murderers such as Frank Kelly, a working-class Democratic operative, took their cues from those far above them on the social and political scale. The tone began with the president. In his proclamation of May 29, 1865, Johnson appointed a governor for Virginia, Unionist Francis Harrison Pierpont. Similar proclamations followed in the coming weeks for six other Confederate states; Johnson also recognized the restored governments in Louisiana and Arkansas established earlier by Lincoln and one he himself had created for Tennessee while military governor. For South Carolina's provisional governor, the president tapped Benjamin F. Perry. Like Pierpont, Perry was a Unionist who had opposed secession, although largely because he believed civil conflict might endanger slavery, and during the conflict he had represented his state in the Confederate House of Representatives. A small planter who owned twenty slaves in 1850, Perry expected tough terms from the federal government, and he was both pleased by the appointment and surprised by the president's disinclination to issue instructions from Washington. Johnson simply urged Perry to "write occasionally" and keep him informed on how the new governor was "getting on in reconstructing the state."[9]

The president's willingness to immediately hand political power back to influential southern whites and, on occasion, onetime Confederate officeholders indicated just how little the past four years had altered his initial attitude toward the war. As had most Democrats in 1861, Johnson regarded the conflict as a partisan squabble among politicians, a spat among white men only. A steadfast Unionist if a proslavery man, his path had carried him to Washington, while Perry's very similar positions had earned him a seat in Richmond under the Confederacy. Now that actual combat was over and Confederate armies had surrendered, Johnson reasoned, the sections could resume their former status. Since slavery had to die so that the North might prevail, Johnson, as he explained it to a Nashville audience in 1864, was "for setting [blacks] free." Yet in the same speech, he reaffirmed his belief that "this is a white man's government." Although the unlettered tailor had never enjoyed the friendship of those planters he once denounced as "aristocrats," he shared their postwar views on civil rights. Johnson was consistently "as decided a hater of the negro," remarked Indiana congressman George W. Julian, "as the rebels from whom he had separated." If the new president was indifferent to slavery, he was dogmatic on who controlled Reconstruction. As had Lincoln, Johnson argued that since secession was unconstitutional, no actual separation of the states had taken place—that the action had been merely an insurrection of individuals. So as commander in chief he alone possessed the authority to return southern persons to the political fold. In his view, members of Congress had no role in the process.[10]

Johnson's appointees agreed. Governor Pierpont had opposed secession, but unlike Perry he had remained loyal to the federal government and had helped lead Virginia's western counties into statehood as West Virginia. Due perhaps to his outsider status in the state capital, upon arriving in Richmond he promptly consulted two former Confederate governors and ignored an appeal from black Virginians asking for protection from violence and retribution. Emboldened by a growing awareness that Johnson, as one politician told a journalist, planned to grant them "the undisputed management of their own affairs," his governors hastened to explain the unchanging times to delighted planters and frustrated Republicans. William Marvin, the president's choice for provisional governor of Florida, advised black veterans that the conflict had been "a white man's war" and warned freed people that they "must not think [that] because you are as free as white people you are their equal, because you are not." The "African has been, in all ages, a savage or a slave," Governor Perry agreed. "God created him inferior to the white man in form, color, and intellect, and no legislation or culture can make him his equal." Former slaveholders were exhilarated by their unexpected good fortune, while dispirited Unionists believed their counsel ignored by Pierpont and Perry. "The Nigs were quite disgusted," crowed Laura Buttolph, daughter of a low-country planter.[11]

"Our poor butchered people want peace," observed a white Carolinian, and all but the most unwavering Confederate loyalists regarded the president's policies as both unwise and unnecessary. Even some planters feared that Johnson's clumsy efforts at appeasement would only attract the wrath of influential Republicans in Washington. Most middle-class whites, and especially those urban dwellers who remembered the hardships of the last two years of the conflict, appeared "crushed and submissive" to northern travelers. Few were willing to openly discuss politics, and many of those who did cursed Jefferson Davis and the 169 South Carolina planters who began the secession drive in December 1860. Although a few southern editors adhered to "the extreme conservative [Democratic] Copperhead standpoint," noticed one journalist, "most [were] guarded" in their opinions, and "their abstinence from political discussion [was] more significant than columns of boldest tirade could be." Working-class whites especially sided against the planters, as had many on the question of land reform. A group of Charleston "Mechanics and Workingmen," after swearing that they had "no shred of sympathy for or desire to elevate the blacks," endorsed emancipation on the grounds that it "made labor respectable." Before the war, a white artisan remarked, they had had to compete against the skilled "slave of the rich man who, himself not a mechanic or laborer, was often a contractor." Overcoming centuries of southern intra-class animosity would be no simple task, but journalists, travelers, and Bureau agents across the region reported that many stood ready to embrace a new order in the name of personal survival and southern prosperity. The country "had the opportunity when Lee surrendered," recalled Johnson's military secretary, "to make our own terms." Senator Charles Sumner concurred: "Never was so great an opportunity lost, as our President has flung away."[12]

Having believed Johnson's distrust of southern landlords to be as pronounced as theirs, former Lincoln supporters were mystified by the president's about-face. "I am fearful [that] President Johnson is reconstructing the Rebels faster than their loyalty will justify," one Illinois voter complained to Senator Lyman Trumbull. Republicans were irate over what they regarded as squandered valor, and if the sacrifice of so many soldiers meant only that planters had lost their bid for independence, the loss had not been worth it. The "people of this country hate slavery & rebellion," protested another of Trumbull's constituents, "and any Administration that will make concessions to either of them after all we have suffered from will soon find that there are few so poor as to do it reverence." Southern Unionists, most of them former Whigs who had risked a good deal in their wartime condemnations of Davis, were particularly bitter. "Union Citizens of Richmond," Charles Palmer reported from his native Virginia, "have since disappeared," demoralized and disempowered by "the sweep of general pardon granted by Pres[iden]t Johnson." Prepared to publicly embrace the Republican Party in exchange for the economic as well as political reconstruction of their battle-ravaged state, those who had denounced secession in 1861 now thought themselves without a defender in the White House. "I believe Virginians and the entire Confederate States," Palmer warned Secretary William H. Seward, "are as *disloyal* to their country & as true & loyall to Jeff Davis and Robert E. Lee as when in their full tide of deluded success and tyranny."[13]

With Congress not scheduled to reconvene until December 4, leading Republicans were unable to do anything more than privately urge the president to exercise caution. Critics quickly dubbed this period "presidential Reconstruction," as Johnson's policies and vetoes generally carried the day until the onset of "Congressional," or "Republican Reconstruction," following the rise of the fortieth Congress. Yet these critical months might be even more aptly characterized as "Confederate Reconstruction," since the president's programs permitted discredited planters and avowed secessionists to temporarily regain power. Believing their military service and unwavering loyalty had earned them a role in the process, southern blacks were dumbfounded by a president they had expected to carry out his predecessor's promises. The first few months of peace, however, allowed for the proliferation of black-run newspapers across the South, and African American editors fought back with the pen. In response to those politicians who argued that blacks "ought [not] to be free until they are fit to use their freedom," the Augusta *Colored American* opined that if any people had "to wait for liberty till they become wise and good in slavery," nobody in the South should be permitted freedom. "The voice of the people should be: 'Loyal men white and black shall govern these States,'" agreed the editor of the Washington *Reconstructionist*. "Rebels must take the back seats in reconstruction."[14]

If Johnson hoped that his provisional governors and those Confederates he had pardoned might reward his leniency with restraint, he was to be disappointed. Although he had called upon returning states to disavow secession and ratify the Thirteenth Amendment, Texas and Mississippi flatly refused the latter requirement. "I am not willing to trust to men who know nothing of slavery the power to frame a code for the freedmen of the State," snapped one speaker. After an anxious Johnson wired a remonstrance to Perry, the South Carolinians empowered with drafting a new constitution admitted that their slaves were emancipated, but only due to "the action of the United States authorities." Even then, eight delegates voted to retain slavery, and the convention chose to repeal rather than disavow their 1860 act of secession. Georgia, however, ratified the Thirteenth Amendment on December 6, 1865, and so twelve days later Seward announced to Congress that the requisite twenty-seven states had approved; Georgia then filed "a claim for compensation" for lost property. Little wonder the process was troubled. Stunned Unionists reported that the vast majority of those elected to the state conventions were the prewar elite. In Texas, one white Republican informed Seward, "nine tenths" of the delegates were "secessionists and last ditch men." Those who supported the Republicans "could not live here safely if the army was withdrawn," he added. C. E. Lippincott, writing from Mississippi, concurred. "Take away garrisons from this Southern Country, and the negroes will be subjected to every outrage." Five years later, on February 17, 1870, Texas ratified the already operational amendment; Mississippi legislators finally did so more than a century later on March 16, 1995.[15]

If possible, the legislators and Congressional delegations then elected by white voters proved even more a catastrophe for the president. Virginia Unionists, still hoping for leadership and direction from the White House, appealed to Johnson "for counsel and advice as to our proper course of action," but they received no response. Among those elected to seats in Congress that December were a good number that had served the Confederacy, four as generals, five as colonels, six as cabinet officers, and nine as congressmen; a few had yet to receive Johnson's pardon. Alexander H. Stephens, the Confederate vice president, was one of Georgia's choices for the Senate. Democrats argued that the election of leading Confederates indicated that southern whites were reconciled to defeat, but Republicans thought differently. Planters planned to resume their old positions by placing "rebels or sympathizers with rebels, into the control of our politics," objected one Massachusetts editor. To allow Stephens to take a seat beside Trumbull and Sumner, fumed another, "would be to give political power to the very men who conspired against the life of the nation." The Republican majority countered that Lincoln had consented to allow them to decide "when or whether members should be admitted to seats in Congress from [southern] States" and refused to accept their credentials. The president protested their exclusion as unmerited, but journalists reported that even in Johnson's Tennessee, "300 Union voters" were denied ballots while "Rebels [won] the election who were not entitled to vote."[16]

For Johnson's critics, even more outrageous and dangerous than southern reluctance to ratify the Thirteenth Amendment or the restoration of Confederate leaders to high national office were the state laws passed in late 1865 and early 1866, known to detractors as the Black Codes. Virtually since the last days of the Confederacy, planters had been clamoring for a new system of laws to reestablish, as one of Governor Perry's constituents phrased it, the "proper subordination of the laboring class" and to control "the savage passions of a people intoxicated with so called freedom." If some southern states refused to ratify the Thirteenth Amendment, they recognized that enough would eventually do so to permanently abolish slavery. "I am sure we will not be allowed even to contend for gradual emancipation," fretted Texas governor James W. Throckmorton in early 1866. "But I do believe we will be enabled to adopt a coercive system of labor." The governor was right. In February, after churlishly acknowledging that slavery had been "terminated" by "force of arms," state legislators unanimously voted down ordinances granting "the negro rights of property and person, [and] to sue and be sued." But in a statute called the Freedmen's Bill—Rights of Negroes in the Courts, the state permitted a freedman the "right to give evidence in cases where he is not interested." Texas lawmakers also established fines of one dollar for "failing to obey reasonable orders, neglect of duty, leaving home without permission, impudence, [and] swearing [at] or [using] indecent language" to an employer.[17]

Each state assembly passed its own code, but many of these legislators had known their counterparts in other states for years, and so a good deal of creative borrowing ensued. Since each was forged on the same legislative agenda—a determination to deny freed people access to land, and so force them back onto the plantations as low-wage laborers—it was simple logic for assemblymen to lift sentences and even entire paragraphs from neighboring state codes. As was the Texas code, Mississippi's statute was granted a reformist-sounding title: An Act to Confer Civil Rights on Freedmen. But the effort fooled nobody. "The spirit of the Legislature, and the white people throughout the State," charged one black editor, "is violently opposed to allowing the negro to become possessors of property." Mississippi's law allowed freed people to "sue and be sued" and even "acquire personal property," but none of the code's provisions, assemblymen cautioned, "shall be so construed as to allow any freeman, free negro, or mulatto to rent or lease any lands." Not surprisingly, black veterans in Mississippi judged "the work of reconstruction [to] be the most difficult in this State." The code's disingenuous title notwithstanding, the so-called Johnson government clearly intended to devise a legal system in which blacks remained semi-enslaved, denied access to land, and relegated to a subordinate economic and social status. Yet for unrepentant Confederates, fines and threats of brief incarceration were not enough. "I know niggers," explained one Mississippi planter, who regarded financial penalties as inadequate to control his workers. "If you will let me tie him up by the thumbs, or keep him on bread and water, that will do."[18]

Closely linked to the rejection of black property rights was the requirement for yearly labor contracts. Moderate northern Republicans might not endorse wholesale land reform, but as advocates of free wage labor, they supported the right of freed people to move about the region, relocate into cities, and even leave the South in hopes of financial betterment. Southern landlords desired just the opposite. South Carolina and Mississippi both crafted strict "vagrancy" laws, which required that black adults provide written evidence of employment by "the second Monday of January" for the coming year. Laborers who broke their contracts and abandoned the plantations within those twelve months not only forfeited all wages but were liable to be "arrest[ed] and carr[ied] back to his or her legal employer." White farmers who offered employment to such "runaways" faced fines of up to five hundred dollars. Texas directed sheriffs to bring "indigent and vagrant minors" before state courts, which might then bind them out under prewar apprenticeship statutes. A soldier stationed in Meridian, Mississippi, alerted his superiors that "under the guise of vagrant laws," legislators proposed "to restore all of slavery but its name," and blacks in Vicksburg gathered as early as June 1865 to protest their "practical reenslavement." Undaunted, Mississippi legislators devised a lengthy list of those who faced arrest under their code: "rogues and vagabonds, idle and dissipated persons, beggars, jugglers, or persons practicing unlawful games or plays." After some deliberation, assemblymen added "fortune tellers" and "common railers" to the roster.[19]

"The new constitution dodged nothing," observed Albert T. Morgan, a soldier and Republican who had settled in Mississippi. Having refused to endow slave marriages with legal status in antebellum years, lawmakers now hastened to codify and define black relationships. African Americans welcomed the move, although not the legislative interference in their private lives enshrined in most Black Codes. "The Marriage Covenant is at the foundation of all our rights," one black corporal remarked, "*now* we have it [and] shall be established as a people." But during slavery and throughout the war, some bondmen and bondwomen found themselves residing with partners not of their choosing, or with near strangers after their spouses were sold away. Mississippi mandated that all blacks "who have not been married, but who are now living together" were "for all purposes in law as married." Planters in state assemblies proposed fines to "punish adultery and concubinage," statutes that black women must have found particularly galling, given the long tradition of sexual abuse on the part of their masters. Southern codes, in imitation of most northern statutes, also banned marriages across the color line. When Aaron Green and Julia Atkinson went ahead with their nuptials in violation of Alabama's prohibition, both were arrested, and Atkinson, a white woman, received a two-year prison sentence.[20]

No lawmaker in any southern state entertained the possibility of granting freed people the basic civil rights afforded them in other parts of the nation. Most of the codes passed during "the Johnsonian period," veteran and attorney Albion Tourgée grumbled, "refused to allow the colored people to testify in courts of justice against white men," a holdover from previous decades, in which bondmen were forbidden to appear as witnesses against whites. In effect, each plantation was once more its own system of justice. As one planter boasted, each landholder was "a judge of police [with the] power to sentence and inflict" punishments. Because the codes invariably applied to all persons of "African ancestry," the few small privileges enjoyed by free people of color during the antebellum era were effectively erased. Blacks, including veterans, were banned from possessing firearms without a license. Legislators insisted that a failure to show proper deference to whites constituted disturbing the peace. "Let a nigger come into *my* office," one sneered, "without tipping his hat, and he'll get a club over it."[21]

Even Kentucky, a slave state that had remained loyal to the Union— albeit one that had supplied a number of troops to the Confederate cause, including former U.S. vice president John C. Breckinridge— passed a similar code that "consign[ed] her negroes to virtual Slavery." For northern Republicans, who had watched in horror as their country regressed on civil rights under a cadre of Democratic presidents during the 1850s, history now appeared to be repeating itself with another Democrat in the White House. "The Rebel army tried repeatedly to take Kentucky during the War, but failed," lamented Horace Greeley, editor of the influential *New-York Tribune*. "Kentucky badly needs reconstruction." Even less trusting of southern whites than were northern Republican journalists, black editors understood that what they were witnessing was the continuation of civil war by other means. The "Rebellion has not ceased; it has only changed its weapons," the editor of Cincinnati's *Colored Citizen* alleged. "Once it followed Lee in arms, now it follows President Johnson in guile and chicanery." Johnson, in fact, did not so much oppose the codes as think them unnecessary due to his reversal of Sherman's order and the Bureau's early efforts at land reform. Those freedmen "without land of their own," he assumed, "will continue to work for those who have it." But for black critics, the codes were the fruit of his efforts, and if the Confederacy, one insisted, "once had its headquarters in Richmond, now it encamps in the White House."[22]

Given free rein by the president, his governors and their assemblies clearly had overreached. Beleaguered Carolina Unionist A. S. Wallace actually welcomed his state's handiwork, which he denounced as a "monument to Legislative folly," as he anticipated its excesses would result in the final overthrow of the planters' monopoly on power. When former governor Perry, who had empanelled the committee to draft the code, and Benjamin L. Orr, the former Confederate senator who replaced him in late November 1865 and signed the bill into law, realized the extent of the political damage, it was too late. Working out of his office at the Citadel, Charleston's military academy, General Daniel E. Sickles used his authority as military commander of the Department of South Carolina to declare the code "null and void." Sickles had lost a leg at Gettysburg to cannon fire, and he had no patience for Confederate defiance; "all laws [should] be applicable to all inhabitants," he decreed. And in Washington, Republicans began to discuss the necessity of the first-ever Civil Rights Bill to undo all of Johnson's damage.[23]

As critical as white Republicans' legislative support was to prove, black editors were especially important in formulating a collective response both to the Black Codes and to Johnson's assertions that he alone controlled the process of state restoration. African American journalists pioneered many of the arguments later employed by Washington politicians and even by the most progressive white Republicans, who had to answer to the more moderate white voters in their home districts. "No State is *republican* in a constitutional and national sense which makes any distinction in civil or political rights among its citizens on account of race or descent," argued the editor of Cincinnati's *Colored Citizen*. Since Article IV of the Constitution "guarantee[d] to every State" a republican form of government, black editors alleged that discriminatory codes violated the basic tenets of popular democracy and so mandated a federal response, a theory increasingly repeated in the corridors of the House and Senate. The publisher of Augusta's *Loyal Georgian* mocked his state code's pretense of "promot[ing] the well-being of the Freedmen" by "educat[ing] them in the arts of labor." What further "training" did former slaves require, he asked dryly, "than they have had all their lives?"[24]

Not content merely to advance their cause in the black press, African Americans peppered friendly Republicans with scores of letters denouncing both the codes and Johnson's appointees. "In most places the freedmen are worse off than when slaves, being exposed to the brutality and vindictiveness of their old masters, without the old check of self-interest," one educated freeman warned Sumner. Blacks in Vicksburg, Mississippi, and Natchez, Tennessee, drafted petitions complaining of their state codes and insisting that their only recourse was access to the ballot. Although Sumner had yet to endorse the national enfranchisement of blacks, he startled many of his Republican colleagues by reading their entreaty to the Senate. In the decades before the war, state courts, special tribunals, and white mobs both North and South had made quick work of those few freemen who attempted to assert their rights, and so African American activism had been restricted to pockets of Ohio, New York, and New England; even there they had encountered discrimination and physical assaults. Long-oppressed southern freemen found their voices and picked up their pens, enraging white conservatives who were unaccustomed to such undeferential behavior. "The Negroes now, aided and seconded by their white allies, are creating the *Second Rebellion*," one Democratic informed Johnson, "a Rebellion against the peace and quiet of the people and the unity of the Nation." Instead of remaining "quiet and orderly," former slaves and "Negro Soldiers" were determined "to strike for the ballot & to assert their equality."[25]

Believing their cause hopeless, a few former slaves thought it wisest to quit the fight. Following the enactment of the Alabama code, freedman William Warner overheard some blacks lamenting "that the democrats have succeeded, and that we are to be slaves again." Some hoped to abandon the South for Liberia, the homeland established for freed slaves by the American Colonization Society and the federal government. The West African nation, which had proclaimed its independence in 1847, never held much appeal for American-born blacks. Its always-meager emigration rate had dropped during the war years from 316 new arrivals in 1860 to 23 in 1864. But with the onset of the codes, 621 emigrants lost all hope in their nation and set sail. A. W. Powers, a former private in the Thirty-fifth Colored Troops, wrote to the society's office in Washington that he was prepared to lead two hundred freed people out of North Carolina. Another group of African Americans considered emigrating with Private Peter Mountain, also a veteran of the Thirty-fifth. The society, however, had been insolvent since the 1830s, after

President Andrew Jackson terminated federal funding for the organization, and the year the war ended, donors contributed only $23,633, hardly enough to relocate thousands of demoralized black southerners.[26]

Many African Americans with the means to do so pushed west instead, and a large number of those black men who remained with the military after Appomattox found themselves stationed in the territories. William F. Bryan wrote to alert Blanche K. Bruce that he had resided in Washington Territory since 1865, had acquired "a homestead" of 160 acres, and that "the same privileges that [he] enjoy[ed were] extended by the laws of the Territory to other colored men." Washington Chavis reported that "the Colard people" were so "well treated" in Kansas that "there will be none of them left in the South in two years." Chavis laughed that the black exodus out of the former Confederacy would leave "the ole rebs [with] very long faces." Yet westward emigration was nearly as expensive and dangerous as was starting life anew in far-off Liberia. Although land in the territories was free under the 1862 Homestead Act, few black families possessed the capital necessary to finance the journey west. As she had done during the war, Sojourner Truth continued to assist freed people who wished to relocate around Rochester, New York. So long as Lincoln lived, Truth was content to volunteer her time at Arlington's Freedmen's Village, but as both the political and physical conditions of the camp deteriorated under the new administration, the sixty-nine-year-old abolitionist decided to return to New York. "God has arisen for the rights of the poor," she assured General Oliver O. Howard, and "justice reigns in spite of presidents." Despite her profound belief in heavenly justice, she worried that blacks were "in hot water" if Johnson remained in the White House.[27]

Truth was right to be concerned. As white violence began to escalate under the codes—for as state legislation reduced black rights and disarmed black veterans, the unimpeded ability of former Confederates to inflict brutality rose—terrified freed people wanted out of the South. While touring upcountry Georgia, Bureau agent James Gillette reported that "would be emigrants [for] Liberia" asked if the agency might transport them "*as* far *en route* as Savannah." D. D. Bell was driven away from his Mississippi home "by the Bulldozers"—whites who delivered a "bull's dose" of whippings. As blacks "never can get justice [in] the U.S.

States," Bell figured, he might as well risk life in Africa. The editor of the Cincinnati *Colored Citizen* thought otherwise and published editorials "utterly opposed to the movement." Particularly in the upper South, few African Americans seriously considered leaving the land of their birth. "We are not Africans but colored Americans, and are entitled to American citizenship by every just consideration," insisted Maryland's L. W. Ballard. "All we want is a chance to work out our fortune and manhood."[28]

Even before the war's end, African Americans had begun to prepare for the Reconstruction battles in a series of conventions designed to formulate demands and maintain contact with activists in other parts of the nation. In the antebellum decades, black abolitionists had held similar gatherings, but the last had been in 1855. In the summer of 1863, black New Yorkers decided to restart the movement, motivated by Governor Horatio Seymour's reluctance to raise black troops in the state. Describing the conflict as "a war between freedom and despotism," Robert Purvis, a Charleston-born freeman who devoted most of his life to antislavery activism in Philadelphia, issued the call for a statewide convention to meet that July in Poughkeepsie. The two-day gathering convened on July 15, just three days before some of the delegates' sons and nephews perished at Fort Wagner. The Reverend Henry Highland Garnet was in attendance, but the conference "Manifesto of the Colored Citizens of the State" was drafted by Purvis, Jonas H. Townsend, and Benjamin F. Randolph, who was soon to become the army chaplain who would deliver a prayer at the rededication of Charleston's AME Church. The widely published "Manifesto" praised the conflict as "one of the most justifiable wars that was ever inaugurated." No longer a mere struggle for sectional reunion, it was "a combat for the sacred rights of Man against the myrmidons of Hell itself, [a] battle for the rights of self-government, true democracy, [and] just republicanism." The delegates censured Seymour for his hesitation to enlist black New Yorkers and called upon young African Americans to sign up when possible, for this was "not a battle of boys but [a] struggle of giants." Most of all, the conventioneers hoped their efforts would revive the moribund convention movement and advance their agenda of equal rights.[29]

It took more than a year, but the fall of 1864 witnessed the rebirth of the movement in what was to be the first of dozens of black conventions that would stretch into 1867. On October 4, 1864, 150 delegates representing Washington and seventeen states gathered in the Wesleyan Methodist Church in Syracuse for a four-day meeting, "the most truly national black convention" held to that date. Although Syracuse was justly regarded as one of the more welcoming of northern cities thanks to its integrated schools and public support for runaway slaves, the sight of so many well-dressed black delegates startled one observer, who loudly wondered where "the damn niggers [were] going." Irish toughs knocked down Henry Highland Garnet and stole his cane. Accustomed to worse, the excited delegates ignored such taunts and crowded into the small church on Genesee Street. John H. Cook gaveled the assembly to order at ten o'clock. Many of those who attended—Douglass, Garnet, William Wells Brown, and future Bureau agent John Mercer Langston—were veterans of the antebellum convention movement, while Garnet had appeared at the Poughkeepsie meeting. Some were local activists, such as Reverend Richard "Daddy" Cain and Octavius Catto, who were new to the national crusade. But the conventioneers wanted to start anew. They announced the formation of the National Equal Rights League, a permanent civil rights organization designed to instigate and oversee local branches across the North and in those parts of the South already under federal arms. Langston agreed to serve as its head.[30]

Over the next three days, the delegates called for an amendment to abolish slavery, demanded equal rights and equal pay for black soldiers, and reaffirmed their belief in the "fundamental principles of this Government." Although they defended the right of freed slaves to accumulate "property" and obtain a decent education, most of those in Syracuse had been born free in the North, and their speeches so frequently emphasized "temperance, frugality, and industry" that a few dissenters grumbled that the freed people's real needs "had not been sufficiently considered by this Convention." But in a keynote address on the third day, John S. Rock spoke eloquently on political rights, shouting that black soldiers had "not gone to the battlefield for the sake of killing," but rather to fight "for liberty and equality." African Americans wanted only what "is asked for the white man; nothing more and nothing less." Black editors across the country covered the convention. "After nearly two centuries of sufferings unparalleled in the world's history," the *New Orleans Tribune's* Louis Charles Roudanez reported, black men meeting in Syracuse promised to "come to the rescue of the country which not only has inflicted these grievances upon them, but which seems yet to be deaf to their plaintive voice." As the word went out to potential leaders of League locals, the exhausted but exhilarated delegates prepared to force the nation's leaders to hear them.[31]

Five months later in March, Douglass and Townshend, this time joined by Reverend Jermain W. Loguen, the Tennessee runaway turned Syracuse minister, kept the momentum going when abolitionists gathered in Albany for the annual meeting of the State Equal Rights League. After Douglass delivered a passionate account of the October meeting, William H. Johnson proposed that his group's original charter be revised so that it "was more in harmony with the spirit of the National Equal Rights League." The members voted their approval, and with that, the first local affiliate of the organization was born.[32]

By the time the next regional convention met the following May, everything had changed. Confederate generals had surrendered, Jefferson Davis had been captured, and President Lincoln had been slain. Freed people did not yet know how bitter a disappointment Andrew Johnson was to be, but with the collapse of the Confederacy, the convention movement turned southward. On May 9, Richmond freedmen crowded into the home of black shoemaker Robert W. Johnson to hear journalist T. Morris Chester speak about the Syracuse conference and the National Equal Rights League. The enthusiastic group promptly organized the Colored Men's Equal Rights League of Richmond. One month later, on June 5, delegates poured into Norfolk's Catherine Street Baptist Church to hear Garnet and stake "their claim for equal suffrage." Meeting at a time when the Thirteenth Amendment had yet to be ratified and only those northern Republicans who held the safest seats bothered to include a single sentence about black voting rights in their speeches, the Norfolk group reminded the nation of black soldiers from Crispus Attucks, whose was "the first blood shed in the Revolution," to those who had perished at "Fort Wagner, and in the death-haunted craters of the Petersburg mine." Shortly thereafter, black Virginians met in Alexandria for a three-day conference to endorse the Norfolk agenda and to demand that their state "be reorganized" on the basis of equal privileges and "the right of suffrage." In the antebellum era, Alexandria had housed the Franklin and Armfield slave trading company, and one delegate marveled that freedmen were now congregating in a town where "only three years ago any man suspected of the slightest tinge of abolitionism" would have been lucky "to escape hanging in the market place."[33]

Although New Orleans had fallen to federal control as early as 1862, it was not until 1865 that the city's African American community, prodded by editor Roudanez, met in a series of conferences from January to mid-May. The final gathering was called to order by Bishop Joseph Jackson Clinton, a "learned, eloquent, and courteous" Philadelphia-born African Methodist. Those men and women who met in the Zion Church understood they had two evils to confront: an already reconstructed legislature that was intensely opposed to black suffrage, and a long history of intra-racial division along lines of class and color. Shortly after the Syracuse convention, however, black envoys Oscar J. Dunn and Captain James H. Ingraham traveled to the city to help organize a branch of the National Equal Rights League. "We regard all black and colored men," Dunn argued, "as fellow sufferers." The Zion assembly took that advice to heart. "We no longer have classes or castes among us," insisted the *Tribune*. "We are made one people and one nation." Shabbily dressed field hands took their places next to wealthy, freeborn delegates of mixed ancestry. "There were seated side by side the rich and the poor, the literate and educated man, and the country laborer, hardly released from bondage." A majority of those present were dark-skinned freedmen, many of them, as Roudanez wrote, "[m]inisters of the gospel, officers and soldiers of the U.S. army," or, as in the case of Dr. Robert Cromwell, former Bureau officials. To the extent that emancipation itself had erased the gulf between bondman and light-skinned freeman, a rift the Black Codes were to further expunge by drawing new lines between whites and those of any measure of blackness, it was but sound policy for Louisiana's African Americans to put aside old differences.[34]

By the time 140 blacks packed Nashville's AME St. John's Chapel on the morning of August 7, the national outlines of the new convention movement had become clear. Although the chosen central committee was comprised of Tennessee residents, the convention's key speakers were experienced in wartime activism and veterans of earlier conferences. Among those who delivered an "eloquent and stirring speech" was the Reverend James D. Lynch. Born free in Baltimore, Lynch served as a missionary along the Georgia-Carolina coast during the conflict and was one of the ministers who had met with General William T. Sherman in Savannah the previous January. Later to serve as Mississippi's secretary of state, Lynch had just come from a conference in Georgia when he addressed the Nashville assembly. In a fiery speech, Lynch denounced white critics of equal suffrage as "copperheads" and "drunken scoundrel[s]," shouting that "when the nation stood trembling on the precipice, the black man came to the rescue." Sergeant Henry J. Maxwell, a South Carolina soldier who had attended the New Orleans convention and would later be stabbed in Charleston, followed Lynch to the pulpit. "We shall be heard by Congress and before the Legislature," Maxwell assured the "overflowing" crowd. "For these rights we will labor; for them we will die. We want two more boxes beside the cartridge box—the ballot box and the jury box." Inspired by the gathering, blacks in Knoxville and Memphis circulated petitions to the legislature demanding political and social equality.[35]

The same pattern held true when California blacks, organized by the Massachusetts-born Frederick G. Barbadoes and by David W. Ruggles, met in Sacramento in October, just as it did when black Pennsylvanians convened in Harrisburg on August 9, and in Cleveland in September and then again in October. At the second conclave, Catto was in attendance, and Langston and Loguen both spoke. Shoemaker Robert W. Johnson represented the Richmond gathering and discussed the "necessity of extending" the theretofore urban movement "into the rural parts of the State." Alabama-born James T. Rapier, who served as a delegate in Nashville, took his seat as a member of the League. The convention condemned colonization "to Liberia or elsewhere" and upheld "the necessity of acquiring property, [and] of educating their children." Demands for voting rights in Pennsylvania were especially acute, since African Americans were not pushing for a new privilege, but renewing an old one; prior to 1838, freed blacks had enjoyed access to the ballot. The Cleveland gathering voted to establish Philadelphia as the League's

Much of the reform activity during the Reconstruction years took place far away from Washington. Starting in July 1863, black activists revived the moribund black convention movement with a meeting in Poughkeepsie, New York. Larger meetings in Syracuse and Albany soon followed, and within weeks of the Confederate surrender, southern blacks organized their own meetings in Richmond and Norfolk. Delegates from earlier gatherings traveled to Alexandria, New Orleans, Nashville, Harrisburg, and Sacramento to help establish a network of activism designed to force their reform agenda on an accidental president and moderate Republicans in the nation's capital. Courtesy of the Schomburg Center for Research in Black Culture.

permanent headquarters and selected ten men, including the absent Douglass, to serve as the organization's vice presidents. Catto was named one of two recording secretaries and instructed to meet with congressmen Stevens and Kelley on a list of issues, from suffrage to schools to streetcar integration.[36]

If the roster of speakers who circulated from convention to convention invariably invoked the memory of Lincoln, they were less confident in his party. The veterans who donned their old uniforms before attending the meetings tended to publicly identify themselves as Republicans, but until black voting rights were assured, theirs was a more symbolic than tangible attachment. Party leaders in Washington continued to skirt the issue of full citizenship, although just before his death in December 1865, Maryland congressman Henry Winter Davis, perceiving the necessity of increasing Republican influence in his border state, publicly endorsed the franchise in all former slave states. When Maryland's African Americans met in a convention in January 1866, they placed voting rights at the top of their list of demands. Sergeant Major Lewis Douglass attended and, more in honor of his father's oratorical skills than in the young printer's abilities, was asked to address the state assembly on their behalf. The northern-born and -bred Lewis judged the convention to be filled with "many ignorant men," a derogatory perception of the black working-class delegates perhaps shared by other educated freemen who traveled the convention circuit. Yet such class divisions existed within white political conventions as well, and the Baltimore group successfully organized a state chapter of the League, threatened to take the state to federal court "for the purpose of making a test question as to the legality of refusing the colored man the right to give evidence in courts," and selected Douglass and William Matthew of Baltimore to lobby lawmakers in Washington.[37]

Black leaders in the lower South were less inclined to openly embrace that progressive an agenda. When Alabama blacks twice met in Mobile in late 1865, the majority of the fifty-six delegates were ministers, and the chairman of the convention was E. S. Winn, a Tuscaloosa freeman and African Methodist elder. Either due to the lack of veterans in the audience, or concerned with the discriminatory codes then being considered by the state legislature, the Mobile group advocated a policy of "peace, friendship, and good will toward all men—especially toward our white fellow-citizens among whom our lot is cast." One delegate went so far as to suggest "that the time has not arrived for extending the elective franchise to the whole colored race," a hint that the previously free elite might settle for a limited franchise. Conventioneers in Savannah did include "the right of suffrage," but they numbered that demand fourth, well behind the right to educate their children. Even then, Savannah's leadership asked only that, if taxed for education, "they may have their proper share of tax raised for schools expended for their benefit," which suggested an implicit acceptance of segregated academies. Only a January 10, 1866, conclave in Augusta was bold enough to send a cover letter and a petition "from three hundred colored citizens" to President Johnson insisting that "the enfranchisement and political equality" of African Americans was their just due in recompense for their role in "sav[ing] the nation from destruction." The open letter was written by delegate Martin R. Delany, who represented South Carolina and served as keynote speaker at the convention; undoubtedly the major's presence in the room had emboldened the group.[38]

That January, delegates from thirteen states and Washington assembled in the District's Fifteenth Street Presbyterian Church in what constituted the first truly national convention since the 1864 Syracuse gathering. Most attendees were from the North and nearby Virginia and Maryland, but Alabama and Florida sent small delegations as well. Both Frederick and Lewis Douglass appeared. The group selected the Reverend Garnet as presiding officer, perhaps due to his role in the instrumental Poughkeepsie conference. But the delegates listened most closely to George T. Downing, who had also attended the Syracuse conference. Previously the owner of a successful hotel in Newport, Rhode Island, and a recruiter for the black Massachusetts Fifth Cavalry, Downing currently managed the House of Representatives dining room, which gave him access to political gossip and also allowed him to quietly lobby progressive Republicans. The convention discussed the Freedmen's Bureau Bill, then awaiting the president's signature, and the prospects of a civil rights act. Hoping for, if not confident of, success in either measure, the group formally resolved their opposition "to foreign colonization to any place" and restated their demand that Congress "guarantee and secure to all loyal citizens, irrespective of race or color, equal rights before the law, including the right of impartial suffrage." Only the vote, they argued, could secure "a republican form of government to the States lately in rebellion." Since the bill extending the life of the Bureau had just emerged from Congress, it made sense to lobby the president about its importance. To that end, the convention deputized Downing, Frederick and Lewis Douglass, attorney and veteran William J. Whipper, and Chicago merchant John Jones to call on Johnson, explain their agenda, and obtain his views on black equality.[39]

On February 7, the five men gained their audience with the president. Johnson was sitting when they entered, "his hands in his pockets, and looking a trifle sour." But when Downing addressed him as "your Excellency" and assured the president that they came "feeling that we are friends meeting a friend," Johnson brightened and shook each of their hands. Downing read a short prepared address that was purposely vague and steered clear of any proposed legislation; he "respectfully" hoped that blacks "may be fully enfranchised, not only here in this District, but throughout the land." Frederick Douglass then added that they had come only "to show our respect, and to present in brief the claims of our race to your favorable consideration." Rather than appeal to natural rights, Douglass pointed to precedent dating back to the Revolutionary era. Blacks were "subject to taxation," he noted, "subject to bear the burdens of the State." Like those early patriots who called for representation commensurate with their financial contributions, "it [was] not improper that [blacks] should ask to share in the privileges" of citizenship as well.[40]

The president responded with a lengthy harangue. His entire public career, Johnson swore, revealed him to be "a friend of the colored man." He had owned slaves until just three years earlier, he confessed, "but never sold one," an admission that, although true, was hardly likely to win over the delegation. Nor was Johnson's assertion that he had been so kind a master that he had virtually been "their slave instead of their being mine." Having thus established his credentials for understanding the South, Johnson then insisted that to push for civil rights at this time could only lead to race war. Clearly unnerved by being addressed by one of the nation's most celebrated orators, but warming to his subject, the unlettered Johnson practically shouted that he did "not like to be arraigned by some who can get up handsomely rounded periods and deal in rhetoric." Frederick Douglass, once an enslaved ships' caulker who had been beaten on the Baltimore docks for the crime of allegedly taking white jobs, and his son Lewis, who had been badly wounded at Fort Wagner, sat stoically while Johnson decried those who "talk about abstract ideas of liberty, who never periled life, liberty, or property." The agenda black Americans proposed, Johnson concluded, might "result in the extermination of one [race] or the other. God forbid that I should be engaged in such a work!"[41]

Thinking the president finished, the elder Douglass opened his mouth to speak, but Johnson cut him off. "I am not quite through yet." Edging close to Douglass, the president asked: "Have you ever lived upon a plantation?" Evidently, Johnson knew nothing of the abolitionist's childhood and was surprised to hear Douglass say that he had. Thinking back to his younger days as an impoverished tailor, Johnson countered with: "When you would look over and see a man who had a large family, struggling hard upon a poor piece of land, you thought a great deal less of him than you did of your own master's negro, didn't you?" Douglass tried to assure the president that he had never done so, but Johnson overrode him again, proposing a conspiracy between "the colored man and his master, combined," to keep the poor white "in slavery" and deny him a share "of the rich land of the country." If granted the franchise, blacks might once more unite with their former masters against white workers. In any case, Johnson added, "the majority" had the right to decide on the ballot. This time, Douglass cut in and observed that in South Carolina and Mississippi, blacks *were* the majority. With barely "repressed anger," the president rose and called an end to the exchange.[42]

As the delegation filed out of the White House, a messenger dashed up to invite the five leaders to the House of Representatives anteroom, where they were quizzed by curious Republicans as to the interview. The group promptly drafted a missive to the *Washington Chronicle*, designed to be an open letter to the president. Inside the executive mansion, Johnson continued to seethe. Turning to his secretary, the president sneered: "Those d[amne]d sons of b[itche]s thought they had me in a trap. I know that d[amne]d Douglass; he's just like any nigger, & would sooner cut a man's throat than not." Twelve days later, Johnson submitted his veto message on the Freedmen's Bureau to Congress.[43]

As the first anniversary of the Appomattox surrender approached in April, southern conventioneers scheduled celebrations "of their freedom, by [staging] processions, speeches, &c." A delegation of white Virginians hastened to the capital to urge Johnson "to forbid negroes to celebrate" the date, but while the president ordered his officers to maintain the peace, he told them he was powerless to halt the parade. Northern newspapers editorialized that the "committee of reconstructed Rebels" indicated that Richmond was not yet prepared to be relieved of the "oversight of Federal troops" but hoped also that those southern whites who "had groaned under the oppression of Confederate tyranny" might join in the festivities. Twenty-five thousand people turned out to join in the Richmond celebration, and the military reported that "good order [was] preserved.[44]

In the wake of their encounter with Johnson, however, those blacks gathering in mid- to late-1866 conventions divided their rhetorical time between demands for voting rights and reproofs of the president's assaults on the Bureau. Delegates meeting in Indianapolis approved resolutions "denouncing President Johnson," praising the Republican leadership in Washington, and advancing "impartial suffrage" as the only solution to the increasingly "miserable" state of southern affairs. A meeting of the Georgia Equal Rights Association agreed that Johnson had "lately shown that he is not as friendly to colored men" as they once had hoped, and they voted to "send colored men from every Southern State" to meet with the president about the Black Codes. Hostile Democrats pushed back. A Memphis editor charged that black Americans and their white allies intended "to raise ten thousand dollars" to finance the Washington lobbying efforts "of Geo[rge] Downing (nigger)," while a Connecticut journal called for support for Johnson's policies, chiding those Republicans whose "devotion to the negro now takes the place of 'support of Government' as a test of loyalty."[45]

The scattered criticisms of the president's program became harder to ignore in September 1866, when a handful of Republican dignitaries banded together with black conventioneers and white abolitionists at Philadelphia's National Suffrage Convention. As the November off-year elections approached, even Thaddeus Stevens shied away from "universal negro suffrage" and declined an invitation to attend the convention. The Pennsylvania congressman, Douglass complained, "feared they would lose several members of Congress by such an avowal." But Johnson's unprecedented decision to campaign across the North that fall on behalf of friendly politicians forced a handful of Republicans into attending. Maryland senator John A. Cresswell, the first man to propose an amendment banning slavery, appeared, as did Massachusetts senator Henry Wilson and Major General Benjamin Butler, then preparing a run for Congress. As the keynote speaker, Douglass spoke of his sons and of those black soldiers who had perished during the war. "We demand suffrage in return for our sacrifices," he shouted, as the audience "rose en masse to cheer him." Warning those reluctant Republicans that black Americans would not settle for second-class citizenship, Douglass demanded the vote for all. "Give it to us now, or we will soon get it without your aid," he threatened. "We will remember our friends, and will not forget our enemies." As "thunderous applause" rolled across the hall, one delegate crowed that the address should be "printed in such large type *that Andy Johnson could read it, drunk or sober.*"[46]

Democrats did their best to ridicule the Philadelphia convention, together with the larger, nearly endless succession of black gatherings, even as Johnson's northern tour—dubbed the "swing around the circle"—proved to be a political disaster for the president's fortunes. White abolitionist Anna Elizabeth Dickinson had spoken "in a most riotous manner" at the conference, and hostile, pro-Johnson editors derided her as "a strong minded female" and accused the delegates of promoting racial "amalgamation." A New Orleans newspaper reasoned that those southern blacks who represented their states were "bogus delegates" on the grounds that Americans of African ancestry were not yet citizens of the republic. If given the right of suffrage, another insisted, black Republicans proposed to "impeach or depose President Johnson, and to revolutionize the Government." One Democrat proposed that Americans would do well to ignore reports from the Philadelphia conference, and in fact to disregard those "conventions (so called) of all kinds, [that] are being continually held all over the North." The black convention movement does "not amount to two cents." But two months later, after the ballots were counted, Republicans picked up thirty-seven seats in Congress.[47]

Congressional Republicans were willing to confront the president on his position that the executive alone was responsible for restoring the Union, just as they had challenged Lincoln on this point. Although in fact Congress had never declared war on the Confederacy, Stevens argued that eleven states had actually seceded and should now be treated as "conquered" provinces. Other Republicans insisted that by separating from the country, the states had regressed back into territories, over which only Congress held jurisdiction. Speaking in Lancaster, Pennsylvania, on the eve of ratification of the Thirteenth Amendment, Stevens observed that the Constitution protected slavery "in every State of the Union where it existed." If the insurrection had been merely one of individuals, then masters might resume their old positions "with their privileges untouched." But if states had seceded, that dissolved old legal "ties between the parties," which allowed for the entire federal government, including Congress, to create new conditions so long as the defeated South was under "military possession." Although Stevens did not say so, even the president, for all of his talk of states' rights, had demanded the end of slavery and a disavowal of secession as the price of readmission to the Union. When the Thirty-ninth Congress convened, it cited Article I, Section 5 of the Constitution regarding their prerogative to judge the qualification of members, excluded members from the former Confederacy, and established a Joint Committee on Reconstruction.[48]

For party leaders, this was far more than a theoretical exercise in constitutional theory. If the same planters who had voted for secession five years earlier could now "stalk back" into political power, as one Ohio congressman put it, both the sacrifices and the gains of the war years had been for naught. Since the Thirteenth Amendment effectively erased the three-fifths clause, which counted five slaves as three people for apportionment and taxation, the Confederate states "could lose nothing if defeated," Massachusetts general Charles G. Loring fretted, and would achieve "a vast increase of relative power in the Government." Noting the lengthy roster of Congressional acts that had contributed to the Union victory, Missouri senator John B. Henderson resolved that the war's success had not been due to "the Executive alone," and so it fell to Congress to decide "whether the causes of the Rebellion had been removed," and if not, to pass further legislation and amendments to "remedy existing evils."[49]

Even those moderate Republicans not yet ready to endorse black voting rights felt the need to respond to Johnson's veto of the Freedmen's Bureau bill, for the agency remained as popular in the North as the Black Codes were despised. As late as February 1866, no less than Lyman Trumbull ridiculed black suffrage as the "most sovereign remedy" to the nation's ills "since the days of Townsend's Sasparilla." But Henry

Winter Davis was hardly the only border-state Republican to understand the necessity of African American ballots. Governor Andrew delivered a lengthy farewell address to the Massachusetts assembly, in
which he urged the continued Congressional exclusion of states who
refused to guarantee "civil rights [to all] men and women, in equality
with the white population." Hinting at Midwestern unhappiness with
the president and his conservative program—a bellwether loud enough
to embolden any centrist politician—the Iowa legislature formally instructed its Washington delegation "to prevent the Rebel States from
resuming their political relations" until they "secured civil rights alike
to whites and blacks." In the Senate, Henry Wilson rose to demand
that in addition to the requirements placed on the South by Johnson,
they also be compelled to "give the freedmen equal civil rights with
the whites, the suffrage to such as have fought for the Union, can read,
and pay taxes."[50]

With that, the question of black voting rights, so vocally demanded
by the black conventions, at long last moved to the Washington agenda.
As a tentative first step, Republican congressman William D. Kelley
introduced legislation to grant blacks the franchise in the District of
Columbia. Sumner regarded the bill not only as an act of justice for the
city's black population, but also as a precedent that might inaugurate "a
policy not only strictly for the District of Columbia, but in some sense
for the country at large." Northern Democrats were as outraged as their
southern brethren. The Founders "did not intend this Government for
the negro race," protested Congressman Andrew J. Rogers of New Jersey. Ignoring the earlier contribution of the roughly five thousand black
patriots who had served their new country, Rogers insisted that "the
Revolutionary war [had been] fought for the liberties of the white race."
One New York Democrat noted that the city's black population had
tripled during the war years, most of them fresh "from the field and
plantation." Somewhat in contradiction to that statistic, as well as to the
petition from black congregants at the First Baptist Church presented
by Senator Wilson, a second New Yorker grumbled that impartial voting rights violated the "will" of the capital's residents. "[T]his was a white
man's government," he bellowed. Such "a detestable measure," a Philadelphia editor added, could only be "enforce[d with] negro bayonets."

An unnamed cabinet member leaked the news that if the bill passed, Johnson would veto it, and he did. But as Washington was under the jurisdiction of Congress, the president could not claim to be defending states' rights with his veto. His disquiet was over race.[51]

Republicans pulled back a step when crafting the first-ever Civil Rights Bill, a bill designed to nullify the Black Codes and clarify federal citizenship, a point that never had been established in the Constitution and that had been muddied considerably in the 1857 Dred Scott decision. Drafted by Trumbull and the Judiciary Committee, the short bill defined citizens as "all persons, irrespective of color or condition, born in the United States" and allowed for fines and imprisonment for "any person depriving any citizen of any of the rights enumerated in this bill." Although a few progressive voices, including Ohio senator John Sherman—the brother of the general—wondered aloud "why anybody should be excluded from the elective franchise merely because he was black," the bill did not contain an explicit suffrage requirement. Even Sherman admitted that since his home state did not allow African Americans to vote, he "could not consistently" demand that southern states do so. Although dismayed by that omission, the editor of Nashville's *Colored Tennessean* grasped hard political realities and endorsed the bill nonetheless. At least the bill protected blacks in their "civil rights," the paper editorialized, "such as *buying, selling, leasing, conveying, etc.*"[52]

Once again, Democrats united in opposition. Despite the fact that the bill said nothing about voting rights, one New Orleans editor charged that the proposed act "alter[ed] the fundamental relations of the central authority toward that of the several states." A Georgia journalist added that far from necessitating a civil rights act, his state's black code revealed "how little need" there was for federal action. "The Southern people have a tender and almost affectionate regard for these helpless people." In Washington, Delaware senator Willard Saulsbury predicted the bill "would lead to bloodshed, war and disunion," while Kentucky senator Garrett Davis dramatically promised that the day the bill became law, "he should feel compelled to regard himself as an enemy of the Government and work for its overthrow." A few Democrats chose to quibble with the bill. One claimed that the three-paragraph act was too long, adding that he "did not believe the situation of affairs was so bad in the South as many gentlemen seemed to say." But former governor Benjamin Perry had little use for polite fictions that the bill's flaws lay in its length or allowance of federal authority. If passed, he fumed, blacks would "serve on juries and hold office, ride with you and your wives and daughters in the cars, eat with you at the hotel, and sit with you in the church."[53]

Confident in their ability to sell the very moderate bill to their constituents back home, Republicans forced a vote in early March. Predictably, the chambers divided along partisan lines. In the Senate, the bill enjoyed a margin of 33 to 12, while the House tally was 111 to 38, with 24 Republican and 8 Democratic congressmen declining to register a vote. Because the measure merely clarified what many Americans regarded as an oversight in the original Constitution, moderate Republicans expected the president to sign it. If not, one New York editor observed, both chambers had passed the act by "more than the required two-thirds" necessary for an override vote. Senator Sherman assured a Connecticut audience that Johnson would "show" the country that Johnson "stood with [Congress] on every material question." The president owed his position to the votes of "Union men," and he "would never throw the power the loyal people gave him into the hands of the copperhead party." Less confident, veterans of Maryland's eight black regiments fired off a petition to Johnson, urging him to "sign the bill." As many as ten Maryland schools "have been burned to the ground," they wrote, and their teachers had been "brutally assaulted, shot at, and maltreated." Nobody had yet been charged under state law.[54]

On March 27, five weeks after his negation of the Bureau bill and hard on the heels of his rejection of the Washington suffrage act, Johnson once again took up his veto pen. Although drafted in part by Ohio attorney Henry Stanberry, and polished considerably by supportive cabinet members, the sentiments were the president's. The bill was "evil" and unprecedented, Johnson charged, as Congress sought to "establish for the security of the colored race safeguards which go infinitely beyond any that the General Government has ever provided for the white race." Continuing the line of thought first employed against Douglass, the president reasoned that no previous Congress had crafted legislation for working-class whites, yet "the distinction of race and color is by the bill made to operate in favor of the colored and against the white race." The president's southern backers endorsed his opinions. "Shall our children see a negro in the President's chair?" questioned a Georgia editor. "Shall the negro intermingle with our daughters, and take an equal place in our household? The president's veto says that he shall not." Perhaps unaware of the bill's margins of victory, an Arkansas publisher observed that Republicans might "scold," but he did not "see what they can do. Their majorities will begin to diminish now."[55]

What they could do was to prepare for an override vote, never before accomplished. Stunned senators reported that Trumbull had shown the president an advance copy of the bill, but that Johnson had raised no objections at that time. Progressives in Washington, who had long since lost faith in Johnson, took heart that their moderate colleagues finally understood the depth of the president's hostility to African Americans. "I see how Senators once lukewarm, indifferent, or perhaps hostile," Sumner marveled, "now generously unite in securing protection to the freedmen by act of Congress." One northern editor observed "that the President's State rights ideas" were essentially "those upon which the South planted itself as a justification for rebellion and treason" and ridiculed his theory that because no previous law assisted immigrants, none was necessary for black Americans. "The foreigner never needed such protection," declared a New Hampshire paper, adding that if often disliked by nativists, immigrants quickly became voters and amassed political clout. Black editors were particularly infuriated by Johnson's reference to his predecessor's policies in his veto message. The president, editorialized the Nashville *Colored Tennessean*, "coldly tramples under foot [Lincoln's] most sacred principles, abandons the people who made him what he is, and couches his official papers in the stereotyped phrases of the old Buchanan and Breckinridge Copperhead regime."[56]

As if determined to drive moderates into the arms of progressive Republicans, just one week later on April 2, Johnson unilaterally decreed that the slaveholders' rebellion had everywhere ended except in parts of distant Texas. The Joint Committee on Reconstruction was then in the process of collecting data on white violence and drafting a report outlining their co-equal authority over the former Confederacy, and the president's proclamation—issued without consulting his cabinet—was an attempt to undercut the right of Republicans to help guide the process. The "insurrection which heretofore existed," the proclamation insisted, "is at an end, and is henceforth to be so regarded." The time had come, the president believed, for white Americans to unite and put the past behind them.[57]

As Congressional testimony increasingly demonstrated that white violence was growing, and that the "insurrection" was far from over, Republican leaders in both chambers began to rally their forces for an override vote. Trumbull, one of the last to break with the president, spoke on the desperate need for such legislation two days after Johnson's decree. "The [Senate] galleries were densely crowded," one journalist scribbled, "with whites and *blacks*." African Americans did far more than watch passively from the balcony. Veterans of the black convention movement paid surprise visits to wavering politicians. William E. Johnson and William C. Gardner, both soon to serve in the South Carolina legislature, led a delegation into the office of New York's Ira Harris. "[A]ll men native born" deserved civil rights, Johnson declared, and for blacks, the bill was "the Magna Charta of our liberties." Such arguments quickly found their way to the Senate floor. Vermont's Justin Morrill denied that bondmen and bondwomen "[had been] assisted to freedom at all." Liberty had come only because the republic had needed fresh troops, and, he declared, "freedom did not come to them, till this nation called on them to help it on to victory." In the House, William Lawrence of Ohio repeated William E. Johnson's assertion that the bill "was not designed for any class or race of people, but to protect the civil rights of all citizens." Horace Greeley's *Tribune* also weighed in on the federal responsibility: "Its honor is pledged to the Four Millions of Freedmen who helped us put down the Rebellion—who scouted, and prayed, and fought for the National cause."[58]

The final vote came on April 9. In the Senate, the bill enjoyed a comfortable margin of 33 to 15, while the House majority was a yet more impressive 122 to 41. Democrats blasted the effort as the handiwork of a radical faction, but in truth Republicans stood united behind both the Civil Rights Bill and the move to override Johnson's rejection. Having overcome what many moderates worried was the historic precedent of defying a presidential veto, Republicans then voted to override Johnson's rejection of the Freedmen's Bureau bill on July 16, and then the following December, they dispensed with his veto of the Washington suffrage bill. "President Johnson can see the law enforced," observed a prescient Massachusetts editor, "or he may practically nullify many of its provisions [by] openly refusing to execute them" and incur the wrath of Congress. White politicians hoped it would not come to that, but Douglass and the small number of blacks who had met with Johnson suspected otherwise.[59]

Rarely had a single piece of legislation been met with such jubilation beyond the streets of Washington as was the Civil Rights Act of 1866. One of Trumbull's constituents wrote to "Congratulat[e] Congress on the victory of today." With the fighting finished only one year before and battlefield scars still fresh, northern soldiers might be prepared to forgive, but hardly to forget, and Illinois voters regarded Johnson's policies as little more than attempts "to give Controll of Congress into the hands of the Rebells." From Bangor and Portland, Maine, to Manhattan, and from Tamaqua, Pennsylvania, to Des Moines, Iowa, triumphant Republicans fired salutes of one hundred guns, waved flags, rang bells, and lit bonfires in celebration, as one Iowa journalist wrote, of the victory over "the Royal Egotist, Humbug, and Knave who sits in the Presidential chair!" In New York City, Chief Justice Salmon P. Chase spoke to a packed Saint Paul's Methodist Church, proclaiming the override "a great triumph" and predicting that "the next step would be to give universal suffrage."[60]

Southern blacks were elated. With "the passage of the Civil Rights Bill," editor Louis Charles Roudanez observed, "there is not a right that a white man can enjoy, to which the colored man is not also entitled." In Norfolk, Virginia, freedmen took to the streets in a spontaneous "parade in honor of the passage" of the bill. White toughs waded into the parade in an attempt to disperse the procession, but marchers fought back and soldiers had to be called out to restore order. One white man was killed and two "mortally wounded." Southern newspapers carried the story under the headline: NEGRO DISTURBANCE IN NORFOLK.[61]

If black activists praised the bill as a means to achieve social equality and integrated schools and transportation, Democratic editors, and not all of them in the South, denounced the "addled brains" of the "Radical revolutionary press" for embracing black political advancement. Although the act was silent on voting rights, conservatives were aware that black conventions had been demanding the franchise for two years, and finally a handful of white Republicans—particularly those with safe districts or secure judicial sinecures—added their voices as well. "As soon as [Republicans] could get President Johnson out of the way," alleged one New Orleans publisher, they would "secure a Fred. Douglass or Sumner" for the presidency. Douglass had yet to clearly identify himself as a Republican, but for alarmed traditionalists who regarded the law as an assault on white prerogative, the black abolitionist assumed a central place in their nightmares. Soon "Fred. Douglass would be President," charged a Pennsylvania editor, with "negro governments in every Southern State, negro Senators and Representatives in Congress, and no bar raised against the perfect equality in society and in politics." Although their fears of an African American in the White House were not to come true during their lifetime, anxious Democrats were right enough on the second score. Within two years, blacks would serve in state constitutional conventions and win election to state assemblies. Within five, a number of men, including black conventioneers "Daddy" Cain and James Rapier, and pilot and navy veteran Robert Smalls, would move on to national office.[62]

White southerners did far worse than simply post angry editorials. Ironically, the end of slavery actually had placed freedmen in greater mortal danger, since they were no longer the expensive chattel of politically influential planters. A Bureau agent in Austin County, Texas, had alerted General Howard to the "week[ly discovery] of negroes found dead, or killed." Provided enough laborers remained in any given area, no whites complained about the murders to state authorities, the agent explained, "since the nigger is not property." A white Tennessean agreed, gloating that a "Nigger's life is cheap now. When a white man feels aggrieved at anything a nigger's done, he just shoots him and puts an end to it." Having attempted to control freedmen through their political systems with the Black Codes—laws that were collectively negated by the Civil Rights Act—whites increasingly turned to extralegal methods to achieve the same objectives. Given that battle-hardened black veterans routinely answered violence with violence, as the Norfolk parade riot revealed, state authorities had sought to disarm African American soldiers before Congress could override Johnson's veto. On January 14, 1866, the commander of Alabama's state militia ordered "the collection of arms and ammunition found in the hands of freedmen." Should any blacks complain about being disarmed, "they will be arrested." The next month, Colonel Charles Whittlesey warned Howard that in North Carolina, local policemen and irregular companies of "Home Guards" had confiscated weapons "from discharged negro soldiers and other freedmen." Regarding that as a violation of Secretary Stanton's orders, Whittlesey directed "that freedmen be protected in their right to bear arms," but well into the spring of 1867, Bureau agents in Mississippi reported that "fire-arms have been taken from freedmen" by local authorities. Efforts by federal officers to "have the arms restored to the owners under the provisions of the Civil Rights Bill have met in most cases without success."[63]

Largely disarmed, black veterans, southern Unionists, and Yankee schoolmasters were routinely targeted for violent removal. Democrats understood that military and community service could be stepping stones to political office, and despite the Civil Rights Act, the reopening of southern schools in the fall of 1866 was met with the "assassinations of several teachers" in Louisiana. One Bureau teacher in rural Alabama complained that so many educators were "threatened" that the schools had to close. "Union men are openly assailed on the streets," he added. When possible, however, blacks and southern Republicans gave as good as they got. When former sergeant major Lewis Douglass was "surrounded by a number of white boys" who resented his "good clothes" while ice skating, he defended himself with his skate blades, "splitting [one's] head with the skates" and taking another's "thumb nearly off." Four days after Congress overrode the president's veto, white Virginian B. S. Whittin was threatened with "a Coat of Tar and Feathers" but single-handedly chased the mob away by promising "to kill the first Traitor" who tried "to carry out any such measures." Nor were threats limited to the South. Whites promising to punish the "miscegenators" attempted to force their way into the Connecticut home of W. H. Davenport, whose wife was an Irish immigrant. Davenport's mother, "an old negress of 50 to 60 years of age," shot and killed the ringleader as he came through the door. That was also the solution of George Band, who methodically killed all of the fourteen men who had "took his wife, hung her to a tree, [and] hacked her to death with knives." But the revenge could not bring his wife back to life, and Band eventually had to flee the county.[64]

That August, Maryland whites—many of them self-proclaimed Confederate veterans—broke up a Methodist camp meeting in Anne Arundel County. Here too the violence was not random, and whites rarely assaulted African Americans simply on account of their color. The attacks were targeted at black men in uniform, who symbolized the revolutionary changes sweeping the country. As the fall elections approached, rumors circulated that "discharged soldiers of the Federal army" planned to march through Baltimore in protest of the state's anti-black codes, and both the city's Democratic mayor and Governor Thomas Swann, a Johnson loyalist, announced that the "Radicals of Baltimore were engaged in treasonable and insurrectionary practices." After conferring with the president, Swann also suggested that those state residents who had fought for the Confederacy and had been disenfranchised by state law as a result should be allowed to vote. The move, Republicans crowed, was "checkmated" by Judge Hugh L. Bond, who ruled that registrars would not allow them to do so, and that any whites who "resort[ed] to armed violence" at the voting stations or against African Americans would see the inside of his courtroom.[65]

Elsewhere in the South, the Civil Rights Act was greeted with renewed violence against black activists and Republican editors. A Norfolk mob destroyed the office of D. B. White's *True Southerner.* Four days before the override vote, three blacks were murdered in Carrollton, Louisiana. In Nashville, a "colored soldier" was attacked by "a large crowd," and black soldiers fought back, wounding several. In a warning to black landholders, whites in Pine Bluff, Oklahoma, "set fire to a black settlement" and left twenty-four "men women and children hanging [from] trees around the Cabbins." In Texas, where twenty thousand black soldiers were mustered out of service, African Americans were "shot down like wild beasts, without any provocation." Tensions were especially high in Charleston, where the Fifty-fourth and Fifty-fifth Volunteers remained stationed in the city. White assaults on servicemen became so frequent that hundreds of black Charlestonians, led by a handful of soldiers, paraded through the streets. When the police arrived with orders to disperse, the marchers showered the police with bricks, badly injuring one police sergeant, whose hat and club were seized as trophies.[66]

Sporadic trouble between black soldiers and white policemen and firefighters—many of them Irish immigrants—exploded into violence in Memphis on May 1, 1866, the day after soldiers of the Third USCT Artillery were disarmed and mustered out. Furious that wealthy whites preferred to hire black porters and hack drivers, working-class whites and immigrants first assaulted black veterans, and then turned their rage on these institutions those soldiers had protected: schools and churches. Activist William Wells Brown, who was then in the city, witnessed arsonists cheering for "white man's government." Determined to restore their lost antebellum world, other whites forced black women to cook meals for them before raping them and burning their homes to the ground. Two days of disorder followed, during which the city government did nothing to quell the violence and assisted in organizing the mobs; one policeman warned blacks that "Your old father, Abe Lincoln, is dead and damned." By the time rioters finished their work, forty-six blacks had been murdered, another seventy wounded, with four churches, twelve schools, and ninety-one homes destroyed. "Soon we shall have no more black troops among us," the *Memphis Avalanche* bragged. "Thank heaven the white race are once more rulers of Memphis."[67]

New Orleans suffered similar violence when the city's blacks gathered on July 30 for a convention at the Mechanics' Institute. Seeking to put an end to the convention movement, at least in Louisiana, former Confederate soldiers bought up every weapon local gun shops had for sale. As nearly two hundred black marchers, led by Lieutenant L. A. Thibault, a veteran of the Seventy-third USCT, approached the Institute, whites began to hurl bricks and rocks. Some marchers responded with shovels and pistol-fire while others fled into the hall. Policemen attacked Dr. Anthony Dostie, a prominent white Republican, shot him five times, and ran him through with a sword. As convention delegates inside frantically tried to construct a barricade of chairs and tables to keep the mob and the police out, black soldiers, Louis Charles Roudanez reported, "were assassinated by scores." Although whites outside randomly shot any black unlucky enough to be caught in the streets, city authorities had drafted "lists of victims" to be eliminated, and anybody wearing a uniform was targeted. As one attacker swore, "We have fought for four years these god-damned Yankees and sons of bitches in the field, and now we will fight them in the city." Thirty-four blacks and four whites lay dead, with almost another two hundred wounded; among those beaten and arrested was Bureau doctor Robert I. Cromwell.[68]

Returning to New Orleans from Texas, Major General Philip H. Sheridan reported that the attack on the convention hall "was no riot; it was an absolute massacre by the police, which was not excelled in murderous cruelty by that of Fort Pillow"—the Tennessee atrocity committed against black soldiers two years earlier. Despite considerable evidence of collusion between the city's police and the white rioters, a grand jury declined to return any indictments, in part because the local district attorney "declined to apply the test-oath to the jurors," thereby allowing known Confederates to sit on the panel. As it became clear that mobs could murder even white Republicans with impunity, some worried activists left the state. "Let Dostie's skin be forthwith stripped and sold to [P. T.] Barnum," gloated the *Mobile Tribune*, "the proceeds to go to the Freedmen's Bureau and negro newspapers, to be sold by them for the benefit of Negroes who have no taste for work." But if the assassinations left the state Republican Party in disarray, it further damaged Democratic prospects across the nation. Cartoonist Thomas Nast sketched a widely reproduced depiction of President Johnson as a smirking king, lurking in a doorway while whites gun down dozens of blacks. The "whole blame of the riot does *not* rest on Mayor [John T.] Monroe" alone, charged Greeley's *New-York Tribune*. White rioters "were simply fulfilling Johnson's prophecies" that "Southern Whites would kill the Blacks if the latter should claim and attempt to exercise the Right of Suffrage." Roudanez was blunter yet. "The rioters of the 30th of July received strength and encouragement from the administration of Mr. Johnson."[69]

Johnson's public attempt to pin responsibility for the carnage on "the radical Congress" and its increasing willingness to enfranchise the "colored population" which "had just been emancipated" gained him little favor among most northern voters. "What have we done to deserve from them such treatment?" wondered the publisher of Augusta's *Colored American*. Mobs "kill, wound, and cowardly beat the colored people, who charge the race with all that is bad." If white southerners hoped to resume those seats in Congress they had been denied a year earlier, Roudanez argued in September 1866, they had only done their cause injury by proving that conditions had actually deteriorated in the former Confederacy. "Already Johnson's policy begins to make emancipation a farce," he editorialized. Although a

The New Orleans riot of July 1866, held just before the off-year elections, helped to convince northern voters that the white South was not yet ready for self-government. Like the Memphis riots of the same year, the New Orleans violence was essentially a continuation of the Civil War; more than half of the whites involved were Confederate veterans, while just less than half of the African Americans had served in the U.S. Army. Voters held Andrew Johnson—seen here as a smirking king—responsible for the rising tide of white violence, and when the November ballots were counted, Republicans captured seventy-seven percent of the seats in Congress. Courtesy Library of Congress.

number of high-profile assassinations, such as those of Octavius Catto and Benjamin F. Randolph, lay in the future, the viciousness of 1866 surpassed the worst moments of violence in the final months of 1865. Convinced that the "murders and outrages" inflicted on blacks and Unionists, together with "the ghastly massacres of Memphis and New Orleans," mandated greater Congressional oversight and further legislation to eradicate white terror, Republicans of all stripes began to ponder the necessity of removing Johnson. Across the South, black veterans ended 1866 as they had begun it, by forming militia units. African Americans in Richmond carried banners through the streets, rifles slung over their shoulders and sabers hanging at their sides. Veterans were once again training in "secret military organizations," worried South Carolina's governor. The next two years were not destined to be tranquil.[70]

CHAPTER SIX

"Andrew Johnson Is But One Man"

The Progressive Alliance Coalesces

THE PAIR WAS DESTINED to raise eyebrows. Born in Gettysburg, Pennsylvania, to a white father and a black mother, Lydia Hamilton Smith accepted the position as housekeeper for Congressman-elect Thaddeus Stevens in 1848. One journalist described her as "comely in appearance, light in color," and other reporters agreed that she was "a light mulatto lady," a "rather small, graceful, composed woman" with "the manners of one never habituated to serve." At fifty-six, the attorney, reformer, and industrialist Stevens was twenty-one years her senior, and by all admissions a curious sight. A congenital deformity of one foot gave him a noticeable limp and, afflicted with alopecia, Stevens lost all of his hair at an early age. He corrected the first with a cane and a specially made shoe, and the second with a dark, ill-fitting wig. By the time she came to work for the agnostic Stevens, the devoutly Catholic Smith had married a black barber, whom one journalist denounced as "a shiftless negro man." They either separated or he died in late 1847, shortly after the birth of their second son. During the time that Stevens served in the state legislature, Smith worked at a hotel in Harrisburg. After his election to Congress in 1848, she and her sons moved first into a small cottage behind his home, and then finally into her employer's house.[1]

Known to his supporters as the "Great Commoner," Stevens always regarded Smith more as a respected family member than as a housekeeper and insisted that guests and relatives pay her proper deference. His family addressed her as Mrs. Smith rather than Lydia. "Much love to you and Mrs. S." wrote a niece in a typical missive. Evidently well educated in a time when class and race, as well as gender, restricted educational opportunities, Smith enjoyed the political discourse found daily in Stevens's parlor. The witty, sarcastic congressman relished the company of a woman described by her priest as "smart as a steel trap, bright, and a good conversationalist." Stevens's critics were less kind. Journalists alleged that he had "seduced [Smith] from her husband, a full-blooded negro," insisted the two "lived in open adultery," and referred to her as his "colored 'housekeeper' and mistress." Even friendly newspapers habitually dubbed her "his famous housekeeper."[2]

The precise nature of their relationship will probably never be known. Toward the end of his life, Stevens once compared himself to former vice president Richard M. Johnson, a Kentucky slaveholder whose mixed-race housekeeper had borne him two light-skinned daughters, whom he had introduced into white society. Although Stevens was already a dedicated antislavery man at the time he met Smith in the late 1840s, their friendship undoubtedly played a role in his growing support for social equality and civil rights. At least in private conversation, Smith was, according to one admiring journalist, "an ardent advocate of her race, untiring in working for its promotion," while the congressman came to endorse the "absolute equality of sex and race." Ever the courageous politician, Stevens, now in the twilight of his political career, emerged as the most uncompromising voice in Washington regarding a complete reorganization of American race relations. "I care not what you may say of Negro equality" he warned his constituents. "I care not what you may say of radicalism; these are my principles, and with the help of God I shall die with them."[3]

As had so many, Smith and Stevens suffered during the war and the early years of Reconstruction. Although still in his teens, Isaac Smith, Lydia's youngest son, volunteered for the Sixth Colored Infantry and saw action in Virginia. During the 1863 invasion of Pennsylvania, Confederate general Jubal Early took special pleasure in burning Stevens's iron foundry near Caledonia to the ground in retaliation for "arming their negroes." Like Judge Hugh L. Bond, Stevens carefully preserved his hate mail, all of it anonymous. One Washington neighbor sent a Christmas message asking God to forgive him "for these great crimes" of seeking "to elevate your black bastards in the Social Scale." From New Orleans, a white supremacist warned Stevens that he had been marked for death. "Your doom is sealed!!!!!! Prepare thy soul for its swift flight. The bony finger has touched your pillow, [and] nothing can change its decree."[4]

Although former Confederates failed to follow through with their threat, Stevens's health was never robust. As 1867 dawned, the seventy-four-year-old congressman began to prepare for the end. Stevens purchased two lots in a cemetery in Lancaster, Pennsylvania—the second, evidently, for Smith—only to discover that the graveyard banned black burials. At length he found that Schreiner's Protestant cemetery, while not exactly integrated, had interred one black body. An associate of the congressman believed that Stevens hoped Smith, who had by now lived with him for nineteen years, would overcome her Catholic sensibilities enough to be buried beside him. Either way, the black-owned *New Orleans Tribune* was pleased to report, the "brave old man" could not "consent to have his bones laid in a cemetery where any of God's children were excluded."[5]

That done, Stevens began to draft his will. Although he estimated the loss of his iron foundry at roughly fifty thousand dollars, he had cash enough left to endow a home and school for orphans. In a curious provision, given the absence of Muslims in postwar Pennsylvania, Stevens demanded that "[n]either poor Germans, Irish or Mohammedans or any others on account of their race or religion" be excluded. "All the inmates shall be educated in the same classes and manner, without regard to color," he stipulated. "They shall be fed at the same table." Stevens had lost his father at an early age to alcoholism, and his bequest of another iron foundry to one nephew was contingent on the young man "abstain[ing] from all intoxicating drink" for five years. Finally, Stevens left Smith either five hundred dollars each year for as long as she might live or five thousand dollars in one payment, as she chose. "Mrs. Smith has some furniture of her own, used in common with mine," he

*Born in 1815 in Adams County, Pennsylvania, Lydia Hamilton Smith was a
light-skinned woman who adhered to the Catholic faith of her white father, a man
of Irish descent. Smith bore her free black husband two sons, but following his
death she took a position as housekeeper with attorney and future congressman
Thaddeus Stevens. Democratic newspapers dubbed her "Mrs. Stevens," and in
his will Stevens bequeathed her a lump sum of five thousand dollars or five
hundred dollars annually for the rest of her life. Smith used the money to buy the
congressman's home, where she had lived for many years. Although historians will
surely never know the precise nature of the relationship between Stevens and
Smith—and Pennsylvania law prohibited a marriage between a white man and a
woman of color—their friendship symbolized the nation's new beginning in race
relations following the war. Courtesy Lancaster County Historical Society.*

observed, and he wished also to allow her to live in his house for one
year after his death."[6]

The alliance, whatever its precise nature, between Stevens and Smith
personified the grander union forming between black Americans and

progressive Republicans by the last moments of 1866, as politicians such as Stevens, horrified by the Black Codes and the rising tide of white violence, embraced earlier black demands for civil and voting rights. Aware that Andrew Johnson had squandered an opportunity to bring about a new day in racial affairs, this developing coalition increasingly agreed on the need for the president's removal. "It is plain there can be no reconstruction till Johnson is impeached and removed," concluded one black editor. But white racism throughout the republic, and not the obstinate president in the White House, was their target. The possibility of impeachment was not central to their crusade; Johnson was merely an obstacle to be eliminated as they labored to move the country forward. Modern studies of the era invariably place the impeachment battle at the center of the story, but contemporary black activists thought otherwise. "The people have something to say in this Republic," commented Louis Charles Roudanez. "Andrew Johnson is but one man. The pro-slavery masses are but a political party."[7]

One indication that the progressive alliance had to push hard not just against an obdurate president but also against a northern public still wrestling with its own racial prejudices was the projected Fourteenth Amendment then moving through the states. Introduced into the Senate in early 1866, the lengthy proposal consisted of five sections. Since the 1857 Dred Scott decision yet stood regarding federal citizenship, Section 1 clarified that any person born or naturalized in the United States was both a federal and state citizen. Seeking to nullify the Black Codes by elevating portions of the 1866 Civil Rights Act into the Constitution, the amendment restricted states from depriving "any person of life, liberty, or property, without due process of law" or denying "to any person within its jurisdiction the equal protection of the laws." Section 3 denied political office to those who had previously taken an oath to support the Constitution and then had willingly "engaged in insurrection or rebellion" against the nation, a wording that exempted Confederate draftees. Dismayed progressives observed that Section 2 did not explicitly enfranchise black voters. Instead, the proposed amendment reduced Congressional representation in "proportion [to] the number of such male citizens" denied access to the ballot. The proposal, Stevens told the House, "was not all he desired, but he was content to accept it for the present." By June 13, both chambers passed the revision. In the House, the amendment was agreed to by the comfortable margin of 128 to 37, every Republican casting his lot with the majority.[8]

As amendments were not regular legislation, Johnson was not in a position to once again employ his veto pen. But he made his opposition known. He informed one audience that he would cheerfully spend twenty thousand dollars of his own money to defeat the amendment. Elsewhere he warned crowds that it threatened "Negro rule," although he well knew that the revision was silent on African American voting rights. Connecticut and New Hampshire promptly ratified the amendment, but South Carolina rejected it by a resounding 95 to 1. Of the Confederate states, only Tennessee, dominated by Governor W. G. Brownlow, Johnson's political enemy, ratified during the course of 1866. "The vilest traitors" controlled South Carolina's government, one white Unionist informed Stevens, adding that he had "slowly but deliberately come to the conclusion that negro suffrage is our only hope." Editor Roudanez agreed: "The rebels were neither entitled now, as Johnson held, nor after ratifying the amendment, as Congress said, to rule the South." Blacks and white Unionists would decide policy. On this, former Confederates and President Johnson proved to be the progressives' best if unintentional supporters. Worried conservatives warned Governor Benjamin L. Orr that South Carolina's lopsided rejection of the moderate amendment would only strengthen the political hand of Stevens and other so-called radicals in Congress.[9]

The defiance in southern state capitols filtered down to city streets, where it manifested itself in further targeted killings. Richmond Democrats celebrated Christmas Day with "savage violence." One white Republican "was hung to the limb of a tree in the Court House yard," while "Seven negroes near the house have been whipped & *one killed*." In Texas, an entire block of black homes near Brenham was torched. Although not yet readmitted to the halls of Congress, the state defiantly selected two prominent secessionists for the federal Senate and elected a Confederate brigadier general as governor. Despite the previous spring's Civil Rights Act, "fifteen men dressed in white clothes" leapt aboard a New Orleans streetcar and shot black rider Robert Spradley "in the hand and thigh." Restaurateur and activist George T. Downing was thrown off a Harlem railroad and beaten by white toughs. Stevens warned the House that southern judges continued to hand down racially based decisions. After committing the same crime, he alleged, "white men only received a slap upon the back, while black men received seventeen lashes, every lash bringing the blood." Nor was corporal abuse the only evidence of white jurists attempting to restore the antebellum social order. In January 1867, Thomas Watkins, a Maryland justice of the peace, refused "to take colored testimony" in the case of Alcinda Warner, a black woman who charged a white man with "assault and rape," including from the victim herself.[10]

On January 3, Stevens rose to introduce legislation that went beyond previous Congressional demands of sharing Reconstruction policy with the president. Repeating earlier Republican assertions that the Confederacy had forfeited its collective statehood by seceding, Stevens argued the states could only be restored by Congress. Echoing Roudanez and other black editors, Stevens added that ratification of the Fourteenth Amendment was not necessarily sufficient for renewed statehood, given the upswing of white violence and the reactionary behavior of state officials. At the same time, Republicans passed a resolution asking the president to provide Congress "with the number and names of persons worth more than $20,000 who had been pardoned." White publishers were apoplectic. A Galveston newspaper worried that Stevens's bill would "invest the North with all the powers of a conqueror, and all the rights of conquest over the South." But the Republican press, including self-identified moderates who were aghast at Johnson's 1866 campaign tour, was uniformly supportive. "There never was a people in such terrible peril as the loyal people of the South, white or black," observed a Boston editor. "Unless Congress proceeded at once and did something to protect those people from the barbarians that are now murdering the whites, and putting into secret graves hundreds of thousands of colored people, it would be liable to the just censure of the world for its neglect, its cowardice, or its want of ability." Even a white Republican from Leesburg, Virginia, assured Stevens that while there was "some small amount of Squirming about the privileges extended to the recent Slaves," there was "no Union man who does not infinitely more fear and dread the domination of the recent Rebels than that of the Recent Slaves."[11]

For moderate Republicans, the trickiest part of the black convention movement's program—a platform increasingly sanctioned by Stevens and Senator Charles Sumner—to endorse was a color-blind franchise. Johnson and the Democrats were united in their opposition, insisting that black Americans were not yet prepared for the responsibility that came with the vote, although a good many blacks both North and South were property-holding taxpayers and far more literate than the president himself. But moderate Republicans fretted that most northern voters were uneasy in pushing for a national franchise. When Sumner raised the possibility of a bill guaranteeing black suffrage across the nation, his Massachusetts colleague Senator Henry Wilson cautioned that not "a square mile of the United States" existed where that issue did not cost Republicans white votes. Fear of a partisan voter backlash in part explained such concerns, but some progressives also thought it hypocritical to impose on southern states a reform not found in many parts of the North. "How can you look Rebel States in the face when you have required colored suffrage of them and fail to require it in the other States?" one wondered. Black activists responded that the obvious remedy was either a nationwide bill along the lines proposed by Sumner, or a renewed effort on the part of northern Republican assemblymen, but appeals to political justice made little headway in early 1867.[12]

For nervous moderates, the hard reality of electoral math provided the more compelling argument for black voting rights. Although suffrage requirements traditionally lay with each state, Constitutional clauses pertaining to apportionment complicated the question. New Englanders had long despised the portion of Article I, Section 3, which allowed slaveholding states to count three of five enslaved residents when it came to the number of Congressional delegates accorded each state. But as the Thirteenth Amendment effectively erased that clause, states of the former Confederacy would be granted even greater clout in Washington following their readmission to Congress. For Missouri Republican Benjamin Gratz Brown, the question was not whether blacks should have the vote, but "whether those who claimed to be their masters shall cast it for them." In the short term, restoration on the basis of white supremacy, as a number of Republican editors complained, meant that "the curious result of the war" was to confer "on a rebel voter in South Carolina a power equal, in national affairs, to that of two loyal voters in New York." Few Maryland Republicans beyond Judge Bond were courageous enough to endorse the black vote, but the editor of the *Annapolis Gazette* protested that his state had "double the white population of South Carolina, [yet] the Conservatives desire that State to have the right to send to Congress five Representatives, being the same as Maryland." In the long term, as states received an electoral count equal to their total Washington delegation, white southern voters would also gain more influence in presidential elections. Abraham Lincoln had demonstrated that a northern candidate could win without southern votes, but that was against a fractured Democratic Party and with the three-fifths clause in place. Looking ahead to 1868, *New-York Tribune* editor Horace Greeley worried that if southern "Blacks are not enfranchised, [no less than antiwar Congressman Clement] Vallandigham could beat Gen. Grant for President."[13]

Grasping the national implications of enfranchising southern blacks, Democrats grumbled about the inevitable next step. Those Republicans who "pretend affection for the black man," bellowed California Democrat Franklin E. Felton, might soon seek to "elevate and enfranchise [the] saffron hued Chinaman." Denied political cover by the White House, even those high-ranking ex-Confederates who promoted reform in the name of sectional harmony were verbally assaulted by Democrats. When former Confederate postmaster general John H. Reagan of Texas published an open letter recommending acceptance of black freedom and voting rights, an old colleague advised him that any "candidate for anything from governor to constable [would] regard it as his duty to denounce you morning, noon, and night." Fiscally minded editors, aware of black demands for public education, charged that with "the mass of ignorant negroes" enfranchised, the new governments in the South were sure to "inaugurate schemes of taxation that will practically be nearly as bad as confiscation itself."[14]

Pragmatic Republicans turned such rhetoric on its head. Few editors repeated black arguments that African American taxpayers deserved representation, or that black veterans had earned the franchise. Instead, many suggested not only that "a million [new] black voters" would render "the colored men respected by the whites," but that competitive political contests in the South could help to advance Republican free labor ideals of industry and social improvement. "They are going to work hard," editorialized one New York publisher. The vote was not merely a right, added another, but a way to "protect the persons and property of both races." The "old Southern order of things is passing away and all things are becoming new." If blacks had the vote, they could not only elect Ulysses S. Grant in 1868, but advance their own teachers and veterans into local and statewide office and protect their rights without recourse to federal power. When white southerners learned "that their only sure hope is not *dis*franchisement but *en*franchisement," observed Greeley, "they will be on praying ground."[15]

As ever, Johnson and southern Democrats did their utmost to injure their own cause. In February 1867, the president infuriated Congress by first commuting the sentences of, and then finally pardoning, four former Confederates who had murdered three Maine soldiers. Secretary of War Edwin M. Stanton ordered them imprisoned for life after trial by a military tribunal, but regarding that order as unconstitutional, Johnson discharged the four. When South Carolina authorities refused to press charges, exasperated Republicans rose in Congress to argue for "the necessity of military interposition to enforce justice, as the Civil Courts are not to be relied upon." Southern whites showered Johnson with thanks for upholding the proposition "that the white race was superior to the black," while southern blacks peppered Stevens with evidence that "Rebel Scoundrils are murdering our Union citizens" as state governments sought only to "collect up all such arms" held by African American veterans. By month's end, twelve states had rejected the Fourteenth Amendment, two more than necessary to prevent its ratification. Moderate Republicans who had anticipated the modest amendment to be the final Reconstruction measure began to agree with Stevens that still more progressive legislation was necessary.[16]

Republicans passed a flurry of legislation in late February and early March. The House Judiciary Committee amended a military bill to suspend all further payments to former masters who had enlisted their slaves in federal forces during the war. Another bill authorized the president to "prevent the infliction of corporal punishment in the late rebellious States," which served to nullify portions of the Black Codes. The House then turned to Stevens's bill, reported out of the Reconstruction Committee, which established "military authority in the Southern States." In what was to become four interlocking acts collectively dubbed the Reconstruction Acts, the House version divided the former Confederacy—with the exception of Tennessee, which had ratified the Fourteenth Amendment—into five military districts, each under the command of a general responsible for seeing federal laws enforced and offenders punished. The Senate version added further requirements before states could send delegations to Congress. States were obligated to ratify the Fourteenth Amendment, to allow "all loyal male citizens twenty-one years of age" to vote "without distinction of race," and to call for new state constitutional conventions. At least temporarily, the bill excluded from suffrage those who had taken an oath of loyalty to the republic but then actively "engaged in rebellion, [given] aid and comfort thereto, or voted for any act of secession." The final version of what was generally known as the Military Reconstruction Act maintained the Senate requirements and stipulated that the current state governments were merely "provisional."[17]

As the army was critical to enforcement of the act, Republicans believed it necessary not only to wrest control of the process over southern restoration from the president, but to simultaneously reduce Johnson's authority over the military. Two other bills, the Tenure of Office Act and the Army Appropriations Act, specified that the president could issue military orders only through the General of the Army, a provision that essentially blocked Johnson from direct communication with the military commanders in the South. Both held that the general and other presidential appointees could only be removed with Senate permission. The laws were designed to protect the positions of Grant, who was serving as the General of the Army and was increasingly a Republican ally, and of Secretary of War Stanton, the most progressive voice in the cabinet. Democrats charged that the laws infringed upon the president's role of commander in chief, but Republicans replied that military oversight was a shared prerogative and that the right to confirm appointments implied an equivalent ability to reject removals. As the collective acts specified precisely what white southerners were required to do prior to readmission, one Republican remarked, Congress had "not interfere[d] with any Southern provisional government which is conducted in good faith, and with a desire to secure equal justice to all men."[18]

Democrats across the nation denounced the package. "The nigger will be the master, the white man the slave," fumed one conservative Manhattan editor, "that or another rebellion." As expected, the obstinate Johnson vetoed almost all of the measures, signing only the bill that ceased military bounty payments to former masters. Ignoring the more temperate draft messages prepared for him by Secretary William H. Seward, Johnson vetoed the acts on both constitutional and policy grounds. Black Americans had no capacity for self-government, he argued. "The negroes have not asked for the privilege of voting," he added, blithely ignoring the demands of dozens of black conventions, and "the vast majority of them have no idea what it means." Also as expected, Congress promptly overrode his vetoes. The president clearly refused to adopt any part of their program, but Republicans trusted that other white southerners might now learn "that they cannot modify the conditions of their return by maintaining a posture of rebellious contumacy." With large majorities against Johnson in both the House and Senate, Roudanez observed, the remaining question was if the laws would "be faithfully executed," or whether the nearly insignificant president planned to continue in his course.[19]

The collective bills indicated that even moderate Republicans finally grasped what black activists had been saying since the passage of the Black Codes. The Civil War yet continued, if by other means than organized military resistance. With the antebellum federal support for slavery gone, white legislators had turned to state venues for restrictive measures, and with Confederate armies vanished from the fields, Confederate veterans resorted to sporadic but targeted violence to achieve their ends. Johnson might think their laws unconstitutional, one Massachusetts editor observed, but Republicans agreed "that the rebellion still exists and they are legislating for a state of war." Abolitionist Wendell Phillips resorted to politically charged military references in defending the package of laws. Although Grant's march toward Richmond had been costly and perilous, Phillips admitted, it had been "more dangerous" still to do nothing, and so Grant, the Republican, had advanced toward his goal. By comparison, General George McClellan, a conservative New Jersey Democrat, had demonstrated the folly of making sure "that a certain step incurred no risk before" taking it. "We hope Congress will not fight this battle on McClellan principles." With Johnson's capacity for mischief diminished, Republicans hoped they could return to the brief moment of promise in the spring of 1865 when so many southern whites had appeared ready to accept the new order. "If the [white] people of the South themselves find no good and substantial grounds of objection to the reconstruction bills," observed one New Yorker, "the wind will be taken out of the sails of Northern conservatives."[20]

Even if southern whites did not acquiesce, in the wake of the Memphis and New Orleans riots most Republicans preferred government action and political justice to sectional reconciliation. "I want ample protection to the freedmen," one constituent lectured Illinois senator Lyman Trumbull, "and if we can't accomplish it any other way keep an army in the south for twenty years to come." Although slow to embrace the egalitarian principles, at least in the opinion of black conventioneers, Republicans at last had incorporated the belief "that the political equality of the negroes follows logically and necessarily upon their freedom." As ever in practical politics, the fact that the votes of southern blacks might sustain the general platform of the northern-based party helped to prod moderates into action, as did the complaints of white Unionists and former Whigs in the South. "Without the colored vote, the white Unionists would have been left in the hands of the rebels," Sumner confided to British abolitionist John Bright. "The colored vote was a *necessity*." Democrats charged that the acts were "punishments" concocted by merciless victors, but southern Unionists responded that secessionists had "lost position by [their] bad conduct" and could "regain it only by [their] good conduct." Speaking in Columbia, South Carolina, John Quincy Adams II added that "universal suffrage" was the result of the Black Codes and not of defeat in 1865. Blacks welcomed the laws as necessary and long-overdue reforms. The laws also, as Washington progressives hoped, had an immediate impact. Only one month after their passage, in April 1867, Bureau agent Alvan Gillem reported from Vicksburg that "whether induced by the passage of the 'Military bill' or by other considerations, the [local] Courts in this district appear more desirous than heretofore to mete out full justice to the freedmen."[21]

Several southern governors agreed that the cost of resistance was too high. Louisiana's James M. Wells issued a proclamation conceding that "the authorities of the State are only provisional." In South Carolina, Governor Orr announced that he would "cheerfully perform" all of the requirements imposed by Congress. Former Georgia governor Joseph E. Brown delivered speeches in Atlanta and Savannah, cautioning whites to "accept the terms of Congress," as "persistent opposition will exasperate the Northern people and may lead to confiscation." Virginia's Roger Pryor, a former Confederate officer, published an open letter in which he urged his state's white citizens to "accept the situation" and to "recognize and respect the rights of the colored race." After two years wasted, Republicans thought the country finally ready to advance on democratization. Black commentators such as Roudanez wondered if Johnson would continue to embolden the now-silenced cadre of white reactionaries, but in a public warning to the White House, new Massachusetts congressman Benjamin F. Butler delivered an address to both chambers of the Maine legislature, "the galleries and floor being crowded to excess," in which he discussed the remedy of impeachment and the possible "necessity of deposing Mr. Johnson." The president could not say he had not been warned.[22]

With the Republican Party formally behind black voting rights, at least in the former Confederacy, the black convention movement, always rightly suspicious of white party leaders, quickly fell into line and embraced the party label. A "Radical Republican Convention" in New Orleans's Economy Hall elected Captain James H. Ingraham, a former Mississippi slave and veteran of the Seventy-third USCT and an early member of the National Equal Rights League, as the proceeding's chairman; praised "the just and patriotic execution of the military reconstruction laws; and demanded "the disfranchisement of all members of secession conventions [and] all editors who advocated secession." On April 13, blacks gathered in Augusta, Georgia, to proclaim their support for "the Republican party," for the abolition of corporal punishment, and for "the right of all colors to hold office." That same day, roughly five thousand people attended a "Radical mass meeting of negroes" in Nashville. So many attendees "pour[ed] in from the country, afoot, on horseback, and in carts and wagons," that organizers had to move the rally outside. Later that month, African Americans meeting at the Virginia State Republican Convention endorsed the federal laws passed to date, but warned that their continuing political loyalty required more than voting rights. Several speakers brought applauding delegates to their feet by shouting that they were "for confiscation," and that "if Congress did not give the negroes lands, they should be taken by violence."[23]

Perhaps the largest convention, and one that demonstrated the possibilities of the emerging progressive coalition, took place in Savannah on April 2. Seven thousand people attended a "great reconstruction meeting," among them James Johnson, a Unionist opposed to secession and briefly Andrew Johnson's appointee as state governor. The interracial assembly praised Congressional Republicans for their leadership and promised to "stand shoulder to shoulder in reorganizing our State Government." When a white speaker patronized blacks in the hall by insisting that "politics is not the study of a day, but of years of toil," delegate James M. Simms seized the podium to remind white delegates that "Colored men were not fools." A former Savannah slave and the brother of runaway Thomas Simms, whose capture in Boston in 1851 and return to Georgia had become an abolitionist rallying cry, James Simms assured the audience that blacks "knew enough to fight right, and they would vote right" too. Black Georgians insisted upon "white and colored aldermen, and white and colored police men, and the sooner people knew it the better." Tunis Campbell spoke next, and he echoed Simms's view that the convention signaled a new and "glorious day" for Georgia, as "white and black men had at last met under the old flag they loved so well to march to Union and victory." Within weeks, the "Black Republican Party" had nominated Simms and Campbell for the state assembly.[24]

Similar meetings were held in Montgomery and Charleston. At the Alabama conference, "both whites and colored citizens" favored "faithful concurrence in the requirements of the military bill" and called for the early meeting of a state constitutional convention. At the Charleston meeting, nearly five thousand blacks packed the hall to hear Francis L. Cardozo, a black teacher with the American Missionary Association and one of the activists instrumental in the recreation of the city's AME congregation two years earlier. Although far fewer whites attended the Charleston convention than in other cities, Cardozo assured the assemblage that South Carolina African Americans were "not opposed to united" action with whites, provided they adopted the Republican label "and intend[ed] to vote for Republican candidates." Blacks would "gladly welcome union with our Southern friends," promised the future South Carolina secretary of state, "but let them join the party which is true." A meeting that July in Columbia approved a platform "essentially similar to that adopted at Charleston." By New Year's Day of 1868, blacks throughout the nation had good reason to celebrate the fifth anniversary of the Emancipation Proclamation. In San Francisco, blacks paraded behind Captain A. G. Denison in two "large cars decorated with American flags [and] filled with the children of the Public and Sunday schools." Only the method "proposed by Congress," noted one speaker, "was the surest way to prevent future rebellions, and to make treason odious and loyalty honorable."[25]

If white Carolinians were reluctant to openly identify with a party so closely associated with Abraham Lincoln, that was hardly the case with Unionists in those corners of the South that had not been part of the Confederacy. Maryland's increasingly radical judge, Hugh L. Bond, attended partisan rallies, called for black voting rights, and worked with black teachers and ministers in the name of educational reform. Baltimore's progressive coalition quickly ran afoul of Governor Thomas Swann, a Johnson supporter and a bitter critic of "negro suffrage." Maryland Democrats urged voters to "sustain President Johnson against the reckless, wicked, and relentless assaults of the radical party." But reformers such as Bond continued to believe that Heaven favored the righteous. Choosing to interpret Republican calls for democratization as "armed opposition," Swann journeyed to Washington to ask the president to help "prevent mobs of Radicals from other States rushing to Baltimore and joining the mobs of Radicals there." The governor also publicly recommended that blacks emigrate "to some more congenial locality where [their] destructive characteristics will furnish no barrier to the enjoyment of social and political rights." Rather than denounce Swann's fears as politically inspired paranoia or join with other southern whites in recognizing the wisdom in working with Congress, Baltimore's chief of police threatened to arrest Republican voters on Election Day.[26]

Black and white Republicans met the challenge by gathering to "condemn the recent course of Governor Swann" and endorse a platform of "manhood suffrage." Conservatives "call us *'negro worshippers,'*" one white conventioneer retorted. But Unionists had stood by the republic, while Democrats had marched south into Virginia to fight for the Confederacy, and so the "subject of *Rebel suffrage* is one of vastly more importance than *negro suffrage*." Black delegate William H. Brown, a Baltimore businessman, rose to praise Bond for his public support for black voting rights. As had many black conventioneers over the previous years, Brown compared the political claims of white voters against those "made sacred by the blood of those who fell at Fort Pillow." As it happened, Bond enjoyed the authority to do far more than merely advocate for black rights. After the chief of police continued to threaten Republican voters, the judge ordered three of his commissioners arrested "on charge of attempting to break the peace." Bond also dragged before his court a Democratic sheriff who was rumored to be "summoning a posse" to aid the commissioners. The judge warned him to desist and added that if the sheriff did "not obey," he would issue a warrant for the sheriff's arrest as well. Bond's actions gained him national attention, and letters flooded in praising "the prudence with which the rebels were checkmated." There on the streets of Baltimore emerged a very different sort of picture from the one journalists painted of events in Washington. Although it was easy for editors to focus on the growing battle between Johnson and Congressional Republicans, the actions of so-called radicals such as Bond and the interracial conventions across the South suggested instead renewed cooperation between whites and blacks who wished to finally bring an end to the Civil War.[27]

When violence flared in Mobile in mid-May 1867, responsible southerners and federal authorities quickly put an end to the disorder. Pennsylvania congressman William D. Kelley had traveled south to address emerging Republican organizations, and on May 14 he was scheduled to speak in Mobile. A group of white hecklers approached the outdoor rally, threatening to "pull him down." Blacks in the audience were well armed, however, and local police moved in to arrest the hecklers. Both sides opened fire. One white attacker and a black defender died in the melee. Unwilling to return to the turmoil of the previous two years, "many of the best citizens of Mobile" published an editorial in the next morning's newspapers, "expressing unqualified condemnation of the parties engaged in the disturbance of the republican meeting last night." The fact that Mobile's police force sought to arrest the hecklers reflected the new tone imposed by the Reconstruction Acts, which put an end to the antebellum regimes and the collusion between policemen and white mobs seen the previous year in Charleston and Memphis. In the Fifth Military District of Louisiana and Texas, General Philip Sheridan ordered mayors under his jurisdiction to "adjust the present police force so that at least half of said force shall be composed of ex-Union soldiers," a command that allowed for the hiring of black veterans. Across the Fourth Military District of Arkansas and Mississippi, General Edward O. C. Ord established fifteen posts for the two thousand soldiers under his command and promptly hauled four whites before army courts for assaulting blacks. One received a sentence of ten years in the state penitentiary. By the fall of 1867, a pleased Bureau agent Alvan Gillem reported, violence against African Americans had virtually ceased in the region.[28]

State authorities continued to function, but when governors or assemblies failed to maintain order, the generals in charge of the five districts moved quickly to fill the legislative void. Ord ordered "all persons who voluntarily exiled themselves upon Lee's surrender, and subsequently returned, to report to his headquarters to take the oath of parole." On another occasion, he banned all concealed weapons. Despite a dramatic decline in violence and unprecedented cooperation between federal commanders and civilian authorities, President Johnson continued in his quest to end Reconstruction. Unable to bypass a Congress that habitually overrode his vetoes, Johnson determined to negate the laws by refusing to enforce them, or by overruling those who did so. When Sheridan removed those Louisiana officials complicit in the New Orleans murders, Johnson reprimanded the general and instructed him to stay his order. Although hesitant to clash openly with his commander in chief, Grant encouraged Sheridan to continue in his course. With that, Johnson decided to replace Sheridan and General Daniel Sickles, a former Democrat and the commander of the Second Military District of South Carolina, who had angered the president by issuing Order No. 32, which "declar[ed] the right of all citizens, without distinction of color, to serve on juries." In a private interview with the president, Supreme Court Chief Justice Salmon P. Chase "remonstrated most earnestly against interference with either Sheridan or [Secretary] Stanton," but Johnson charged ahead, replacing Sheridan with a conservative Democrat, General Winfield Scott Hancock. The new commander immediately removed eight black Republicans on the New Orleans City Council and replaced them with whites. Grant overruled Hancock, prompting one Democratic editor to sneer that "Grant is as good a nigger radical now as anybody." In Texas, with Sheridan gone, violence spiked, and Texas Republicans pointed to at least sixty-two murders in December 1867 and January 1868 as evidence of a "perceptible increase" in political assassinations.[29]

Recent votes in Congress indicated that even moderate Republicans no longer supported the president, but their belated awareness that dropping Vice President Hannibal Hamlin from the ticket in 1864 had resulted in catastrophe did not necessarily mean that they were ready to remove Johnson from office. Each new tactic from the president, however, cost him crucial support among those centrists who had reluctantly concluded that their wisest course was to endure Johnson's presence until his term expired on March 4, 1869. Previous presidents had removed generals, but Johnson's immediate predecessor had done so for incompetence. In 1863 Lincoln had famously placed Joseph Hooker in command of the Army of the Potomac despite distrusting the general's personal politics. So determined was he to brook no disagreement from subordinates, that Johnson now ordered the federal government to withhold all advertising patronage from those editors who failed to endorse his Reconstruction program. He fired one Illinois-based tax collector "merely because [he] cannot think as the President does" on larger policy matters. As early as December 1865, a Republican doctor in Bloomington, Illinois, mailed Trumbull a petition demanding "the Impeachment of President Johnson—or the Tennessee Tailor," and in the following month a gathering of "German radicals in St. Louis" denounced Johnson and called for his impeachment for failing to enforce federal laws.[30]

For Johnson, removing innocuous tax collectors and reinterpreting federal legislation to conservative generals was not enough to end Congressional Reconstruction. Since the generals in the field ultimately answered to Stanton, that meant that the secretary, like Sickles and Sheridan, had to be replaced. Although a Democrat early in life and briefly attorney general in the James Buchanan administration, Stanton had impressed Lincoln enough to be named secretary of war in early 1862, and the convert to Republicanism was the most progressive holdover in Johnson's cabinet. Having lost a wife and daughter to illness and a beloved brother to suicide, Stanton could be morose and brusque, and in meeting after meeting he bluntly informed the president that federal laws must be enforced. Waiting until Congress adjourned, on August 5, 1867, Johnson mailed Stanton a one-sentence missive, telling him that his "resignation as Secretary of War [would] be accepted." Johnson's request was designed to sidestep the Tenure of Office Act, and Stanton knew it. The following day he posted an equally curt reply, informing Johnson that "public considerations" constrained him from resigning "before the next meeting of Congress" in late November. Several delegations of prominent Republicans hastened to the War Department to urge Stanton to hold firm. Seven days later, when it became clear that his secretary was not inclined to quit, Johnson announced the suspension of Stanton and the interim appointment of Grant. The president also threatened to fire General John Pope, whose jurisdiction stretched over the Third Military District (including Georgia, Alabama, and Florida), unless he ceased to carry out the instructions of Congress. On December 28, when Pope continued to follow those instructions and, as had Sickles, ordered that African Americans be allowed to serve on juries, he too was fired despite Grant's objections. Several conservative journals, including the *New York Times* and the *Boston Daily Advertiser*, grudgingly concluded that impeachment was now the only remedy, as did the *Chicago Tribune*, which had previously run editorials against removal.[31]

When Congress reconvened late that fall, Johnson, in compliance with the Tenure of Office Act, formally notified Congress of his actions and requested its compliance with Stanton's removal. Instead, the Senate Committee on Military Affairs voted 35 to 6 not to accept his dismissal. On November 25, the House Judiciary Committee, by a vote of 5 to 4, moved to impeach the president for violating the Tenure of Office Act and attempting to circumvent the Reconstruction Acts. The president hoped that Grant would remain in the War Department until Stanton appealed the question to the Supreme Court, which might then strike down the law as unconstitutional. Grant had only agreed to serve in the cabinet as a way of limiting the president's damage in the South, however, and he saw little logic in allowing the president to ruin both of their political careers. Desperate, Johnson made yet another overt appeal to racism, warning Congress in his December 3 message that Republicans were not content with granting blacks political rights, but intended "that they shall rule the white race." Even in the president's home state, white Unionists lost all patience with Johnson. An infuriated Tennessee assembly, by a party line vote of 50 to 20, formally resolved to instruct the state's senators and congressmen "to vote for the impeachment of Andrew Johnson." Texas Unionists agreed. Johnson "ignores the loyal white men of the South," one complained, "and desired to keep the right of citizenship" from black men. "He is doing more to bring disgrace upon this nation than Jeff Davis."[32]

If Grant was looking ahead toward the November 1868 elections, activists far outside of Washington's corridors understood that more was at stake than the careers of a few white politicians. With a different executive in charge, one willing to enforce the laws passed by Congressional majorities, the hard-won era of military and civilian cooperation might continue to change the political face of the South, and with that, the entire nation. Despite all of the bills passed by Congress, from the Civil Rights Act to the Reconstruction Acts, the fundamental flaw with the Republican program, Wisconsin senator Timothy Otis Howe admitted, was their naïve hope that the president would not simply ignore legislation passed over his veto. For their part, the enemies of reform confidently expected Johnson to continue to do just that until his last day in office. Southern conservatives should be "playing possum," counseled one Alabama Democrat, until they could retake control of their states and then "tear up their nigger constitutions and make new ones on their own definitions of republicanism." A white Louisiana journalist concurred, writing that if Johnson could just hold onto office, "the Radical work from first to last will be swept from the statute books and reversed, and the 'bottom rail' of the fence (the nigger) will be placed where it belongs."[33]

Although they recognized that the problem with America was far deeper than one man, black editors correctly regarded Johnson as a major impediment to progress, and they wanted him gone. Louis Charles Roudanez observed that the "unfortunate policy" of allowing the reactionary minority to reclaim power in the South had produced the New Orleans "massacre," and Philip A. Bell, the self-proclaimed "thoroughly radical" editor of the San Francisco *Elevator*, denounced "his obstinacy Andrew Johnson" and his "disorganizing plans." Johnson's December message to Congress especially drew their ire. The Military Reconstruction Act, "the work of the wisest Congress ever assembled," Bell argued, was "contemptuously repudiated by one man obtruding his individual opinions against the wisdom of the Representatives of the whole people." Since a handful of "Southern men, emboldened by President Johnson," argued the black editor of Augusta's *Loyal Georgian*, sought to accomplish "through the agency of the Democratic organization, what they failed to do through the agency of bayonets and bullets," it would be "not a blunder but a crime" not to impeach. "The removal of Andrew Johnson would be a lifting from the Southern people a greater load than any under which they have ever suffered," agreed a Charleston editor.[34]

Never one to back down, Johnson continued to rail against "the effort to Africanize the half of our country." At one particularly tumultuous cabinet meeting, Johnson and Grant argued over the Tenure of Office Act, with Johnson denouncing the law as unconstitutional and so of no legal standing. Grant replied that until the courts ruled, the law would have to be obeyed. With the Senate refusing to consent to Stanton's dismissal, Grant quit the cabinet, returning the keys to his office and alerting the president by messenger that he was obliged to return to his former position as General of the Army. Johnson then offered the cabinet post to General William T. Sherman, and when that gambit failed, to Adjutant General Lorenzo Thomas. Ironically, the choice of Thomas was a last-moment bid to appeal to progressive Republicans, as Thomas's 1863 Special Order No. 45 had helped to establish the policy of turning abandoned plantations near Vicksburg over to female and aged slaves. Since that promising policy had foundered due to Johnson's early edicts, the attempt placated nobody, and Thomas, who did not desire the position, found himself briefly arrested for violating the Tenure of Office Act. Stanton remained "camped in the war office," one editor laughed, and Johnson "made no progress in [actually] ousting Stanton," while the Republicans were nearly united "in favor of removing the arch disturber of the nation's peace.'"[35]

On February 24, 1868, following several days of deliberations, Thaddeus Stevens closed the Congressional debates by speaking in favor of his resolution to impeach. So weak that his remarks could only be heard by those sitting nearby, Stevens insisted that impeachment was both a political and a legal procedure. For two years, starting with his attempts to govern the defeated Confederate states without consulting Congress, Johnson had committed a series of "crimes" against the republic. Echoing black editors and activists across the nation, Stevens insisted that the coming vote was not "the temporary triumph of a political party," but was undertaken to see whether "the whole continent shall be filled with a free and untrammeled people or shall be a nest of shrinking, cowardly slaves." The House of Representatives voted 126 to 47 in favor of his resolution on impeachment. One week later, the House adopted eleven articles, most devoted to the Stanton affair. Speaking in support of the charges, Congressman Kelley, who personally had witnessed violence in Mobile, reminded his colleagues what was at stake: "The unsheeted ghosts of the two thousand murdered negroes in Texas, cry, if the dead ever invoke vengeance, for the punishment of Andrew Johnson."[36]

The progressives' course proved harder in the Senate. Republicans required a two-thirds vote to convict. While they numerically possessed that margin, virtually every party member would have to vote for removal to achieve it. Radicals argued that by emphasizing the Stanton firing in the eleven articles—a legal tactic designed to win over nervous Republican moderates—the House failed to address the more fundamental question. Had the president, by removing generals for partisan reasons and then instructing them to ignore the political requirements of the Reconstruction Acts, wielded his constitutional authority as commander in chief to damage the equally legitimate authority of Congress to pass legislation? The absence of a sitting vice president complicated matters. Ohio Republican Benjamin F. Wade, the president pro tempore of the Senate, was next in line for the presidency. Democrats despised Wade as among "the first to secure the nigger suffrage enactment," but moderate Republicans were equally uncomfortable with his advocacy of women's rights and inflationary monetary policies. Republican industrialists in New England regarded him as too friendly to the National Labor Union, which had been founded two years earlier in 1866. Although Wade assured reporters that he did "not covet the position," some moderates thought it wiser to ride out one final year with a politically weakened president than turn the reins of power to one of the most radical men in the Senate. Black progressives, not surprisingly, saw the matter differently. Roudanez praised Wade both for his support for the National Equal Rights League and for appearing on the same stage with feminists Lydia Maria Child, Elizabeth Cady Stanton, and Susan B. Anthony.[37]

The Senate proceedings began on March 23, with the case for removal presented by House managers Stevens and Benjamin F. Butler, once a formidable courtroom attorney. The debates paused while Johnson's defense attorneys prepared their case, and then commenced again on March 30. The folly of House Republicans not granting greater attention to Johnson's refusal to enforce the franchise provisions of the Reconstruction Acts quickly became clear. A group of seven moderates, most of them from the border states and worried about how their votes would be received in the fall elections, seized upon the technicality that as Stanton was a Lincoln appointee, his case was not covered by the Tenure of Office Act. Maine's William Pitt Fessenden, the one member of the cadre from New England, was also the sole moderate who understood that a vote to acquit would result in him being "denounced as a traitor, & perhaps hung in effigy." But his concerns about Johnson were assuaged by remarks the president made at a private dinner party, in which he promised to cease his interference with Congressional acts and appoint the respected General John M. Schofield to the War Department. On the final vote, a majority of Republicans supported conviction, but with seven defections, including Fessenden and Trumbull, the tally of thirty-five to nineteen fell one vote short of the necessary two thirds. African Americans and southern Unionists, focused more on the course of democracy than on legal trifles, were disconsolate. One white Georgia Republican reported to Sumner that when news reached him of the acquittal of "one of the great tyrannical usurpers," it "made many a truly loyal hearts Beat sad." For black Americans, the defection of party moderates, just as the Republicans' endorsement of southern suffrage began to win them over, was a rude awakening. "The Republican Party professes to be a reform party," fumed San Francisco editor Philip A. Bell. But when Johnson's guilt was proven "beyond doubt, and his conviction would restore peace and quietude, we find Republican Senators quibbling about technicalities, and standing in the way of the reform which his removal would produce."[38]

Black radicals had to be satisfied with the presidential nomination of Ulysses S. Grant, who was tapped by the Republicans at their May 21 convention in Chicago only four days after the Senate vote on acquittal. They took heart too in the ratification of the Fourteenth Amendment, which became operational on July 9 when South Carolina, having rejected the amendment in December 1866, became the twenty-eighth state to ratify. Progressives were disappointed that Wade lost the vice presidential nomination to Congressman Schuyler Colfax of Indiana, although they found some solace in the fact that Colfax had voted to impeach. When "Grant becomes President," Bell prayed, "a great many wrongs would be made right."[39]

When the Democrats met two months later in Manhattan, some border South delegates hoped to vindicate Johnson by nominating the accidental president in his own right. On the first ballot he received sixty-five votes. That test of strength proved inadequate, as that was less than one third of the total necessary for nomination, and on the twenty-second ballot the convention finally selected former New York governor Horatio Seymour. To provide geographical balance, the convention then chose General Francis Preston Blair Jr. of Missouri, a former Republican congressman and member of the powerful Blair dynasty. Yet if the party opted to steer clear of the impeached president, its candidates virtually endorsed his program and tactics. Democrats remained bitterly opposed to black suffrage, in part due to racism but also in recognition, as one Texas editor bluntly put it, that "nigger voters could not be induced to vote against [Republicans] to any extent." With the black vote, southern Republicans could be competitive; without it, Democrats would carry virtually every race. On the eve of the convention, Blair published an open letter that undoubtedly secured his nomination. Since black votes in the South would ensure Republican control of both the Senate and House for the foreseeable future, he observed, the only method for "undo[ing] the Radical plan of reconstruction" was for the next president to simply "declare the reconstruction acts null and void; compel the army to undo its usurpations at the South; [and] allow the white people to reorganize their own governments." Johnson's disinclination to enforce laws he regarded as unconstitutional, prior to any rulings by the Supreme Court, of course, together with his meddling with the generals who tried to carry out the provisions of the Military Reconstruction Act, were precisely what nearly cost him his position. Blair's public letter all but guaranteed weary voters another four years of tension between Congress and a Democratic White House. Seymour did not endorse the letter, but neither did he attempt to rein in his irrepressible running mate. "A year ago Frank Blair was a Republican," editor Bell sighed, "now he is a rebel."[40]

Progressives feared that the failure to convict Johnson would be interpreted by southern conservatives as federal acquiescence in renewed violence, and the nomination of Seymour and Blair did little to dissuade anybody of that view. At a Missouri ratifying convention, a marketer did brisk sales of images of Seymour, Blair, and assassin John Wilkes Booth. "The rebel leaders at the South have commenced their work of persecution of Union men, white as well as black," the *Elevator* reported, warning that "emboldened by the [nomination] of their candidates," southern whites "would again establish their Confederacy." Assisting in this counterrevolution was the declining number of soldiers in the South. Each year brought new reductions as the War Department became engrossed with Indian affairs on the Great Plains. Hoping to keep Grant out of the presidency, or at least recognizing that their window of opportunity between an indifferent Johnson government and a potentially confrontational Grant administration was limited, southern Democrats resorted to what editor Bell dubbed a new "reign of terror." In Opelousas, Louisiana, "armed Democrats" demolished the office of the pro-Republican *Progress*, lynched its French-born editor, and shot as many as "one hundred negroes." Worried Bureau agents reported "that both white and colored citizens are arming themselves" and begged Washington to increase the number of military patrols before November 3 so as to ensure fair balloting. "No white radical or colored will be allowed to vote at the next Election for president unless he votes the democratic ticket if the government don't give us protections," complained Georgian Howell C. Flournoy. "During the rebellion I was more than forty times reported for arrest for my Union Sentiments," he added, "but I have never Seen such times in my life."[41]

Even in Mississippi, one of the three states that had yet to ratify the Fourteenth Amendment and so a jurisdiction that only held local and statewide elections in 1868, violence became commonplace. Near Yazoo, Democrats regularly galloped past a newly built black church "where the Republican party could hold meetings," endeavoring "to *scare* the freed people from their right to vote." A Bureau agent in Montgomery informed his superior that "many Union Men, & freedmen have been murdered," most of them highly visible Republicans targeted for "assassination." As the dwindling army patrols could not be everywhere and usually bivouacked in urban areas, Democrats typically waited until the dark of night and went after rural activists. Near Northport, Alabama, "a gang of men disguised" broke into the home of Moses Hughes. When they could not find Hughes, who had crawled up the chimney, they shot his wife "through the Brain & left her dead." The "plain truth," the agent stated, "is the Rebellion is flourishing in these parts."[42]

Republicans were far from safe in southern towns either. The Reverend Benjamin F. Randolph was murdered in Cokesbury, South Carolina, as he boarded a train. A former Union chaplain who had delivered a prayer at the rededication of Charleston's AME congregation, Randolph remained in the city, where together with Reverend E. J. Adams he published the *Journal* and then the *Advocate*. In 1867, Randolph became vice president of the Republican state executive committee before

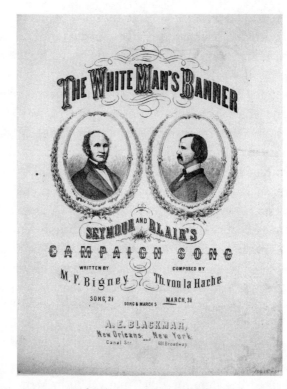

The presidential contest of 1868 pitted General Ulysses S. Grant and running mate Schuyler Colfax against Horatio Seymour, the former governor of New York, and Francis P. Blair Jr., a onetime free-soiler and Republican turned Democrat. The Democrats ran an unabashedly racist campaign, and Blair's denunciations of Congressional Reconstruction were so rancorous that the party's national committee urged him to confine his campaigning to Illinois and his adopted state of Missouri for fear that he would sink the ticket. Where African Americans could vote, they cast their ballots for Grant, and their roughly seven hundred thousand votes gave Grant his victory; most likely, Grant became the first president to win with a minority of the white vote. Courtesy Library of Congress.

serving in both the state constitutional convention and the state senate. He was on an October "electioneering tour" when three whites rode up to the train platform and pumped at least five bullets into his body. Writing to Republican governor Robert K. Scott, who was a Pennsylvania-born former Union general, Richard H. "Daddy" Cain, now also a member of the South Carolina senate, charged that this "bold act of the Democracy has emboldened those of this city and the lives of the leading men of our party are threatened." Cain was informed that he, too, as well as the governor, had "been marked out as victims, before *election*," and that Democrats "contemplated Assassinations" of "every leading Republican" in the state. As a rising black politician, the Oberlin-educated Randolph, southern whites recognized, would soon earn a seat in the national House of Representatives, and the whites sought to eliminate such ambitious African Americans while their influence and reputation were yet local. Cain too feared that his black constituents would not cower from a fight, and he cautioned Scott that if any more prominent blacks were murdered, "the people here swore to burn [Charleston] to ashes and have no mercy on the Democrats."[43]

On many occasions, landlords and employers resorted to economic coercion against Republicans, an effective tactic in a time when voting was open and public. Voters had to obtain a large "ticket" from a party functionary, and then on Election Day deposit that in an enormous bowl or crate marked with a party preference. John Roberts, a Georgia planter, evicted the similarly named James Roberts "from his planta-tion, telling him that no Radical negro could stay on his place." The editor of a Georgia Republican paper reported that landlords "threaten to turn colored men away from their employment if they did not vote as the employer dictates." Despite such coercion, southern blacks proudly carried, waved, and even pinned to their clothing campaign badges em-blazoned with Grant's image. In Mississippi, one new voter "defiantly" wore two badges on his lapels, and so his white neighbors could better see them, he marched down the sidewalk, rather than in "the middle of the street, where other niggers go." When one freedman was reluctant to pin his on, his wife grabbed it and "bravely" wore it "upon her own breast."[44]

More commonly, Democrats employed violence. In New Orleans, whites fired at Republican marchers, "killing men and women, one with a baby in her arms." One month before the election, "three disguised men" dragged the Reverend Psalm Porter from his home and "shot him through the right thigh." Benjamin Jackson was driven out of Baker County, Georgia, after "professing to be a Radical in politics," and James Miller was "killed for expressing radical sentiments at a church" rally.

Another "body of men" called on Basil Weaver, a thirty-year-old former slave, dragged him into the woods, and "gave him thirty or forty lashes," pausing between whippings to ask "what he was politically—a Republican or a Democrat." Despite the Civil Rights Act and the Fourteenth Amendment, Bureau agent Charles Rauschenberg lamented, court remedies were difficult to achieve, as "the prosecutors were being either killed or driven away," while "frightened negroes" were reluctant to testify "for fear of meeting the same fate" and all-white juries were "imbibed with the same spirit of hatred and prejudice as the criminals."[45]

Terrorists especially targeted Republican functionaries, who were critical to disseminating party information, setting up political rallies at churches, and handing out ballots. When an Atlanta-based activist named Walker journeyed into the countryside, "a party of white men" surrounded the home of the freedmen where Walker was spending the night and threatened to torch the house unless Walker came with them. Vowing to "deliver himself and trust to the Lord," Walker went with them. He was found the next day "with two bullet holes in his breast." Two days before the election, one Bureau agent informed his superiors that he knew of "five freedmen who have been murdered for political opinion within the last two weeks." A black editor in Galveston urged his readers not to respond to "murder" with violence, "but to take notice of our desperadoes, and conquer them through the military authority." Some black veterans, however, declined to rely on the ever-decreasing federal military. A group of armed whites burst into the cabin of Perry Jeffrey late on the night of November 1, following his refusal to attend a Democratic rally on the grounds "that he intended to vote for Grant." The attackers fired eleven shots into his home, wounding his son, but Jeffrey returned fire, "causing them to leave & dropping one of their hats."[46]

As they had since black men began to don blue uniforms five years earlier, southern whites chose to characterize acts of self-defense in the same language they had once used to describe slave revolts. A group of alarmed Georgians warned Bureau agents that five black veterans, including James Roberts, were "drilling and organizing colored people with the intention of inciting riot and insurrection." White neighbors of planter S. H. Carter assured him that Ralph Jones, previously one of his slaves, was "drilling companies and getting up ammunition with the intention of murdering *all*." When approached by the agent, Roberts admitted that Republicans intended to protect themselves on Election Day, but he remarked that the true cause of white "enmity" was due to his "being a radical" Republican. Democrats waylaid Jones after he left Carter's estate, and "shot [him] in the leg with a pistol or rifle," but the wounded man lived to vote on November 3.[47]

Election Day in 1868 was like none held before. Although black men could still not vote across much of the North, for the first time, African Americans in the South shared in selecting the nation's next president. Blacks of both genders understood what the election meant for their future. In California, one black woman announced that she had not purchased any new clothes for several months, for if "Grant was not elected, she would never want anything more to wear, for she would die." Georgia agents reported that "many" black voters were refused the ballot on the grounds that they "had not yet paid their poll-taxes," but when they could, "all the freedmen, who appeared in strong force, voted the republican ticket." White Carolinians tried the same tactic, but with less success, as the black-owned Charleston *Free Press* had informed readers that "every man who is registered could vote," and that the poll tax restriction was one of the illegal "wiles of the enemy." In Louisiana, rural voters marched in protective groups to county courthouses to cast their tickets. In New Orleans, "several Republican clubs of colored men, in uniform, with torches and a drum corps, paraded through the streets" in imitation of the northern "Wide Awake" groups who had marched for Abraham Lincoln in 1860.[48]

Grant's success over Seymour in the popular vote by 52.7 percent to 47.3 percent was closer than many seasoned observers expected, given the general's enormous popularity among northern voters and federal veterans. But his electoral margin of 214 to 80 was far more impressive, and Republicans attributed their margin of victory to roughly four hundred thousand African American votes. White violence in parts of the South kept Georgia and Louisiana in the Democratic ranks—with Texas, Mississippi, and Virginia not casting presidential ballots—but Seymour carried only six other states, including his own New York and nearby New Jersey. In two states, Iowa and Minnesota, white voters approved amendments to their state constitutions that enfranchised blacks.

Out West, where Republicans won California and Nevada, Democrats concluded that southern violence had hurt the party's fortunes by convincing moderate voters that a Democratic victory would mean further chaos. "We should no longer sanction the bloody deeds" of white vigilantes, advised one Nevada Democrat. "Let us no longer oppress the negro and deny him a home in the land that gave him birth. The people are disgusted with the everlasting negro equality question and the assertion that this is a white man's government." A New Orleans Democrat concurred, admitting that Democratic violence had "driven [blacks] into the Republican ranks, and fenced them in there." Publisher Philip A. Bell hailed the outcome as even more significant than Lincoln's 1864 reelection, for it "firmly establishes the reconstruction acts of Congress, and shadows forth the speedy accomplishment of equal suffrage for all citizens." Weary of both white viciousness and Andrew Johnson, black voters everywhere agreed. In December, a Bureau agent reported from Montgomery that African Americans in his district were "doing quite well" and were "happy and contented." Both blacks and whites, he added, had ceased to file labor grievances against one another, and the agent had "strong hopes & expectations that a better state of things will speedily be brought about since General Grant is Elected President."[49]

Tragically, Thaddeus Stevens did not live to witness the victory. Never vigorous, the congressman was further weakened by the long hours devoted to the battle over impeachment. By the summer of 1868, as he entered his seventy-sixth year, his colleagues realized he was dying. Stevens was cheered by the ratification of the Fourteenth Amendment in July, and when friends visited and tried to discuss his condition, he steered the conversation back to public affairs. He had every confidence that Grant would win in November, and when told that Congressman John Morrissey of New York was placing bets on Seymour, Stevens, ever witty and caustic, smiled and muttered, "I like him for his pluck." By August 11, his doctor decided against further treatment. Two black clergymen, William Hall and James Reed, arrived to find Stevens lying in bed, with Lydia Smith kneeling at its foot in prayer. "Mr. Stevens, you have the prayers of all the colored people in the country," Reverend Hall stated, asking for permission to pray over him. Stevens nodded but made no reply. He died just before midnight.[50]

A contingent of black Zouaves came to collect his body and carry him to the national Capitol rotunda, where he lay in state with the soldiers standing guard. Three days later, a small but solemn ceremony was held in the rotunda, and politicians and reformers gathered to pay their final respects. Across Pennsylvania, crowds turned out to see the special three-car train carrying his coffin rumble by. At Independence Hall in Philadelphia, flags flew at half-mast. Twenty-two thousand mourners, half of them African Americans, attended his funeral service in Lancaster on August 15. The legislature of South Carolina, increasingly dominated by white and black Republicans, passed resolutions of "regret" at the passing of "a man who was in favor of the abolition of slavery at the time when slave drivers cracked their whips in Congress." Frederick Douglass, who kept a portrait of Stevens in his home, praised the congressman for holding "the highest place among the statesmen who grappled with the issues raised by the recent slaveholders' rebellion."[51]

Even in the shades, Stevens drew rebukes from his southern critics. One Georgia editor huffed that had the congressman been "as honest as his friends claim, he should have married Mrs. Lydia Smith, though on his death bed." The old rumors gained new life when Stevens's will was read, and antagonistic journalists placed the word "housekeeper" in quotation marks when discussing his bequest to her of five hundred dollars a year. But in the District of Columbia, blacks erected "the first monument to Thaddeus Stevens" by year's end. Rather than purchase a chunk of stone, African Americans pooled their money to finance a school, saying that "no tribute could have been more appropriate" to the "venerable statesman."[52]

Among the first to take a seat in the August 14 rotunda ceremony was Charles Sumner, who privately praised Stevens for being ever "austere & fixed" on the questions of "Slavery & the suppression of the Rebellion." His demise, Sumner assured a British correspondent, while a personal loss to his friends and family, did not signal an end to progressive reform. "His death will make no essential change" in Washington, Sumner insisted, as the laws and amendments he had championed had prepared the path for the rising generation of black veterans, ministers, educators, and party activists. The wars of Reconstruction had lost a valued officer, but the Reconstruction Acts enabled hundreds of activists to rewrite state constitutions, stand for local office, and arrange runs for statewide positions. As Ulysses Grant prepared to take the oath of office, black Republicans across the country readied themselves for a new burst of activity. "We have nothing to fear in the great battle, now waged for our rights on this continent," editor Bell promised, "if we play a faithful part in the drama of American reform."[53]

CHAPTER SEVEN

"We Knows That Much Better Than You Do"

Voting Rights and Political Service

R ARELY HAD THE WORLD CHANGED so swiftly. Just ten years after President Abraham Lincoln, in his final public address, advocated voting rights for the "very intelligent [blacks], and on those who serve in our cause as soldiers," Blanche Kelso Bruce, a former slave, raised his right hand to take the oath of office as a U.S. senator from Mississippi. Garbed in a black suit and starched white cotton shirt, his black waistcoat adorned with a fourteen-karat-gold pocket watch, the stout, slightly balding statesman looked older than his thirty-four years. His dark "wavy" hair and newly trimmed van dyke revealed his mother's heritage, while his light skin was the legacy of his father and former master. Preceded in the Senate by Hiram Revels, who had served a partial term from 1870 to 1871, Bruce took his oath less than two decades after Chief Justice Roger B. Taney announced that blacks were not citizens in the country of their birth. "Unpretending and unostentatious," the *Memphis Planet* conceded, "he moves quietly on, the honoured representative of four millions of colored people."[1]

Born in 1841 in Farmville, Virginia, the child then known as Branch and his five siblings were slaves because their mother, Polly Bruce, was a slave. Blanche later insisted that his father, Pettis Perkinson, had treated him as "tenderly" as he had treated his white children, and the young slave—who changed his name to Blanche while still in his teens—was employed as a domestic to his half brother and taught to read. But in an act that demonstrated that the war truly could be a conflict of brothers, in 1861 Blanche's white half brother William left to join the Confederate cause. Blanche decided "to emancipate [him]self" and decamped for the abolitionist stronghold of Lawrence, Kansas, where he found employment as a teacher. The decision nearly proved a fatal one when in August 1863 the town was sacked by Confederate guerrillas led by William Clarke Quantrill. The raiders murdered 183 men and boys, slaughtering anybody above the age of fourteen, but Bruce was able to hide in bushes behind his house. "Quantrill's band certainly would not have spared a colored man," Bruce later wrote.[2]

After the war, Bruce briefly attended Oberlin College, the rural Ohio school widely known for its abolitionist origins and progressive attitudes on educational integration. His meager financial resources soon forced him to withdraw, but while working on a Mississippi River steamboat, Bruce heard about opportunities for ambitious black men in the lower South. Arriving in Mississippi in February 1869, at a time when the state had not yet been readmitted to Congress, Bruce settled in Bolivar County, a devoutly Republican region with a four-to-one advantage in black voters. As a reminder that southern-born blacks too might be carpetbaggers, he quickly won elections for sheriff, then tax collector and superintendent of education, all while editing a local newspaper. Senators were then chosen by state assemblies, and on February 3, 1874, Bruce was chosen by the Mississippi legislature to serve in the national Senate. He journeyed north toward Washington to begin what would become the first full term served by an African American senator. There he joined black Congressmen John Adams Hyman of North Carolina and Robert Smalls, who succeeded Richard "Daddy" Cain in South Carolina's fifth district. Congressman John Roy Lynch, one of the youngest members of the House, continued to represent Mississippi's sixth district. "A turn in fortune's wheel" was one white editor's characterization of just how dramatically the political world had been turned upside down.[3]

As the only man of color in the chamber, Bruce sought to position

himself as the servant of his state's entire population and dispel any notions that he was a single-issue politician. That meant seeking to appease his state's other senator, James L. Alcorn. Just one month into his
term, Bruce stepped across the aisle to converse with Alcorn, a conservative Republican and former Confederate officer who routinely cau-
cused with the chamber's Democrats. Alcorn had not seen fit to honor the
tradition of escorting his junior colleague to his swearing-in ceremony,
but Bruce was not a man to carry a grudge. The two were engaged in
"harmonious conservation" when above them in the gallery, two white
observers began to loudly discuss the novelty of "a nigger coming over
to sit with Democrats in the United States Senate." The second man, a
Marylander, admitted that Bruce "looks clean, and maybe he will keep
his place and be respectful." But most senators, well aware of just how
far their country had progressed since 1861, accepted his presence, if
perhaps grudgingly. "He has made a most favorable impression upon
the members of the Senate and those with whom he came into contact,"
observed one black editor. In politics, power and influence could trump
race. If Mississippi Unionists preferred their senator to be white, the reality was that Bruce held the seat, and he shared their vision of regional
prosperity, even if they did not share his of an interracial democracy.
One Pennsylvania Republican visited Bruce's office and was surprised
to find a "small army of white Mississippians" in his waiting room, all of
them "ready to swear by you." The northern man thought that curious.
He had never before met white southerners, and he "had a lurking idea
that these people were all down on a negro on general principles." But
Reconstruction was an era of new opportunities, and southern whites,
whether they dreaded it or accepted it, had seen this day coming for
nearly a decade.[4]

Former slaves such as Bruce and Smalls did not ascend to positions of
power overnight. As both of their life stories suggest, their stations
owed much to ambition and drive and, as with any successful politician,
to a certain amount of luck and opportunity. They also owed the offices
to thousands of voters and hundreds of black registrars and poll workers. But before there was a Republican organization in the South, there

The first African American to serve a full term in the Senate, Blanche K. Bruce
(left) was born a slave in Virginia in 1841. After becoming free, Bruce attended
Oberlin College, a hotbed of antislavery activism, and when the U.S. Army
turned down his application to serve, he opened a school for black children in
Mark Twain's Hannibal, Missouri. After his six years in the Senate, Bruce was
appointed Register of the Treasury by President James Garfield, making his
signature the first by an African American to appear on federal currency.
Courtesy Library of Congress.

was a white-created political society that served as their first introduction
into partisan politics, and that, as much as the reality of administrative
life in the 1870s, explained why Senator Bruce labored as hard for white
Unionists as he did for his black constituents. Founded in Philadelphia
in 1862 during the bleakest days of the war, the Union League was designed to support Lincoln's policies and promote his party's fortunes.
The League quickly spread to Chicago and Manhattan, and for the duration of the war, its membership consisted largely of army officers and
entrepreneurs. The group hoped to expand, and as the fortunes of war

turned, the League grew in size. The Philadelphia group, which financed the construction of an elegant building on South Broad Street, served as the national council, with each state and territory granted a sub-council. For local chapters to join, all that was required was the presence of at least nine loyal men. Members contributed dues, which varied according to region, and the League elected officers, including a president, vice president, and treasurer. Member William O. Stoddard bragged that the structure was "the most perfect party skeleton ever put together for utter efficiency of political machine work."[5]

Despite its reputation for staid patriotism and its old-money stewardship, the League formally endorsed black voting rights as early as 1866. To better facilitate the enrollment of illiterate freedmen, the League headquarters prepared a simple pamphlet for distribution to "every Radical who could read." The pamphlet contained an instructional dialogue, a conversation between "a white Republican and a colored citizen" meant to be read by two members at organizational meetings. Francis L. Cardozo, the Charleston-born freedman and educator, and Tunis Campbell took turns reading the dialogue at meetings across South Carolina, and according to Reverend Henry McNeal Turner, Campbell's readings inspired "the whole house [to] ring with shouts, and shake with spasmodic motions." Men willing to join—and virtually every black veteran did—stepped forward to take a solemn oath: "I pledge my life, my fortune, and my sacred honor. So help me God." Although the League caught on quickly in the urban South, with chapters formed in Nashville, Richmond, and Savannah in late 1865 and early 1866, chapters also emerged in rural areas, particularly on large plantations, such as Davis Bend. By the end of March 1866, one black Charlestonian estimated that there were two thousand chapters across the nation, and if most African Americans were not yet prepared to wholly embrace the Republican Party, the councils endorsed the progressive agenda and vilified Andrew Johnson. The Charleston chapter passed resolutions in support of the Freedmen's Bureau, condemned the president's veto of the agency, praised those Republicans who voted to override, and criticized "rebels, and poisonous [Democratic] Copperheads, in rejoicing over and approving the veto." So political was their agenda that when speakers ventured into plantation districts to recruit new members, black veterans usually came armed and stacked their rifles behind bushes near the organizers, leaving their wives to guard the weapons while they listened.[6]

With the passage of the Military Reconstruction Act, League promoters found it safe to recruit in isolated upcountry regions previously removed from army patrols. Prior to the arrival of soldiers, one Democratic editor complained, "the contaminating influence of mischievous counselors" took hold "only in the cities and villages, [and] along the main thoroughfares." Yet when protected, the League saw new chapters emerge in virtually every county, particularly since those "counselors" were also the same activists who had been organizing in the South since the first troops landed in New Orleans and in the Carolina low country. The "freedmen have been organized in loyal Union Leagues," one journalist reported, "through the influence of the preachers in their churches, the Northern teachers in their schools, and the officers of the Freedmen's Bureau." Since African Americans already knew and trusted men such as Campbell and Turner, it proved effortless to fold the new organization into previous reform efforts. At the Syracuse "Loyal League Convention" in 1866, the membership virtually mirrored that of the earlier Equal Rights League meetings, and when Charleston blacks organized their chapter, its leadership included most of the men who had met to reorganize the city's AME church the year before. After Republicans in Washington finally incorporated black suffrage into their 1867 laws, southern chapters, often calling themselves the "Colored Union League," simply merged with the party. When League officials announced a conference in Greenville, South Carolina, blacks and some whites traveled from as far away as twenty miles to start the chapter and hear "eloquent orators of the [Republican] party."[7]

Aghast at the prospect of black suffrage, southern Democrats originally hoped that the black Leaguers might evolve into a third party, leaving the Republicans to organize among the white Unionist minority. But when League members met in Mobile in May 1867, they made their position clear to their opponents: "We are Republicans and you Democrats or Conservatives may as well know it by now." Formal fusion with national Republicans came at a cost, however. By mid-1867, local chapters began to distance themselves from the land-reform issue.

Many League officers were urbanites or born free before the war, and carpenters and shoemakers were less inclined to endorse land redistribution schemes than were rural freedmen. But while chapters in both Columbia, South Carolina, and Mobile voted down resolutions demanding immediate confiscation, the latter did warn that "the future conduct of the late rebels" might require it "as an imperious necessity." The desire of local members not to damage the national party by burdening them with what northern voters regarded as a truly radical program did not mean that they opposed other forms of land assistance to black agriculturalists, or the sale of public or abandoned lands on generous terms. Nor did it keep black League officers from working with white Bureau officials when it came to intervening in labor disputes between planters and their laborers. Some recruiters clearly regarded their public position as a tactical retreat, and perhaps one to be abandoned as soon as black voters could move into the ranks of legislators. Well into 1868, potential recruits at League meetings in both North Carolina and South Carolina were assured that the organization favored a policy of "forty acres in real estate for each negro."[8]

Suspicions among southern Unionists as to the true agenda of black-dominated League councils, together with rural white aversion to the Republican label, hindered the emergence of a truly interracial movement. But recognizing the League's ability to attract black voters, the Union Republican Congressional Executive Committee assumed oversight of League activities in the South just after the passage of the Reconstruction Acts. Republican funding efforts remained hidden behind closed doors, but any efforts at disguising the partisan nature of League conferences—which, in any case, black attendees had little interest in doing—vanished when highly visible northern Republicans journeyed south to speak at League meetings. In June 1867, Senator Henry Wilson addressed a Union rally in Richmond, calling those in the audience fellow "members of the great Republican Party." Wilson's speech was delivered at the elegant Ballard House hotel, but he then accompanied officers of the chapter as they recruited at an AME congregation in Charlottesville. Wealthy southern whites were far more comfortable with the white-dominated Republican Party than with the often-secretive League chapters, and if white Unionists were displeased with the tributes to the martyred Lincoln that were standard at each conference, black Leaguers were infuriated by occasional Unionist resolutions calling for the "colonization of the colored race when such a measure shall become practicable." But for black veterans, the dwindling number of federal soldiers in the South meant that a new organization had to take the army's place, and those clubs willing to offer both political education and physical protection proved especially attractive to black veterans.[9]

As Congress required each Confederate state to draft a new constitution, the next step was for League chapters to organize statewide party conventions. Those conferences, in turn, were expected to cobble together platforms for potential inclusion in the new constitutions, organize slates of candidates to serve as delegates to constitutional conventions, and prepare League members and Bureau agents for the difficult work of registering rural voters, a requirement of the Reconstruction Acts but also a process that had slowed due to Johnson's tampering with the generals in the field. When South Carolina Republicans met in Charleston in March 1867, and then again that July in Columbia, black Leaguers dominated the meeting and endorsed a radical program. Hoping to appeal to white farmers and black agriculturalists, the delegates disregarded the protests of white businessmen in the halls and recommended the abolition of imprisonment for debt, the integration of public schools, legal protection for "the poor man's homestead" against seizure, government assistance for "the aged, infirm, and helpless poor," heavy taxes on "large land monopolies," and "mild confiscation" designed to facilitate "the division and sale of unoccupied lands among the poorer classes." Although black delegates were not in the majority that April when Virginia Republicans convened in Richmond's "African Church," two delegates seized the podium to deliver "inflammatory speeches," in which they "demand[ed] higher pay" for black workers of "at least $40 per month." League members, many of them also Bureau agents and teachers, controlled the Republican convention in Montgomery, and when the party met in Louisiana, delegates resolved to "stand firm" with Congress and adhere to a "strict non-affiliation with pro-rebel [Democratic] politics."[10]

To encourage the registration of eligible voters, General John Pope, who commanded the Third Military District prior to his December

1867 removal, appointed a series of interracial three-man boards of registration for each of the three states in his district. Among those selected for Georgia was Tunis Campbell. Since considerable travel was involved, Pope offered fifteen cents for each urban voter registered and up to forty cents for voters in remote rural districts. Democrats denounced the registration efforts as inspired by a "diabolical hatred of everything Southern," and white Georgians murdered one registrar and tried to poison Campbell, prompting black veterans to patrol the grounds around his home. In upcountry plantation districts, registrars brought drums to rallies to attract potential voters. Party organizers in both sections of the republic had long employed music and even cannon to gather and energize crowds, but for southerners—and perhaps for nervous whites more than for African Americans—drums conjured up distant memories of the bloody 1739 slave rebellion near Stono, South Carolina. At one Mississippi rally, Democrats tried to silence the music, warning Republicans that they "cannot beat that drum here." The state was "a white man's country," he added, "and we don't allow that." When possible, Democrats chopped the heads out of Republican drums, and militant whites stuck broken drumsticks into their hatbands to counter the ribbons and badges donned by Leaguers.[11]

As the day for voting on convention delegates approached, League activists found themselves working long hours without rest. In rural districts, local authorities tried to hide the polls in out-of-the-way locations or house them on estates of hostile Democratic landlords. In many parts of the South, whites chose not to vote, hoping that by boycotting the proceedings they could discredit the new constitutions. In Columbus, Georgia, only twenty-five whites voted. Although black voters held the majority in Alabama, officials in white-dominated Crenshaw County set up a rope barricade, so that "every [black] voter had to run the gauntlet of their jeers and threats" while employers stood to one side and "watched to see whether their hands had voted." Expecting such tactics, Leaguers petitioned military commanders to move polling sites to defensible areas, protect ballot boxes, and appoint honest election officials. Predisposed to expect difficulties between white Democrats and black Republicans, League officers were surprised to discover occasional tensions between ambitious local freedmen and equally aspiring black outsiders. In Vicksburg, former Davis Bend slave and Union scout Albert Johnson had worked his way up through the black convention movement, only to find himself running against Thomas Stringer, a Maryland-born freeman who had arrived in Mississippi as a teacher and Methodist missionary. Already accustomed to intra-party competition in the North, white Republicans regarded such competition as healthy, although some fretted that so many of the seven hundred thousand new southern black voters were undereducated. (National party leaders, of course, harbored similar doubts about working-class whites and Irish immigrants.) Running for a seat in the South Carolina constitutional convention, former slave Beverly Nash spoke for many black Leaguers when he admitted that if many freedmen were "not prepared for this suffrage," they could quickly learn. "We may not understand it at the start, but in time we shall learn to do our duty."[12]

The Louisiana state convention was among the first to gather, meeting in November 1867 at the New Orleans Mechanics' Institute, site of the previous year's attack on black conventioneers. Southern blacks and northern-born white carpetbaggers occupied roughly two thirds of the seats, with most of the remainder representing Lincoln's widely despised restored state government. The black delegates steered clear of land reform but otherwise embraced the label of "Radical Republican," and many of the policies they engraved into the new state constitution reflected that designation. Pinckney B. S. Pinchback, a former captain in the Seventy-fourth USCT and the publisher of the New Orleans *Weekly Louisianian*, drafted the clauses that guaranteed all citizens "without distinction of race or color or previous condition" equal access to public transportation and business licenses. Dr. Robert I. Cromwell, the Virginia-born Bureau official who had been beaten in the 1866 riot, also took a hand in the provisions pertaining to accommodations. "Whites who did not approve of these privileges to the colored man," he remarked, "could leave the country and go to Venezuela or elsewhere." Under the proposed constitution, any adult male who had lived in Louisiana for one year could enjoy "all political and civil rights."[13]

The Alabama convention began at nearly the same time, assembling on November 5. Although conservative editors fumed that the delegates would "Africanize" the state, the convention was dominated by seventy-eight whites, fifty-one of whom were southern Unionists; only eighteen blacks completed the roster. Among the minority, however, was Alabama freeman James T. Rapier, who had attended schools in both Nashville and Canada. A renowned orator, Rapier was regarded as a most "dangerous man to meet on the stump." Upon being elected a delegate from Lauderdale County, Rapier was promptly appointed chairman of the platform committee. In response to rising violence, Rapier advocated disfranchising select former Confederates, if at least temporarily, a position that led one antagonistic editor to charge that he intended to "disfranchise every thinker, every man of property and every man of honor." Rapier lost that fight, but as in Louisiana, he and black delegates were successful in assuring voting rights for "all colored male persons of the age of 21 years." Alabama's black men already enjoyed the right to vote due to the Reconstruction Acts, but laws could be overturned more easily than state constitutions or federal amendments, and with Johnson yet in office, progressives such as Rapier wished to enshrine suffrage rights in every level of government.[14]

As they did across the South, Democrats in Georgia vented their frustrations at their new powerlessness in a series of angry editorials lampooning black delegates. Of the thirty-three men of color who met in Atlanta in December, "one or two have all the appearance of being in line direct from the Congo," sneered one Macon editor. "The prevailing costume is a condemned Yankee army overcoat," another wrote, ignoring the fact that military service was ever a selling point for American voters. When delegates arrived in black suits and white cravats, racist editors ridiculed that too, insisting that the clothes "probably belonged to their masters." Delegate and future state assemblyman William Golding was indeed a semiliterate former slave, born on a Liberty County plantation. Yet this staunch advocate of public education, some Democrats conceded, was "ever respectful to the whites." He was not, however, naïve, and the cautious Golding arrived with a bodyguard "of his own color." Aaron A. Bradley was another former slave, previously owned by South Carolina governor Francis Pickens. But the literate shoemaker had opened a school for black children in Savannah in 1865, where he worked with freedmen in the cause of land reform. Georgia-born Henry McNeal Turner was also literate, having been ordained an

AME minister in Baltimore and educated at Missouri's Trinity College. A chaplain with the First Regiment USCT, Turner took his seat beside delegate Tunis Campbell. Another hostile editor described the soft-spoken Turner as "the most favorable specimen of this class of animals in the collection," but publishing offensive editorials was virtually the only recourse for unreconstructed journalists. When North Carolina's convention met in January 1868, the delegates voted to expel a reporter from the *Carolinian* "for using the term 'nigger' in his report."[15]

Among the various state constitutional conventions, perhaps the most remarkable was that which met on January 14, 1868, at the Charleston Club House. As the 124 delegates filed into the hall, the white men instinctively found seats in front, while the African American delegates moved toward the back. But polite acts of deference could not mask the fact that men of color dominated the convention. Eight years earlier, South Carolina had been the first state to secede upon news of Lincoln's election, but now seventy-six of the men who gathered to reform the state's constitution were black; forty-one of them had been born slaves, and they represented all but three counties. As elsewhere, reactionary editors poured out their impotent rage in racist insults. Although most of the former slaves in attendance were, like Robert Smalls, atypical bondmen, the incendiary *Charleston Mercury* dubbed the gathering the "Congo Convention" and even attacked Daniel H. Chamberlain, a white Yale graduate who had led the black Fifth Massachusetts Cavalry before settling in the state, as a "buccaneer" from "Hell, and Boston." Freedmen in the room included Francis L. Cardozo; Robert Brown Elliott, a Liverpool-born attorney; William J. Whipper, a Pennsylvania lawyer and veteran of the Thirty-first USCT; and "Daddy" Cain. As at the North Carolina convention, some delegates called for the removal of disrespectful journalists from the hall. Whipper countered that barring anybody from the convention, even Roswell T. Logan, the reporter from the *Mercury*, was "unworthy of our character." Landon Langley, a veteran of the celebrated Fifty-fourth and a former Bureau agent, saw it differently. "I am not willing for that rebel sheet to burlesque this body," he snapped, "I want it excluded." At length, Logan was allowed to remain, although not before being slapped by a white delegate.[16]

For all of their bigoted characterizations of these conventions, Democrats were aware that the Charleston gathering was unusual in its black majority. African Americans served in the largest numbers in states with high percentages of blacks, where the numbers of white Unionists were smallest, and where federal occupation was longest. Blacks formed the majority of delegates only in South Carolina and Louisiana; in Texas, blacks made up just eleven percent of the membership. On average, whites comprised fifty-five percent of the overall representation. In all, 265 men of color served in the eleven state constitutional conventions in the former Confederacy, and at least 107 of them had been born slaves (although nineteen had found their way to freedom prior to 1861). Twenty-eight had lived all or parts of their lives in free states, but many had arrived with the army, and forty were veterans. Although disproportionately mixed-race and from towns or cities rather than the countryside, a good many were ministers or artisans who had ties to the slave community and owed their political positions to first-time black voters. Since skilled urban blacks, whether enslaved or free, had greater need of literacy than did rural bondmen, most enjoyed some education; among the black South Carolina delegates, at least eighty-two percent were literate, and ten percent, including the Oberlin-educated Reverend Randolph, had achieved a college or professional education, especially impressive in an era when only a small number of privileged white males attended college.[17]

Although radical critics were quick to charge that the urban background and mixed ancestry of so many delegates explained the failure of the new constitutions to implement land reform, the reality is that African American members were invariably outvoted by white Unionists. Compared to the reactionary Democrats who ridiculed their efforts, the white Republicans inside the convention halls appeared progressive, but as prosperous landlords and urban businessmen, they betrayed their Whiggish roots and displayed as much hostility to such allegedly radical nostrums as labor organization and property redistribution as did northern Republicans. Determined to protect suffrage rights and educational opportunities within the constitutions, even the most radical black delegates understood that they had to give way on some issues to obtain others. Even then, black delegates had to confront those white allies, such as the Unionists at the Virginia convention, who advocated literacy tests or "an 'intelligence qualification' for voting," or those

Louisiana Republicans who denigrated the few black delegates "who are only able to [sign with] their marks." Reporting on the conventions, Unionist editors but grudgingly endorsed black voting rights, and only then to "keep down the rebels." When southern Unionists spoke of land reform, they thought in terms of creating a free-labor world of small farmers through incremental steps rather than with wholesale redistribution. As one Republican explained, he was "utterly opposed [to] confiscation of large estates and the gratuitous division among the freedmen," particularly since the plantations would eventually "be broken up by sale, device, or by the burden of taxation" on white landlords. Such men comprised the majority of delegates in nine of the eleven states.[18]

That hardly meant that some black delegates did not try. In North Carolina, delegate John H. Williamson, a former slave (and future state assemblyman) continued to remind colleagues "that Lincoln promised them 40 acres of land." Inspired by his words, black delegates uniformly voted against a white-authored report "against confiscation." But after northern allies such as editor Horace Greeley warned the Richmond convention that Congress would never sanction confiscation, most delegates instead turned their energies to education, voting rights, and equal access to public accommodations. In Texas, the handful of black delegates demanded and won provisions for free homesteads, and eight of the new constitutions protected debtors from losing their farms. In Charleston, delegate Randolph—who had but nine months to live— advocated maintaining Bureau schools until a state board of education could be established. When whites protested that the state was too insolvent to afford a statewide system, blacks simply ignored their obstructionism and instead addressed the issue of compulsory school attendance, a thorny issue in a time when black parents required their children's labor on the farm for much of the year. Smalls understood the dilemma but agreed with Elliott and Cardozo that mandatory education was crucial to both black prosperity and the future of their race should conservatives ever seize control of the state assembly. "We know that when the old aristocracy and ruling power of this state get into power," Cardozo warned, "they will take precious good care that the colored people shall never be enlightened."[19]

As if to prove that point, the *Charleston Mercury* replied that "Southern [whites] do not intend to be mongrelized" and warned that the new constitution could only be "preserved by the bayonet for all time to come." One Boston editor observed that Robert Barnwell Rhett Sr., the *Mercury*'s fire-eating publisher, "was largely instrumental in getting up one rebellion" and had "ambitions to start another." Rhett had been successful in helping to guide his state out of the Union in 1860, but just eight years later, he stood helpless against the tide of history. Thanks to secession, governmental changes under the Johnson state regimes, the admission of new states in the West, and Congressionally mandated reforms, Americans framed no fewer than thirty-two state constitutions between 1861 and 1870. Conservatives across the nation ridiculed the southern documents as the shoddy creations of men ill-prepared for the solemn responsibility of state building, and for generations of twentieth-century whites, these criticisms became accepted as fact for those who took a dim view of Reconstruction reforms. In reality, these constitutions stood the test of time. When South Carolina altered its 1868 constitution after nearly three decades, it was only to remove the clauses pertaining to voting rights, in order to implement discriminatory Jim Crow restrictions. Virginia maintained its constitution until 1902, when it took similar steps to purge African Americans from the voting rolls.[20]

Aware of just how historic these constitutional reforms were, conservatives attempted to defeat their ratification with an orchestrated campaign of intimidation and violence that surpassed even that waged against Grant voters in the presidential election later that fall. Letters stacked up on Senator Charles Sumner's desk detailing almost daily instances of coercion, which only served to convince Republicans in Washington that southern Democrats could not yet be trusted to resume power. Bureau agents reported from Mississippi that Democratic newspapers were "publishing the names of all Freedmen who voted for the Constitution & calling upon the Citizens not to Employ or Encourage them in any way." Landlords threatened their tenants that unless they voted "*against* the *Constitution* when it comes before the people for adoption," they would have "neither houses nor land next year," a tactic that merely reminded freedmen of the need to acquire their own farms.

In counties where whites held the majority, Bureau agents often found it difficult to force employers to appear before them unless their summonses were delivered by military patrols. When agent Jarod Moore tried to file "cases where Freedmen have been discharged" for voting for the new constitution, several landlords informed him that Mississippi's Black Codes were yet in effect, and that they did "not recognize any 'Nigger' Bureau."[21]

Similar reports reached General Oliver O. Howard from South Carolina, where Georgetown-area "Southern sympathizers discharged their colored men for voting as they thought best." Captain James Gillette, stationed in Montgomery, Alabama, reported that "not less than a hundred freedmen" had visited his office to complain of being "discharged for exercising political rights in voting." Black fathers worried about their ability to feed their families, but they understood also that if white Democrats could defeat ratification, their dreams of better economic conditions would vanish along with their voting rights. Black ministers urged their flocks to stand united, and congregations often promised to assist those whose votes cost them their employment. "In them times colored preachers so 'furiate de women," South Carolinian Andy Brice later recalled, "dat dey would put on breeches and vote de 'Publican radical ticket" if their husbands declined to do so. As the votes were counted in Mississippi that July, both sides "conceded that the 'Radical Party' have a majority of votes," despite the fact that large numbers of blacks were "summarily discharged" for supporting the constitution.[22]

As voting was a public activity, bribery also proved an effective tactic. William Kellis, a former Confederate captain and a Mississippi justice of the peace, promised Thompson Edwards "Money if he would vote the democratic ticket." Edwards evidently took the cash, but his friend Will Henderson, who was employed by the commissioner of elections, tried to "persuade him not be bought but to vote as he pleased." Henderson reported the incident, but added that despite the fact blacks in the county were "threatened & intimidated," virtually "all the Colored men" voted to ratify the new constitution. Even a few whites were offered incentives to reject the constitution. Charles Marshall was promised a "gold watch and chain" if he would vote no, and when he demurred, the mayor of his small town loaned him one hundred dollars. After their efforts failed, Kellis and a sheriff went in search of Henderson "and threatened to shoot him," but Henderson fled into the woods.[23]

Henderson knew what awaited him at the jail if he allowed himself to be arrested. In Greenville, Alabama, George McClellan "wantonly stabbed" a black Republican, but when the case was brought before a local court, the all-white jury voted to acquit. When Jacksonville freedman Riley Williams announced that he planned to support ratification, John Cunningham, a former Confederate private, attacked Williams, "kicked him down, [and] kicked out several teeth," shouting that he "could lick any damned Son of a bitch, white or black, who voted for the Constitution." An army captain had Cunningham arrested, but his friends promptly posted bail, leaving the officer to hope that the ex-soldier could be tried by a military tribunal rather than a civilian court. When state courts refused to condemn white terrorism, others grew bolder. Shortly after the McClellan affair, four whites waited until midnight and then invaded the Greenville home of League member Abram Butler. They stripped Butler naked and whipped him with hickory switches, swearing "that Yankees and niggers like him were trying to get the government away from them."[24]

White extremists were especially vicious when it came to dealing with northern soldiers who settled in the South, or with black Republicans primed for higher office. Sixteen Mississippians murdered Albert Tipton, a white colonel from Ohio. "You have been a Yankee soldier," one sneered. "You fought against us and are now going to vote against us and we will kill you." Tipton's offense was compounded by the crime of marrying a black woman. Despite the fact that she was able to identify one of the men who took her husband "away," the civil authorities "refused to take any steps in the matter." On nearly the same late July 1868 day, Texas Democrats shot and killed two Republican organizers, Harry Thomas and George Brooks, believing that with its "effective leadership" out of the way, the black community in Millican—which included Frederick Douglass's brother Perry Downs—would be easier to control. Ironically, southern Democrats pointed to the ratification violence as evidence that the former Confederacy would never be quiet as long as black activists worked for political reform, and while the army protected their endeavors. The fact that "blacks could only vote at the point of a bayonet," Republican William M. Dickson responded, was evidence that Johnson's policies had failed and that "the rebellion is not subdued." The North and the South had achieved but "a truce, not a lasting peace," he concluded, and it was "at least better to know it before we disband our armies."[25]

When Election Day arrived in Vicksburg, "some 200 freedmen" banded together to march to the polls behind "Banners, Pictures and U.S. Flags." Knowing that they were sure to lose the ratification battles, whites again either opted not to vote, or chose to turn out to harass black voters. Rhett's *Mercury* encouraged whites to boycott the ratification election, for "to co-operate with [Republicans] in the Southern States now" only aided "them in the purpose of ruling the white race, by the black." In spite of the protective shield of numbers, a Vicksburg "mob" assaulted the procession, tearing down the flags and banners and clubbing the freedmen. Some of the black men brought their wives and children with them to witness the marvel of voting, and whites beat them too. In most locales, blacks marched in clusters to polling stations but met only angry stares. It was a "solemn farce," growled Savannah's George Anderson Mercer, to see the "crowds of ignorant negroes from the country" coming into the city to vote, with whites "eschewing altogether any participation in this outrage upon the Constitution."[26]

Despite knowing that they faced violence simply for wishing to cast a ballot to help shape the future of their country, African Americans turned out in overwhelming numbers to vote. In Mississippi, nearly eighty percent of all eligible black men registered to vote and did so in the summer elections. Perhaps only 2,500 whites across the state were disqualified from voting by the Reconstruction Acts; far more significant in explaining the ratification victory was the refusal of many whites to assist the process, together with the loss of twenty-seven thousand white Mississippi males who perished during the war. "The colored population are exceedingly numerous, and have taken possession of the polls," complained one Texas editor. By virtue of refusing to be cowed or bribed or bludgeoned into not voting, the "bottom rail" was on top, he added, "and [white] scalawagism [was] in the zenith of its glory."[27]

With voting rights in the former Confederacy protected both by the

Reconstruction Acts and new state constitutions, the Equal Rights League returned its attention to states in the North and West. Since roughly three out of four northern black men between the ages of eighteen and forty-five had served with the military during the conflict, most men of voting age could argue that their service had earned them the right of ballot. As veterans resolved at a meeting organized by Iowa's Sixtieth USCT, "he who is worthy to be trusted with the musket can, and ought, to be trusted with the ballot." The League had its work cut out for it. Only New England, with its small black population, allowed blacks to vote, and even there, Connecticut retained a widely ignored whites-only clause in the state constitution. Voters in New York consistently opted to retain the $250 property qualification imposed only on African Americans, and in most states Republican leaders, mindful of the issue's unpopularity, refused to advance voting rights legislation or allow for statewide referendums. When put to statewide tests, white voters invariably refused to overturn restrictive laws; in 1867, initiatives failed in Ohio, Kansas, and Michigan. Three years after the Syracuse convention and the formation of the Equal Rights League, only federal action aimed at the South had advanced the cause of black suffrage.[28]

Prodded by black activists and their own progressive faction, who routinely introduced petitions demanding voting rights, Congressional Republicans acted where even moderates conceded that the federal government had clear authority. Republicans enacted color-blind suffrage in the District of Columbia, and when the Nebraska and Colorado territories sought admission to the Union, Sumner demanded that the word "white" be stricken from their proposed constitutions as the price of statehood. Democrats pointed to the hypocrisy of New York or Ohio senators demanding of territories what they did not require of their own constituents, but Republicans, promised Louis Charles Roudanez, were "determined to make a straight and outright fight on the issue." Victory also arrived in Wisconsin, where the state supreme court unanimously ruled "that colored men are entitled to vote" on the grounds that an 1849 referendum on removing restrictions on black voters had been improperly decided. Although the decades-old proposed amendment to the state constitution had carried by a vote of 8,263 to 4,075, election officials had ruled that the change could not be ratified on the grounds that most of the 31,759 voters who had cast a ballot in that election had not taken a position on the amendment. Wisconsin blacks who had lived in the state for one year were immediately eligible to vote, the court ruled, but activists were aware that none of these federal- or court-mandated victories reflected democratic triumphs.[29]

If any single event convinced activists that state-by-state suffrage fights were not the appropriate method for enfranchising blacks, it came in New York in the spring of 1867. The state planned to meet and revise its constitution, and Republican governor Reuben E. Fenton urged New Yorkers to at long last do away with the 1821 property requirement imposed on blacks. Of the 20,806 black males—some of them minors—living in the state as of 1865, about twenty-one percent already owned property enough to vote. Should the state adopt a color-blind franchise, another 11,000 black men would obtain the ballot. Although some 720,000 New Yorkers had turned out to vote in the previous year's gubernatorial election, Fenton had won by a slim margin of 8,000 votes. Republicans had never done well in Manhattan or Brooklyn, but as many poorer blacks resided in those areas, franchise reform would aid the party in traditionally Democratic strongholds. Writing in his *New-York Tribune*, Horace Greeley turned Democrats' arguments against them, observing that it was only fair to restructure the state along lines imposed by Congress on the defeated South. When a bill for a convention came before the assembly, Fenton supporter Charles S. Hoyt offered an amendment allowing "every male citizen of the age of twenty-one years, without distinction of color" to be "entitled to vote." But moderate Republicans united with unwavering Democrats to oppose the revision, and Hoyt's amendment failed by an overwhelming vote of 90 to 33. Those blacks who could vote had "sent Governor Seymour home and Reuben E. Fenton to Albany," one fumed, but even the governor could not get party moderates to follow his lead.[30]

More resistant still were the states in the upper South that had never formally allied themselves with the Confederacy and so were not subject to the Reconstruction Acts. Kentucky and Delaware made no moves toward enfranchising black men. In Missouri, Republicans won handily in 1868, but despite large majorities in the assembly, party leaders failed to prod nervous junior legislators into supporting a proposed black suffrage amendment. The same held true in Maryland, where black activists counted on the vote to push for educational reform. When the Republican state convention backed away from a color-blind franchise, Judge Hugh L. Bond organized a May 1868 counter-convention of party radicals, but the meager turnout for the protest rally underscored the moderates' concerns. Bond denounced those assemblymen who preferred "expedient" pragmatism, insisting that "only courageous, inexorable battle for the right brings true glory." Whatever the truth of that maxim, blacks along the southern border remained disenfranchised.[31]

Largely stymied on the state level, Republicans at length gave in to radical demands and in February 1869 introduced the Fifteenth Amendment. The proposed constitutional revision was brief and consisted of two sections. Section 1 held that "citizens of the United States" could not be denied the right to vote "on account of race, color, or previous condition of servitude." A number of progressives, including Sumner, objected to the amendment's negative wording, preferring a simple assertion of the right of blacks to vote. Radicals feared that southern states might simply find new grounds, such as literacy tests or poll taxes, to evade the spirit of the amendment. Feminists complained that the carefully worded revision appeared designed to deny women the right to vote, while congressmen from the new state of Nevada worried that a more inclusive phrasing could enfranchise Chinese and Irish immigrants. A few Republican moderates suggested that a better solution would be to give freedmen a few years to become literate and acquire property, or that the proposed amendment should instead base representation in the House on the number of voters in any given state rather than the total population. Radicals responded that freedmen were endeavoring to do just that, and as Roudanez editorialized, "when the fifteenth amendment is adopted, Maryland will become a Republican State, and the white Union men of Kentucky and Delaware will be heavily reinforced."[32]

Democrats remained uniformly hostile, but black veterans and conventioneers continued to lobby undecided congressmen. John Mercer Langston assured Oberlin students that the amendment was "the logical and legal consequence" of the previous two amendments, and that "consequent upon the triumph of the abolition movement, its coming was inevitable." Regarding "the elective franchise as the one great power by which all civil rights are obtained," Frederick Douglass set "to work with whatever force and energy" he possessed "to secure this power for the recently emancipated millions." The tally in the House came to 144 to 44, with 35 abstentions; in the Senate, Republicans mustered 39 votes to 13 nays, with Sumner among the 14 who chose not to vote. Congress required Virginia, Georgia, Mississippi, and Texas to ratify as the price of Washington representation, although the last never did. Well aware that he owed his election to southern black votes, President Grant issued a statement endorsing the revision and warning "the [white] race more favored heretofore by our laws" that it was wrong to withhold "legal privilege of advancement to the new citizen." The adoption of this third Reconstruction amendment, he added, "completes the greatest civil change, and constitutes the most important event that has occurred, since the nation came into life."[33]

As the amendment moved through the states, Democrats resorted to the same arguments they had employed since resisting black liberation during the war. Republicans countered by hinting that their opponents were as disloyal as southern planters and praised black men for their military service. Although they brushed aside Democratic charges that they only wished to obtain black Republican votes, even moderates hoped that black voting rights would serve to dampen election-year racist rhetoric. "There isn't a Democrat fool enough," Greeley argued, "to treat [blacks] as Democrats now do after they shall have been armed with votes." When Georgia ratified in late March 1870, the amendment became law, and Douglass delivered a celebratory speech entitled "At Last, At Last, the Black Man Has a Future." Only ten years after South Carolina slaveholders had seceded, Douglass thundered, black Americans were "free, the black man is a citizen, [and] the black man is enfranchised." Black Republicans in Mississippi, as elsewhere across the South, celebrated ratification with "grand mass meetings." Democrats had fought the amendment in California, but with ratification "the colored people" of Los Angeles and San Francisco took to the streets in celebration. The Los Angeles Artillery fired "one hundred salutes to commemorate the event," after which the Reverend J. E. M. Gilliard, "the colored lecturer," spoke of the long struggle for political equality in both his state and his nation, reserving special praise for "Lincoln, Stanton, John Brown, [and] Grant."[34]

In areas where black voters did not hold a majority of ballots, voting rights did not translate into African American political service on the state level. But in the former Confederacy (as well as in Missouri and Washington, D.C.) blacks won seats in state assemblies and served their regions in virtually every capacity. Many of those who stood for election had first served in their state constitutional conventions; Pinckney B. S. Pinchback, who had written the clause in the Louisiana constitution pertaining to public transportation and acted as president of the Union Progressive Club, first served in the state senate before filling out a five-week window as the era's only African American governor. Six other men earned the title of lieutenant governor, 60 acted as militia officers, 9 were secretaries of state, and 112 won election to state senates. Most impressive of all were the 682 men elected to state legislatures. Contrary to popular writings and images common to the mid-twentieth century, however, only in South Carolina, where 316 African American men held state office during the period, did people of color enjoy a majority in the lower houses. In Tennessee, only twenty men won state positions between 1868 and 1876; in Missouri, the number was one. On average, few than twenty percent of southern political offices during the peak of Reconstruction were in the hands of black men.[35]

Even so, whether they were thrilled or horrified by this change, South Carolina had gone from having a state assembly dominated by slaveholders to one dominated by men of color. More impressive yet, as far as progressives were concerned, was the far larger number of blacks who served their states and counties in appointive or lesser elective offices. Particularly in rural areas, where majority black populations dominated, African Americans served their constituents as coroners and constables, judges and jury commissioners. Seventy-nine men, including future senator Blanche K. Bruce, assisted new school districts on state boards of education. Another 232 served either as justices of the peace or as county magistrates, and 113 were county commissioners. Only one served as district attorney, but forty-one were sheriffs and twenty-five were deputy sheriffs. In the decades before the war, jailors and wardens incarcerated and executed men like Denmark Vesey, but now nine African American men held the former position and four the latter. No less than 146 black urbanites served on city councils in Richmond, Petersburg, Norfolk, Nashville, and Memphis. In Virginia, William Hodges, a literate freeman who had been arrested in 1830 for helping runaways forge freedom papers, served as superintendent for the poor in Norfolk.[36]

Hodges was typical of Virginia officeholders in that he had been free before the war. But outside of Virginia, Louisiana, and the District of Columbia, a majority of those who held political office had been born into bondage. In South Carolina, at least 131 men who served the state were former slaves. Among them were Robert Smalls, elected to the assembly in 1868, and Aaron A. Bradley. While still in his teens, Bradley had escaped and made his way to Boston, where he read law and became an attorney. A good many were veterans. William J. Whipper, born free in Philadelphia and also a lawyer, had enlisted in the Thirty-first USCT; naturally pugnacious, he had been court-martialed for fighting with a white lieutenant and had accompanied Frederick and Lewis Douglass to the White House to confront Andrew Johnson. He too was elected to the South Carolina assembly in 1868, the same year that Chaplain Benjamin F. Randolph took his seat in the state senate. Whipper and Randolph had been educated as young men, but other new assemblymen had learned to read while in the army. Black voters were always impressed by military service, and Stephen A. Swails, the Utica boatman who had fought with the Fifty-fourth, had wounds to prove it. He joined Randolph in the senate in 1868, while Sergeant William H. W. Grey, who also had fought at Fort Wagner with the Fifty-fourth, represented Charleston County in the assembly.[37]

African American politicians made the greatest impact in South Carolina, winning fifty-two percent of the elections for state or national office during the Grant years. By 1872, men of color—a large percent of them were mixed-race—occupied sixty-two percent of the seats in the house; with a black majority in the lower chamber and a Republican majority in the Senate, progressives chaired more than half the assembly's committees and succeeded in elevating two blacks into the speaker's chair and a third into the position of president pro tempore of the senate. The governor, Brigadier General Robert K. Scott, was a white Republican who had arrived in the state with the Freedmen's Bureau. Although Assemblyman Francis L. Cardozo boasted a British university education at a time when few white elites attended even a few years at an American college, reactionary Carolinians complained that black politicians had transformed the state into "a new Liberia." Essayist Louisa McCord denounced the legislature as the "crow-congress" and the "monkey show," but when a delegation of unconvinced New Jersey Democrats arrived to tour the state, they were pleasantly surprised to discover that Judge Jonathan J. Wright, the only black member of the state supreme court, "conducted himself with great modesty and propriety." The fact that the group expected to find Wright, an Ithaca-educated veteran of the 1864 Syracuse convention who had arrived in the region with the American Missionary Association, anything but a jurist of wisdom and "good manners" said more about the Newark delegation than about the quality of southern black activism.[38]

A similar coalition of white progressives and African American legislators held sway in Louisiana. Following the April 1868 elections, Henry Clay Warmoth, a Missouri attorney and veteran of the battle of Vicksburg, moved into the governor's mansion; his lieutenant governor was Oscar J. Dunn, the New Orleans–born freeman and veteran who had served in his state's 1865 black suffrage convention. Like South Carolina, Louisiana was witness to an old and often crippling division within the African American community between light-skinned freemen and those blacks liberated by the war. So many of the fifty-six Republicans in the Assembly were of mixed ancestry that the press was unsure of just how to count black legislators. Clearly, however, a majority of Louisiana's "colored" politicians, including Pinchback, had some white ancestors and had never been enslaved. Yet as in the Columbia, South Carolina, statehouse, even those black freedmen were atypical in their skills and literacy. One friendly reporter found the twenty senate Republicans—at least seven of whom were African Americans—to be "quiet, intelligent looking men." Dunn, who presided over the chamber, was a "portly colored gentleman of commanding presence, who seemed perfectly at home in his position." Due in part to the state's complicated racial history, both Dunn and the moderate Warmoth promised to work with all races and both parties to improve their battered state.[39]

By comparison, Georgia's black politicians were less affluent than their South Carolina and Louisiana counterparts. Before the war, 5.3 percent of Louisiana's African American population enjoyed freedom, but Georgia's 1860 freed population was a minuscule 0.8 percent, and most of them were impoverished former slaves. A few legislators, such as Tunis Campbell, hailed from the North, but of the state's black assemblymen, eighty percent had been born into bondage somewhere in the South, and not a single black politician born in Georgia had been born free. The state's antebellum code defined free people of color as "all negroes, mulattoes, and mestizoes, and their descendants, having one-eighth negro, or African blood, in their veins." But if Georgia assemblyman Henry McNeal Turner was characteristic of other South Carolina–born freemen in that he was mixed-race, the former Union chaplain and Bureau agent had no use for racial distinctions. "We need power and intellectual equality with the whites," Turner told one audience. "It does not matter whether he be a pretty or ugly negro; a black negro or a mulatto, whether he were a slave or a free negro; the question is, is he a negro at all?" All Americans who were not white bore "the brand of negro oppression," and the only issue that mattered to him was whether fellow Republicans pursued an agenda that assisted their constituents.[40]

Hostile newspapers portrayed the black assemblymen as rigidly partisan and determined only to aid their black constituents. Black Republicans in Florida, reported one journalist, resolved to assist no man "who had voluntarily been in the Rebel army." But Alonzo Webster, editor of the *Charleston Advocate*, a black weekly designed to serve the low country, countered that he "scorn[ed] the idea of the white or black man's party. The broad basis on which we are to predicate our legislation should be that of principle, and not of complexion." Under Republican governments, progressives sought to reform every aspect of society. South Carolina legislators passed bills expanding married women's property rights, modernized divorce proceedings, funded medical care for the poor, protected minors against parental abuse, and held white fathers financially responsible for their mixed-race children. Republicans were equally active on the local level. Nashville provided food and firewood to the indigent, and Petersburg regulated the rates charged by carriage drivers, paved dirt streets, and established a board of health. Democrats complained of the rising costs associated with free public schools and improved hospitals, but Republicans replied that they were dealing with the destruction wrought not just by the war, but by decades of planter neglect. Warmoth observed that Louisiana lacked a single paved public road, and New Orleans lacked a modern water filtration plant and so suffered from regular outbreaks of malaria and yellow fever.[41]

The new sense of public responsibility filtered down to ordinary citizens, who displayed a newfound assertiveness. Armed with the Civil Rights Act of 1866 and assisted by black sheriffs and jurors, southern blacks began to sue when denied those "advantages and privileges," as attorney and future Virginia congressman John Mercer Langston put it, "which are so indispensable to rational and useful enjoyment of life that without them citizenship itself loses much of its value." Aware that many of Johnson's conservative judicial appointees were not sympathetic to equal rights, Congress created nine new circuit judgeships, which allowed Grant to appoint more Republicans to the bench. (At the time, circuit court judges did not hear only appeals but also both criminal and civil jury cases.)[42]

When Mississippi state court judges refused to accept blacks as jurors, Governor Adelbert Ames, a Maine-born general, issued an executive order in April 1869 mandating that "all persons, without respect to race, color or previous condition of servitude, who possess the qualifications" would be allowed to serve. Aware that civil rights cases stood no chance before all-white juries, Ames, who had survived both Fredericksburg and Gettysburg, was determined to advance democracy on every level. Conservatives gave way on Ames's jury order but insisted that "social equality must be the work of time, not of legislation." Having arrived on the southern mainland only twelve years after the first English settlers, black Americans thought they had waited long enough, and if juries proved necessary for equal rights, they were as willing to appeal to courts as had their former masters in earlier years when asserting their legal rights as slaveholders. One hostile editor resorted to sarcasm, writing that "poor oppressed whites" should thank Ames for relieving them of jury duty," while warning uncomplaining blacks that they had "no right to complain" about having to "bear some of [the] burthens" of government. Other editors grumbled that African Americans, unwavering in their demands for equality, "saunter around town in their best clothes," while some black women even "haul their babies around in carriages." So determined were freedpeople not to accept their old roles, another groused, that it was nearly "impossible to hire one to wash and cook, or to cut wood and work the garden."[43]

African Americans used the Civil Rights Act to sue for a variety of grievances. Although most aspects of the Black Codes had been nullified by federal law and state constitutions, some southern communities continued to employ children as apprentices under old vagrancy statutes. Pea Powan went to court to obtain a writ against planter and former slave owner James C. Harris, who had detained Powan's four minor children. In Mississippi, Elvira Harrison, Lucinda Jones, and Lizzie Alexander sued a county court prosecutor who arrested them for vagrancy when they refused to provide him with a certificate of employment. Stephen Jackson, a Kentucky freedman, used the 1866 law when employer Elijah Bohen refused to pay him the promised $160 "for ten months labor" in planting corn and raising hogs. Jackson produced two witnesses who corroborated his story, and the jury not only found for Jackson, they assessed damages at $169.62.[44]

Unwavering in their refusal to accept any slights, no matter how trivial, blacks proceeded to make life miserable for those who refused to accept a new day in race relations. An African American Chicagoan named Smith sued Dan Rice, a Democratic activist and traveling circus owner, when an usher tried to seat him in the section reserved for blacks. Smith "desired to sit elsewhere, and upon being refused, made complaint." William A. Hayne, a South Carolina–born Bureau teacher and state assemblyman, sued barber J. Lombardo for refusing to shave him. Despite the fact that Lombardo was himself mixed-race, the "aristocratic barber of Charleston" accepted only white customers, and when Hayne demanded a shave, "the legislator was disparaged as a 'nigger.'" Hayne sued for one thousand dollars, the same amount that a Mr. Sauvinet collected when denied service in an all-white New Orleans saloon.

"We may be on the eve of a greater change than any of our suppositions imply," marveled one black editor.[45]

For those long denied any legal rights, even the smallest mistreatment deserved redress, but the issue of public transportation was no trivial matter. As cities again began to grow in the years after the war, streetcar lines expanded too, and for black workers inexpensive transport was crucial to their employment. Despite Salmon P. Chase's efforts in Washington and the successful Philadelphia campaign waged by Octavius Catto, most streetcars around the nation remained stubbornly segregated, if more by tradition than by law. As early as 1862, General Nathaniel P. Banks won the right for black soldiers to ride on New Orleans cars, but African American civilians still walked beside the tracks each day or rode on special cars marked with a black star. Richmond began to construct its system in 1865 as Virginians rebuilt their burned capital, but one newspaper warned black Virginians not to expect to buy "first class seats until they are fully recognized as a first class people." Even after Catto's triumph in 1867, the mayor of Philadelphia publicly announced that he did not permit "the ladies of his family to ride in the cars with colored people." Trains and steamboats also retained separate cars or floors for black passengers. Only Massachusetts, in 1865, had passed a pioneering law requiring the integration of all public accommodations.[46]

Such practices belonged to the discredited antebellum past, Roudanez argued from the pages of his *Tribune*. "This law, known as the Civil Rights Bill," made the black American "a citizen to all intents and purposes, and has so far repealed all laws giving railroad companies the right to make rules and regulations discriminating against him on account of race." Pinchback agreed, telling the Louisiana Senate that it was "unjust and monstrous" that men and women born in America were routinely denied "decent accommodation" on "Steamboat, railroad cars, or conveyance here in our native country." Nor was this a private matter in which individual companies could decide policy. Since streetcar companies had to make agreements and sign contracts with the cities in which they operated, John Mercer Langston added, those deals were "fundamentally with the entire community," not merely the white portion of it, and so it was the legal "duty of the common carrier of passengers to receive all persons." As for the commonly heard argument that "no white lady would ever ride in a car with colored women" who were not her servants, Roudanez laughed, that only served "to convince the world that, though claiming to be a lady, she [possessed] very low manners." Should a white not care to dine beside "such self-made men as Frederick Douglass, Minister [to Haiti] Ebenezer Bassett, and [then-state] Senator Revels, at a hotel table," he could eat "his meals at his room." Perhaps due to their relatively privileged backgrounds, no black editor argued against the existence of "first class accommodations" or expensive hotels. They simply denounced the exclusion of "wealthy, intelligent or respectable" blacks from dining rooms that "welcome and entertain all white persons, whatever may be their character."[47]

So common was racial exclusion from elegant hotels, that when Sarah Wall Langston—the future congressman's mixed-race wife—returned to Manhattan from Haiti and was escorted to a dinner table by the ship's captain, white guests assumed she was Cuban. Her husband heard two well-to-do women speculating as to her ethnicity, and when one insisted that Sarah was black, the other remarked: "Why, they wouldn't let a nigger into this hotel and into the dining room." Shortly thereafter, John Mercer Langston was refused a seat at a hotel dining room in Columbus, Ohio, while he was paying a call on then-governor Rutherford B. Hayes.[48]

Prodded by Roudanez's editorials and Pinchback's speeches, a number of New Orleans activists worked to force streetcar integration in 1867. Then–state senator Pinchback routinely boarded cars reserved for whites; because of his light complexion and political position, conductors rarely asked him to leave, although they sometimes stacked packages around him in a makeshift wall. In late April, a conductor forcibly removed William Nichols from his car and had him arrested, but on the advice of Warmoth, then preparing for his gubernatorial race, the city dropped the charges. Hoping to use the incident to compel integration, Nichols sued the conductor for "assault and battery and false imprisonment." The streetcar company responded by dropping its formal policy of racial exclusion but adopted the practice of simply remaining stationary if blacks boarded the cars. Some whites stepped off when blacks took a seat, but the result was that few streetcars moved, and since white passengers had to reach their destinations too, the company finally gave way. Nichols dropped his suit against the conductor, having won the day.[49]

Manhattan streetcars were similarly segregated by custom rather than by state or local ordinance. As in the South, the companies that began to build lines in the decade before the war were privately owned but signed contracts with the city. As a result, as one black passenger observed, "riding, for colored folks, depended upon the whims of respective stage drivers." Emboldened by successes in Washington, Philadelphia, and New Orleans, New York City's black community renewed their efforts to force the state to adopt a uniform policy. As early as 1864, activists had rallied around a black war widow who was arrested for refusing to leave a whites-only car. In May 1871, blacks organized a concerted effort. On the same day, numerous riders boarded omnibuses on the Fifth Avenue line, while others marched into "fashionable barrooms and restaurants" and demanded service. "Sambo appears to have worked himself into a phrenzy for enforcing the civil rights bill in the matter of transportation," one conservative editor sneered. But the assault on white prerogative forced the hand of Republicans in the state assembly, and in the following year they too passed legislation banning discrimination in public accommodations.[50]

Some cities in the South proved more resistant. Ironically, urban segregation had been more common in the antebellum North, and before the war, southern free blacks and slaves who were hired out by their masters often resided in hovels beside elegant townhomes. But the end of slavery erased the region's chief form of social control, and conservatives were determined to replace bondage with newer varieties of racial domination. Richmond streetcars allowed blacks to ride, but only by clinging to the outside. Mobile relegated blacks to the rear of the cars and erected iron lattices to maintain racial divides. But when war hero Robert Smalls was warned to stand on the rear platform of a Charleston car, a coalition of blacks and white Republicans promised to boycott public transportation so long as "colored men, women, and children are refused admittance to the cars" while "the worst class of whites may ride." African Americans in Mobile filed suit against the president of the

Dauphin Street Car Company in April 1867, and when the company offered only to create separate "Star Cars" for African Americans, "vast
throngs of white and black gathered by the various lines of the city railway." Many of the whites sought to deny black riders seats, but in cities
where the majority of passengers were African Americans, lengthy boy-
cotts could cripple private businesses. The Mobile company was "obliged
to take [separate] cars off, for the negroes did not support them, and they
were run at a dead expense." Even after companies in Charleston, Nashville, and Mobile formally ended segregationist policies, individual
drivers and white riders often made travel difficult for black riders. After dealing with an incident in Vicksburg, one elderly black decided to
move to Kansas, where he hoped "every man was treated rite and where
they had some law." "I could tell you of the ignorance of the South for a
hole day," he complained to Blanche Bruce.[51]

As the potential emigrant was to discover, few cities in postwar America embraced integration, which meant that black activists and their attorneys kept courts busy. When a Cincinnati commuter was ejected from
a streetcar, he sued the conductor and pocketed eight hundred dollars.
A Washington conductor ordered Sojourner Truth off his car, and when
she refused, he stopped the car and attempted to pull her off. The sixty-
eight-year-old abolitionist held on with both hands but injured her
shoulder. She sued, and the conductor "lost his situation." One white
rider in Washington so objected to sitting beside a black man that he
pulled a pistol "and swore he would blow the nigger's brains out." The
black rider remained resolute, so it was the furious white passenger who
stepped off. As late as 1871, a black man sued and collected against a
Baltimore company for refusing to carry him. The federal court decision settled the matter, one black editor was pleased to report, "and
colored people will be permitted to pay their fare and have their rides
like other people. The world moves on verily."[52]

When railroads and steamboats pursued similar policies, black activists sued them as well. Emma Coger, a twenty-year-old teacher from Illinois, was assaulted while traveling by steamboat from Keokuk, Iowa.
Told to take her meals in the pantry with the servants, Coger found a
seat beside other "ladies" in the main dining room. Three of the five
white women at her table left rather than dine with her, and when that

failed, the captain yanked her chair away and dragged her from the room. Coger sued for damages and collected, even though the captain offered up a number of witnesses who claimed the "yellow girl" had instigated the altercation. A Washington jury awarded activist Kate Brown fifteen hundred dollars after an Alexandria, Virginia, guard beat her savagely for boarding a "ladies" car. Black politicians were particularly quick to resort to legal avenues. In three separate cases from 1871, Pinchback sued the New Orleans, Jackson, and Great Northern Railroad for twenty-five thousand dollars after it sold him a first-class ticket for a sleeping car and then denied him the compartment. Georgia assemblyman James M. Simms collected eighteen hundred dollars in damages against the Richmond, Fredericksburg, and Potomac Railroad for ejecting him from a steamer it operated between Washington and Richmond. Hannibal C. Carter, then preparing for a successful run at the state assembly, won ten thousand dollars in damages from the Mississippi and Tennessee Railroad "for ejecting him and his wife from a car on the train assigned to the white people alone." The Indiana-born politician was not accustomed to backing down. Carter had risen to the rank of captain in the Seventy-fourth USCT but had been reprimanded for signing a petition to the secretary of war on the matter of unequal pay. At a Republican rally in 1868, white terrorists fired at his group, but the veteran was armed and shot back. Five black men sat on the jury that awarded him damages, and Carter was able to use the money to finance his campaign; certainly his willingness to sue the railroad also earned him the gratitude of black voters.[53]

Secure in their abilities, having worked their way up the political ladder from veteran to Union League member to assemblyman, six African American legislators sought higher office in the fall 1870 elections. Particularly in Mississippi, Louisiana, and South Carolina, where black residents held the majority, ambitious men set their sights on Washington. Joseph H. Rainey, born a slave in Georgetown, South Carolina, had fled with his wife during the war but returned in time to attend the 1865 black convention in his native state. Although not a veteran, Rainey joined the Union League, served in the state constitutional convention, and won election to the state senate in 1868. Robert DeLarge and Robert Brown Elliott also represented South Carolina, while Jeffrey Long won his seat from Georgia, Benjamin S. Turner represented Alabama, and

Josiah Walls captured Florida's only Congressional seat. Two of the six had served in the army, with Walls rising to the rank of sergeant; and two, Turner and DeLarge, had worked for the Bureau. Three of the men, as newspapers routinely observed, were "bright mulattoes," although four of them, including Rainey, had been born into slavery. All but Long had served in their state assemblies. Four of the men represented the states they were born into; Walls was a former slave from Winchester, Virginia, and Elliott had arrived in the South from Boston. Congress "will soon have its full proportion of darkey members," jeered one New York journal.[54]

The fact that three of South Carolina's four congressmen were African Americans attracted considerable attention in the national press, and with good reason. Nothing more aptly symbolized a new day in American democracy than men of color representing the state most identified with slavery, nullification, and secession. Symbolism, however, was hardly synonymous with influence. As a state senator, Rainey had chaired the finance committee. Turner had sat on the Selma city council. Walls had been elected mayor of Gainesville and served in both Florida's house and senate. In Washington, however, many northern Republicans, either due to their own inherent racism, or out of fear of looking too socially progressive in the eyes of their constituents, kept their distance. Speaker James G. Blaine offered them unimportant committee assignments; upon being sworn in, Rainey was "assigned a seat in the furthermost corner of the Hall." The Republican press patronized them. The Cleveland *Plain Dealer* described Rainey as a "snuff-colored contraband" who "dresses unusually well for a Southern member of Congress." Through their speeches, at least, they were able to address issues generally ignored by northern members of their own party, and Congressman Long—who was elected only to serve in a short, four-month session during the winter of 1870 and 1871—used his time on Capitol Hill to address white violence against southern freedmen. Although reelected in 1872, Elliott finally decided he could have a greater impact on the state level where real social change was being effected; seventy-eight percent of black officeholders during the era functioned on the local level. Elliott resigned his seat in favor of a post in the South Carolina assembly, which promptly elected him speaker.[55]

Just months earlier, Hiram Revels had raised his right hand to take the oath of office as U.S. senator from Mississippi. Born to free parents in North Carolina in 1822, Revels and his family moved out of the South after the Vesey plot and Nat Turner revolt led to a backlash against free blacks. Revels first enrolled at a Quaker seminary in Indiana before attending Knox College, an Illinois institution founded by antislavery Presbyterians. Revels began his ministry with AME congregations in Kansas and Missouri, where he was briefly arrested for "preaching the gospel to Negroes." When the war came, he served as a chaplain with Maryland's first black regiment and then with the Freedmen's Bureau in Mississippi. A brief time spent as alderman in Natchez prepared him for a term in the state senate, and when Mississippi ratified the Fifteenth Amendment in January 1870, Revels was selected by the state assembly to fill the seat resigned by Senator Albert Gallatin Brown in early 1861. Senators George Vickers and Willard Saulsbury Sr., Democrats from Maryland and Delaware, respectively, rose to challenge Revels's right to take his oath, citing Taney's 1857 Dred Scott decision that blacks were not citizens of the United States. But the majority, led by Sumner and pointing to the Fourteenth Amendment, swatted away the objection. "Dred Scott is a dead African [American slave]," observed Horace Greeley, "while Hiram Revels is a live American citizen."[56]

Revels served only thirteen months, and his service in the Senate was more emblematic than effectual. But for black Americans, the sight of Revels sitting beside Sumner and speaking in a chamber once home to slaveholders Jefferson Davis and John C. Calhoun was symbol enough. "The colored people are rejoicing over the advent of the colored Senator Revels," huffed one Virginia editor. Revels took a room with George T. Downing, the black hotelier and longtime activist, and black political groups around the country peppered him with invitations to speak. That July, black Republicans in Kansas, Missouri, and Nebraska staged a series of "Emancipation Day" celebrations, with "grand dinners and speeches." Southern whites, even those Unionists who supported the Republicans, were less ecstatic. "Since Revels was elected," one complained to an unsympathetic Adelbert Ames, "it is surprising how grasping the niggers are and the great number flocking here from other states clamorous for office." A handful of northern progressives, however, lobbied for either Revels or Douglass to be placed on the ticket as Grant's running mate in 1872.[57]

It was just as well that they were not. By the election, popular discontent with the growing corruption within the Grant administration, together with northern weariness over the seemingly endless Reconstruction battles, led some white reformers to believe that Grant should be denied a second term. Among those calling themselves Liberal Republicans, the name of editor Horace Greeley was bandied about as a possible choice. Black Republicans were horrified. Although hardly unworried by reports of scandals within Grant's cabinet, African American activists shared none of the moderates' desires to heal sectional wounds by deemphasizing civil rights in the former Confederacy. The president had enthusiastically endorsed the Fifteenth Amendment, and that was enough for southern freedmen. "*Grant Secured* to *us the privilege* of exercising that franchise," one Mississippian assured now-senator Ames, and "You know how the name of Grant sounds to the Colored voters." Black Republicans debated the matter at their 1871 Southern States Convention of Colored Men, but the convention resolved to stand firm behind Grant. In early 1872, just before white Liberal Republicans met in Cincinnati in their mini-convention, southern blacks convened again, this time in New Orleans, to make it clear that their desire was that Grant would "be the choice of the party." For the blacks who continued to assemble and drill in "negro militias," the fact that their president was a former general meant a good deal.[58]

When the majority of Republicans, meeting at their regular convention in Philadelphia in early June, renominated Grant but replaced the scandal-plagued Schuyler Colfax not with Revels but with Massachusetts senator Henry Wilson, a handful of Republican defectors banded together with the Democratic Party to endorse a ticket of Greeley and Missouri governor Benjamin Gratz Brown. Blacks were having none of it. Wilson was a known radical and a supporter of Reconstruction, while the Democratic convention's band saluted the ticket by playing "Dixie." The Republican platform condemned corruption and endorsed the three recent constitutional amendments but announced that "local self-government, with impartial suffrage, will guard the rights of all citizens more securely than any centralized power." African Americans, who had largely admired Greeley, now thought him hopelessly naïve, as they well knew that most southern whites, if returned to power, would deny blacks the right to vote. "This means that they would repeal the work of ten years past," John Mercer Langston argued. "The teachers, men and women, who have gone South, are to be given over to the Ku Klux." If the platform "means 'State Rights' again," black Republicans would not "follow any one out of the Republican party." For politically astute observers such as future congressman Langston, the problem with Grant was that his willingness to turn a blind eye to Washington corruption fractured the progressive coalition, not that he was too tough on white reactionaries.[59]

Black activists were particularly tough on former white allies and those they regarded as African American apostates. John Mercer Langston little knew what to make of the feud—largely over foreign policy—between Grant and Charles Sumner, but he personally urged the senator to "remain in the Republican party" and not go with Greeley. When Sumner persevered in his defection, Langston informed him that he "could not, and would not follow him." Louisiana governor Warmoth also abandoned Grant, and as Pinchback put it, was "driven practically out of the Republican party [after] he espoused the cause of Mr. Greeley." After the Reverend J. Sella Martin, a South Carolina–born freedman who led congregations in Boston and Washington before returning to the South with the American Missionary Association, stood for election to the Louisiana assembly as a Greeley supporter, he fell "from the grace of the Church" and was forced to resign his ministry. After Martin claimed that "thousands of colored men in their heart of hearts followed Charles Sumner" and supported the fusion ticket, Langston publicly rebuked him. It was "simply untrue," Langston wrote, that even "five hundred [black] men in any part of the country were influenced by Mr. Sumner or anybody else" to vote for Greeley. Four years later, a despondent Martin locked himself into a hotel room and swallowed an overdose of laudanum.[60]

Douglass also weighed in, writing an editorial for the pamphlet *Grant or Greeley—Which? Facts and Arguments for the Consideration of*

the Colored Citizens of the United States. Like Langston, the great abolitionist was less interested in defending the ethical lapses of Grant's appointees than he was in attacking a purported "reform" movement that
openly called for the "overthrow of negro supremacy." Douglass thought
that phrase, voiced at the Democrats' Baltimore convention, absurd.
"Where has the negro been supreme in this country?" he wondered.
Philip A. Bell, editor of San Francisco's *Elevator*, had little doubt that
black voters would spurn the fusion ticket of Greeley's men and Democrats. "They are the same men, who ten years ago, flung the lash at the
slave markets of the South," he editorialized, "they are the men who
refused sitting in a street car, alongside with a colored man, and who
now, when aware of your growing political importance, pretend to be
your friends and claim your votes." Neither writer had to worry. Grant
won handily, capturing fifty-five percent of the popular vote. Black
southerners, one Baptist preacher assured a northern visitor, had little
trouble distinguishing between what he dubbed "the Union ticket and
the Rebel ticket." The minister conceded that black voters did not always know a great deal about the candidates at the top of the tickets, but
they knew what the parties stood for. "Yes, sir; we knows that much
better than you do!" Freedmen knew their former masters "from skin to
core, better than you do or can do, till you live amongst 'em as long, and
see as much of 'em as we have."[61]

By the time Grant began his second term in March 1873, white violence, ever a threat in the southern countryside, had grown worse yet,
until Reconstruction had effectively ceased in portions of the country.
Yet during that same year, Blanche K. Bruce turned down Adelbert
Ames's suggestion that he run for lieutenant governor of Mississippi; his
gaze was instead already on Washington and the bigger prize of a Senate seat. In assessing Reconstruction's relative successes and failures,
Republican journalists tallied votes and watched with concern as black
activists vanished during a rural canvas, or as white mobs kept black
voters away from southern polls. Harder to quantify was the impact
that Bruce's election to the nation's highest chamber had on black
Americans across the republic. "I am a Louisianan and an exile from my
dear old State," F. W. Kornman wrote Bruce from Manhattan. She and
her husband hoped the new senator would send her a small portrait

photo, "the picture of the first man of the colored race who has risen sublimely above *prejudices* and *passions* of *race* and boldly stood up for the right [as] no conqueror on the battle ever so much deserved the laurel wreath of fame as you do."[62]

CHAPTER EIGHT

"An Absolute Massacre"

White Violence and the End of Reconstruction in the South

WILLIAM DENNIS NEVER GAINED the national fame of war hero Robert Smalls. Unlike Blanche K. Bruce, he never raised his right hand to take the oath of office as a United States senator. He was neither wealthy nor politically connected, as was Judge Hugh L. Bond. Dennis was merely a foot soldier in the wars of Reconstruction, and like Octavius Catto, one of its casualties. Born a slave in Virginia in 1844, he somehow found his way north to Manhattan during the chaos of war. Only twenty years old, he enlisted in the Forty-fifth USCT on July 11, 1864, and was witness to the final months of the conflict. When fighting stopped, he remained in the army and was finally mustered out in Mississippi. He settled in Meridian, a simple "laborer" according to the traveling census taker, and became active in the Union League and the Republican Party.[1]

Shortly before Grant's bid for a second term, white Democrats, many of them former Confederates, took to marching through the streets of Meridian, hoping to intimidate Republicans into staying away from the polls. One afternoon, nearly five hundred "Ku-Klux cavalry" trooped by the home of Mayor William Sturges. The group was led by A. G. Horn, editor of the city's *Mercury*, who glared at the northern-born white mayor's house, shouting: "We must get that d[amne]d rascal."

Refusing to be intimidated, black Republicans organized their own "negro militia." Their captain was thirty-year-old William Clopton, another Virginia native who had joined the Fifty-fifth when he reached freedom in Tennessee. According to one unsympathetic account, Clopton concluded an afternoon's drills by promising his men that with "one hundred" such troops "he could annihilate one thousand white men." At almost the same moment the muster was concluded, a fire broke out in a store owned by a former Confederate. Freedmen did not start the blaze, but Clopton allegedly aimed his pistol at those attempting to extinguish the fire, "thanking God the rebels' property was burning." After the town's AME congregation rang its bell in hopes of pulling the throng off the streets, the sheriff dispatched a posse to arrest Clopton, who was "placed under guard in the Court House."[2]

That night, white Democrats staged a meeting designed to show that they had "at last determined to check the mad and destructive career of the bad negroes and their white" allies. Dennis, together with J. Aaron Moore, a black Methodist minister and state assemblyman who served on the Meridian town council, and D. Warren Tyler, called a second meeting at the African Church. They "desired peace," they assured the crowd, and the three "made speeches regretting that a better feeling did not exist" with their white neighbors. "The Union party was growing at all times," Dennis promised, and Grant was sure to be "triumphant" in 1872. There was no need for violence. The sheriff, however, chose to regard their speeches as "very inflammatory," and the fact that the prudent Tyler had carried a gun to the meeting was enough for him to order the arrest of Tyler and the Reverend Moore.[3]

When the trial of the three began, Judge E. L. Bramlette promptly lost control of his courtroom. A Mr. Brantley was deposed regarding some comments Tyler—whom he dismissed as "this boy here"—had made "about the Democrats getting frightened." But the "very rude and angry" Tyler shouted that Brantley was a liar. Not accustomed to being spoken to in such a fashion by a black man, Brantley raised his cane and advanced on Tyler, only to be held back by the city marshal. What exactly happened next depended on the political persuasion of the reporter. Mayor Sturges swore that Tyler had no weapon beyond a "pocket-knife," but hostile whites claimed he "drew a repeater and commenced firing at Brantley." Nearly all of the spectators who crowded the courtroom, it appeared, were armed, and "an indiscriminate firing commenced." Judge Bramlette was shot "through the head and instantly killed"; several whites were wounded, and Clopton and four other blacks died in the melee. Badly wounded, Dennis leapt from the second-floor window to the brick pavement below, but whites pouring out of the courthouse caught him and "cut his throat." The mob chased Reverend Moore as well. He escaped, so they "went and burned his house." Tyler also jumped from the window but was caught as he ran down an alley and "instantly killed." The mob, now carrying "double-barreled shot guns," surrounded Mayor Sturges's home. "They treated [him] respectfully," he admitted, but warned him that he "must take a Northern-bound train" or be killed. "I yielded," Sturges confessed.[4]

Just one month earlier, in February 1871, Democrats in Camden, New Jersey, had resorted to similar tactics to depress the Republican vote. Some of the roughly four hundred black voters in the town had voted as soon as the polls opened, hoping to avoid trouble. One of those who arrived later was John Gillen, a twenty-four-year-old black South Carolina native. Gillen and another black man, John Ray, were standing in the Republican column to vote—candidates often waited in separate party lines to obtain their "ticket"—when "the line was broken up by white men." Squire Henry and Francis Souders, a constable, shoved their way into the line, and Souders, who was armed with a pistol and a blackjack, intimidated three black voters into leaving the polls. The two whites arrived with a crowd of Democrats, many of them from Pennsylvania and twelve of them Philadelphia policemen. Gillen was determined to vote, and the other blacks who remained in line began to push Henry. "This thing has been going on long enough," Souders shouted, pulling his gun and shooting Gillen. Both Souders and Henry began to beat Ray, while the blacks in the room "kicked out" at Henry. A jury found Souders guilty of starting what the press dubbed "the Camden riot" but recommended "mercy" on the grounds that Gillen had lived to testify against him. Eleven months later, Souders, still a constable, was arrested again for assaulting John Quinn, an African American. It was during the intervening months that a white Democrat assassinated Octavius Catto in Philadelphia.[5]

Revolutionary movements can be stopped by violence, provided enough politicians are assassinated, enough party registrars are eliminated, and enough voters are intimidated into remaining home on Election Day. For one too-brief moment, South Carolina had congressmen who reflected the state's demographics; its elections were the most democratic the state would see prior to 1965, when both women *and* African Americans would again enjoy the ballot. But as the Indian wars in the West drew fast-moving cavalry out of the southern states, leaving behind only ever-dwindling numbers of infantry—most of whom were stationed in urban areas—white violence rose accordingly. In the first year after the passage of the Military Reconstruction Act, two thousand soldiers monitored elections in Louisiana. Within just two years, that number was reduced by nearly three quarters, to 598, and by the time Grant stood for reelection, only 421 soldiers guarded the vast state's 51,843 square miles. The concomitant spike in white vigilantism marked the beginning of the end of Reconstruction in much of the former Confederacy. In Florida, Secretary of State Jonathan Gibbs estimated that at least 153 blacks were assassinated in Jackson County alone during the three-year period after the election of 1868. By the time he left office in March 1887, Congressman Robert Smalls claimed that fifty-three thousand African Americans had been murdered, mostly in the South, in the years since emancipation.[6]

Black Republicans and their allies quickly came to describe all white vigilantes as members of the Ku Klux Klan, but it was hardly that simple. Had black activists and the federal government faced one enormous, highly centralized organization, ending the violence on the countryside would have been more easily accomplished, even with the declining number of cavalrymen. Founded in Pulaski, Tennessee, by six Confederates on the day before Christmas in 1865, the group was named after the Greek word for circle, *kyklos*, and initially was little more than a social club for discontented veterans. By the spring of 1867, however, it had adopted a hierarchical, military-style organization, and former slave trader and Confederate general Nathan Bedford Forrest emerged as its Grand Dragon, or national leader. Members took an oath to support "a white man's government" and were thereafter required to carry arms at

This cartoon, which appeared in Harper's Weekly, *drew attention to the connections between the Confederacy, Klan activity, and the Democratic Party. Here, a "pirate" flying the flag of white supremacy, sails the "New Alabama," a reference to the CSS* Alabama, *the notorious Confederate raider that was finally sunk in 1864 off the coast of France. An American warship responds with a shell labeled "Equal Rights to All." Courtesy Library of Congress.*

all times. Massachusetts congressman Benjamin F. Butler, the former officer who had freed black runaways at Fort Monroe, understood that the Klan was not a response to defeat itself, but was instead an extralegal attempt to halt the political reforms engendered by Reconstruction. Having "lost on the open field of battle," Butler argued, former slaveholders had drafted the Black Codes. The Civil Rights Act of 1866 and the new state constitutions mandated by Congress had erased those attempts to circumvent the Thirteenth Amendment. So "now by stealthy midnight assassination" Klansmen sought to deny black Americans "the rights guaranteed to [them] by the constitution of the country." What white southerners could not achieve by working within the political system, Butler charged, they would accomplish through "force, fraud, and murder."[7]

Klan members typically operated in their home counties, which meant that they knew which local black activists to target, but also that those activists knew them as well. In hopes of disguising their identities, night riders "wore caps over the head and eyes," Carolina freedwoman Frances Andrews remembered, "but no long white gowns." A few Klansmen hoped to frighten southern blacks into believing that they were the ghosts of dead Confederates, but nobody was fooled. "Preacher Pitts' brother was one," Andrews claimed. Former slave Lorenza Ezell agreed that all blacks knew which of their white neighbors were involved. "Spite dey sheets and things," Ezell pointed out, "I knowed dey voices and dey saddle hosses." A third black witness, A. P. Huggins of Mississippi, stated that "many of them [had] served in the confederate army." After the Klan adopted military-style ranks, former privates naturally fell into line behind their old captains and lieutenants. A few blacks even noted that the companies stretched back into the antebellum years, when armed whites had ridden nightly patrols in search of blacks who had wandered away from their masters' estates. "There wasn't no difference between the patroles and the Ku Klux that I knows of," added freedman J. T. Tims. "If th'd ketch you, they would whip you." In some cases, Klansmen were the sons of older Confederates. "The men who were too old, and the boys who were too young to go to the war," surmised Mississippi Republican Horatio Ballard, "are to-day the least 'reconstructed' portion of the community."[8]

Klan activity was most common in upcountry regions, where federal cavalry was scarce and where struggles over land were most acute. White farmers who had not owned slaves before the war banded together with planters in the name of labor control, as the former feared that too-independent black yeomen posed competition and the latter wished to impose greater restraints over those freedmen who had used the scarcity of labor to obtain beneficial sharecropping agreements. Consequently, vigilante bands identified as Klan locals were synonymous with Democratic voters and activists. As fewer blacks resided in upcountry districts, the intimidation of a small number of voters—or the elimination of a few Republican registrars and poll workers—could tip the balance in state and local elections. As one Ohio editor charged, "the national triumph of the Democratic party" would mean the "reign of the bowie knife, of the revolver, and of ruffianism" across much of the South. So open was Klan violence in many counties, and so openly affiliated with Democratic politicians were its members, that "Ku Klux" quickly transformed into a verb. An African American woman complained that she was "Ku-Kluxed" after refusing to work for a particular white family, while an aggrieved black Georgian threatened to "Ku-Klux the Ku-Klux" vigilantes.[9]

As a national institution, the Democratic Party recognized the dangers of placing its hopes on racially inspired violence. Although long accustomed to employing racist appeals in every section of the republic, some Democrats worried that continual Election Day violence would attract the wrath of Grant and the more progressive Republicans in Washington. And if the intimidation of some black voters won elections in those counties already balanced between blacks and whites, rumors of white coercion also inspired blacks to turn out in large numbers in districts where they barely held the majority. Even northern moderates feared that left unabated, "the faintest gleam of a Democratic triumph" could lead to greater "tumult, violence, incendiarism, and bloodshed on the part of the Ku Klux, bushwhackers and unreconstructed rebels of the South." So long as northern politicians thought the violence sporadic and isolated, they were inclined to ignore the issue. But once partisan-minded men understood, as one of now-senator Adelbert Ames's worried constituents wrote, that "a democratic organization [was] forming in this state, which must resemble in its purpose somewhat the 'Ku Klux' organization," they began to take notice. Every Democrat elected to Congress through violence was one more vote against national Republican policies.[10]

Klan violence was rarely random, and white raiders did not simply assault blacks for being black. Carolina assemblyman Benjamin F. Randolph, who was murdered on the eve of the 1868 election, was typical of those targeted for removal. During that same year, Klansmen killed two other black legislators in South Carolina and another in Arkansas. In Camilla, Georgia, Democrats opened fire on a Republican parade, killing or wounding twenty black marchers, and a black Georgia assemblyman was dragged from his home and nearly beaten to death. Black politicians were not safe even within the walls of southern statehouses. After Tunis Campbell rose in the Georgia Senate to protest his expulsion—the federal Congress demanded his reinstatement—he was warned that there were "eight men stationed on the front and side gallery, above the Republican members," each armed with "revolvers." When Campbell refused to be silenced, a number of nervous "Senators then moved away [from] his seat." Klansmen also assaulted any black male for "acting the Big Man," since assertive freedmen tended to be the type of freedmen to join the Union League or attend political rallies.[11]

White Republicans, regardless of where they were born, attracted almost as much violence as their black brethren. Despite hailing from Georgia and once having owned slaves, Unionist William Hugh Smith had opposed secession and fled to federal lines in 1862. After being elected governor of Alabama in 1868, Smith was routinely harassed by Democrats who hoped to intimidate him into quitting his office as he spoke around the state. In Sumter County, Smith gave a speech at the courthouse, while one listener, very much "in liquor," stood close to the governor "with a large knife in his hand, drawn," while several others "came in with revolvers on their persons." Smith was finally drowned out by "insulting remarks" from the audience, but he was allowed to depart alive. Northern men were often less lucky. Charles Stearns, an abolitionist who settled in Georgia, ran for judge in Columbia County and won by twelve hundred votes. As he traveled his circuit, however, mobs attended his courts, shouting that Stearns had been "elected by nigger votes and the niggers had no right to vote." Having fought beside free-soilers in "Bleeding Kansas," Stearns was no coward, but after Democrats dragged him from his home and savagely beat a black employee, the judge resigned his position and returned to Massachusetts. "It seems that no Yankee who does his duty can live down South," one of Ames's correspondents reported after witnessing the murder of a Republican chief of police. "[T]he assassin can do his bloody work without fear of punishment, so long as he confines himself to the butchery of northern men."[12]

Although white violence spiked on the eve of Grant's election, it dissipated only slightly during his first term in office and spiked again during the 1870 off-year elections. When Republicans staged a rally in Norfolk featuring John Mercer Langston, recently appointed dean of the Howard University law school, and ex-governor Henry H. Wells, a Rochester-born general who had gained fame for his role in cornering John Wilkes Booth in a Virginia barn, armed Democrats shoved their way close to the podium. Langston attempted to speak over their jeers and catcalls, but when the small band of outnumbered policemen tried to "quell the disturbance," whites fired "several volleys from small arms." As the audience scattered "in every direction," a few blacks returned fire. Miraculously, nobody was killed, but John T. Daniel, a prominent white Republican, was shot in the head, and "many whites and blacks were wounded." The next morning, patrols found a dead black man, "badly cut" and tossed into an alley near the rally. "The ex-rebels at Norfolk have been emulating the example of friends at Mobile and New Orleans," complained one Republican, "yet they insist that the South is as tolerant of Republican sentiments as the North."[13]

In the years prior to the war, crowds of African Americans, whether praying peacefully in churches or talking in low voices on city street corners, always unnerved whites, and some former Confederates blamed the escalating violence on northern Republicans who encouraged blacks to vote and stand for office. Black veterans required no encouragement, of course, but as former governor Benjamin F. Perry explained in a public letter of 1871, "the colored people of South Carolina behaved well during the war and would have continued to do so but for the unprincipled carpet-bagger, who came among them and stirred up hatred to the white race." All of the "lawlessness and violence" sweeping the state was the logical result of "organized colored troops" and postwar black militia companies. On the advice of Republican governor Robert K. Scott, a former general and Bureau official, black veterans organized the "National Guard Service of South Carolina," and President Grant ordered an additional twelve infantry and four cavalry companies into the state. The show of force was strictly defensive. But soldiers could not be everywhere, and their transfer inevitably dampened violence in one location, only to allow it to erupt in another. Just two weeks before the

Norfolk riot, a Democratic mob in Greene County, Alabama, assaulted Congressman Charles Hays during a campaign stop. Although born in the county and once a Democrat, Hays had joined the Republicans in 1866 and so was hated by his neighbors. As with Langston, the crowd first tried to shout him down, and when that failed they dragged him from the stage. A number of freedmen intervened, but the Democrats were better armed. Fifty-eight blacks were shot, four of them mortally, with only two whites injured.[14]

If black officeholders symbolized what African Americans could aspire to, predominantly black or interracial schools, churches, and Union League halls—which were frequently one and the same thing—paved the way for such achievement. As they had virtually since Appomattox, whites torched them almost as rapidly as blacks could construct them. When League members in rural North Carolina returned to their homes after a "Flag Raising" in Halifax, they found a white mob standing in "a line a Cross [the] public Road with gun and pistle." In urban areas, such as New Orleans, where federal troops remained stationed, Democrats rarely dared to burn schoolhouses. Instead, they organized gangs of "boy regulators" to barge into classrooms and demand that all students of color leave. That tactic, however, attracted the attention of powerful Republicans when two of the youthful victims turned out to be Governor Pinckney B. S. Pinchback's sons. Teachers and schools in the countryside proved safer targets. Schoolmarm Maria Waterbury and her female colleagues were repeatedly hounded by the "Ku-Klux," who constantly surrounded their cabin late at night. "Tramp, tramp went their feet on the porch," she wrote, "and we heard them try the locks on the doors, and whistle to each other." During the first six months of 1871, vigilantes burned twenty-six schools in one Alabama county alone. Waterbury prayed loudly during such moments, but "when the morning began to dawn" she reported the incidents to the authorities. "There is an eternal hatred," one state investigating committee concluded, "existing against all men that voted the Republican ticket, or who belong to the Loyal League, or [are] engaged in teaching schools."[15]

To unreconstructed whites, those men and women who did not stand with them were against them. Most white Unionists were former Whigs, and although southern businessmen hardly welcomed the new dawn of racial egalitarianism, neither were they interested in fighting on in a cause they had never much cared for. Constitutional Unionists in Virginia, Kentucky, and Tennessee had carried their states for candidate (and former Whig) John Bell in 1860, and Democrats feared that fair elections might provide the Republicans with a permanent lock on the Electoral College. As a result, no act of interracial cooperation, no matter how innocuous, escaped the notice of the Klan. When Octavia Otey, an Alabama widow, rented her land to black farmers, hooded horsemen galloped onto her property, asking whether her tenants were "humble and respectful" to her and demanding one of them by name. Otey refused to comply, and after that her livestock began to disappear. South Carolina Democrats organized an "Agricultural and Police Club" in 1870, whose bylaws required members to ostracize whites who declined to join. White Republicans, organizer George Tillman sneered, would be treated "as a whole nigger would be treated," and members were to "pass him and his whole family with silent contempt." When social ostracism failed, there was always the noose. John W. Alvord toured the South in 1870, and Christmas found him in Kentucky. His hotel, he discovered, was run by "an ex-rebel," one of the Kentuckians who had marched across the border to fight for the Confederacy, and the local "headquarters of the ku-klux or 'marauders'" was close by. Just how near the reverend discovered when he awoke to find that "a white man was hung to a tree in the court-house yard," with "six or seven colored men" whipped and another murdered.[16]

In an era when party machinery relied on a handful of activists to distribute ballots, guard ballot boxes, and encourage the timid to vote, the elimination of just a few individuals could turn a close election. Carolina riders draped in sheets and hoods surrounded the home of Sherrard Butler, who they knew had picked up 360 election tickets from the Abbeville courthouse the previous day. Since the ballots—colored red with Lincoln's profile on them—had been printed in Columbia, they could not be quickly replaced. But the Klansmen were armed and Butler's family was at home, so he surrendered the tickets. The next day, more than two hundred blacks were unable to vote after the Republicans ran out of ballots. Georgia Klansmen paid a similar call on Henry Lowther, charging that he "had taken too great a stand against them in the republican party." The men, whom Lowther later identified as Democrats, let him live but carried him to a swamp and castrated him. Political vigilantes were crueler still toward A. R. Wilson, a black registrar from Burleson County, Texas. Wilson was first "fearfully mangled with knives" and then lynched. Republicans in Washington estimated Klan membership at only thirty thousand by the 1870 elections, yet targeted assassinations of key activists threatened to destroy the entire Republican Party in the South. "For Godsake," pleaded a white Texas judge, "send help immediately for it is impossible for union men to remain here unless we are protected."[17]

Because the killings of Republican activists attracted the attention of Washington, white supremacists were generally content to harass black voters. In Atlanta, a federal marshal tried to avoid problems by having Republicans line up on one side of the courthouse, with Democrats on the other. White "toughs" pressed into Republican lines, spitting in the face of the marshal and making it nearly "impossible for a man to crush through to the polls." But in a few high-profile cases, Democrats went after those men they regarded as "real enemies." The same month in which Klansmen shot South Carolina assemblyman Benjamin F. Randolph also marked the first-ever assassination of a sitting member of Congress. In Monroe County, Arkansas, the secretary of the Democratic Committee emptied a double-barreled shotgun into Congressman James M. Hinds, a white Unionist and the former attorney general of Minnesota. The killer later claimed he had been intoxicated, prompting one Republican editor to agree that he had been "drunk unquestionably with that kind of rot-gut which is now firing the hearts of the rebels throughout the South, a virulent hatred of northern men."[18]

Although the murder of a white congressman earned Klansmen the ire of President Grant, the national publicity the killing generated served its larger purpose of warning Republicans of the dangers of party activism. Once word of Hinds's execution spread, a relatively small number of Democrats found they could intimidate tens of thousands of Republicans, sometimes without bloodshed. Typical was the admonition nailed to the door of Bob Martin, a black Greensboro shopkeeper. "You're getting' too damn smart," read the warning. "The white folks round Burke's Cross-Roads don't want any sech smart niggers round thar." On occasion, courageous judges ordered men who violated the voting rights of black Americans taken into custody. Nat Ward of Memphis was twice arrested "on charges of intimidating negroes at the polls," as were Joseph Pearl and Martin Burke of Greenbush, New York. But in remote rural districts, night riders promised swift retaliation for those who contacted the authorities. Mississippi's Dike Michee paid a visit to his brother, a prominent Republican, but found his brother gone and his pregnant sister-in-law murdered. When Michee asked his father why the crime had gone unreported, the old man replied that the killers had "beat him & cut all the hair off his head and threatened that if he came to town to make any report they would injure him."[19]

By the dawn of 1871, the Republican organization was in tatters in portions of the South. Party activists, one South Carolina freedman lamented, had been "scattered and beaten and run out." Republicans had "no leaders up there [in Union County]—no leaders." In Louisiana, Republicans charged that more than two thousand supporters had been "killed, wounded, or otherwise injured" in the final weeks leading up to Grant's reelection. Polling numbers supported the allegations. Republican ballots in Louisiana fell from sixty-nine thousand in the previous election to thirty-three thousand, and in three Georgia counties that were home to black majorities, the president failed to garner a single recorded vote. Southern Democrats swore to carry "the election peaceably if we can, [but] forcibly if we must." Authorities in Louisiana's St. Landry Parish stumbled across a "pile of twenty-five bodies" of black Republicans dumped in the woods, and following that atrocity, the Klansmen marched the survivors to the polls "and made them vote the Democratic ticket." When informed of the violence throughout the South, Senator Ames fretted that no party could have hundreds of its "best and most reliable workers" eliminated and yet remain a viable organization.[20]

In hotly contested districts across the South, however, militant Republicans did more than merely worry about Democratic violence. John Price, the progressive white editor of the *Little Rock Republican*, was ready to respond in kind. If Democrats wanted a war, he editorialized, "let us be prepared to give it to them at once, and all along the line." Like black veterans in both sections of the country, Price was not prepared to give up on freedoms so hard-won. While moderate Republicans in Washington urged appeasement, Price denounced "the pernicious delusion that a policy of conciliation should be adopted towards the malignant and unreconstructed adherents of the 'lost cause.'" In South Carolina, freedmen stockpiled guns and transformed their Union League chapter into a black militia. A Democratic company, known as the Sweetwater Sabre Club, escalated tensions by firing shots into the home of League member Ned Tennent. Summoned by a large bass drum, one hundred black militiamen turned out to protect Tennent's home. Although the white mob was larger, they intended intimidation, not battle, and they dispersed. When Klansmen torched a black church near Chester, South Carolina, veterans fought back. "The darkies killed some of de Ku Klux and dey took dere dead and put dem in Pilgrim Church," remembered former slave Brawley Gilmore. "Den dey set fere to dat church and it burnt everything up to de very bones of de white folks."[21]

In those states still controlled by Republican legislatures and governors, Democratic editors tried to whip up popular support with melodramatic stories of alleged riots and rapes. Under the sensational headline of A CASE FOR A ROPE, the Macon *Daily Telegraph* accused Tuskegee postmaster W. P. M. Gilbert of planning a riot that threatened "the lives of many hundred innocent women and children." White allegations of black sexual misconduct had once been limited to times of slave rebelliousness, but such charges grew commonplace during Reconstruction. After black militiamen confronted a smaller party of white vigilantes in Georgia's Dawson County, the *Telegraph*'s editor characterized that as "a threatened negro riot." Assuring his readers that Georgia was "as peaceful and law respecting as any State in the Union," he insisted that the only solution to armed blacks fell within "Judge Lynch's jurisdiction." Where black Republicans resided in large numbers, however, resorts to the noose were more easily advocated than accomplished. In Memphis, a fight between "five negro soldiers" stationed in the city and dockworkers resulted in the stabbing of one of the whites. A white policeman tried to arrest the soldiers, but one pulled his pistol and the five retreated to their barracks, where they were supported by "a dozen or fifteen" other black soldiers. Fifteen Texas Klansmen fared even less well when they tried to intimidate blacks by marching through the freedmen's section of Millican. Organized by George Brooks, the later-assassinated

League head, blacks opened fire on the group. The Klansmen scattered, leaving the street littered with masks, sheets, and two pistols. Brooks's men added the revolvers to their small arsenal.[22]

The prospect of renewed civil war, this time between black and white militias, led southern governors of both parties to appeal to the federal government. State authorities attempted to dampen white violence by raiding farmhouses and country taverns believed to be Klan hideouts, sometimes capturing documents and robes. But only in states that enjoyed large pockets of white Unionists, such as Tennessee and Arkansas, could underfunded governors mount credible challenges to Democratic vigilantes. South Carolina governor Robert K. Scott dispatched militia units against the Klan in 1869 and 1870, but his meager forces were so unsuccessful that he was reduced to begging black militiamen to disband and pleading with upcountry Democrats to stop the killings. Furious that the Freedmen's Bureau was finally discontinued in 1870, black Republicans were in no mood to unilaterally disarm, and white Unionists worried that unless the Democratic Party put an end to the "lawlessness and outrage," the federal government would be forced to step in. "If we don't enforce the law ourselves it will be done for us," admitted southern Unionist Benjamin Hill. "The Ku Klux business is the worst thing that ever afflicted the South."[23]

To bolster beleaguered state governments, Republicans used their majorities in both the House and Senate to pass a series of laws between May 1870 and June 1872, commonly dubbed the "Enforcement Acts." Designed to enforce the Fifteenth Amendment, the first of the bills was introduced by Ohio congressman John Bingham, who conceded that black voters were routinely harassed in his own state. Assisted by the Secret Service, established in 1865, and the Justice Department, created in June 1870, Congress authorized Attorney General Amos T. Akerman to use federal marshals to enforce the Constitution and investigate assaults on black voting rights. Although born in New Hampshire, the fifty-year-old Akerman had moved south to teach in the 1840s; a former Whig opposed to secession, he had nonetheless accepted a minor post in the Confederate quartermaster corps. But with war's end, Akerman announced himself a Republican, condemned Andrew Johnson's policies, and endorsed black voting rights. Despite the fact that the laws were

unprecedented in their scope and power, designed as they were to uti-
lize federal machinery to supervise and enforce local elections, Democrats were surprisingly mute over Akerman's actions, perhaps because
he had been one of them for the past three decades. So enthusiastic were
southern Republicans in his appointment that two newspapers in Georgia, where Akerman had made his home since 1850, endorsed him for
the vice presidency for 1872.[24]

Rather than criticize an adopted son of the South, Democrats simply
insisted that there was no cause for additional legislation. "There are no
Ku-Klux outrages," maintained a New Orleans editor, "nor is there any
need of martial law." Despite the hundreds of murders that preceded
each election cycle, one Alabama judge told a Congressional committee
investigating white violence that he "did not believe any such organization as Ku-Klux existed" in his state, and that blacks "were as safe there
as in any state in the Union." Almost at the moment the judge spoke
those words, John Tyler Jr., the editor of the *Montgomery Advertiser* and
the son of the former U.S. president and Confederate official, revealed
just how little he accepted the reforms of the previous decade. Tyler
wondered how long the "southern people" would have to endure such
"wrongs," suggesting that blacks and white Unionists had no right to
define themselves as "southerners." For the handful of Democrats who
had never accepted defeat and now fought on, having exchanged their
uniforms for hoods, the arrest of Klansmen was a blatant assault on
"southern" rights. Among those who recognized that white vigilantism
was combat by another name was sixty-year-old abolitionist Wendell
Phillips. "There was still a state of war with the South," he warned a
Manhattan audience in the spring of 1871. "Let General Grant lay his
hand on the leaders in the South," he shouted, "and you will never hear
of the Ku-Klux again."[25]

Following ratification of the Fifteenth Amendment, Phillips and
other old crusaders largely moved on to other issues, particularly wom-
en's suffrage and the emerging labor movement, but black activists continued to lobby Washington-based Republicans regarding their newly
won rights. In March 1871, following a black convention in Atlanta,
Georgia state senator Tunis Campbell journeyed to the capital to meet
with Grant about conditions in his part of the South. Black Tennesseans

forwarded a detailed petition to Congress denouncing poll taxes, and the Southern States Convention of Colored Men met in the house chamber in Columbia to demand additional legislation to protect those liberties earned during the war. "If we look over all the Southern States," remarked Louisiana delegate J. H. Burch, "we will find the highways and the byways marked by the bleaching bones of white and colored men, who have fought, bled, and died that colored men might assume, even in South Carolina, the rights and privileges of manhood." Worried about the coming elections, the president and his attorney general crafted a bill aptly named the Ku Klux Klan Act, which Grant signed into law on April 20, 1871. Democrats dubbed the president "Kaiser Grant" and charged him with trying to usurp power, but Akerman advised that appeasement was useless. Nothing was "more idle than to attempt to conciliate by kindness that portion of the southern people who are still malcontent," he counseled. "They take all kindness on the part of the Government as evidence of timidity." Even as Campbell returned from Washington, his supporters warned him to take care on his journey, as they feared "rebels" planned to ambush him on his "way home."[26]

If some black activists were apprehensive about the dedication of northern reformers, they had no such concerns about Akerman. Since his election to the Georgia constitutional convention of 1867, he had stood with progressives, an especially brave position given the potential dangers to family. Although chronically unwell, the tall, lean Dartmouth-educated Akerman struck visitors as a man "of learning" with a "disposition to deep meditation." As was the case with many southern Unionists, the self-proclaimed "dedicated opponent of Klanism" was not so much a proponent of black social equality as he was an attorney determined to uphold the rule of law and the authority of the federal government. Hoping to crush white vigilantism for good, the attorney general instructed district attorneys to resort to "extraordinary means" to destroy the Klan. On Akerman's advice, Grant declared martial law and suspended the writ of habeas corpus in nine Carolina counties, powers granted him under the Klan Act. To better supervise the trials of those captured by army patrols, Akerman left Washington for the South, where he oversaw the prosecutions. Many of those brought before the court were tried by interracial juries, and once they received lengthy prison sentences in northern penitentiaries, most of the convicted were prepared to "puke," or confess, as Akerman indelicately put it, and identify others in their group. Although the Justice Department only obtained 168 convictions, Akerman's informants guessed that as many as two thousand vigilantes fled the state rather than face arrest.[27]

"Peace has come to many places as never before," Frederick Douglass enthused. "The scourging and slaughter of our people have so far ceased." But the aging abolitionist was overly optimistic. The Klan Act allowed federal marshals to guarantee protection to witnesses and jury members, but absent more troops, such promises often proved hollow. As one district attorney working in Kentucky warned his superiors, white supremacists "never fire on United States soldiers, but they do not hesitate to shoot Marshals whenever an opportunity is presented." Federal judges also lived in fear. When prosecutors could not prod captured vigilantes into turning state's evidence, they had to rely on black victims. Those brutalized might recognize their tormentors' voices, but juries demanded exact identifications. "The offences under these laws most complained of are perpetrated in the night time and under the additional protection of disguises and disciplined caution," one Mississippi Unionist complained to Adelbert Ames, "and direct testimony is of difficult procurement." At a late 1871 convention in Columbia, Pinchback and South Carolina congressman Robert Brown Elliott, who had a far better sense than Douglass of conditions in the South, implored Washington to send more troops and "complete that [work] which is so auspiciously begun." Frederick G. Barbadoes had traveled all the way from California for the conference, and none of the delegates intended to back down. But neither were they confident that Akerman and his attorneys could put a complete halt, as Pinchback observed, to "the murder of the prominent representative men of our class."[28]

White vigilantism did not end in 1871, but it changed. Democratic mobs were less likely to assault blacks at the polls, where marshals were inclined to station themselves. Groups of night riders near urban areas also attracted the attention of army patrols. But small groups and even single assassins continued to prey on Republican leaders, and on occasion, white gangs rioted against black neighborhoods in ill-defended up-country towns. Intimidation continued as well, and both carpetbaggers and scalawags awoke to find empty coffins with their names inscribed on them dumped near their doors. In Alabama, a lone gunman lay in wait for a U.S. marshal as he returned from a political rally and "shot at him as he passed," reported a black journalist, "but owing to the darkness missed his aim." As ever, vigilantes sought to eliminate ministers, understanding how the murder of one influential community leader might terrify an entire congregation. "One smart nigger in some localities would control the votes of two or three hundred niggers," observed a visiting New York attorney. The "Democrats wanted to get those recognized leaders out of the way; if they could not scare him out, then they would kill him."[29]

As Tunis Campbell was to discover, there was more than one way to eliminate black leaders. Since his arrival on the Georgia coast, conservative Democrats had despised him for his efforts at land reform and voter registration, denouncing him in the press as an "old reprobate" and an "old black Ku klux." When elected to the state senate, the Democratic majority expelled him and the other black senators, only to see them reinstated in 1870 by an order of Congress. Rumor had it that assassins hoped to murder him on his journey back from Washington and his meeting with the president. Finally, in January 1875 an all-white grand jury indicted Campbell, who also served as a justice of the peace, for the false imprisonment of a white man two years earlier. Campbell had fined Isaac Rafe one hundred dollars for breaking into two homes owned by blacks. Although the county contained three times as many African Americans voters as white citizens, the jury empanelled to hear the case contained only one black, but two whites who once had had run-ins with Campbell. Even then, the jury failed to return a verdict, and the judge, a Confederate veteran, warned them that he would sequester them for nearly a week unless they reached a decision soon.[30]

For farmers who were needed in their fields, the threat was enough. The jury found Campbell guilty but recommended mercy and a modest fine. The judge refused, stripped Campbell of his office, and ordered him taken to the Chatham County jail and then the state penitentiary. Campbell and his attorneys appealed for a bond, but the judge snapped that he "would not take a bond for the sum of a million dollars." One friendly journalist described the trial as a "farce," but the hostile Macon

Daily Telegraph sneered that the "King of the McIntosh County Congos" was finally out of the way.[31]

On the morning of January 12, 1876, prison guards arrived at the jail to collect the former justice. Handcuffed and attached to a chain twelve feet long, Campbell was dragged through the streets of Savannah as a warning to other Republicans. Georgia had already begun to institute a series of prison work camps, and Campbell and 119 other convicts were leased to Colonel T. J. Smith, who compensated the state $1,154 for their labor. Worried about Campbell's powers of persuasion, Smith at first kept him under heavy guard, but soon he too was won over by Campbell's eloquence. Smith put Campbell in charge of his blacksmith shop, fed him from his own kitchen, and finally permitted him to preach three times a week. Despite this, Campbell's friends hoped to win his early release. A number of prominent blacks, including a good many current and former legislators, editors, and ministers, petitioned Governor James Milton Smith on his behalf. But Smith, a Democrat and former Confederate captain—and the man who had appointed the trial judge in Campbell's case—rebuffed their efforts. Finally, after one year, the sixty-five-year-old activist was released. Convinced that local Democrats would trump up another case if he returned to the coast, Campbell instead moved to Washington, and then after several years on to Boston, where he died in 1891.[32]

In counties far removed from the security of barracked soldiers, white supremacists occasionally staged quick strikes on Republican strongholds. Following a hotly contested election for governor, heavily armed Louisiana Democrats attacked the Colfax courthouse on Easter Sunday, April 13, 1873. The handful of whites inside the building were allowed to surrender and flee, but African Americans held on until the building was torched. Most of those killed were executed after they had laid down their arms. By the time two marshals arrived two days later, they counted at least sixty-two bodies. Survivors claimed that as many as twenty more bodies had been tossed into the Red River. The next year, three former Confederate officers launched a new paper in nearby Alexandria. Named the *Caucasian*, the tabloid, as an early editorial explained, was designed "to take a bold stand [and] assert the dignity of our manhood" by putting an end to the "tame submission to this most desolating war of the negro upon us." To the extent that the editors re-garded a color-blind franchise as tantamount to "war," peace was only possible if African Americans agreed to return to their antebellum con-dition. Within a month of the newspaper's first edition, white Demo-crats along the Red River met to organize a new paramilitary group called the White League, essentially a less clandestine Klan.[33]

By year's end, the White League had emerged as a statewide militia, and similar groups, sometimes known as Rifle Clubs, Red Shirts, or Knights of the White Camellia, appeared first in eastern Texas and then in other parts of the South. By claiming the right to muster as county militias, the groups sought to achieve the same ends as the Klan while escaping prosecution. Taking advantage of a severe recession in 1873, they hoped to act while much of the nation was focused on economic concerns, and they rightly guessed that Democrats would pick up seats in the off-year elections, which would further dampen Republican en-thusiasm for tough measures. Of the disorder that shook the South that fall, one third of the riots took place on or during the week before the election, with half of the mayhem starting with Rifle Clubs attempting to break up Republican rallies or scare black voters away from the polls. In New Orleans, only eight years after the 1866 riots, five thousand White Leaguers marched through the streets, demanding the resigna-tion of Governor William Pitt Kellogg, a Vermont-born Republican. When thirty-five hundred Republicans confronted them, both sides opened fire. In Washington, Grant summoned his cabinet for an emer-gency meeting and issued a proclamation commanding "turbulent and disorderly persons to disperse and retire peaceably to their respective abodes." To enforce that, the president rushed troops into the area, and within weeks the Seventh Cavalry arrived to restore order.[34]

A declining number of soldiers could not police so vast a region. White Leaguers in Coushatta, Louisiana, rounded up a number of Re-publicans, including six African Americans, a federal marshal, and a deputy sheriff, and staged a trial in which the defendants were accused of fomenting black "insurrection." The extralegal proceedings ended only when the men agreed to resign their positions and leave the state within twenty-four hours. In South Carolina, former slave and Union League organizer Ted Tennent, who had escaped an earlier lynching by summoning black militiamen with fife and drum, was again harassed by a mob, this time for allegedly ordering the burning of the plantation home of a Democratic leader and former Confederate general. Government investigators in the South spoke to 150 witnesses in Mississippi alone, among them Republican registrars ordered to leave town or face arson and prospective voters who turned away from the polls after finding them surrounded by armed whites. In one instance, White Leaguers prevented undertakers from selling caskets to the families of murdered Republicans. If northern moderates were increasingly uncomfortable with Grant's use of force in the South, black Republicans prayed only for greater enforcement of the law. Democrats engaged in "systematic warfare upon Republicans, white and colored," John Mercer Langston charged, which "necessitated the use of the army to maintain the peace, and protect the loyal people of the South." The army would have to remain in portions of his South for decades to come to shield governors, marshals, sheriffs, and the basic "operations of the Government," Langston believed, as the only alternative was the end to democracy.[35]

Langston had no shortage of evidence. One month before the battle in New Orleans, white and black militiamen engaged in skirmishes around Vicksburg, Mississippi. "Armed bodies of men are parading the streets both night and day," one Republican warned Grant, and "the City Authorities are utterly unable to protect the lives and property of the Citizens." That December, white vigilantes surrounded the courthouse, demanded that the black sheriff leave the county, and installed a white Democrat in his place. For Governor Ames, it was bad enough when toughs tried to intimidate Republicans into not voting, but the forced removal of elected officials was an even greater affront to popular government. Ames appealed yet again to the president, warning that freedmen and black veterans had no intention of backing down. "Give us guns and we will show the scoundrels that the colored people will fight," Abraham Burriss wrote the governor. "Arm us; let us protect ourselves, and show the scoundrels, assasans, that we have men of valor to come in contact with."[36]

Many of the generals who ascended to the presidency have discovered that life as chief executive was far different from that of army officer. During the war, Grant had given orders, and they had been followed.

Whatever else his failings as president—and his inattentiveness to the personal ethics of his appointees earned him the ire of clean-government advocates—Grant labored mightily to force change on a resistant South. Moderate Republicans grew weary of the violence in the South, and many northern politicians discovered it easier to turn a blind eye to the bloodshed, particularly as their constituents were far more concerned with rising unemployment in their own cities. A strike staged by black workers at a Washington railway company inspired the increasingly erratic Horace Greeley to denounce them as a "lawless mob" who refused wages that "thousands" of white laborers would "be glad" to settle for. Hoping to yet achieve a southern policy that combined force with conciliation, Grant backed demands for amnesty legislation that would remove the Fourteenth Amendment's prohibition on holding office for the final handful of high Confederate officials. The final Senate vote on the measure, thirty-eight yeas and only two nays, reminded progressives just how outnumbered they were in Washington corridors, as did the response of Missouri senator Carl Schurz when Grant sent a special message to Congress on the situation in Louisiana. Once a young revolutionary, the Prussian-born Schurz had followed Sumner into the Liberal faction in 1872, and rising in the Senate, he accused Grant and the military of trampling upon white civil liberties. By then, Akerman had resigned, collateral damage in a power struggle with the Interior secretary over grants of land to the Union Pacific Railroad. On the eve of the 1876 presidential contest, only black Americans stood by the unpopular Grant. The president, Douglass mused, "proved himself a better republican than he was supposed to be when first nominated and voted for."[37]

The lingering economic downturn also fueled a backlash against government spending on every level. Most voters were furious with state aid to railroads and other "lavish expenditures," and the grim mood of the electorate led southern scalawags to fear for their futures and carpetbaggers to advocate cutbacks. South Carolina's Daniel H. Chamberlain, a Massachusetts-born army officer who had led black troops during the war, shifted to the center following a narrow election victory in 1874, which won him the governor's office, and denounced state programs to aid those sharecroppers and tenant farmers hit hard by the depression. Some scalawags openly abandoned the Republicans for the

Democrats, a plausible move for former Whigs as the postwar national Democratic Party had abandoned its Jacksonian radicalism in exchange for pro-business policies largely indistinguishable from Republican economic programs. Others merely dropped the untenable label of Republican and embraced that of Redeemer, pretending to have "redeemed" their region from carpetbagger rule. Savvy black observers such as Bruce understood that the change in nomenclature meant little enough, since scalawags had never been enthusiastic about black political rights, and they encouraged black voters "not to fritter away your strength upon a divided ticket" but to stick with the Republicans. Although black activists knew they could not carry many close districts with only Republican ballots, they had never cared for scalawags such as Mississippi's senator James L. Alcorn, a former Whig who endorsed black voting rights only as a practical necessity. "The time has arrived when the Colored men should shake off the unprincipled rascals who ride into office at their expense," one registrar counseled Senator Bruce.[38]

White progressives living in the South were accustomed to the calculated moderation of scalawags and carpetbaggers. When Cynthia Everett, the dedicated Freemen's Bureau teacher who remained in South Carolina even after the agency was defunded, alerted Governor Robert Kingston Scott to the "lamentable conditions of juvenile prisoners in the Charleston Jail," the Republican governor instructed an aide to inform Everett that he had no "power" to deal with the problem. Such indifference did little to end Reconstruction in some parts of the South, but far more serious was the increasing willingness of Republican authorities to ignore the dangers posed by Democratic paramilitary units. Scott, at least, had mobilized black militiamen to protect the polls. But after being harassed by armed Red Shirts at a Republican rally, Governor Chamberlain abandoned his statewide speaking tour and gave up any attempts to disarm the vigilantes, despite being warned by Adjutant General Henry W. Purvis, an Oberlin-educated African American, that the extralegal gun clubs were not part of the state militia and constituted a threat to the government.[39]

Quickly running out of allies and options in the South, black activists turned back to their few reliable partners in Washington. With Grant on the eve of retirement, that meant the president's personal foe, Charles

Sumner. Secure in his safe Senate seat and facing increasingly poor health, Sumner was prepared for one final assault on southern folkways. Furious that growing numbers of black children attended inferior, segregated schools, despite the fact that a number of state constitutions and Congressional stipulations supposedly guaranteed equal access to education, the Massachusetts senator began to prepare legislation as early as 1870 that would expand on the rights promised by the 1866 Civil Rights Act. Sumner consulted with a number of black leaders, and his initial bill was crafted in conjunction with Howard University law dean John Mercer Langston. Sumner hoped the bill, which banned segregated inns, railroad, stage, and streetcar lines, schools, churches, juries, and even cemeteries, would pass in tandem with the conciliatory amnesty act. South Carolina lieutenant governor Alonzo Ransier, a Charleston-born freeman, endorsed the bill, stating that black Americans could not engage in "the pursuit of happiness" while forced to educate their children in substandard schools and constantly "defend [their] lives and property in the courts." To those who claimed the bill was unconstitutional, Sumner replied that it was authorized by the Thirteenth Amendment, which had not only abolished slavery but put an end to all "badges of slavery" and racial inferiority. Ominously, Illinois senator Lyman Trumbull, an early Lincoln backer and one of the authors of both the 1866 statute and the Thirteenth Amendment, kept the bill from coming to the floor in 1870. The bill's flaw, Trumbull warned, was that it was not really about civil rights but instead pushed for "social equality." Undeterred, Sumner reintroduced the bill twice more in 1871, with similar results.[40]

In five short years, the political climate in Washington had cooled considerably. White northerners had turned to other pursuits, and they tired of reading of the perennial election riots in the South. Speaking in Nashville, Senator Schurz shouted that although he had once been a radical, he was now ready "to stretch out my hand to all men who, having stood against us during the civil war, are now ready to work for the restoration of universal peace, harmony, friendship and true brotherhood." White supremacists, of course, desired none of these things, but as a reminder that the South was only solidly for the Democrats if Washington turned its back on reform, Tennessee Republican Gilbert

Haven, a white Unionist, wrote to encourage Sumner to fight for his bill "with all the vehemence of your soul." The Reverend Haven had boarded a train with four black men, one of them also a minister, and where Haven had been escorted to "an elegant car," the four black passengers had been forced to ride "in a dirty, ill-ventilated, close-packed, unswept car, as mean as mean could be." Those who lamented the inherent injustice of segregation, Sumner believed, had existed in the South since 1865 but were increasingly being silenced by mobs and reactionary politicians.[41]

Black activists and politicians continued to press their wavering allies in Washington, peppering Congress with tales of continuing segregation, mostly but not exclusively in the southern states. Douglass wrote of being denied dinner on a Potomac River steamboat after returning from the Caribbean on an official investigation requested by President Grant. Despite holding the position of lieutenant governor, Louisiana's Oscar J. Dunn was refused a first-class rail ticket in his own state. Meeting in a convention in Cincinnati, the black press also endorsed a supplemental act to the 1866 Civil Rights Act, at least in part as convention delegates Pinchback and Lewis H. Douglass remained active in both politics and journalism. Other appeals to Congress were more graphic, yet drew the link between atrocities and unequal accommodations. "The roasting of a poor negro lad with kerosene at Port Jervis a few days ago by two or three white brutes," Pinchback's *Weekly Louisianian* observed, "is but the crystallization of a sentiment, which in less defined form shut Frederick Douglass from a hotel in St. Louis." One of Bruce's constituents urged him to "Tell there in Congress how Howard Banks & his poor little Boy were brutally murdered here" in Vicksburg, and "how one of our oldest preachers was shot down." In Mississippi, the entire black membership of the state house and senate forwarded a petition along to Ames, demanding the "passage of an act equal in the purpose and intended effect of the Sumner Civil rights bill." The roster of names included also fourteen white Republican members of the house and another ten white senators. The Republicans had attempted to pass a state law similar to Sumner's, but Democrats stole the house version of the bill from the "Office of the Secretary" shortly before the assembly went out of session.[42]

If a handful of courageous white Unionists affixed their names to a public petition, Democrats were quick to exploit the specter of yet another extension of federal authority. As so often in politics, reality and rhetoric proved to be poor companions. A number of southern states already had even more stringent civil rights acts on their books, yet that did not stop what Langston dubbed "extreme articles from Southern journals" from warning their readers that mixed schools would inevitably lead to mixed marriages. "You may be sure the Democrats are not slow to play on this aroused prejudice," fretted one visiting Republican editor. Sumner's annual efforts to pass his bill surely led to the defection of more southern Republicans, who turned their coats and took the name of Redeemers, but while black politicians regretted the loss of their votes in state assemblies, they did not much mourn their absence in caucus chambers.[43]

When the Forty-third U.S. Congress met in December 1873, Congressman Butler reintroduced the bill, while Sumner, across the hall, again submitted a Senate version. Despite the concerns of southern Unionists, both versions were unambiguous when it came to school integration. Rising in opposition in the House on January 5, 1874, was the aged Alexander H. Stephens of Georgia, the former vice president of the Confederacy. Twelve years earlier, Stephens had famously described slavery as the "cornerstone" of his new nation, and now he assured the chamber that black southerners had "no desire for anything partaking of the character of social rights." Congressman Elliott responded the next morning, the galleries packed with reporters, black Washingtonians, and even General William T. Sherman, who desired to hear the rejoinder. Noting how Stephens's address of 1861 had "shocked the civilized world," Elliott hoped that the "progress of events has swept away that pseudo-government which rested on greed, pride, and tyranny." The black congressman concluded with a flourish. "The results of the war, as seen in reconstruction, have settled forever the political status of my race," he observed, and the "passage of this bill will determine the civil status, not only of the negro, but of any other class of citizens who may feel themselves discriminated against." Blacks in the gallery rose in applause, and it took several minutes for the chairman's gavel to quiet the chamber.[44]

Even then, it required one final event, and a major revision in the act, before it obtained the necessary majority. Although he had only turned sixty-three in January 1874, Sumner suffered from heart disease. By February he rarely left his bed. As each visitor came to pay his final respects—Douglass, George T. Downing, Massachusetts congressman George F. Hoar—Sumner's response was always the same. Rising from his pillows, the senator grabbed each visitor's hand tightly, whispering: "You must take care of the civil-rights bill,—my bill, the civil-rights bill, don't let it fail." Shot through with morphine to ease his pain, the senator died on the afternoon of March 11.[45]

Sumner's death served as a rallying cry for the bill's supporters, but his removal from the Senate also facilitated passage in an unfortunate way. With the great abolitionist not present to argue for some of its most crucial features, Republicans stripped the bill of its provisions for integrated cemeteries and, most especially, for schools. That earned the measure the required majority, but even then, 90 of the 162 Republicans who voted for the final version of the bill in February 1875 either planned to retire or were lame-duck members who had lost their seats the previous fall. Grant, who had endorsed the original measure, signed the act on March 1. Progressives were less than jubilant. "To let the colored people ride in cars, stop at hotels, and go to places of amusement, while they are denied equal school education," complained the editor of the Boston *Commonwealth*, "can bring no satisfaction to a thoughtful and logical mind." Speaking at a convention of black newspapermen, Georgia assemblyman Henry McNeal Turner agreed, denouncing the act as a "patched up apology for a Civil Rights Bill." Even after the bill's passage, Turner added, he had been "shoved out of first-class hotels" in New Jersey. Other activists, such as Pinchback and Langston, defended the bill as the best they were likely to get. Langston admitted to one Virginia audience that while he would have liked "to see the bill passed with that provision [on schools] retained," he believed that a weakened bill provided the basis for future reforms. Pinchback gave the final effort an equally lukewarm endorsement, noting that the first moment a white man was "debarred access to the public schools, or to all the conveniences and luxuries of modern transit," he would immediately claim a "violation of his rights of Citizenship" and seek redress in the courts.[46]

Aware that Grant had but months left in his second term, Democratic governors made little effort to see that the law was enforced. Some restaurants evaded the law by not applying for a license, since the act, as one black member of the Georgia legislature discovered, "only applied to those establishments for the carrying on of which a license was required." During the summer of 1876, more than a year after the law's passage, Benjamin Tanner, a Methodist minister, reported that he was rarely able to board first-class cars anywhere in the South. "In Atlanta everything is separate," he protested. "You go to the depot, and you find three sets of rooms—*to wit*, 'Ladies' Rooms,' 'Gentlemen's Rooms,' and 'Freedmen's Rooms.'" A few governors openly challenged the lame-duck executive and his marshals to enforce the law. Even before the Supreme Court struck the law down in 1883, arguing that the Fourteenth Amendment only prohibited discrimination by the states, rather than by individuals, the law had been effectively nullified by Democratic obstructionism, the complications and cost involved with filing suits, and white retaliation against black southerners who did so.[47]

By the time the Reverend Tanner returned North, the contest to replace Grant was already under way. The Republicans tapped Ohio governor Rutherford B. Hayes, a major general and a former congressman who had voted for the Civil Rights Act of 1866. Meeting in St. Louis in late June, the Democrats selected New York governor Samuel J. Tilden, a reformer who had taken on the power of his own party's corrupt Tammany Hall machine. But Tilden was also a mainstream Democrat in that he promised his southern supporters that he would end "the rapacity of carpetbag tyrannies." As was traditional, neither candidate campaigned, but Hayes's promises of clean government won back most of the Liberal Republican bolters of 1872, including Carl Schurz. Hayes also announced that he "wanted to plainly talk of the rights of the colored man," but precisely what, if anything, he planned to do to halt the violence was left unsaid. Black Republicans were accustomed to northern politicians sounding moderate while attempting to appeal to white voters, and many hoped that like Lincoln and Grant before him, Hayes might be a better champion of black rights as a president than as a candidate. Even so, Senator Bruce's constituents urged him to push for an uncompromising man. "We want no milk & cider Candidates for the

Presidency," one wrote on the eve of Hayes's selection. "We must have a man who will *use* the Strong arm of the law to suppress violence & punish offenders or political liberty is at an End in Miss[issipp]i."[48]

Reports flooded in to Hayes's campaign headquarters in Columbus, Ohio, that a number of southern states, including Louisiana and South Carolina, were lost without increased federal forces. Black legislators in the South Carolina assembly passed a resolution, formally "protesting against the [further] removal of Federal troops," soldiers that one Georgia editor decried as the "pimps and tools" of black Republicans. But the escalating Indian wars on the Great Plains left the public clamoring for more soldiers in the West. (The army's defeat near the Little Bighorn River in Montana Territory came just two days before the Democrats nominated Tilden.) Nine years earlier, with the passage of the Military Reconstruction Act, roughly twelve thousand soldiers had guarded rural voters and patrolled southern streets. By the summer of 1876, only twenty-eight hundred federal troops provided a largely symbolic occupation of what had been eleven Confederate states. Despite the rise of the Klan and other vigilante groups, the ratio of one soldier to every 708 southern civilians had been gradually reduced to one for every 3,160 people. As South Carolina congressman Joseph H. Rainey explained on the floor of the House, it was not merely a matter of black voters arriving unmolested at the polls. On occasion he had difficulty reaching his constituents. During one campaign swing, the congressman was riding toward a rally in Bennettsville when he and a number of supporters were confronted by a small army of more than one hundred armed Red Shirts. Through a stroke of astonishingly good luck, one of the few army patrols still stationed in South Carolina suddenly galloped into view. Had the soldiers not happened along, Rainey assured the chamber, a number of people "alive at this time," including himself, "would have been numbered among the dead."[49]

With United States troops declining in numbers, black Carolinians and aging USCT veterans once more began to drill. African American militiamen in Aiken County, a black majority county opposite the Georgia border, had been organized six years earlier by Governor Scott, and after renewed election violence in 1874 their numbers swelled to eighty members. Former Confederate general M. C. Butler responded by riding into the county town of Hamburg at the head of two hundred men and a cannon. After the black militiamen barricaded themselves in their quarters, the whites opened fire and readied the cannon. The blacks fled, but seven, including the town marshal, were shot as they ran; the marshal's body was then mutilated. Emboldened by their success in the heavily black region, another former Confederate general and Democratic activist, Martin W. Gary, published a thirty-nine-point agenda by which his party might achieve victory that fall. The entire proposal was founded upon military force. Point 12 encouraged "every Democrat [to] feel honor bound to control the vote of at least one negro, by intimidation, purchase, [or] keeping him away" from the polls. If intimidation failed, Gary recommended escalation. The "necessities of the times require" that some South Carolina Republicans "should die," he bluntly observed. "A dead Radical is very harmless," Gary added, while a voter merely driven away from the polls could return and be "very troublesome, sometimes dangerous, [and] always vindictive."[50]

Attorney General Alphonso Taft warned Hayes that he had given up trying to prevent voter fraud in Mississippi. A weary, abused Adelbert Ames had resigned his office during the previous March, and the new governor was John M. Stone, a Democrat and former Confederate colonel. "Are we to have *Soldiers?*" Sheriff William H. Hancock asked Senator Bruce. Only with military protection would the Democrats "allow the Colored voters to exercise their right of franchise." In a fair election, Hancock guessed, the Republicans could "carry the state by twenty or thirty thousand votes," but without guards Tilden would take Mississippi, "this is a certainty." Jefferson L. Edmonds informed Bruce that while trying to register blacks in Clay County, he had been "met by a mob twice and warned to leave or die." At each campaign stop, blacks asked Hancock whether they would receive safeguards that fall. The sheriff had no answer but urged African Americans "to organize and register" regardless. "What use," one replied, "for we cannot vote, unless there are Soldiers to protect us in doing so."[51]

Northern Republicans, even those who did endorse continuing federal force in the former Confederacy, understood that a solid Democratic South complicated Hayes's electoral math. Grant had carried Indiana and New York—the latter, with thirty-five votes, the Electoral

College's prize—but now the former appeared lost, as Governor Tilden enjoyed far greater support in his home state than had editor Greeley. Party leaders hoped to keep South Carolina in the Republican camp, but with "Mississippi, Louisiana, and Florida secured [by the Democrats] the chances are two to one in favor of the Rebel party," one black activist warned Bruce. A worried Pennsylvanian hoped that Congress might pass yet another law, which would not only secure blacks the right to vote but prosecute "each and all persons" who attempted to "intimidate or hinder" southern voters. The problem, of course, was that even the current laws simply went unenforced in the South, and with Sumner gone, few Republicans in Washington showed any interest in new legislation. "Assassinations, and the taking of men from jail by Mob violence and breaking their necks is very Common," a Republican reported from Columbus, Mississippi, correctly predicting that there "will be only one party voting in Miss in Nov[embe]r next."[52]

Anti-black rioting broke out in early September in Charleston. But two companies of federal troops remained stationed in the port, and within twenty-four hours the city's streets were clear and quiet. The violence simply moved upcountry to Ellenton, where six days of rioting in mid-month led to the death of somewhere between twenty-five and one hundred African Americans. As Election Day approached, chaos returned to Charleston. Unwilling to give up their political rights, black militiamen took control of the courthouse. Colonel Henry J. Hunt appealed to both sides to lay down their arms, but Charleston's mayor, a Republican, replied that "a Negro had as good a right to be on the street armed as a white man." The city's Red Shirts finally agreed to disperse, but elsewhere in the state Democratic activist (and future governor) Benjamin R. Tillman, who stood by the polls while holding a pistol, carried his precinct by a vote of 211 to 2. "Quite a number of Col[ored] were killed," one black Republican reported to Bruce, "many were killed in order to controle them."[53]

Election Day found Senator Bruce back in Mississippi, but to no avail. Despite the state's black majority, its eight electoral votes went to Tilden. The Democrats carried every southern state that housed no federal troops, but fraud and violence so plagued South Carolina, Louisiana, and Florida, that Republican-controlled vote-counting boards threw out the results and declared the three states and their combined nineteen electoral votes for Hayes. Due to the intimidation common to every southern state, Tilden captured a popular majority of 250,000 more ballots than Hayes and won 184 electoral votes, one vote shy of the required majority. If all three of the disputed states remained in the Republican column, however—and they had all gone for Grant four years earlier—the Ohioan would win by a single electoral vote. Democrats continued to insist their candidate had carried the disputed states, and it appeared that no clear winner would exist to take the oath of office on March 4. Hayes assured Douglass and other black leaders that he would never bargain their rights away, and that any Republican administration would uphold "the 13th, 14th, and 15th amendments." But the electoral deadlock created an unprecedented crisis. As part of a package of deals agreed to by his advisors and backers in early 1877, Hayes promised to remove the final detachments of federal troops in the South. The Congressionally established bipartisan election commission then rewarded all three of the contested states to the Republicans.[54]

What came to be dubbed the Compromise of 1877 marked the end to any remaining federal effort to protect black citizens in the former Confederacy. But despite modern attempts to impose a precise chronology on the period, Hayes's election did not bring about any neat conclusion to Reconstruction. The declining number of soldiers in the South already meant that black Republicans had been in harm's way since 1870, and while activists condemned the symbolic removal of the final troops, no progressive was naïve enough to believe that twenty-eight hundred soldiers stationed in a handful of urban areas provided their party or their property with adequate security. Nor did black office-holding suddenly stop on either the federal or state level. Perhaps to silence his northern black critics, Hayes appointed Douglass marshal of the District of Columbia. Blanche K. Bruce remained in the Senate until 1881, and while Alabama's Jeremiah Haralson, Louisiana's Charles E. Nash, and North Carolina's John Adams Hyman all retired or lost their seats in 1877, Mississippi congressman John Roy Lynch won a third term in 1882. Congressman Robert Smalls served five terms into 1887, as did James O'Hara of North Carolina. Thomas E. Miller of South Carolina, former Howard University law professor John Mercer Langston, and

North Carolinians Henry P. Cheatham and George Henry White won elections well into the 1890s, and in White's case, into the first year of the twentieth century.[55]

Particularly in southern towns and cities, blacks continued to enjoy positions of influence and power. In Jackson, Mississippi, Republicans persisted in dominating the city's affairs throughout the 1880s, and an integrated police force maintained order generally absent in the countryside. Black men sat on town councils in Little Rock, Chattanooga, Memphis, Nashville, and Charlotte. In Florida, black control of statewide offices declined after 1877, and Florida congressman Josiah T. Walls left office in March 1875. But in twenty-three Florida towns, African American office-holding *increased* 123 percent between 1876 and 1889, as blacks won election as mayors, city councilmen, tax collectors, city treasurers, and sheriffs. As late as 1891, Langston pointed out in an Indianapolis address, 2,393 African Americans were employed by the federal government in Washington, drawing combined annual salaries of $1,370,000. Among them was former senator Bruce, who worked as the recorder of deeds. "The civil service law as enforced at present," Congressman Langston observed, "has absolutely eliminated the color line in the Government departments." Even in the South, twenty-five percent of those who passed the competitive exam under the 1883 Pendleton Civil Service Reform Act were blacks who then obtained federal positions.[56]

Although aware that the new president was not the crusader they had hoped for, black activists were pragmatic enough to understand the political realities that limited Hayes's options. As Pinchback, then serving on his state's board of education, reminded one audience, the Democrats controlled the House, and therefore the nation's budget. Following the removal of the final troops from the South, the House voted only to approve appropriations for the military provided "it should not be used in the Southern States." So long as Democrats across the nation resorted to race-baiting and condemned Reconstruction-era reforms, black activists, Langston conceded, had no choice but to stand behind the president. White Republicans might be less than enthusiastic when it came to civil rights, he confided to a group of blacks meeting in Newport, Virginia, but "all the [anti-] black laws of every state and of the nation were

THE WARS OF RECONSTRUCTION

made by the Democratic party." Even so, most African Americans hoped to bring Grant back for a third term, after Hayes announced he would not run for reelection in 1880. James Edward Bruce, a black journalist in Chicago, regarded the fifty-eight-year-old Grant as "the only man who can silence the *Copperhead* [Democratic] element in the South."[57]

The black conventions that stretched back to the Syracuse meeting of 1864 continued, each designed to enlist a new generation of activists in the fight for democracy. An 1879 conference in Nashville featured Pinchback, Congressman Lynch, and Henry Clay Bruce, the senator's half-brother and a Kansas-based activist. The organizers wished to enlist younger members in the cause, but also to "present the actual conditions of our people" to an increasingly ambivalent nation and "to state our grievances, and to propose such remedies as we think the situation demands." Conventioneers routinely publicized specific assaults, naming victims and dates of murders and, when possible, the names of perpetrators "of lynchings in the South that have come under our notice." At one 1890 meeting, Pinchback encouraged "young persons of both sexes" to join the new Citizens' Rights for the Colored Americans organization. Let the subject "be constantly agitated in the family circle, in public meetings, in the pulpits, and in the press," Pinchback urged. Some, such as Ida B. Wells, born in Mississippi in 1862, began to do so, in her case motivated by the 1892 lynching of three of her friends. So busy did the older generation of activists remain that the demanding schedule of speeches and conferences took a toll. While speaking in Philadelphia, the seventy-four-year-old Douglass's legs gave out, and he had to be helped from the stage. "Our lives have been long in the land and we have both," he assured his old ally Downing, "done something to leave the world better than we found it."[58]

Douglass died in 1895, shortly after what was probably his seventy-seventh birthday, but Langston and Pinchback, eleven and fifteen years younger, respectively, battled on. Both dedicated themselves to fighting the rising tide of Jim Crow segregation and the pseudo-scientific racism that accompanied it. Although he moved his family to Washington in 1893, the former governor helped to organize the Comité des Citoyens (Citizens' Committee), a New Orleans–based group that sponsored

Homer Plessy's legal challenge to segregated train cars. Langston traveled about the country denouncing the new "Jim Crow car Infamy" and drafting editorials designed to counter essays, such as that published by former Kansas senator John J. Ingalls, that derided the "intellectual traits, qualities, and characteristics" of African Americans. In the House, Congressman George Henry White, born only nine years before his state seceded from the Union, routinely took to the floor to condemn the rash of lynchings across the South, which he placed at almost two hundred each year by the mid-1890s. When younger blacks turned defeatist and once again began to consider the possibility of emigration, aged activists such as Langston always had the same response: "When anyone wants you to go to Africa say no, 'you want to stay home.' Let the Democrats go."[59]

Sadly, fighting to preserve rapidly vanishing Reconstruction reforms increasingly meant doing so outside the South. Appointed the Register of the Treasury by President James A. Garfield, Blanche Bruce remained in Washington; his position, to which he was reappointed by William McKinley, meant he was the first African American to have his signature printed on federal currency. Bruce died suddenly of diabetes in March 1898 at the young age of fifty-seven. Langston died the year before, also in Washington, at age sixty-seven. Congressman White decided not to seek reelection in 1900, after North Carolina revised its constitution to effectively disenfranchise black voters. "I cannot live in North Carolina and be treated as a man," he told a Chicago reporter before relocating his family to Philadelphia. White was also furious with his party for dropping any references to lynching or discrimination from their 1900 party platform. Pinchback refused to break with the Republicans and campaigned for McKinley, yet he warned his audience at New York's Cooper Union that "whenever colored men have been deprived of the ballot, unjust class legislation has speedily followed [and] race antagonism has been intensified." Pinchback hoped to be repaid with a federal appointment, and the Colored Citizens League of New York lobbied hard for an unspecified but "just tribute" for Pinchback's long labors. But no appointment was forthcoming.[60]

By then, the wars of Reconstruction had entered a new campaign, as writers, activists, and intellectuals sought to impose their visions of the period on American readers. For white southerners and Democrats of all stripes, that meant depicting the era in the bleakest possible terms, thereby hoping to convince future generations never to again attempt such reforms. For black scholars, activists, and artists, that meant defending the reforms of Pinchback, who lived on in Washington until 1921, and of former congressman Thomas E. Miller, who died in Charleston on the eve of his eighty-ninth birthday in 1938. In some cases, it meant keeping alive a father's legacy, as it was for Roscoe Conkling Bruce, who attended Harvard University with another young black man, William Edward Burghardt Du Bois, better known as W. E. B. And so 1901 saw the last black member of Congress until 1928, but it also saw the publication of Du Bois's historical evaluation of the Freedmen's Bureau in the *Atlantic Monthly* and a critical review of Booker T. Washington's accommodationist *Up from Slavery*. The battle was far from over.[61]

CHAPTER NINE

"We Shall Be Recognized As Men"

The Reconstruction Era in Memory

B ORN ON CHURCH STREET in Great Barrington, Massachusetts, in the year that House Republicans impeached Andrew Johnson, William Edward Burghardt Du Bois descended from a long line of African American activists. His father, Alfred, had served in the Twentieth Regiment of New York Colored Troops and seen action in Louisiana, although his record was not one of distinction. Having suffered numerous bouts of dysentery and diarrhea, Alfred deserted eight weeks before the war ended at Appomattox. But several generations earlier, following the death of his first wife, the boy's maternal great-grandfather, Revolutionary War veteran Jack Burghardt, married the former slave who called herself Elizabeth Freeman. Just prior to their 1790 marriage, while still known as Mum Bett, Freeman had helped to destroy slavery in Massachusetts by suing her violent, ill-tempered mistress, Annetje Ashley, and demanding her freedom.[1]

Quitting his regiment before his tour was up was only one of Alfred Du Bois's sins, since he was most likely already married on the day in 1867 when he stood before the altar with Mary Silvina Burghardt. But the family was otherwise respectable, and William's mother's family had long owned land in the western part of the state. Barrington offered decent schools, and the bright youth William—who later became known as W. E. B.—quickly became the "favorite" of its "stern and inflexible" schoolmarm, Miss Cross. As a light-skinned youth, whose racial background, he once remarked, included "a flood of Negro blood, a strain of French, a bit of Dutch, but, thank God! no Anglo-Saxon," Du Bois faced little discrimination from white students, and when he decided to attend Fisk University, the predominantly white First Congregational Church donated funds to assist with tuition. Arriving in Nashville in 1885, Du Bois "was thrilled to be for the first time among so many people of [his] own color." But he also came face to face with southern racism. While walking down a Nashville street, the seventeen-year-old student bumped into a white woman. He immediately apologized, but instead of accepting his explanation, the "furious" woman spat: "How dare you speak to me, you impudent nigger!"[2]

As a New Englander, Du Bois had always dreamed of attending Harvard University, and as his graduation from Fisk approached, he wrote to express interest in "the degree of Ph.D. in Political Science." Harvard would not accept Fisk credits, but based on his grades and letters of recommendation, the university awarded him a scholarship. He received his second bachelor's degree in history, *cum laude*, and after graduate work at the University of Berlin, he returned to Harvard, becoming in 1895 the first African American to earn a Ph.D. His dissertation, *The Suppression of the African Slave Trade to the United States of America, 1638–1870*, was published the following year in Harvard's Historical Studies series. A one-year research position at the University of Pennsylvania allowed him to begin work on what would become *The Philadelphia Negro*, a book that chronicled the assassination of Octavius Catto. After weighing several offers, Du Bois accepted a position teaching history and economics at Atlanta University.[3]

During his time in Atlanta, Du Bois became acquainted with Booker T. Washington, the former Virginia slave who ran the city's Tuskegee Institute. Washington, famous for his 1895 "Atlanta Compromise" speech, in which he offered to forgo the struggle against segregation and disenfranchisement in exchange for the right of economic advancement for the black community through vocational training, had offered the young academic a job teaching mathematics, but Du Bois was already beginning to side with Washington's critics, such as Congressman George Henry White. The 1899 lynching of Sam Hose clarified Du Bois's thinking. A black farmer who lived just outside Atlanta, Hose murdered a white neighbor after the man pulled a gun on him during an argument over debt. Rumor spread that Hose had also raped the man's wife. A mob of nearly two thousand Georgians removed Hose from custody, chopped parts from his body, doused him in kerosene, and burned him alive. As Du Bois walked down Main Street, he noticed that Hose's burnt knuckles were on display in a grocery store window. From that moment on, Du Bois admitted, he "began to turn aside from [his academic] work." He could no longer act the "calm, cool, and detached" scholar "while Negroes were lynched, murdered, and starved."[4]

Although relations between the two men remained cordial as late as 1902, Du Bois and Washington ultimately parted ways on the meaning of Reconstruction and its legacy. "During the whole of the Reconstruction period two ideas were constantly agitating the minds of the coloured people," Washington wrote. "One of these was the craze for Greek and Latin learning, and the other was a desire to hold office." For Du Bois, his university degrees represented not merely his personal ambitions, but also a belief in his race. Washington disagreed, writing: "It could not have been expected that a people who had spent generations in slavery, and before that generations in the darkest heathenism, could at first form any proper conception of what an education meant." Du Bois finally concluded that Washington's views on the era's successes revealed nothing more than one-sided concessions. In 1896, 130,344 black Louisianans had been registered to vote. Just four years later, that number plummeted to 5,320. In 1901, he penned a critical review of Washington's *Up from Slavery*, which two years later he expanded into the essay "Of Mr. Booker T. Washington and Others" for his book *The Souls of Black Folk*. From then on, Du Bois waged a two-front battle. To one side stood white reactionaries such as Benjamin R. Tillman, the South Carolina governor and senator, who lectured Du Bois that black men "of course should never have received the ballot [but for] the fanatical abolitionists under the leadership of Thad Stevens and Chas. Sumner." To the other was Washington, whose accommodationist approach enjoyed a tremendous following among southern businessmen and those black journalists he helped finance. The editor of the Kansas City *American Citizen* scoffed that Du Bois placed "his trust in the promulgation of flowery sentences," while "Mr. Washington puts his trust in work" and understood that "mortgages cannot be paid off with flowery speeches." One Indianapolis editor thought Du Bois too harsh in suggesting that Washington was "too cold toward the higher education of the Negro," insisting that all the Tuskegee educator wanted was laws that "restrict the suffrage by educational or property qualifications" uniformly imposed on both races. Washington's influence was so great that it was the rare black journalist, such as the editor of the *Cleveland Gazette*, who agreed with Du Bois that Washington's positions had a "malevolent influence upon race progress."[5]

Dedicated to agitation and "aggressive action," Du Bois planned a gathering of like-minded men for Buffalo, New York, in July 1905. The hostility of Buffalo hoteliers forced the delegates to relocate to the Canadian side of the Niagara Falls, and the fact that the first twentieth-century conference dedicated to equal rights in the United States was forced to meet in a foreign country made the enormity of the struggle all too clear. But the thirty men who arrived—*Boston Guardian* editor William Monroe Trotter demanded the exclusion of women—drew up an uncompromising list of demands, starting with the "duty to vote." Newspapers friendly to what critics dubbed "the Tuskegee Machine" ignored the conference, but the group met again the following year, this time at Harpers Ferry, West Virginia, to commemorate the one hundredth anniversary of John Brown's birth. A third meeting of the Niagara Movement in New York City three years later resulted in the founding of the National Association for the Advancement of Colored People (NAACP). Still teaching at Atlanta University and determined to set the historical record straight, Du Bois also found time to write a biography of Brown, a project that began as a chronicle of Nat Turner and other "Negro insurrections from Toussaint [Louverture] down to John Brown." On every possible front, Du Bois was prepared to wage a new campaign in the wars of Reconstruction.[6]

By the time Du Bois published his Brown biography in 1909, the battle over Reconstruction's legacy had been under way for decades. One of

Shortly after writing a critical review of Booker T. Washington's accommodationist Up from Slavery, *Dr. W. E. B. Du Bois and editor William Monroe Trotter launched the Niagara Movement. Speaking at the conference, Du Bois—pictured here in the middle row in a white hat—denounced the nation's retreat from the reforms of Reconstruction but guaranteed eventual success: "And we shall win. The past promised it, the present foretells it. Thank God for John Brown! Thank God for Garrison and Douglass! Sumner and Phillips, Nat Turner and Robert Gould Shaw, and all the hallowed dead who died for freedom! Thank God for all those to-day, few though their voices be, who have not forgotten the divine brotherhood of all men white and black, rich and poor, fortunate and unfortunate." Courtesy University of Massachusetts Amherst.*

the earliest salvos was fired in 1881 with the publication of Jefferson Davis's two-volume memoir, *The Rise and Fall of the Confederate Government.* Having lost his estate during the war, Davis and his wife resided on a plantation near Biloxi, Mississippi, the permanent houseguests of wealthy widow Sarah Dorsey. Like so many political memoirs, the

1,561-page history was designed to settle old scores, earn the author generous royalties, and rewrite the past. The famously thin-skinned former president devoted almost as many angry pages to attacking generals Joseph E. Johnston and P. G. T. Beauregard as he did to Abraham Lincoln, and priced between ten to twenty dollars (depending on the binding), the volumes were beyond reach of most of his impoverished admirers. But Davis was anxious to prove "that the existence of African servitude was in no wise the cause of the conflict," a statement considerably at odds with his many pronouncements during the secession crisis. He also reduced Reconstruction reforms to the "imposing [of] an oppressive peace on honorable men who had laid down their arms." The rambling, disjointed memoir proved a critical and financial failure, but it joined a series of volumes designed to glorify the Confederacy as an admirable "Lost Cause" waged in the name of states' rights against federal despotism. Already in print were Alexander Stephens's equally thick two-volume set, *Constitutional View of the Late War Between the States*, and E. A. Pollard's *The Lost Cause*, which defended slavery as an institution that "elevated the African" and "protected the negro in life and limb."[7]

Eight years after the publication of Davis's memoir, white southerners founded the United Confederate Veterans (UCV). Appearing at a time when some districts continued to send black congressmen to Washington, the organization served to rally whites of all classes behind a sanitized view of the antebellum era and a critical appraisal of postwar reforms. Affiliated groups, such as the United Daughters of the Confederacy (UDC), joined the UCV in hosting "Confederate celebrations" and raising money for statuary. In 1892, the UCV created a committee designed to promote the "proper" history of the era; the committee also compiled lists of recommended and condemned histories of the war. The UDC pored over textbooks and primers that "slandered" the South by suggesting that Confederates had fought to preserve slavery, an effort that earned the scorn of General James Longstreet, who resided in Georgia until his death in 1904. "Why not talk about witchcraft if slavery was not the cause of the war," he marveled. "I never heard of any other cause of the quarrel than slavery." Longstreet's honesty made him unpopular among UCV leaders, who refused to invite him to veterans' reunions. (He sometimes came anyway, to the cheers of his men.) But the general found company in the Grand Army of the Republic (GAR), an equally determined organization of northern veterans. GAR reunions rang with speeches identifying slavery as "the direct and inviting cause" of secession, and Massachusetts legislators made sure that schoolchildren identified the war with "treason and rebellion." Black veterans especially linked the struggles of the past with those of the present. When the Massachusetts Colored Veterans Association gathered in 1884, organizers urged that a monument be built in Washington to "the patriotic negro." But perhaps more pressing was their resolution demanding "full equal protection of the laws" for all black Americans.[8]

If anathema to black veterans, the views promoted by the UCV and the UDC were embraced by a handful of influential northern conservatives. Two distinguished historians, James Ford Rhodes and William A. Dunning, were born in Ohio in 1848 and New Jersey in 1857, respectively. Neither of these Democrats endorsed secession in their works, although Dunning, who began teaching history at Columbia University in 1886, was critical of both southern Unionists and northern carpetbaggers. As had southern reactionaries during the previous decade, Dunning equated an egalitarian, color-blind franchise with black "domination," praising those whites who, "subjugated by adversaries of their own race, thwarted the scheme which threatened permanent subjection to another race." Rhodes, who began to publish his eight-volume *History of the United States from the Compromise of 1850* in 1893, concurred that Republican Reconstruction Acts constituted "an attack on civilization [and] did not show wise constructive statesmanship in forcing unqualified Negro Suffrage on the South." Former congressman John Roy Lynch, who died in Chicago in 1939 at the age of ninety-two, penned a stinging rebuttal designed, as he observed, to "present the other side." Lynch accused Rhodes—who was not a professionally trained scholar but a wealthy industrialist—of consciously twisting data and misusing "alleged historical facts" so as "to magnify the virtues and minimize the faults of the Democrats and to magnify the faults and minimize the virtues of the Republicans, the colored men especially." But Britain's Oxford University rewarded Rhodes with an honorary degree, and fellow Columbia University historian John W. Burgess defended

Dunning, denouncing Reconstruction as "the most soul-sickening spectacle that Americans have ever been called upon to behold."[9]

Even more dangerous, black activists believed, was the outpouring of sentimental novels and highly fictionalized memoirs that romanticized the old South. Since far more people read these short novels than waded through dense multivolume historical tomes, they had a far greater ability to influence popular opinion than Davis or Dunning or Burgess. Typical was James Battle Avirett's *The Old Plantation: How We Lived in Great House and Cabin Before the War*. As the subtitle suggested, Avirett, a onetime Confederate chaplain, painted an image of a benevolent slavery, in which a happy if inferior people had been "steadily emerging from the shadow of paganism" thanks to their "daily contact with the older, stronger civilization" when Lincoln foolishly sought "to hurry Almighty God in His slower, wiser purposes with this race." That freedmen "were not fitted for the ballot" was a point he thought beneath debate. Myrta Lockett Avary and J. W. Daniel went further still. Daniel's 1905 *A Maid of the Foot-Hills* glorified those common whites who armed themselves as Red Shirt vigilantes to liberate "the oppressed citizens" of the South. Although her 1906 *Dixie After the War* purported to be a work of popular history, Avary invented dialogue and offensive black dialect. In her retelling of the Reconstruction years, black Union Leaguers committed endless acts of brutality and rape against innocent whites. When Virginia males retaliated by lynching a black rapist, Avary had her villain apologize to the vengeful mob: "But fo' Gawd, gent'mun, ef a white man f'om de Norf hadn't put't in my hade dat a white 'oman warn' none too good fuh."[10]

Avirett and Daniel were old enough to remember the final antebellum years and the war, so their fictions tended to end with Reconstruction rather than start in the postwar period. That, together with his spectacular financial success, was what set Thomas Dixon Jr. apart. Born in the village of Shelby, North Carolina, during the last year of the war, Dixon was only eleven when his state elected former slave John Adams Hyman to Congress. He later recalled seeing his first Klansmen when he was five. Dixon was initially frightened while watching the hooded men ride silently past his window, but his mother assured him that "they're our people—they're guarding us from harm." He later discovered that a beloved uncle, a Confederate colonel, was a prominent Klansman. Following an education at Baltimore's Johns Hopkins University, where he became friendly with fellow student Woodrow Wilson, the tall, lanky Dixon tried his hand at acting, preaching, and state politics. But after witnessing a 1901 theatrical adaptation of Harriet Beecher Stowe's *Uncle Tom's Cabin*, a furious Dixon was inspired to try his hand at an anti-Reconstruction novel. Lifting the infamous Simon Legree from Stowe's pages, Dixon recast the erstwhile slave driver as a scalawag who united with former slaves and carpetbaggers to plunder the region. As in Avary's work, whites organized as Klansmen to rescue their state from race war and barbarism. Released by the New York publisher Doubleday, Page and Company in 1902—a year after Congressman White quit his state in disgust—*The Leopard's Spots: A Romance of the White Man's Burden* was a runaway bestseller, and that begged a sequel.[11]

Three years later Dixon produced what he announced was the second of a projected trilogy on the postwar years. More ambitious than its predecessor, *The Clansman: An Historical Romance of the Ku Klux Klan* shifted back and forth between Washington and the South Carolina countryside. Hoping to appeal to northern readers as well, Dixon opened his novel with a sympathetic cameo of Lincoln, who in Dixon's retelling wished only to restore the South as it had been. But his assassination had goaded "club footed" Congressman Austin Stoneman—a thinly disguised Thaddeus Stevens—to "punish" the South by encouraging black troops, "answerable to no authority save the savage instincts of their officers, [to] terrorize the state." If Avirett's antebellum blacks were content in their benevolent bondage, liberation and political rights had transformed Dixon's African Americans into murderous rapists. In a plot line borrowed from Avary, Dixon's Gus, a former bondman and Stoneman's henchman, raped a fifteen-year-old white girl. The Klansman of the title, former Confederate soldier Ben Cameron, served as Grand Dragon of a vigilante unit dedicated to white supremacy, and he and his men captured and executed Gus. His love Elsie Stoneman, the congressman's daughter, defied her father and took her stand with the white South. Du Bois was so incensed by the novel that he complained to Walter Hines Page, the North Carolina–born editor and vice president

of Doubleday, Page and Company. Page admitted that the plot promoted his "enemies' doctrine" but added that he thought it necessary to
provide Dixon with the same literary "freedom" that he gave critics of
racism. Understanding too well that Doubleday, Page existed to sell
books, Du Bois did not bother to reply.[12]

Perhaps believing that the debate was lost with popular audiences,
Du Bois and Lynch instead returned fire in an academic venue. Then in
his mid-sixties, the former congressman wrote *The Facts of Reconstruction*, in which he blamed Johnson's policies for sowing the seeds of failure
in Mississippi. In December 1909, Du Bois drafted an essay on Reconstruction for the annual meeting of the prestigious American Historical
Association (AHA) in Manhattan. In the bluntly titled "Reconstruction
and Its Benefits," Du Bois challenged the Dunning-Rhodes view that
the postwar years constituted a "tragic era" of black misrule. The reforms of the period gave the South three critical things it had lacked: "1.
Democratic government. 2. Free public schools. 3. New social legislation." If anything, he argued, the only flaws in Republican policies had
been to defund the Freedmen's Bureau in 1870 and not engage in more
effective "distribution of land and capital" for the next "forty years."
White scholars in the audience listened politely, but few were persuaded.
The influential *American Historical Review* published the essay, although
editor J. Franklin Jameson refused Du Bois's request that he capitalize
the word "Negro." The vast majority of white historians, however, ignored both scholarly defenses and remained loyal to the Dunning view.
No other black historian would speak at the AHA until thirty-one more
years had passed.[13]

Du Bois's careful research was no match for new media. If Dixon's
novels reached far greater audiences than did either Lynch or Dunning,
it would be a motion picture that would embed the notion of Reconstruction as a vindictive failure in the white mind for much of the twentieth century. Filmmaker D. W. Griffith, the son of a Confederate cavalry
officer, had already made a number of short movies about the Civil
War. His dream was to film Dixon's first two novels, especially *The
Clansman*, which Dixon had already adapted into a successful stage play.
Griffith offered Dixon ten thousand dollars for the rights to the play and
hired Dixon to co-author the script. In a time when movies typically

lasted ten minutes and ran on a single reel, Griffith envisioned an epic production filmed in color; budget concerns forced him to abandon the use of color film, but his final cut ran just over three hours. The plot adhered faithfully to Dixon's novel, with Gus, still lacking a surname and played by white actor Walter Long in blackface, dying at the hands of hooded vigilantes in the name of southern civilization. At an advance screening, the film contained its original name, until Dixon enthused, "It should be called *The Birth of a Nation*," reflecting his belief that a unified country of white supremacists had emerged from the ashes of Reconstruction.[14]

Having spent themselves into considerable debt in making the film, which ran well over budget, Griffith and Dixon had to ask an unheard-of ticket price of two dollars. Ever the savvy businessman, Dixon, who was already plotting a sequel to be based on the third volume of his trilogy, *The Traitor*, thought to cash in on his university friendship with Woodrow Wilson. The Virginia-born president was already on record as a critic of Reconstruction, having depreciated black voters as "ignorant dupes" who "blindly followed the political party which had brought on the war of their emancipation." Dixon was able to arrange the first-ever showing of a film at the White House, assuring the president that as viewers of the movie would be transformed into "sympathetic Southern voters," there "will never [again] be an issue of your segregation policy." Enthralled by the film, Wilson pronounced it "like writing history with lightning," adding, "My only regret is that it is all so terribly true." Black editors were horrified by the president's endorsement. One Indianapolis publisher wondered "how Mr. Wilson and his associates could view the picture favorably," and while Wilson's domestic policies had already alienated northern black voters, he had no wish to disaffect white progressives. Wilson promptly informed AME bishop Alexander Walters that he had not approved of the film, and the White House quietly spread word that the comment had been mistakenly attributed to Wilson by advisor Joseph Tumulty.[15]

The African American community was alarmed over the passions aroused by the film, and no wonder. Houston audiences screamed "lynch him!" while watching Gus pursue actress Lillian Gish. In Lafayette, Indiana, a theater patron shot and killed a black teenager after watching the movie, and advocates of residential segregation passed out flyers demanding new ordinances outside St. Louis theaters. Du Bois and the NAACP called for a boycott of the film and urged the National Board of Censorship to reverse its stamp of approval. After a call to the White House confirmed the fact that the president had seen and liked the film, a majority of the Board endorsed the movie, although Rabbi Stephen Wise, a dissenting member, denounced it as "indescribably foul and loathsome." A Boston theater made national news by refusing to sell tickets to blacks, assuming they were there to protest. In fact, they were, and among the crowd were *Boston Guardian* editor William Monroe Trotter and the Reverend Aaron W. Puller. When Trotter demanded a ticket, a policeman "punched Trotter in the jaw" and arrested both men for "inciting a riot." Judge John G. Brackett, the Republican son of former governor John Quincy Adams Brackett, saw it differently, ruling that "the two persons responsible for the near riot were the policemen" and that the theater owner was in violation "of the equal rights laws" of the state for selling tickets only to whites.[16]

After Supreme Court Chief Justice Edward White, once a Confederate soldier and still a Klansman, publicly endorsed the film, the black press redoubled its efforts to have the film banned. Griffith had a First Amendment right to his views, numerous editors argued, just as theater owners had a similar right not to book a film designed "to inflame racial passion." Trotter succeeded in having the film banned in Lynn, Massachusetts, and following more white-on-black violence, most Manhattan theaters stopped showing the film. Ohio governor Frank B. Willis, a Republican and the son of a Civil War veteran, barred the film from his state on the grounds that it was "mob-inciting," although the uproar over his decision only motivated whites in other states to flock to still-open theaters, making *Birth of a Nation* the highest grossing film until 1939.[17]

Worse was to follow. The infant film industry, like any business enterprise, spawned imitations of a successful product. Within months the stunning financial returns of *Birth of a Nation* motivated Fox Films to churn out a short silent, *The Nigger*. Based on a play of the same name by Edward Sheldon, the film was essentially Dixon's epic without the battle scenes. In the movie, an unnamed African American—portrayed by the assistant director in blackface—literally frothing at the mouth, assaulted a white girl wandering through the woods and committed what a subtitle describes as "the usual crime." Klansmen with blood-hounds tracked and lynched the rapist, but determined to escalate the violence over that in *Birth*, the black man was then burned at the stake. Once again, the black press condemned the film. The film was "as vicious, harmful, and mob-inciting as any" in Dixon's movie, the editor of the *Cleveland Gazette* remarked. "Only a thoroughly prejudiced white could fail to see this." A representative of the trade journal *Moving Picture World* joined the chorus, charging that the artless film was a "brutal appeal to the most dangerous human passions and prejudices." If vulgar and lacking cinematic merit, Sheldon's film merely preyed upon the same central theme disseminated by Dixon and Dunning: that the key flaw in Reconstruction was that it had unchained vulgar, brutal African American men.[18]

Realizing that reasoned editorials about the truth of Reconstruction were no match for popular media, Du Bois and the NAACP began to explore the idea of filming a response to *Birth of a Nation*. Two possibilities were *Lincoln's Dream*, a screenplay promoting racial understanding and integration, and *Rachel*, a play by Angelina Grimké, the talented daughter of former Charleston slave and Harvard-educated NAACP activist Archibald Grimké. Carl Laemmle, the German-born, Jewish founder of Universal Studios, was interested in the first, but only if the NAACP could raise ten thousand dollars to help with financing. With that, Du Bois lost interest, but in 1920, black filmmaker Oscar Micheaux responded with *Within Our Gates*. Shot on a limited budget and with borrowed costumes, director-screenwriter Micheaux turned the tables on *Birth* through the story of black schoolteacher Sylvia Landry, who worked at an underfunded rural school in the South. In Micheaux's reversal, Landry barely escaped being raped by a white man, and the film included a graphic lynching of Landry's mother and father. In the wake of the Chicago race riot of 1919, Illinois's Board of Censors approved the film, but only after the lynching and rape scenes were cut. The black editor of Chicago's *Broad Axe* fumed that the cuts rendered the silent film "hardly intelligible," but he gave its accuracy high marks, particularly "the opposition of the Southern white woman" to Landry's pleas of assistance, and "the financial straits of the school." In St. Paul, Minnesota, where the film was shown intact, the *Appeal* praised Micheaux's courage in showing "lynching in all of its gruesome details."[19]

White audiences failed to support the film, which in turn failed to alter the general public's negative view of Reconstruction. Perhaps the lowest moment came in 1929, when political journalist and popular historian Claude Bowers completed *The Tragic Era: The Revolution After Lincoln*. As destructive as the so-called Dunning School theories might be, they reached only the small handful of white men who could afford a university education, or in some cases the students of those graduates trained by Dunning or Burgess. But Bowers was an influential editorialist with the *New York Journal* and an important Democrat; he served as the temporary chairman of the Democratic National Convention in 1929 and would later be appointed ambassador to Spain and Chile by Franklin Delano Roosevelt, who admired Bowers's writings. *The Tragic Era* skirted the edges of fiction, but his lively, caustic style appealed to lay readers, and the thick volume, published by Houghton Mifflin and offered as a selection by the Literary Guild, was nearly as popular as *Birth of a Nation*. Certainly it was much influenced by the film, as the central villain was the "abnormal" Stevens, while liberation unchained "simple-minded" blacks who became infamous for their "lustful assaults" on white women. White vigilantes were the heroes of his tale, who put an end to "carpetbag crimes." The book received glowing reviews, apart from that in the NAACP's official magazine, *The Crisis*. "It seems to me that the *Tragic Era* should be answered," former North Carolina slave Anna Julia Cooper informed Du Bois, who was the magazine's editor. Although the Oberlin- and Sorbonne-educated Cooper was the fourth African American woman to earn a doctorate, she deferred to Du Bois, writing confidently, "*Thou* art the Man" to do it.[20]

As it happened, Du Bois was then trying to do just that, if only in a small way. Du Bois had largely given up teaching for activism and scholarship, and he held the position of Director of Publicity and Research for the NAACP. He was contacted by Franklin H. Hooper, who invited him to write a lengthy article on "The Negro in the United States" for the *Encyclopaedia Britannica*. When the galleys for the piece arrived, Du Bois was stunned, and he dashed off a series of letters to

Hooper explaining why he was "very much dissatisfied" with the editor's changes. Gone was the reference to the Black Codes as being "slavery in everything but name." Banished also as the number of African Americans lynched during Reconstruction and the positive achievements of black politicians in the South. The word "Negro" lost its capitalization. In response, Hooper grudgingly agreed to capitalize "Negro" but refused to restore Du Bois's claim that "it was the Negro loyalty and the Negro alone that restored the South to the Union; established the New Democracy, both for white and black, and instituted the public schools." Admittedly, Du Bois's sentence slighted white Unionists and northern Republicans, but that was not the editor's concern. Rather, Hooper made it clear that he could not "conscientiously allow" Du Bois's depiction of the era's many successes "to pass," as he regarded that "largely a matter of opinion." Du Bois refused to agree to the cut, and the volume eventually went to press without his essay.[21]

Du Bois was hardly alone in pushing back against the prevalent view of the era. He was joined in the fight by a number of black writers, journalists, and academics. Canadian novelist and journalist Albert Evander Coleman penned the descriptively titled *Romantic Adventures of Rosy, the Octoroon: With Some Account of the Persecution of the Southern Negroes During the Reconstruction Period*. Although born and educated in Ontario, Coleman had traveled extensively around the South as a young reporter for the *New York Herald*, and black editors publicized the novella as based on "incidents that he personally" witnessed "while journeying up and down the Mississippi River in 1868." Another writer, Howard W. Odum, born in Georgia in 1884, told the story of "Black Ulysses," a former slave and "story teller," in 1931's *Cold Blue Moon*. Set in the final days of the Civil War and the Reconstruction era, Odum's collection of stories, rather like Micheaux's film, reversed the popular stereotypes of the early twentieth century by depicting a white planter, known simply as "Old Colonel," as a man who had sexually abused black women and sired several mixed-race daughters. Perhaps to better highlight the rampant inhumanity of his own time, Odum had one of the daughters demonstrate her humanity, even to her despised father, by caring for him on his deathbed.[22]

Nor was Du Bois the only writer who wished to highlight the

advances made in public education just after the war. The January 1920 issue of the *Journal of Negro History* featured more than fifty pages of documents pertaining to "Some Negro Members of Reconstruction Conventions and Legislatures." Speaking to a gathering of educators, Roscoe Dunjee, the editor of Oklahoma City's *Black Dispatch* and the reputed grandson of President John Tyler, reminded his listeners—who included several state senators and mayors—that it was a "fact" that public education in the South had first appeared "when black men controlled the politics" of the region. Although white novelists and film-makers routinely emphasized "the evil effects of Negro control," Dunjee added, it was only black legislators and their carpetbagger allies who "gave to the poor white and black children the foundation" for modern school systems. Black ministers also kept alive the memory of the time when black politicians had held "positions of honor and responsibility in almost every walk of civil life." They reminded their congregations of the service of "Daddy" Cain, Blanche Bruce and Hiram Revels, and Robert Brown Elliott, "statesmen who did not suffer in comparison with the ablest white men of the same rank." In a time when white university men were taught that black officeholders were "ignoramuses and buffoons," an almost-underground movement within the black community sought to remind the coming generation that the only "bloody debacle of Reconstruction [had come] when the Negro was driven out of politics." As Will W. Alexander, the president of New Orleans's black Dillard College, assured one audience, it was only when congressmen such as George Henry White gave up the struggle that "ignorance got hold of the government at the end of Reconstruction."[23]

For Du Bois the scholar, the final straw was the 1930 publication of Tennessee journalist and businessman George Fort Milton's *The Age of Hate*. In the rambling, 787-page account of Andrew Johnson's battle with the Republicans, it was progressives who were the haters, and none more so than Thaddeus Stevens, called the "Caliban of the House" by Milton. In characterizing the Radical leader as Shakespeare's deformed slave, Milton reduced Stevens and other progressive reformers to vengeful demagogues, angry politicians with "hatred stamped upon [their] brows." Within the year, publisher Alfred Harcourt wrote to Du Bois, reporting that he had heard rumors that the historian was at work on a major reevaluation of Reconstruction, and saying that he would be interested in seeing the manuscript. Du Bois replied that he envisioned two volumes, the first to cover the period from 1860 to 1876, and a second book designed to cover "the part which Negro troops took in the World War." Although he intended to rehabilitate Stevens and Sumner as advocates of democracy, his central purpose was to focus on "the real hero" of the era, "the slave who is being emancipated." Du Bois admitted that he was "aghast at what American historians [had] done to this field," denouncing the "chorus of agreement" as to the period's failings as being grounded in white bigotry rather than dispassionate research and analysis.[24]

The final result was *Black Reconstruction in America*. At 746 pages, the thick volume ran almost as long as Milton's jeremiad, and for many readers, the most revelatory section was its final chapter, "The Propaganda of History." His previous experience with the American Historical Association taught him that simply setting out the facts was not enough; he needed to openly engage other authors. Bravely, Du Bois named names, starting with James Ford Rhodes. The Ohio businessman, Du Bois observed, neither had been "trained as an historian" nor had enjoyed a "broad formal education." Rhodes ignored evidence, Du Bois charged, that did not support his preconceived theories of black inferiority, such as the Congressional report on Klan atrocities. Although Dunning was "less dogmatic" a scholar, his "propaganda against the Negro" had been passed on to his graduate students, whose collective work "has been one-sided and partisan to the last degree." Bowers's *Tragic Era* and Milton's *Age of Hate* were, respectively, "absolutely devoid of historical judgment" and a failed "attempt to re-write the character of Andrew Johnson." Yet in all of these accounts, he wrote, the "chief witness in Reconstruction, the emancipated slave himself, has been almost barred" from testimony. At times, Du Bois himself abandoned his claims of detached critic, calling Dunning a "copperhead" and Rhodes "an exploiter of wage labor." But his central theme was accurate enough. Regarding African Americans and their white allies as inferior beings and warped Calibans, these writers saw little "need to waste time delving into" the many successes of "Reconstruction history."[25]

As they had for the previous quarter century, editors at the *American*

Historical Review ignored both Du Bois's and the book's existence, not bothering to send it out for review. Historian Avery Craven charged that Du Bois employed "abolitionist propaganda and the biased statements of partisan politicians," and *Time* magazine dismissed Du Bois as an "ax grinder" who filled his pages with a Reconstruction "wonderland in which all familiar scenes and landmarks have been changed or swept away." Trying to change the old narrative was precisely Du Bois's purpose, of course, and rather to the author's surprise, the Book-of-the-Month Club adopted *Black Reconstruction*, with southern-born white journalist Jonathan Daniels praising the book as a necessary corrective "for much white history about a period in which the Negro played a great part." Yale University's William McDonald mixed praise with doubt in his *New York Times* review, writing that while Du Bois's analysis was "shot through with Marxian economics," he was "absolutely justified in his rancorous onslaught on American historians" such as Dunning and Milton. A reviewer for the New York *Daily Mirror* agreed that the study was a "bristling piece of scholarship that should disturb complacent historians."[26]

The book sold only 376 copies during its first year, but the black press, long frustrated by what they regarded as a racist retelling of their past, warmly embraced it. During what was then National Negro History Week, black teachers and ministers "presented masterful reviews" of the volume for audiences across the nation. Rarely able to afford private libraries, black professionals formed "Book Lovers' Clubs" to discuss and swap the book, perhaps one explanation for its meager sales. In a widely reprinted essay, William Pickens, the son of South Carolina slaves and an NAACP chapter organizer, hailed *Black Reconstruction* as "the most significant book of the last half hundred years." Confident that black audiences would be familiar with Du Bois, Pickens thought "every white man should read it, if he wants to let a bit of light into the caverns of darkness." Aware that most whites yet envisioned the Reconstruction-era southern legislatures as they had seen them in *Birth of a Nation*, one black editor also hoped to get the book into the hands of white readers so they would know the truth, "that Negro legislators" had been "different only in the color of their skins." Progressive reformers such as Robert Smalls had done far "more than eat peanuts and spit at silver spittoons, mostly missing the mark."[27]

Once again, black teachers and editors discovered that even elegantly written monographs were no match for romantic fiction. Within twelve months of *Black Reconstruction*'s appearance came Margaret Mitchell's sprawling *Gone with the Wind*. Set against the background of war and Reconstruction in Georgia, the novel covered the years from 1861 to 1873, as Mitchell's protagonist Scarlett O'Hara grew from sixteen to twenty-eight years of age. Long interested in the American past, provided it was taught on her terms—years earlier, as a student at Smith College in Massachusetts she had demanded to be transferred to another history class when she discovered that a young black woman had enrolled in the same course—Mitchell insisted that her novel was based on years of research, and it drew heavily on the writings of Dunning and Ulrich B. Phillips, the author of 1918's *American Negro Slavery*. Published by Macmillan in June 1936, *Gone with the Wind* ran for more than one thousand pages and was priced at an unheard-of three dollars. Despite its cost, the book sold nearly one million copies by year's end, or roughly thirteen times more copies each day than Du Bois sold in an entire year. The novel's black detractors were furious to discover that Mitchell was awarded the Pulitzer Prize the following year. Her story was "well told" but otherwise "resented by thinking Negroes," complained editor Frank Marshall Davis. Mitchell "twist[ed] reconstruction era facts into a web of lies." Since Du Bois had uncovered facts "that whites had ignored or hushed up," Davis wondered why prize committees heaped praise on *Gone with the Wind* but ignored *Black Reconstruction*. "Nobody knows whether the Pulitzer Committee will ever look with favor upon a colored writer."[28]

If black critics had little use for the novel, southern whites devoutly believed that Mitchell had told their story. Mitchell hagiographer Darden Asbury Pyron, a historian at Florida International University famous for hanging up large Confederate flags at his dinner parties, defended her novel "as a revisionist history of the planter class." As for her racial stereotypes, Pyron insisted that Du Bois's *Black Reconstruction* had "made no headway at all on the popular mind," yet he praised Mitchell for digging deeply "into [other] primary and secondary sources to make her work as historically accurate as she knew how." The black editor of the Kansas City *Plaindealer* saw it differently. "The anger of the South with the North for freeing the slaves," he complained, "was passed on to a little white girl, who grew up to write a book, titled *Gone With the Wind*."[29]

Before the year was out, the novel was optioned by Metro-Goldwyn-Mayer, a studio largely financed by Louis B. Mayer's far-sighted decision to purchase the exclusive film rights for *Birth of a Nation* in Britain. Assuming the worst, black journalists such as Elizabeth Lawson feared that *Gone with the Wind* was "likely to repeat in all essential respects Griffith's rotten *Birth of a Nation*." Even before the film was scheduled to be shot on California back lots, the NAACP launched a campaign against the movie, and although most of their complaints about the novel's inaccuracies were not addressed, they were able to temper some of the book's more egregious racial content. Much of Mitchell's depiction of Reconstruction, however, made the transition to celluloid. Late in the film, words appear on the screen, explaining to audiences that as "tattered Cavaliers" returned home after the war, they confronted "another invader, more cruel and vicious than any they had fought, the Carpetbagger." The words, a loose paraphrase of Bowers's description—"Then came the scum of Northern society, soldiers of fortune"—were projected against a scene of two well-dressed men, one white and the other black, sitting beside large carpetbags in a carriage, as tattered veterans limped beside them. While black audiences were generally pleased to witness Hattie McDaniel win an Academy Award for her performance, they were less enthusiastic about the fact that she won for playing Mammy. In a February 1940 celebration of Lincoln's birth held, fittingly, at Catto Auditorium in Philadelphia, speakers derided the film as "propaganda designed to tear down all the principles for which Abraham Lincoln sacrificed his precious life."[30]

Just as *Birth of Nation* had spawned imitators, so too did *Gone with the Wind*'s enormous success inspire other studios to return to the Reconstruction era. During the early 1940s, the Walt Disney Studios began work on *Song of the South*, based on the "Uncle Remus" stories of Joel Chandler Harris. Set in the 1870s and filmed on a cotton farm on the outskirts of Phoenix, Arizona, the film adopted a more romanticized view of the postwar period. Absent were both rapacious carpetbaggers and glorified Klansmen in favor of scenes of content, singing sharecroppers and a jovial Remus who regaled white children with stories of Br'er Rabbit (themselves sanitized of their original African American trickster elements). Black critics charged that the script gave "the impression of an idyllic master-slave relationship" in the postwar period, and Disney himself inadvertently revealed the patronizing nature of the project by laughing that they had "dug up a swell little pickaninny" to play the role of the black child. (Hattie McDaniel once again assumed the mammy role.) The NAACP took "sharp issue" with the popular *Parents' Magazine*, which endorsed the film, and a number of black-owned theaters refused to screen it. Although the musical, which mixed live actors with cartoon animals, lacked the historical pretensions and inaccuracies of *Gone with the Wind*, black publishers thought its depiction of the struggles of the Reconstruction years "cast insipience on the Negro Race of today."[31]

Once again, the African American press instead endorsed an alternative, in this case the cartoon short *Brotherhood of Man*. Based upon a pamphlet produced by the American Missionary Association entitled *Races of Mankind*, the 1947 cartoon was financed by the United Auto Workers. Black newspapers advertised it as "a healthy antidote to an Uncle Tom cartoon movie such as Disney's *Song of the South*," pointing out that it was the first children's film "to show the equality of men, whatever their race or color." African American publishers proved slightly more forgiving the following year, when actor James Baskett, who had played Uncle Remus in the Disney film, died of heart disease at the age of forty-four. Most black editors, however, could not resist observing that Baskett had been unable to attend the Atlanta premiere of *Song* due to the city's segregationist policies, regulations that had also kept Hattie McDaniel away from Georgia several years earlier when *Gone with the Wind* premiered.[32]

The year 1947 also saw the appearance of the first major nonfiction account of the postwar era since Du Bois's volume. Published as part of Louisiana State University Press's prestigious History of the South series, E. Merton Coulter's *The South Since Reconstruction, 1865–1877* gave new life to the old Dunning-Bowers view. Both of Coulter's grandfathers had served in the Confederate military; one had been indicted for Klan activities but escaped punishment after being acquitted by an all-white jury. Coulter, who taught at the University of Georgia and was an avowed segregationist, had little use for Du Bois's attempts to rehabilitate the period. "No amount of revision," Coulter asserted in his introduction, "can explain away the grievous mistakes made in this abnormal period of American history." Republican reforms in South Carolina and Louisiana, Coulter added, "were the world's classic example of Negro rule," worse even than "Haiti, for the black emperors of that benighted country" governed people who "had never known any other kind of rule but bad." Harvard-educated historian John Hope Franklin, who was then teaching at Howard University, provided a searing critique in the *Journal of Negro Education* of both Coulter's use of data and his analysis, but most white scholars integrated Coulter's findings into their lectures and textbooks. Thomas A. Bailey, author of *The American Pageant: A History of the Republic*, one of the best-selling undergraduate textbooks, agreed that white Radicals had employed former slaves as "unwitting tool[s] of their own schemes." Unlike Coulter, Bailey had been born and educated in California and spent most of his career teaching at Harvard, Cornell, and Stanford universities, yet his assessment that "gun-supported reconstruction of the South, begun so brutally in 1867" and resulting in integrated southern legislatures that often "resembled the comic opera," reflected the works of Dunning and Bowers and even of Thomas Dixon Jr.[33]

For yet another generation of African American veterans, returning home from a global battle against fascism to discover their neighborhood theaters showing films such as *Song of the South* was a depressing reminder of how little had changed on the home front. Another was the 1957 Pulitzer Prize–winning biography *Profiles in Courage*, ostensibly written by Massachusetts senator John F. Kennedy. The book contained a series of biographical vignettes, one of them dedicated to Lucius Lamar, an associate justice of the Supreme Court. As a young congressman, Lamar was an avid secessionist who had drafted Mississippi's ordinance of secession. Kennedy was especially critical of senator and governor Adelbert Ames, writing that "no state suffered more from carpetbag rule than Mississippi." Kennedy thought it revealing that "two former slaves held the offices of Lieutenant Governor and Secretary of State," although he neglected to add that the latter, James D. Lynch, had been freed as a child by his white father, a minister, who had him educated in New Hampshire. Kennedy also hammered away at the tax increases during the period, a peculiar criticism from a New England Democrat who supported public education. Much of the research for the book was provided by Georgetown historian Jules Davids, who had taught the senator's wife in a course that required her to read Henry Steele Commager and Samuel Eliot Morison's popular textbook *The Growth of the American Republic*, which referred to slaves as "Sambo" and black children as "pickanninies." The bibliography for the chapter included *The Tragic Era*.[34]

By then, John Hope Franklin's pioneering black history textbook, *From Slavery to Freedom: A History of Negro Americans*, had been in print for eight years. In the late 1950s, Daniel J. Boorstin invited Franklin to publish a volume on Reconstruction as part of his series, Chicago History of American Civilization. The book, slimmer than the volumes it posed a response to, and so more readable, was published in 1961, just after Franklin accepted a position with Brooklyn College and became the first African American to head a major history department. Throughout *Reconstruction: After the Civil War*, Franklin carried on a polite but firm debate with the consensus view. Whereas earlier historians had disparaged carpetbaggers as "depraved, dissolute, dishonest and degraded," Franklin argued that the vast majority were "teachers, preachers [and] discharged Union soldiers" of "good intentions." As had Du Bois several decades earlier, Franklin praised Congressman Thaddeus Stevens as a crusader who was "deeply committed to the principles of Negro suffrage" and who regarded voting rights as a step toward democracy, not as a punishment for the white South. Determined to change the tide of mainstream scholarship, Franklin kept the focus in Washington, and even then most of the African Americans who served in Congress received but a cursory mention. Bruce appeared only once, Revels twice. Franklin also avoided what he regarded as Du Bois's "strong Marxist bias." But the thoughtful, elegantly crafted study, he admitted, was designed to be a break with "the prevailing view, usually ascribed to Dunning, that little good came out of the reconstruction experience."[35]

With the onset of the 1960s, the country's attitudes toward race, at long last, began to shift. Thanks to a new generation of African American activists, politicians slowly embraced civil rights reforms that would constitute a second Reconstruction. Where Du Bois's scholarship had been ignored, at least in predominantly white universities, Franklin's book was widely praised. Reviewing the volume for the *American Historical Review*, the journal that had opted not to review *Black Reconstruction*, Hans L. Trefousse pronounced the book "excellent" and lauded Franklin's tone as an "exercise [in] remarkable restraint." Trefousse had recently crafted a balanced biography of Benjamin F. Butler, so he was among those scholars prepared to accept a new synthesis. Franklin's depiction "completely demolishes the traditional picture," he concluded. British historian Alan Conway was equally ready to rethink a period whose scholarship had "long been dominated by historians who reflect the attitudes which were so graphically portrayed in D. W. Griffith's screen classic *The Birth of a Nation*." Conway too commended Franklin for his "balanced, objective study of a complex period," and Edgar A. Toppin, reviewing the book for the *Journal of Negro History*, also thought it "judicious" and crafted with "objectivity" and "fairness." Among the handful of dissenters was Avery Craven, who had criticized Du Bois's volume years earlier. Born in 1885 in Iowa, Craven had spent most of his career at the University of Chicago, although at this time he was teaching at the University of South Carolina. In a bizarre review that never once mentioned the author's name, Craven sniped that it had become "quite clear that scholars sitting in Northern libraries reading the official documents are not reconstructing Reconstruction in a very realistic way." For Craven, the fact that Franklin, born in Oklahoma and educated at Fisk, had written much of the book while living in New York was indictment enough.[36]

The one scholar more qualified than any other to critique *Reconstruction* did not do so. Three years earlier, on March 2, 1958, more than a thousand celebrants had turned out at Manhattan's Roosevelt Hotel to commemorate Du Bois's ninetieth birthday. Singer and activist Paul Robeson, the son of a slave, sang. John Hope Franklin praised the pioneering scholar and chided those "so-called respectable people" who had stayed away that night, fearing "the McCarthyites and the cold war

hawks." Shortly thereafter, the still intellectually active Du Bois de-
parted for Ghana to oversee the *Encyclopedia Africana*. Organizers of
the 1963 March on Washington, timed to coincide with the centennial of
Lincoln's proclamation, hoped that he might return to speak, but Du
Bois was finished with America. He praised Reverend Martin Luther
King Jr. as "honest, straight-forward, well-trained, and knowing the
limits" of the nation when it came to civil rights; but he intended to remain in Africa. Du Bois followed the news of the march on Ghana Radio and considered attending a demonstration at the American embassy
in Accra. But he was tired and went to bed. He died in his sleep just before midnight on August 27 at the age of ninety-five. Just hours later,
roughly 250,000 Americans—eighty percent of them black—began to
assemble at the Lincoln Memorial for the day's program of music and
speakers.[37]

By the time Reverend King stood in Lincoln's "symbolic shadow" and
reminded his white brethren that they had "defaulted" on the promises
made by the government in the wake of the Civil War, mainstream scholars and professional historians were rediscovering Du Bois's and Lynch's
writings and assimilating Franklin's findings into their lectures. Within
the decade, in most corners of academe, the Dunning School was in full
flight, the victim of too many televised images of fire hoses and police
dogs spraying and attacking peaceful civil rights activists. Following
one final tour of theaters in the early 1970s, the Disney Company pulled
Song of the South from the rotation of classic films from its vaults. But
Gone with the Wind was twice re-released to theaters, in 1971 and 1974,
and its two-night television premiere in 1976 set new records for view-
ership. That record—broken, ironically, the following year when the
miniseries *Roots* premiered—served as a reminder that the romanticized
view of the Old South, and the concomitant idea that Reconstruction
was, as Charleston tour guides still insist, "the most undemocratic moment in South Carolina history," lives on in the popular imagination.[38]

The Spirit of Freedom Monument

ADMITTING GUILT, whether for individuals or for nations, is not easily done. Modern politicians have mastered the art of the no-fault apology, in which the burden of a remark, or of a misdeed, is placed on the offended, on the victim. *If* that person was insulted, or *if* the act or policy in question was wrong, then the perpetrator purports to be sorry. Equally common today is the passive-voice admission of wrongdoing. Mistakes *were* made, politicians sigh, careful not to concede just who committed the error. Although such tortured constructions make voters weary, the tendency to dissimulate is understandable. People who plan to stand for reelection to office rarely wish to admit failure, much less actual culpability. And members of a nation who rightly regard themselves as residents of a more just and democratic society than many others on the planet are collectively loath to admit that good and honorable policies were consciously overturned by a reactionary minority while thousands of people across the nation found it easier to look the other way.

We study history, however, not as a quaint exercise in antiquarianism, but to understand the present. History, properly understood, is a series of meandering roads that all converge on the modern day. If we consciously ignore unpleasant parts of that journey, or seek to redraw that map, so that the country's first era of progressive reform instead resembles a tragic era of corruption and bad government, then we fail to understand the contemporary world. It remains far simpler to point the finger at other nations, at tyrants who were so determined to erase their misdeeds that they literally airbrushed victims of government purges from old photographs. Most Americans boast that they would never endure such fictions, insisting that their own nation faces up to hard truths. But then they rewrite it, in novels and plays and films that libel dedicated activists who sacrificed their lives for democracy and voting rights, or they sanitize it in historical dramas that privilege romance over causation and emphasize big-screen spectacle over a tough-minded critique of past wrongs.

One of the many virtues of the Reconstruction era, perhaps, was the willingness of men and women on both sides of the political divide to defend their deeds. South Carolina governor Benjamin Tillman had no compunction in telling W. E. B. Du Bois that Thaddeus Stevens had erred in his advocacy of voting rights for the freedmen. Charleston-born Francis L. Cardozo, who as secretary of state became the first African American elected to a statewide office in the country, was just as adamant in defending Republican policies. Later critics such as John F. Kennedy lamented increased taxes in the period, but speaking before South Carolina's Columbia Union League in 1870, Cardozo thought that progressives had "cause for congratulating" themselves when it came to increased debt. Antebellum Democrats, he chided, had wasted "several millions [in] building the State House," while black legislators instead funded interracial schools and created a state Land Commission. Public monies devoted to the Commission, Cardozo added, furnished impoverished farmers of both races "with an opportunity to purchase homes on easy terms, [and] destroys the hope so *fondly* cherished of restoring the former state of things."[1]

Indiana Republican Oliver P. Morton was equally resolute in defending the policies President Ulysses Grant pursued in the former Confederacy. "We hear it said that the Republican system of reconstruction is a failure," the former governor remarked shortly before his death in 1877. Since Americans insisted they believed in democracy and a government based upon the consent of the governed, the laws and amendments enacted by Reconstruction-era legislators and congressmen were "just and immutable." If Reconstruction had failed, Morton charged, it was only because it had been "resisted by armed and murderous organizations, by terrorism and proscription the most wicked and cruel of the age." Postwar reforms did not come to an end because they had fulfilled their objectives, Morton insisted. Nor were they repealed because they were ineffective. They were instead systematically destroyed through targeted assassination and violence, a grim reality that modern audiences often prefer not to hear. Easier it is to believe that there was something flawed or venal about the period, which somehow softens the misdeeds of white vigilantism and alleviates the memory of the murders of activists such as Octavius Catto or the Reverend Benjamin F. Randolph.[2]

Although rarely easy, facing up to uncomfortable truths can be historically enlightening. If nothing else, an honest gaze backward serves as a reminder of just how recently these events took place. By the November day in 1939 when former congressman turned historian John Roy Lynch died at the age of ninety-two, Martin Luther King Jr. was ten years old. In 2000, the North Carolina legislature commissioned a report about Election Day rioting in 1898, during which nearly two thousand white Democrats dismantled the printing press of Wilmington's only black newspaper, forced the town's African American leaders to flee, and shot Republican voters down in the streets. One commission member, a white contractor, resisted the investigation, warning that it would "keep old wounds open." His first thought was that "everybody made mistakes 100 years ago, let's deal with today," as if the murder of as many as one hundred black voters was little more than a gaffe better forgotten. But as the commission pored over old newspaper clippings and archival correspondence, the businessman came to a new understanding of the past. "My opinion changed," he conceded, "and I was surprised to learn the depth of feeling that existed and that it was not that long ago."[3]

For others, clinging to comfortable untruths is preferable to coming to terms with a complicated and often troubling past. If historians largely abandoned the Dunning School of Reconstruction half a century ago, it lives on in some corners of academe, and especially in the popular consciousness. Although films now avoid the brutal racism of *Birth of a Nation*, they either tiptoe around the thorny issue of Civil War causation, perhaps fearing that a candid discussion of slavery will alienate some ticket buyers, or they perpetuate the myth that vindictive northern Republicans dealt severely with the defeated Confederacy. In 1993's *Gettysburg*, writer-director Ronald F. Maxwell, in an effort to play down the debate over slavery's expansion as the basis for secession and to emphasize that James Longstreet was no proslavery ideologue, had the general comment, "We should have freed the slaves, then fired on Fort Sumter." The historical Longstreet, of course, routinely admitted in later years that slavery had been the cause of the war, and the real general might have wondered why the slaveholding states were fighting on for independence if their slaves had already been freed. The fact that writers of a film produced in the last decade of the twentieth century wished to transform Longstreet into a closet abolitionist reveals that it is more marketable to reduce a screenplay to a one-dimensional discussion of tactics and maneuvers than to seriously investigate *why* so many Americans died at Gettysburg.[4]

Five years later, *The Day Lincoln Was Shot*, written and directed by John Gray for the TNT television channel, concluded with a crawl stating that the real tragedy of Abraham Lincoln's death was that it left the process of Reconstruction in the hands of radicals such as Stevens who desired to "punish" the South. Curiously, neither those words nor Longstreet's strange remark appeared in the books on which *Gettysburg* and the TNT film were based, Michael Shaara's 1974 novel *The Killer Angels* and popular writer Jim Bishop's similarly titled 1955 account of the Lincoln assassination, which suggests that Maxwell and Gray either turned to outdated sources on the period themselves or harbor popular misconceptions about Reconstruction-era reforms. More recently, Steven Spielberg's 2012 *Lincoln* depicted Stevens as a principled if pragmatic crusader who regarded freedom and black rights as simple justice, although the black activists who lobbied for emancipation and equal rights are oddly absent from the film. Yet for some Americans, the progressive reforms Republicans like Stevens championed appear so modern that journalists could not accept them as accurate. When 1993's *Sommersby*, set in postwar Tennessee, featured a black Republican judge, at least one

Florida film reviewer derided the courtroom scene as fanciful and ahistorical.[5]

Both Dunning and Bowers remain in print, as do all three of Thomas Dixon Jr.'s novels. These writings *should* remain accessible, if only as historical documents themselves, or as gloomy reminders of how white Americans willfully misremembered the Reconstruction decades for much of the last century. Yet in posting a review on the nation's largest website for book buyers, one recent Dunning reader condemned Reconstruction as "a period of excessive punishment of the [white] South for their beliefs in their God-given right to secede from a nation that had lost sight of the Constitutional constraints on an increasingly tyrannical Federal government." As had Dixon, the reviewer hinted that black voting rights and military occupation all but justified "subsequent guerrilla-based irregular warfare." Twenty-first-century purchasers of Bowers praised the author for accurately drawing Stevens as "a true scoundrel," an ardent "crusader for negro equality," and a man who "hated the South and it's [sic] white population" and so labored to make Reconstruction "as harsh and unforgiving as could be." A third reader was so incensed after reading Bowers that he claimed to "detest the devilish personalities in *Tragic Era*, [and] would like to smack them around a bit, tar and feather them and run them out of American history." A self-described historian pronounced Bowers "simply the best book ever written on The Reconstruction and the post-War for Southern Independence Era—period." The reviewer found it especially refreshing that one could still buy books "written well before either publisher [-imposed] or self-censorship due to political correctness became the norm."[6]

Tempting though it might be to dismiss a dozen modern glowing online reviews of a discredited, highly fictionalized work published during the 1920s as the last gasp of a handful of die-hard neo-Confederates, the theory that "much vicious hatred was inflicted upon the defenseless South after the Confederacy was defeated"—as yet another modern reader of Bowers put it—remains all too commonplace. Thomas DiLorenzo, an economist once affiliated with the League of the South Institute—which continues to advocate secession—recently argued that "twelve more years of violence and lawlessness under military rule during 'Reconstruction' [made it] unarguably [sic] the worst episode of anarchy ever witnessed on American soil." Not that the former Confederacy was "lawless" due to white vigilantism, but rather that the presence of soldiers protecting black voters was itself somehow "violent." The Sons of the Confederate Veterans provided research for Joy Masoff's elementary education textbook, *Our Virginia: Past and Present*, which erroneously suggested that "thousands" of African Americans fought for the Confederacy, and they also supplied the text for Virginia governor Robert F. McDonnell's 2010 Confederate History Month proclamation, which failed to mention slavery. As a result, perhaps no other topic in the American past betrays such a stunning disconnect between what historians regard as the facts and what the general public believes to be true.[7]

When it comes to remembering the war and its aftermath, statues and monuments have become especially contested terrain, nearly as bloody as the sites they commemorate. A bronze bust of Nathan Bedford Forrest erected in Selma, Alabama, in 2000 vanished from a city park. When a group calling itself Friends of Forrest raised money for a replacement, local activists argued against erecting it in a public space. One member of the Friends group replied that "in this country, we're allowed to venerate our heroes." He added that Selma already had a monument to Martin Luther King Jr. and that they simply wished to "enjoy the same treatment," as if equating a wealthy slave trader, Klan leader, and Confederate officer who allowed for the massacre of black troops at Fort Pillow with a minister, pacifist, and civil rights martyr made for some sort of historical parity. Other members of the group accused their critics of violating the "civil rights" of whites and of "presentism," that is, of using recent standards to condemn past behavior. Opponents of the new bust, however, said nothing that had not first been uttered during Forrest's lifetime. "While we extended our power," what was left of the planter class "respected" the federal government, one Republican argued in 1866. "When we laid aside our weapons and prepared to welcome" the white South back into the Union, former Confederates "mistook humanity and good feeling for fear."[8]

The rancorous debate in Selma appeared almost sedate by comparison to the bitter discussion in Charleston over the proposed Spirit of Freedom Monument. The brainchild of African American social studies teacher Henry Darby, the statue was designed to memorialize black abolitionist Denmark Vesey and two of the Africans who also swung from the gallows during the summer of 1822, Jack Pritchard and Monday Gell. In a city filled with statues and plaques and busts to slaveholding Founding Fathers and Confederate officers, Darby thought it wrong that Vesey, whose burial place is unknown, had no marker of any sort. After years of lobbying, in 2007 the city of Charleston allocated twenty thousand dollars toward the statue and approved a design. Most members of the city's Arts and History Commission voted to support the project, which features Vesey, a carpenter and lay minister at the city's AME congregation, holding a Bible in one hand and tools in the other. One dissenting member complained that Vesey was an unsuitable subject for a monument. "Is it appropriate to massacre individuals," he wondered, "or to slowly win one's freedom through the process? That's what it boils down to." In reality, two years before Vesey's conspiracy, the state assembly had passed new legislation banning self-purchase and private manumissions, but the lone dissenter declined to explain what peaceful "process" existed for Carolina bondmen.[9]

Other critics promptly weighed in. One local radio talk-show host claimed Vesey, who had purchased his freedom in 1799 but whose children remained enslaved, was "a guy who didn't want to just kill his oppressors, he wanted to kill all white people—women, children, everybody." Assuming that the ultimate goal of slave rebelliousness was the murder of whites, rather than the liberation of black Americans, the radio host denounced Vesey as "a would-be terrorist." Yet another opponent wrote to the Charleston *Post and Courier*, insisting that Vesey's plan, which was to culminate in the escape of thousands of black Carolinians to Haiti, "was nothing more than a Holocaust." Rather more surprising, a professor of history at the Citadel, a college originally housed in an armory constructed in the wake of Vesey's conspiracy, also expressed doubts about building a monument "to a man bound and determined to create mayhem." The professor, Kyle Sinisi, who taught a course called "The War for Southern Independence," also darkened the skins and inflated the numbers of those mixed-race freedmen—the small handful of self-styled "browns" who owned slaves—by opining that "many black freedmen owned slaves." Sinisi added that slavery had yet to "gain the stigma attached to it today," a theory evidently unknown to the dozens of enslaved Americans who ventured their lives in 1822 to win freedom for themselves and their families.[10]

Complicating matters was the question of just where to erect the monument. Proponents instinctively thought of Marion Square, one of the largest parks in the city. The Square also had symbolic value. The original Citadel was nearby, as was the 1865 AME church designed by Robert Vesey Sr. (A more recent AME church now sits at that location.) But a tall pillar topped by a statue of proslavery senator John C. Calhoun dominates the square, which remains owned by two militia companies founded in the nineteenth century, neither of which looked favorably on a memorial to a free black who orchestrated a slave conspiracy. By 2000, supporters of the Spirit of Freedom had settled upon Hampton Park. Having once been home to the Union cemetery at the Race Course and Jockey Club, the site also resonated with those who wished to remember the first Memorial Day and the heady postwar moments of hope. Although yet short of necessary funds to transform the small model into a full-size statue, the city staged a groundbreaking on February 1, 2010. Despite unusually cold winds, hundreds turned out to celebrate what Mayor Joe Riley praised as "the indomitable spirit of humanity's desire for freedom." Speaking at the ceremony, the Reverend Joseph Darby laughed away the morning's chill. "God ordered this weather for everyone who said it would be a cold day" in South Carolina "before there was a statue for Denmark Vesey," he remarked.[11]

Once again, critics peppered the local newspaper with letters of complaint. As before, most writers charged that Vesey had planned to murder "every man, woman and child in the city," while another, with shades of Thomas Dixon Jr., added "arson and rape" to the inventory of the abolitionist's alleged crimes. Tour guide and writer Mark Jones insisted that "any number of African Americans in Charleston" were more deserving of statues than Vesey, Gell, and Pritchard, as the rebel leaders had intended to use "violence" to liberate the city's slaves. Advocates of the memorial responded that Charleston, and indeed most of the nation, had erected hundreds of statues to white soldiers and statesmen who employed war and revolution to achieve independence or to resolve the nation's woes. Requiring all shrines to African Americans to

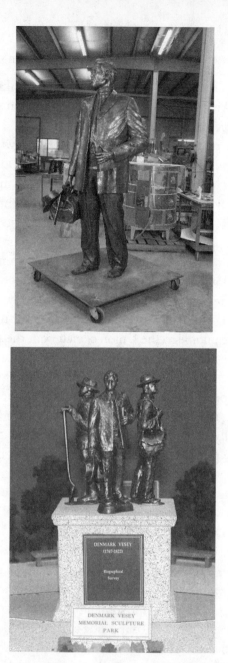

The yet-unfinished Denmark Vesey monument is designed to commemorate the long history of African American struggle in South Carolina. When completed, it will be one of the very few memorials to black Americans in Charleston, a city otherwise brimming with statues and monuments to slaveholding politicians and Confederate leaders. Although Vesey was hanged in 1822, the black abolitionist's son Robert Vesey resurfaced in Charleston at war's end and took part in the rededication ceremony at Fort Sumter in April 1865. The younger Vesey, a carpenter like his father, also designed the rebuilt AME Church in Charleston, replacing the one razed by Charleston's white population forty-three years earlier. Courtesy Charleston Post and Courier *and sculptor Ed Dwight.*

memorialize only pacifists, some noted, was an ahistorical double standard. As historian Bernard E. Powers Jr. observed, once peaceful change had been rendered impossible by the state legislature, "violent revolution [was] inevitable." Although Vesey, who had purchased his freedom decades earlier, was no longer a slave at the time of his rebellion, in his old age he was "the voice of the voiceless," Powers remarked. "There's something uniquely American about that."[12]

Many Carolina whites thought otherwise. One persistent letter writer announced himself "bitterly opposed" to the statue, charging that the proposed Spirit of Freedom Monument "could be Charleston's parallel to the 1990s O. J. Simpson verdict." If likening a lay minister who hoped to free thousands of enslaved Americans, including some of his children, with a wealthy athlete accused of murdering his white wife struck many newspaper readers as poor history, it was hard to tell from online postings on the *Post and Courier*'s website. One writer, failing to note that the rebels had intended to commandeer ships in the harbor for escape to Haiti, instead claimed that conspirators had planned to "create their own oppressive regime" in the state, "in which they could become the elite." As a reminder of just how interconnected the antebellum years were with the Civil War and its aftermath, another writer thought to add that Lincoln "was far more racist than Robert E. Lee, Stonewall Jackson, or Jefferson Davis." The Confederate president's unsuccessful last-minute proposal to arm a small number of black men was inflated into a plan "to eventually end slavery and give blacks full equal rights." Vesey "was no Sparticus [sic]," mused a third.[13]

So nervous were many whites that critics proposed a number of other candidates for the memorial. Demonstrating that recent history is easier to navigate than a contested past, letter writers advocated black physicist and astronaut Ronald McNair, who died in 1986 aboard the space shuttle *Challenger*. Another suggested rock music pioneer Chubby Checker, while a former president of the College of Charleston advanced the name of Georgia-born John C. Frémont, a white alumnus of the college. More appropriate suggestions included war hero and congressman Robert Smalls, who died in Beaufort, South Carolina, in 1915. As part of the city's Civil War commemoration, two small markers to Smalls had been erected in various parts of Charleston. The Reverend

Darby welcomed the tributes to the congressman but observed "that had Smalls not succeeded in commandeering a Southern ship," he would "have been executed like Vesey." Smalls or Frémont or the black soldiers in the Massachusetts Fifty-fourth should be remembered by history, Darby agreed, for "they were as much advocates of freedom as was Denmark Vesey." But a proper remembrance of the past demanded more than just counter monuments to men like Smalls or Martin Luther King Jr. It required a full, complete accounting of a troubled, complex past, which included the mass execution of men found guilty of conspiring for their freedom.[14]

The statue remains unbuilt. Denmark Vesey's monument is a bare spot in a park on the outskirts of the city. For both the detractors and proponents of the proposed statue, the dispute, bitter though it might be, pertains only to the prewar enslavement of Africans and African Americans in antebellum Charleston. For Robert Vesey, who spent the years from 1822 to 1865 virtually in hiding, the struggle was far longer. But the end of war meant a new day for the aged former slave, and for his son Robert and daughter-in-law Anna. Reconstruction made it possible for Robert Sr. to rebuild his father's church and to join Charleston's Mechanics' Association; and it gave his son, Robert Jr., the opportunity to open an account at the city's branch of the Freedman's Savings Bank. Reconstruction meant long-deferred dreams were at last realized. By the time the elder Robert Vesey died in 1870, the former slave Robert Smalls, whom he knew from the Fort Sumter rededication ceremony, had helped craft a state constitution that allowed both men to cast a ballot. Robert Vesey Jr., born in 1832, surely lived to see Smalls elected to the national House of Representatives from Carolina's Fifth District; but like his infant son who perished in 1874, he probably died before witnessing the way a new kind of war murdered the promise of Reconstruction.

A single statue cannot re-create, cannot memorialize a multifaceted past. But if the Spirit of Freedom Monument is ever completed, perhaps a fourth figure should be added to the pedestal, that of Robert Vesey Sr., when he was a twenty-two-year-old carpenter. Denmark Vesey had once considered taking his second wife, Susan, and their free children and emigrating to Liberia. But his son Robert and his other children remained enslaved, so Vesey resolved "to stay, and see what he could do for his fellow creatures." For black Americans and their radical Republican allies, Reconstruction *was* that better future, the nation's first truly progressive era. If activists won permanent voting rights or integrated transportation in Pennsylvania and New York, the era's reforms ended in most of the republic by 1901. No forest of statues can make up for that lost potential or can erase the guilt of those who drove activists like George Henry White from office. But when as many monuments, South *and* North, are erected to Benjamin F. Randolph, Octavius Catto, and James M. Hinds—reformers who lost their lives during the wars of Reconstruction—as currently venerate proslavery politicians and Confederate generals, we will know that Americans have finally come to understand the meaning of those decades.[15]

ACKNOWLEDGMENTS

Finishing a book is always highly satisfying, yet strangely worrisome. A long journey is at long last complete, but the final submission of a manuscript also means there can be no more revisions, no corrections or changes after further contemplation. The one task that involves no trepidation, however, is thanking old friends and colleagues who read all or parts of the manuscript, saved me from more than a few errors, and simply made the entire process of research and writing more enjoyable.

I first met John Belohlavek, who provided his customarily sensible comments on several chapters, at the 1988 meeting of the Society for Historians of the Early American Republic (SHEAR). I knew virtually nobody at the conference and John was the toast of the meeting due to his most recent book, but he took pity on me, asked me what I was working on, and bought me a drink. Our annual martinis at SHEAR are now for me the highlight of the convention. Two other old and wise friends, Stan Harrold and Hugh Davis, also read portions of the manuscript. Stan's liberal use of his red pen and his assaults on adjectives are not for the faint of heart, but he is invariably right on both grammar and content. The impact that Hugh, who remains the leading authority on Reconstruction in the northern states, had on this volume should be clear to anybody reading the endnotes.

I have taken advantage of the kind natures of Carol Lasser, Gary Kornblith, and the forgiving Stacey Robertson—whose surname I really *do* know how to spell—for some time now. They know everything there is to know about nineteenth-century reform and antislavery, and without complaint they read any pages I send their way. John Quist and Mitchell Snay also put aside their own important work long enough to read some of this manuscript, and Mitchell's superb biography of Horace Greeley came out just as I was getting to the 1872 election. John probably figures that after all this time I owe him a few favors, but since I have seen him kneel and pray about colonization in the Oberlin College chapel—in period garb, no less, and with Gary and Hugh, come to think of it—I suspect we are just about even.

Robert Cook and Richard Follett not only invited me to speak at the University of Sussex, they agreed to read portions of this volume, and their knowledge of the period and the battles in Washington is unparalleled. I am grateful also to Wayne Stevens, Le Moyne College's indefatigable research librarian, who is ever willing to track down the most obscure pamphlet or document. Thanks also to Le Moyne's Committee on Research and Development for their generous support for the images reproduced here.

This project began with a call from Dan Green, my wonderful and supportive agent, who knows more history than most historians and reads my manuscripts with a careful and discerning eye. Peter Ginna is an absolutely fantastic editor, always flagging a poorly crafted sentence or a paragraph that begs for clarification, yet never trying to soften or correct my voice.

Special thanks go to dear pals Alan Gallay and Donald R. Wright. I have now known Alan for thirty-three years, and he has probably read every word I have written since we met in graduate school in 1980. Only a true friend would write something as blunt as "I'm just not buying this" in the margins of my manuscripts, but Alan is always as reassuring as he is perceptive. Don clearly missed his calling as an editor, but he is so gentle in his assessments that I invariably turn to him with my first drafts. Both, as I may have remarked before, are lovely people to have a drink with.

Most of this book was written during the 2011–2012 academic year, while I was teaching as the Mary Ball Washington Professor at University College Dublin. I am grateful to the Fulbright Commission and to the department at UCD—especially to John McCaffery, the head of school—for giving me the time to finish this project. While in Ireland, I had the opportunity to try out some of these ideas and chapters at Belfast's Queen's University, the University of Sussex, and the University of Nottingham (where like Robin I wore green, if not much to the amusement of those in the audience), and so special thanks to Brian Kelly, Catherine Clinton, Anthony Stanonis, Richard Follett, Robert Cook, Bevan Sewell, and Celeste-Marie Bernier for their kind hospitality, probing questions, lively discussions, enjoyable dinners, and delicious wines.

My daughters, Kearney and Hannah, had little to do with this volume. But they are wonderful and perfect and brilliant and make my life better in every way. They are now starting to read my backlog of books, and one day they may get to this one too. I hope they like it.

Leigh Fought, to whom this book is dedicated, read the entire manuscript and filled the margins of each page with shrewd comments and brilliant suggestions for revision. During our time in Ireland, we learned to tap away at either end of our dining room table without interrupting the other's writing, at least not too often. Most of our afternoons in Dublin ended with lengthy walks along the Dodder, as we ran ideas past one another and talked over what we had written that day. Leigh probably thinks that she monopolized those strolls with her thoughts on Frederick Douglass and the women in his life, but as with everything regarding Leigh, it was all to my advantage.

Prologue: Robert Vesey's Charleston

1. Sidney Andrews, *The South Since the War* (Boston, 1866), 1; Edwin M. Stanton to Abraham Lincoln, March 25, 1865, in Abraham Lincoln Papers, Library of Congress (hereafter LC); Henry Mayer, *All on Fire: William Lloyd Garrison and the Abolition of Slavery* (New York, 2005), 577; Phillips, it seems, did not attend, since the ceremony is not mentioned in James Brewer Stewart, *Wendell Phillips: Liberty's Hero* (Baton Rouge, 1986).

2. Bruce Levine, *Half Slave and Half Free: The Roots of the Civil War*, rev. ed. (New York, 2005), 241; Bernard E. Powers, *Black Charlestonians: A Social History, 1822–1885* (Fayetteville, AR, 1994), 70.

3. Walter J. Fraser, *Charleston! Charleston! The History of a Southern City* (Columbia, SC, 1990), 272; Leon Litwack, *Been in the Storm So Long: The Aftermath of Slavery* (New York, 1979), 178.

4. Paul Escott, *After Secession: Jefferson Davis and the Failure of Confederate Nationalism* (Baton Rouge, 1977), 224; *Milwaukee Daily Sentinel*, May 4, 1865.

5. Andrews, *The South Since the War*, 1; Mayer, *All on Fire*, 578; *New-York Tribune*, April 18, 1865; *Philadelphia Illustrated New Age*, April 18, 1865.

6. *Philadelphia Illustrated New Age*, April 18, 1865; Philip Dray, *Capitol Men: The Epic Story of Reconstruction Through the Lives of the First Black Congressmen* (New York, 2010), 19–20; Fraser, *Charleston*, 273; Henry Wilson, Speech of April 1865, in *The Freedmen's Book*, ed. Lydia Maria Child (Boston, 1865), 259.

7. Elizabeth Leonard, *Lincoln's Forgotten Ally: Judge Advocate General Joseph Holt of Kentucky* (Chapel Hill, 2011), 198–99; Joseph Holt, *Treason and Its Treatment* (New York 1865), 6–7.

8. Mayer, *All on Fire*, 582; Dray, *Capitol Men*, 81–82; Powers, *Black Charlestonians*, 71. Citadel Square is now Marion Square.

9. Stephen Budiansky, *The Bloody Shirt: Terror After Appomattox* (New York, 2008), 18–19; *Boston Daily Advertiser*, August 11, 1865; *New-York Tribune*, April 13, 1865.

10. *New York Herald*, May 22, 1865.

11. *New York Herald*, May 22, 1865. On the 1790 creation of the exclusive brown organization, see Robert L. Harris, "Charleston's Free Afro-American Elite: The Brown Fellowship Society and the Humane Brotherhood," *South Carolina Historical Magazine* (hereafter *SCHM*) 82 (1981): 304. For Vesey's betrayal by Peter Desverney and George Wilson, see my *He Shall Go Out Free: The Lives of Denmark Vesey* (Lanham, MD, 2004), 2nd ed., 154–62. For the letter signed by a number of the city's browns, including brothers John, Francis, and Anthony as well as their father, Peter Desverney, who died that year at the age of seventy-three, see Elizabeth Collins, *Memories of the Southern States* (Taunton, UK, 1865), 89.

12. Andrews, The *South Since the War*, 2; Walter B. Edgar, *South Carolina: A History* (Columbia, SC, 1998), 378; on the *Charleston Mercury* and its advocacy of a "slave republic," see edition of February 13, 1861.

13. Philadelphia *Christian Recorder*, October 14, 1865.

14. Wilbert L. Jenkins, *Seizing the New Day: African Americans in Post-Civil War Charleston* (Bloomington, IN, 1998), 39; W. E. B. Du Bois, *Black Reconstruction, 1860–1880* (New York, 1999 ed.), 231.

15. *South Carolina Leader*, December 9, 1865; see also Bill of Sale, September 10, 1808, Vol. 4A, p. 97, South Carolina Department of Archives and History. At the trial of his slave George Evans, James Evans confirmed that Denmark's wife Beck had once belonged to John Barker. See Records of the General Assembly, Governor's Message, South Carolina Department of Archives and History; Steven Hahn's influential and persuasive *A Nation Under Our Feet: Black Political Struggles in the Rural South from Slavery to the Great Migration* (Cambridge, 2003), as the subtitle suggests, situates this political movement on the countryside, where indeed a good many veterans and former drivers organized black voters. Yet as a number of other scholars have emphasized, African Americans in urban areas and those freed before the war disproportionately held local and state office during the era.

16. Robert A. Vesey, August 30, 1871, Register of Signatures of Depositors in Branches of the Freedman's Savings and Trust Company, 1865–1874, Reel 23, National Archives (hereafter NA), Washington, D.C.

17. Christopher M. Span, *From Cotton Field to Schoolhouse: African American Education in Mississippi, 1862–1875* (Chapel Hill, 2009), 64; *Milwaukee Daily Sentinel*, May 4, 1865; *Boston Daily Journal*, August 17, 1866; *Albany Evening Journal*, March 29, 1866; *New Orleans Tribune*, October 29, 1867.

18. Michael W. Fitzgerald, *Splendid Failure: Postwar Reconstruction in the American South* (Chicago, 2008), 158–59; *New Orleans Tribune*, July 7, 1867; James M. McPherson, *Abraham Lincoln and the Second American Revolution* (New York, 1991), 19.

19. Fraser, *Charleston*, 285; *New Orleans Tribune*, October 29, 1867; New Orleans *Weekly Louisianian*, July 9, 1871.

20. Andrew L. Slap, *The Doom of Reconstruction: The Liberal Republicans in the Civil War Era* (New York, 2006), 74; James K. Hogue, *Uncivil War: Five New Orleans Street Battles and the Rise and Fall of Radical Reconstruction* (Baton Rouge, 2006), 24–25;

Edmund L. Drago, *Black Politicians and Reconstruction in Georgia: A Splendid Failure* (Baton Rouge, 1982), 76.

21. This, of course, is to reduce often complicated theses into a single paragraph, and on occasion authors working within what one may call a single theoretical school differ substantially in their approaches. Anne Sarah Rubin, *A Shattered Nation: The Rise and Fall of the Confederacy, 1861–1868* (Chapel Hill, 2005), argues that an emotional attachment to the Confederacy continued to unite whites, while J. Mills Thornton III, "Fiscal Policy and the Failure of Radical Reconstruction in the Lower South," in *Region, Race and Reconstruction: Essays in Honor of C. Vann Woodward*, eds. J. Morgan Kousser and James M. McPherson (New York, 1982), argues that Republican financial policies, and especially the need to tax to pay for new services, drove farmers into the arms of the so-called Redeemers (many of whom, ironically, were former Whigs who often sided with Republicans on national economic issues).

22. The two leading voices in this school are Thomas Holt, *Black over White: Negro Political Leadership in South Carolina During Reconstruction* (Urbana, IL,1977), and Michael Fitzgerald, *Urban Emancipation: Popular Politics in Reconstruction Mobile, 1860–1890* (Baton Rouge, 2002). Here too, there is a small historiographical gulf between the two, since Holt emphasizes the split between browns and blacks, while Fitzgerald contrasts class backgrounds and the factionalism within the black political community; Eric Foner, "Reconstruction Revisited," *Reviews in American History* 10 (1982): 89, provides a brief but illuminating critique of this view.

23. Hahn, *A Nation Under Our Feet*, which was clearly inspired in part by the model of a separate black nation in Eugene D. Genovese, *Roll, Jordan, Roll: The World the Slaves Made* (New York, 1974).

24. For this view, see Eric Foner, *Reconstruction: America's Unfinished Revolution, 1863–1877* (New York, 1988). Here too, of course, this is to somewhat oversimplify Foner's complicated argument, which is developed over the course of a lengthy volume. Written in the 1980s, however, much of Foner's volume was crafted in opposition to the traditional, anti-Reconstruction Dunning school of thought. Thanks to Foner's efforts, so-called revisionist scholars writing in the years after the publication of his volume no longer have to reply to the old, critical view of Reconstruction. My chief complaint with the term "revisionist" is that a large number of important scholars, from Du Bois, *Black Reconstruction*, first published in 1934, to John Hope Franklin, *Reconstruction After the Civil War* (Chicago, 1961), eloquently denounced the views advocated by white historians such as U. B. Phillips and William A. Dunning. To the extent that a number of black politicians and white activists continued to defend Reconstruction long after 1877, one might well describe critics like Phillips and Dunning as the true revisionists.

25. This very accurate depiction of northern racism can be found in works on Reconstruction from C. Vann Woodward, *Reunion and Reaction: The Compromise of 1877 and the End of Reconstruction* (New York, 1951), to Heather Cox Richardson, *The Death of Reconstruction: Race, Labor, and Politics in the Post–Civil War North, 1865–1901* (Cambridge, MA, 2001).

26. Charles Stearns, *The Black Man of the South and the Rebels* (Boston, 1872), 103; *Vermont Journal* (Windsor, VT), March 31, 1866; Jeffrey D. Wirt, *General James Longstreet: The Confederacy's Most Controversial Soldier: A Biography* (New York, 1993), 410–11. Wirt adds that "Other former Rebel officers and politicians echoed Longstreet's sentiments, not only in Louisiana but throughout the region."

27. Slap, The *Doom of Reconstruction*, 74–75; John Diertrich to Lyman Trumbull, July 16, 1866, in Lyman Trumbull Papers, LC; *Annapolis Gazette*, September 6, 1866. As Annette Gordon-Reed rightly observes in her slim but perceptive new biography, *Andrew Johnson* (New York, 2011), 5, "America went from the best [chief executive] to the worst in one presidential term." By comparison, Howard Means, *The Avenger Takes His Place: Andrew Johnson and the 45 Days That Changed the Nation* (New York, 2006), although often critical of Johnson, is an unpersuasive attempt to demonstrate that he was essentially carrying out Lincoln's policies.

28. Michael Perman makes this point in "Counter Reconstruction," in *The Facts of Reconstruction: Essays in Honor of John Hope Franklin*, eds. Eric Anderson and Alfred A. Moss Jr. (Baton Rouge, 1991), 27; two recent and excellent accounts of the massacre of 1873 are LeeAnna Keith, *The Colfax Massacre: The Untold Story of Black Power, White Terror, and the Death of Reconstruction* (New York, 2008), and Charles Lane, *The Day Freedom Died: The Colfax Massacre, the Supreme Court, and the Betrayal of Reconstruction* (New York, 2008). Lane's account of the Court's indifference is continued in Lawrence Goldstone, *Inherently Unequal: The Betrayal of Equal Rights by the Supreme Court, 1865–1903* (New York, 2011). On Randolph's 1868 assassination, see *New York Times*, October 19, 1868.

29. Colonel Whittlesey to General Oliver O. Howard, February 16, 1866, in Register of Letters Received by the Commissioners of the Bureau of Refugees, Freedmen, and Abandoned Lands (hereafter Freedmen's Bureau Papers), Roll 23, NA.

30. James L. Alcorn to W. D. Frazer, March 20, 1880, in Blanche K. Bruce Papers, Howard University; interview with John Davenport, in *The American Slave: South Carolina Narratives*, ed. George Rawick (Westport, 1972), 242. On Lee A. Nance, see Eric Foner, ed., *Freedom's Lawmakers: A Directory of Black Officeholders During Reconstruction*, 2nd ed. (Baton Rouge, 1996), 158.

31. Carl R. Osthaus, *Freedmen, Philanthropy, and Fraud: A History of the Freedman's Savings Bank* (Urbana, IL, 1976), 180–84; death of Robert A. Vesey, January 15, 1874, in Charleston City Death Records, 1821–1914, South Carolina Department of Archives and History.

32. Ethan J. Kytle and Blain Roberts, "'Is It Okay to Talk About Slavery?': Segregating the Past in Historic Charleston," *Destination Dixie: Tourism and Southern History*, ed. Karen L. Cox (Gainesville, 2012), 143. The guide's comment, ironically, mirrors the thoughts of South Carolina Governor Benjamin Perry, who equated black suffrage with southern whites "giving up the rights of their state and all constitutional and republican government." See Benjamin F. Perry to F. Marion Nye, May 25, 1867, Perry Papers, Wilson Library, University of North Carolina. What is now called the Old Exchange building was in 1822 a post office and bank, but in the past its vaults

had served as a dungeon. On the night before his execution, Denmark Vesey and four other condemned blacks were moved from the jail-workhouse complex to the vault; that morning they were carried to the gallows beyond the city limits. See my *He Shall Go Out Free*, 189–90.

Chapter One: *"An Eagle on His Button"*

1. Jefferson Ellis, Company Descriptive Book, April 1863, Compiled Military Service Records of Volunteer Union Soldiers, U.S. Colored Troops, 54th Massachusetts Infantry, Reel 5, NA; Louis J. Kelsey, Reel 10, Ibid.; Daniel A. Kelley, Reel 10, Ibid.; George W. Dugan, Reel 5, Ibid.; Robert J. Jones, Reel 10, Ibid.; Samuel Kinney, Reel 10, Ibid.; George Alexander, Reel 5, Ibid; Joseph K. Barge to Blanch K. Bruce, February 17, 1876, in Blanche K. Bruce Papers, Howard University.

2. Eric Foner, ed., *Freedom's Lawmakers: A Directory of Black Officeholders During Reconstruction*, 2nd ed. (Baton Rouge, 1996), xxv; Enos Smith, Company Descriptive Book, April 1863, Compiled Military Service Records of Volunteer Union Soldiers, U.S. Colored Troops, 54th Massachusetts Infantry, Reel 15, NA; Henry Kirk, Reel 10, Ibid.; John Simmons, Reel 15, Ibid.

3. Robert S. Levine, *Martin Delany, Frederick Douglass, and the Politics of Representative Identity* (Chapel Hill, 1997), 20–27.

4. Martin R. Delany, *The Condition, Elevation, Emigration, and Destiny of the Colored People of the United States, Politically Considered* (Philadelphia, 1852); Martin R. Delany, *Blake: Or, the Huts of America*, ed. Floyd Miller (Boston, 1970).

5. Charles V. Dyer to Abraham Lincoln, April 26, 1863, in Lincoln Papers, LC; Peter Page to Abraham Lincoln, May 1, 1863, Ibid.

6. Margot Minardi, *Making Slavery History: Abolitionism and the Politics of Memory in Massachusetts* (New York, 2010), 151; Martin R. Delany to Edwin M. Stanton, December 15, 1863, in *Freedom: Series II: The Black Military Experience: A Documentary History of Emancipation, 1861–1867*, eds. Ira Berlin, Joseph P. Reidy, and Leslie S. Rowland (Cambridge, 1983), 101–2; Leon Litwack, *Been in the Storm So Long: The Aftermath of Slavery* (New York, 1979), 96.

7. Levine, *Delany*, 222; Philip Dray, *Capitol Men: The Epic Story of Reconstruction Through the Lives of the First Black Congressmen* (New York, 2010), 12.

8. James Oakes, *The Radical and the Republican: Frederick Douglass, Abraham Lincoln, and the Triumph of Antislavery Politics* (New York, 2007), 144–45; Adam Goodheart, *1861: The Civil War Awakening* (New York, 2011), 335; Hans L. Trefousse, *Ben Butler: The South Called Him Beast!* (New York, 1957), 79; Benjamin F. Butler to Secretary of War Simon Cameron, July 30, 1861, in *Private and Official Correspondence of Gen. Benjamin F. Butler*, eds. Benjamin F. Butler and Jessie Ames Marshall (Norwood, 1917), 1: 185–88; Steven Hahn, *A Nation Under Our Feet: Black Political Struggles in the Rural South from Slavery to the Great Migration* (Cambridge, 2003), 70.

9. James G. Hollandsworth, *Pretense of Glory: The Life of General Nathaniel P. Banks* (Baton Rouge, 2005), 128; David Goldfield, *America Aflame: How the Civil War Created*

a Nation (New York, 2011), 280; Garland H. White to Edwin M. Stanton, May 7, 1862, in *Freedom: Series II*, 82–83.

10. Frederick Douglass, *Life and Times of Frederick Douglass* (New York, 1962 ed.), 337; Edward A. Miller Jr., *Lincoln's Abolitionist General: The Biography of David Hunter* (Columbia, SC, 1997), 97; Steven V. Ash, *Firebrand of Liberty: The Story of Two Black Regiments That Changed the Course of the Civil War* (New York, 2008), 32–33.

11. Thomas Wentworth Higginson, *Army Life in a Black Regiment* (Boston, 1870), 272–73; Dray, *Capitol Men*, 12; Laura M. Towne, *Letters and Diary of Laura M. Towne, Written from the Sea Islands of South Carolina* (Cambridge,1912), 71; Geoffrey Perret, *Lincoln's War: The Untold Story of America's Greatest President as Commander in Chief* (New York, 2004), 204–5; Salmon P. Chase to Abraham Lincoln, May 16, 1862, in Lincoln Papers, LC; David Hunter to Abraham Lincoln, June 25, 1862, Ibid.; Ash, *Firebrand of Liberty*, 33; Miller, *Lincoln's Abolitionist General*, 101–2. Typical of those who fled their masters was Friday Albright, a waiter who quit the Hilton Head estate of James Kirk and joined Hunter's unit on May 11, 1862. See Company Descriptive Book, May 1862, Compiled Military Service Records of Volunteer Union Soldiers, U.S. Colored Troops, 1st Colored Infantry, Record Group 94, NA.

12. *Cincinnati Daily Gazette*, August 7, 1871; Glenn David Brasher, *The Peninsula Campaign and the Necessity of Emancipation: African Americans the Fight for Freedom* (Chapel Hill, 2012), 205; Philip Shaw Paludan, *The Presidency of Abraham Lincoln* (Lexington, 1994), 146–47; Willie Lee Rose, *Rehearsal for Reconstruction: The Port Royal Experiment* (New York, 1964), 186–87; *Journal of the Senate*, July 17, 1862, 37th Cong., 2nd Sess. (Washington, 1863), 872; Scott French and Carol Sheriff, *A People at War: Civilians and Soldiers in America's Civil War*, 192.

13. Rose, *Rehearsal for Reconstruction*, 193; Litwack, *Been in the Storm So Long*, 68; Higginson, *Army Life in a Black Regiment*, 2–3, 276.

14. Higginson to James, November 24, 1862, in Higginson Papers, American Antiquarian Society; Sarah Parker Remond, *The Negroes & Anglo-Africans as Freedmen and Soldiers* (London, 1864), 6; James M. McPherson, ed., *The Negro's Civil War: How American Negroes Felt and Acted During the War for the Union* (New York, 1965), 213; Higginson, *Army Life in a Black Regiment*, 34. White observers invariably recorded not merely the words spoken by black leaders but also what they regarded as slave dialect. Although these documents demonstrate that even white Republicans and northern abolitionists carried racial and class baggage, it would also be ahistorical to rewrite such quotations into modern English.

15. Ash, *Firebrand of Liberty*, 36–37; interview with John Franklin, in George Rawick, ed., *The American Slave: South Carolina Narratives* (Westport, 1972), 84.

16. David Donald, *Lincoln* (New York, 1995), 430; Frederick J. Blue, *Charles Sumner and the Conscience of the North* (Arlington Heights, IL., 1994), 134–35; Thomas A. Jenckes to Abraham Lincoln, September 11, 1862, in Lincoln Papers, LC.

17. Dudley Taylor Cornish, *The Sable Arm: Black Troops in the Union Army, 1861–1865* (Lexington, 1987), 162; John David Smith, "Let Us Be Grateful That We Have Colored Troops That Will Fight," in *Black Soldiers in Blue: African American Troops in the*

Civil War Era, ed. John David Smith (Chapel Hill, 2001), 44–45; Governor M. L. Bonham to General P. G. T. Beauregard, July 22, 1863, in Berlin, ed., *Freedom: Series II*, 579–80.

18. Hannah Johnson to Abraham Lincoln, July 31, 1863, in Berlin, ed., *Freedom: Series II*, 582–83; James M. McPherson, *Tried By War: Abraham Lincoln as Commander in Chief* (New York, 2008), 205.

19. *Liberator*, January 2, 1863; *Boston Journal*, January 2, 1863; *Philadelphia Inquirer*, January 1, 1863; *New York Herald*, January 1, 1863.

20. San Francisco *Elevator*, July 3, 1872; Charles Sumner to John Murray Forbes, December 28, 1862, in *The Selected Letters of Charles Sumner*, ed. Beverly Wilson Palmer (Boston, 1990), 2: 136.

21. Bruce Tap, "Race, Rhetoric, and Emancipation: The Election of 1862 in Illinois," *Civil War History* 39 (1993): 101–25; Perret, *Lincoln's War*, 296–97; *Liberator*, February 20, 1863; Ulysses S. Grant to Abraham Lincoln, August 23, 1863, in Lincoln Papers, LC.

22. Edward A. Miller Jr., *The Black Civil War Soldiers of Illinois: The Story of the 29th U.S. Colored Infantry* (Columbia, SC, 1998), 22; Minardi, *Making Slavery History*, 167.

23. David W. Blight, *Frederick Douglass's Civil War: Keeping Faith in Jubilee* (Baton Rouge, 1989), 160–61; *Hartford Daily Courant*, March 7, 1863; Justin D. Fulton, a progressive white minister, also hoped that "freedmen with arms in their hands will not submit to be disfranchised." See his *Radicalism: A Sermon Preached in Tremont Temple, on Fast-Day* (Boston, 1865), 35.

24. W. E. B. Du Bois, *Black Reconstruction, 1860–1880* (New York, 1999 ed.), 97; John A. Andrew to Francis G. Shaw, January 30, 1863, in Berlin, ed., *Freedom: Series II*, 86–87; *Liberator*, February 20, 1863; Robert Gould Shaw to Elizabeth Lyman, February 20, 1863, in *Blue-Eyed Child of Fortune: The Civil War Letters of Colonel Robert Gould Shaw*, ed. Russell Duncan (Athens, GA, 1992), 292–93.

25. Ronald C. White Jr., *A. Lincoln: A Biography* (New York, 2009), 541–42; Blight, *Frederick Douglass's Civil War*, 158–59.

26. Douglass, *Life and Times*, 342; Margaret Washington, *Sojourner Truth's America* (Urbana, 2009), 305; Charles R. Douglass, Company Descriptive Book, April 1863, Compiled Military Service Records of Volunteer Union Soldiers, U.S. Colored Troops, 54th Massachusetts Infantry, Reel 5, NA; Lewis H. Douglass, Reel 5, Ibid.; Stephen Ennis, Reel 5, Ibid.; Peter Smith, Reel 15, Ibid.; Thomas F. Smith, Reel 15, Ibid.; Robert J. Simmons, Reel 15, Ibid.

27. Russell Duncan, *Where Death and Glory Meet: Colonel Robert Gould Shaw and the 54th Massachusetts Infantry* (Athens, GA, 1999), 1–2; Lewis H. Douglass, Company Descriptive Book, April 1863, Compiled Military Service Records of Volunteer Union Soldiers, U.S. Colored Troops, 54th Massachusetts Infantry, Reel 5, NA; William S. McFeely, *Frederick Douglass* (New York, 1991), 225; Washington *National Intelligencer*, July 8, 1863; Lewis H. Douglass to Amelia Loguen, June 18, 1863, in Walter O. Evans Collection, Savannah; Kate Clifford Larson, *Bound for the Promise Land: Harriet Tubman, Portrait of an American Hero* (New York, 2004), 203–4.

28. Robert Gould Shaw to Sarah Shaw, July 3, 1863, in Duncan, ed., *Blue-Eyed Child of Fortune*, 373; Towne, *Letters and Diary*, 114; Lewis H. Douglass to Amelia Loguen, September 28, 1864, in Douglass Papers, Evans Collection, Savannah.

29. Lewis H. Douglass to Amelia Loguen, August 27, 1863, in Evans Collection, Savannah; McFeely, *Douglass*, 226; Joseph E. Stevens, *1863: The Rebirth of a Nation* (New York, 1999), 309.

30. Stevens, *1863*, 309; Lewis H. Douglass to Frederick and Anna Douglass, July 20, 1863, in *The Black Abolitionist Papers, Vol. V: The United States, 1859 to 1865*, eds. C. Peter Ripley and Michael Hembree (Chapel Hill, 1992), 240–41; Washington, *Sojourner Truth's America*, 306.

31. Certification by Dr. James Macune Smith, October 6, 1863, in Compiled Military Service Records of Volunteer Union Soldiers, U.S. Colored Troops, 54th Massachusetts Infantry, Reel 5, NA; Lewis H. Douglass to Amelia Loguen, August 15, 1863, in Evans Collection, Savannah; Nathan Sprague, Company Descriptive Book, September 1864, Compiled Military Service Records of Volunteer Union Soldiers, U.S. Colored Troops, 54th Massachusetts Infantry, Reel 15, NA; E. D. Townsend, Special Order 122, March 19, 1864, Reel 5, Ibid. According to Dr. Smith's report, Douglass developed "gangrene of left half of Scrotum." Although Lewis returned home and married his fiancée, Amelia Loguen, he was never able to have children.

32. Henry Gardner, Company Descriptive Book, June 1864, Compiled Military Service Records of Volunteer Union Soldiers, U.S. Colored Troops, 8th Infantry, Record Group 94, NA; Samuel Turner, 1st Colored Infantry, June 1863, Reel 15, Ibid.; James Allen, Massachusetts 54th, Reel 5, Ibid.

33. Samuel Gridley Howe to unknown, November 13, 1863, Company Descriptive Book, Compiled Military Service Records of Volunteer Union Soldiers, U.S. Colored Troops, 2ndInfantry, Record Group 94, NA; Edward North to unknown, October 27, 1863, Ibid.; Edward L. Stevens, Company Descriptive Book, January 1864, Compiled Military Service Records of Volunteer Union Soldiers, U.S. Colored Troops, 54th Massachusetts Infantry, Reel 15, NA.

34. Hahn, *A Nation Under Our Feet*, 97–98; Keith P. Wilson, *Campfires of Freedom: The Camp Life of Black Soldiers During the Civil War* (Kent, 2002), 98–99.

35. Higginson, *Army Life in a Black Regiment*, 25; McPherson, ed., *Negro's Civil War*, 212; Harriet Beecher Stowe, "The Education of Freedmen," *North American Review* 128 (1879): 614.

36. Ira Berlin, *Generations of Captivity: A History of African-American Slaves* (New York, 2004), 257; Claude H. Nolen, *African American Southerners in Slavery, Civil War, and Reconstruction* (Jefferson, 2001), 129; Joe M. Richardson, "Christian Abolitionism: The American Missionary Association and the Florida Negro," *Journal of Negro Education* 40 (1971): 35; Laura W. Wakefield, "'Set a Light in a Dark Place': Teachers of Freedmen in Florida, 1864–1874," *Florida Historical Quarterly* 81 (2003): 405; E. S. Wheeler to General Ullmann, April 8, 1864, in Berlin, ed., *Freedom: Series II*, 618.

37. Joseph T. Glatthaar, *Forged in Battle: The Civil War Alliance of Black Soldiers and White*

Officers (New York, 1989), 226; Wilson, *Campfires of Freedom*, 88–89; J. M. Mickley to Adjt. Gen. , January 31, 1865, in Berlin, ed., *Freedom: Series II*, 620–621.

38. Glatthaar, *Forged in Battle*, 178–79, 248–49; Lewis H. Douglass et al. to Edwin M. Stanton, January 1865, in Berlin, ed., *Freedom: Series II*, 340–341; William D. Matthews to James H. Lane, January 12, 1863, Ibid., 69–70.

39. John F. Bartholf to E. B. Tracy, September 24, 1864, in Compiled Military Service Records of Volunteer Union Soldiers who Served with U.S. Colored Troops, 2nd U.S. Colored, Record Group 94, NA; Allen C. Guelzo, *Lincoln's Emancipation Proclamation: The End of Slavery in America* (New York, 2004), 218.

40. David Donald, *Charles Sumner and the Rights of Man* (New York, 1970), 154; Kate Masur, *An Example for All the Land: Emancipation and the Struggle over Equality in Washington, D.C.* (Chapel Hill, 2010), 101; Salmon P. Chase to Jay Cooke, September 1, 1863, in *The Salmon Chase Papers: Correspondence*, ed. John Niven (Kent, 1997), 4: 129; John Lee, Company Descriptive Book, January 1864, Compiled Military Service Records of Volunteer Union Soldiers, U.S. Colored Troops, 54th Massachusetts Infantry, Reel 10, NA; Philip Foner, "The Battle to End Discrimination," *Pennsylvania History* 40 (1973): 270.

41. John B. Boles, *Black Southerners, 1619–1869* (Lexington, 1983), 195; John Cimprich, *Fort Pillow, A Civil War Massacre, and Public Memory* (Baton Rouge, 2005), 72; Gary W. Gallagher, *The Union War* (Cambridge, 2011), 98; Richard M. Reid, *Freedom for Themselves: North Carolina's Black Soldiers in the Civil War Era* (Chapel Hill, 2008), 258.

42. Charges and Specifications Preferred Against Private Alfred Lee, July 29, 1865, Compiled Military Service Records of Volunteer Union Soldiers, U.S. Colored Troops, 54th Massachusetts Infantry, Reel 10, NA; *New Orleans Tribune*, August 10, 1865.

43. Charges and Specifications Preferred Against Private Grimm Z. Smith, June 28, 1865, Compiled Military Service Records of Volunteer Union Soldiers, U.S. Colored Troops, 54th Massachusetts Infantry, Reel 15, NA; Grimm Z. Smith, Company Descriptive Book, January 1864, Compiled Military Service Records of Volunteer Union Soldiers, U.S. Colored Troops, 54th Massachusetts Infantry, Reel 5, NA. Three Margaret Smiths appear in the 1850 federal census for Charleston, but only one of them was white. That Margaret Smith, born in 1810, owned thirty-eight slaves in 1850 and one of them was a ten-year-old boy; if the birth date Private Smith gave to recruiters was correct, he was born in 1840. See South Carolina, federal census, page 114, NA.

44. John H. B. Payne to unknown, June 11, 1864, in *A Grand Army of Black Men: Letters from African-American Soldiers in the Union Army 1861–1865*, ed. Edwin S. Redkey (Cambridge, 1992), 208–9; Herman Belz, "Law, Politics, and Race in the Struggle for Equal Pay During the Civil War," *Civil War History* 22 (1976): 198–202; Litwack, *Been in the Storm*, 83. When black Kentucky private Perry Hawkins complained too often about pay and conditions for black soldiers in Texas, he was court-martialed "on the charge of exciting mutiny in July 1865" and sentenced to eighteen months at hard labor. He died on December 19, 1865, before his sentence could be concluded.

See (author unknown) *History of the 116th Regiment U.S.C. Infantry, From Its Organization to the Present Time* (Philadelphia, 1866), 45.

45. Hugh L. Bond to Edwin M. Stanton, August 15, 1863, in Berlin, ed., *Freedom: Series II*, 202–3; James H. Adair, November 11, 1863, Compiled Military Service Records of Volunteer Union Soldiers, U.S. Colored Troops, 2nd Infantry, Record Group 94, NA; Levin Barrett, September 1863, Ibid.; James Mathews, Claim for Compensation for Enlisted Slave, June 24, 1863, Reel 15, Ibid.

46. Eric Foner, *The Fiery Trial: Abraham Lincoln and American Slavery* (New York, 2010), 254; Douglass, *Life and Times*, 346–47; Francis George Shaw to Abraham Lincoln, July 31, 1863, in Lincoln Papers, LC; Frederick Douglass to Abraham Lincoln, August 29, 1864, Ibid.; John A. Andrew to Abraham Lincoln, May 27, 1864, Ibid.

47. *New Orleans Tribune*, August 23, 1864; Hans L. Trefousse, *Thaddeus Stevens: Nineteenth-Century Egalitarian* (Chapel Hill, 1997), 140; Charleston *Missionary Record*, July 5, 1873; *Cincinnati Daily Gazette*, August 7, 1871.

48. Daniel Ullmann, *Address by Daniel Ullmann Before the Soldier's and Sailor's Union of the State of New York* (Washington, 1868), 3; Glatthaar, *Forged in Battle*, 166–67; Wilson, *Campfires of Freedom*, 112–13; Jason Marsh to Lyman Trumbull, January 8, 1866, in Trumbull Papers, LC.

49. Cornish, *Sable Arm*, 215–16; Washington, *Sojourner Truth's America*, 320; Foner, *Fiery Trial*, 317.

50. McFeely, *Douglass*, 231; Glatthaar, *Forged in Battle*, 248–49; Richard Bailey, *Neither Carpetbaggers Nor Scalawags: Black Officeholders During the Reconstruction of Alabama, 1867–1878* (Montgomery, 1991), 109; Eric Foner, *Reconstruction: America's Unfinished Revolution, 1863–1877* (New York, 1988), 9; Foner, ed., *Freedom's Lawmakers*, 154.

51. Anne Sarah Rubin, *A Shattered Nation: The Rise and Fall of the Confederacy, 1861–1868* (Chapel Hill, 2005), 102–3; Foner, *Fiery Trial*, 252–53; Donald, *Charles Sumner*, 118–19; Abraham Lincoln to John A. Andrew, February 18, 1864, in Lincoln Papers, LC. On the election returns in 1860, see my *Year of Meteors: Stephen Douglas, Abraham Lincoln, and the Election that Brought on the Civil War* (New York, 2010), appendix.

52. *Albany Evening Journal*, March 31, 1866; Nat Gadsden, Register of Signatures of Depositors in Branches of the Freedman's Savings and Trust Company, Reel 21, NA; Charles W. Singer to unknown, September 18, 1864, in Redkey, ed., *A Grand Army of Black Men*, 213–14; Blight, *Frederick Douglass's Civil War*, 164; Louis P. Masur, *Lincoln's Hundred Days: The Emancipation Proclamation and the War for the Union* (Cambridge, 2012), 226. On the Confederate military's enslavement of free blacks in 1863, see Stanley Harrold, *Border War: Fighting over Slavery Before the Civil War* (Chapel Hill, 2010), 186–87.

53. "The Freedmen at Port Royal," *North American Review* (1865), 27; Holt, *Black over White*, 49; Foner, ed., *Freedom's Lawmakers*, 117; Glatthaar, *Forged in Battle*, 246.

54. John Cimprich, "The Beginning of the Black Suffrage Movement in Tennessee, 1864–1865," *Journal of Negro History* (hereafter *JNH*) 65 (1980), 186; Jim Cullen, "'I's A Man Now': Gender and African American Men," in *Divided Houses: Gender and the Civil*

War, eds. Catherine Clinton and Nina Silber (New York, 1992), 85; Foner, *Reconstruction*, 9; Glatthaar, *Forged in Battle*, 79.

55. Rose, *Rehearsal for Reconstruction*, 245; Litwack, *Been in the Storm So Long*, 269.

56. Hahn, *A Nation Under Our Feet*, 89–90; *New Orleans Tribune*, October 25, 1864; William M. Dickson, *The Absolute Equality of All Men Before the Law, the Only True Basis for Reconstruction* (Cincinnati, 1865), 6.

57. Blight, *Frederick Douglass's Civil War*, 186; *New York Herald*, July 19, 1865.

Chapter Two: "To Forget and Forgive Old Scores"

1. David Warren Bowen, *Andrew Johnson and the Negro* (Knoxville, 1989), 51; Annette Gordon-Reed, *Andrew Johnson* (New York, 2011), 38.

2. Paul H. Bergeron, *Andrew Johnson's Civil War and Reconstruction* (Knoxville, 2011), 27; Bowen, *Andrew Johnson and the Negro*, 51, is critical of Johnson's behavior during the early years of the war; James Oakes, *Freedom National: The Destruction of Slavery in the United States, 1861–1865* (New York, 2012), 483, is kinder, calling the military governor the president's "strongest ally in the struggle to get slavery abolished in Tennessee." On Johnson's presidential aspirations in 1860, see my *Year of Meteors*, 58–60; on his being chosen in 1864, see John C. Waugh, *Reelecting Lincoln: The Battle for the 1864 Presidency* (New York, 1997), 197–201.

3. Charles Johnson to Andrew Johnson, January 29, 1860, in *The Papers of Andrew Johnson*, ed. LeRoy P. Graf (Knoxville, 1972), 3: 404–5; Samuel Johnson to Andrew Johnson, 1867, Ibid., 12: 183; Andrew Johnson to Samuel Johnson, 1867, Ibid., 12: 237.

4. Gordon-Reed, *Johnson*, 38–39; Andrew Johnson to Robert Johnson, 1854, in *Papers of Johnson*, 2: 230–31; David Nichols, ed., *Ernie's America: The Best of Ernie Pyle's 1930s Travel Dispatches* (New York, 1990), 304–6. On the state constitutional amendment, see John Cimprich, *Slavery's End in Tennessee, 1861–1865* (Tuscaloosa, 1985), 104–5, 116.

5. David Donald, *Charles Sumner and the Rights of Man* (New York, 1970), 207–8 and note 7; David Goldfield, *America Aflame: How the Civil War Created a Nation* (New York, 2011), 418; Salmon P. Chase to Abraham Lincoln, November 25, 1863, in Lincoln Papers, LC; Abraham Lincoln to Michael Hahn, March 13, 1864, Ibid.; Michael Hahn to Abraham Lincoln, May 11, 1864, Ibid. The final vote on emancipation in Louisiana was 70 to 16.

6. Gerald S. Henig, *Henry Winter Davis: Antebellum and Civil War Congressman from Maryland* (New York, 1973), 234–35; Benjamin F. Wade to Abraham Lincoln, March 13, 1864, in Lincoln Papers, LC; David Donald, *Lincoln* (New York, 1995), 510–11. Even Secretary Chase encouraged Lincoln to avoid the ten percent figure in favor of a "simpler & clearer declaration" as to who was a loyal citizen of each state. See Salmon P. Chase to Henry Ward Beecher, December 26, 1863, in *Chase Papers*, 4: 225–26.

7. Peter Kolchin, *Unfree Labor: American Slavery and Russian Serfdom* (Cambridge, 1987), 289; Frederick Douglass to Abraham Lincoln, August 29, 1864, in Lincoln Papers, LC; Leslie A. Schwalm, *Emancipation's Diaspora: Race and Reconstruction in the Upper Midwest* (Chapel Hill, 2009), 65.

8. *New Orleans Tribune*, April 6, 1865; Eugene D. Genovese, *Roll, Jordan, Roll: The World the Slaves Made* (New York, 1974), 150–51; C. A. Morton to James A. Seddon, April 2, 1863, in Berlin, ed., *Freedom: Series I*, 762–63; James A. Seddon to Jefferson Davis, November 26, 1863, in Robert F. Durden, ed., *The Grey and the Black: The Confederate Debate on Emancipation* (Baton Rouge, 1972), 48–49.

9. Joseph P. Reidy, "Coming from the Shadow of the Past: The Transition from Slavery to Freedom at the Freedmen's Village, 1863–1900," *Virginia Magazine of History and Biography* 95 (1987): 408; *National Anti-Slavery Standard*, April 14, 1866; *Morning Oregonian* (Portland, OR), May 4, 1866. Norris's story was first reported on June 24, 1859, in the *New-York Tribune* and was published even before Lee's role in defeating John Brown's raid at Harpers Ferry made him relatively famous.

10. James Oliver to Simeon S. Jocelyn, January 14, 1863, in *The Black Abolitionist Papers, Vol. V: The United States, 1859 to 1865*, eds. C. Peter Ripley and Michael Hembree (Chapel Hill, 1992), 5: 173; Harriet Jacobs to Lydia Maria Child, March 18, 1863, Ibid., Hiram W. Allen to A. G. Draper, November 17, 1863, in Berlin, ed., *Freedom: Series I*, 92; Leon Litwack, *Been in the Storm So Long: The Aftermath of Slavery* (New York, 1979), 399.

11. Edmund L. Drago, *Black Politicians and Reconstruction in Georgia: A Splendid Failure* (Baton Rouge, 1982), 5–6; Leigh Fought, *Southern Womanhood & Slavery: A Biography of Louisa S. McCord, 1810–1879* (Columbia, MO, 2003), 178; interview with Savilla Burrell, in George Rawick, ed., *The American Slave: South Carolina Narratives* (Westport, 1972), 151; interview with Sara Brown, Ibid., 142.

12. Eric Foner, *Nothing But Freedom: Emancipation and Its Legacy* (Baton Rouge, 1983), 80–81; Julie Saville, *The Work of Reconstruction: From Slave to Wage Laborer in South Carolina 1860–1870* (Cambridge, 1994), 151–52; Robert L. Paquette, "The Drivers Shall Lead Them: Images and Reality in Slave Resistance," in *Race, Slavery, and Southern History*, eds. Robert L. Paquette and Louis A. Ferleger (Charlottesville, 2000), 31–58; Stephanie McCurry, *Confederate Reckoning: Power and Politics in the Civil War South* (Cambridge, 2010), 244–45.

13. Gary W. Gallagher, *The Union War* (Cambridge, 2011), 116; Christopher M. Span, *From Cotton Field to Schoolhouse: African American Education in Mississippi, 1862–1875* (Chapel Hill, 2009), 53–54; Andrew Ward, *The Slaves' War: The Civil War in the Words of Former Slaves* (New York, 2008), 162–63; Michael W. Fitzgerald, "Emancipation and Military Pacification: The Freedmen's Bureau and Social Control in Alabama," in *The Freedmen's Bureau and Reconstruction*, eds. Paul A. Cimbala and Randall M. Miller (New York, 1999), 48–49.

14. *Cincinnati Daily Enquirer*, February 16, 1866; Albert T. Morgan, *Yazoo: Or, on the Picket Line of Freedom in the South* (Washington, 1884), 42; Drago, *Black Politicians and Reconstruction in Georgia*, 8–9.

15. William C. Davis, *Look Away: A History of the Confederate States of America* (New York, 2002), 150; Armistead L. Robinson, *Bitter Fruits of Bondage: The Demise of Slavery and the Collapse of the Confederacy, 1861–1865* (Charlottesville, 2004), 201.

16. Litwack, *Been in the Storm So Long*, 142–43; Leslie A. Schwalm, "Sweet Dreams of

Freedom: Freedwomen's Reconstruction of Life and Labor in Lowcountry South Carolina," *Journal of Women's History* 9 (1997): 9; Laura M. Towne, *Letters and Diary of Laura M. Towne, Written from the Sea Islands of South Carolina* (Cambridge, 1912), 85.

17. Schwalm, "Sweet Dreams of Freedom," 26; Sarah Parker Remond, *The Negroes & Anglo-Africans as Freedmen and Soldiers* (London, 1864), 25; George C. Rable, *Civil Wars: Women and the Crisis of Southern Nationalism* (Urbana, IL, 1989), 255; Ira Berlin, *Generations of Captivity: A History of African-American Slaves* (New York, 2004), 258–59.

18. *Memphis Daily Avalanche*, January 31, 1867; Litwack, *Been in the Storm So Long*, 48; Francis Thomas Howard, *In and Out of the Lines: An Accurate Account of Incidents During the Occupation of Georgia by Federal Troops in 1864–65* (New York, 1905), 204.

19. Davis, *Look Away*, 146–47; Martha Hodes, *White Women, Black Men: Illicit Sex in the Nineteenth-Century South* (New Haven, 1997), 100; Joan E. Cashin, *First Lady of the Confederacy: Varina Davis's Civil War* (Cambridge, 2006), 143; Sidney Andrews, *The South Since the War* (Boston, 1866), 65; Genovese, *Roll, Jordan, Roll*, 98–99.

20. *New Orleans Tribune*, July 22, 1865; McCurry, *Confederate Reckoning*, 298–99, 255–56.

21. Litwack, *Been in the Storm So Long*, 312–13; Beverly Tucker, Company Descriptive Book, May 1863, in Compiled Military Service Records of Volunteer Union Soldiers, 1st Colored Infantry, Reel 15, NA; Howard N. Rabinowitz, *Race Relations in the Urban South, 1865–1890* (New York, 1978), 18–19; William P. Connor, "Reconstruction Rebels: The *New Orleans Tribune* in Post-War Louisiana," *Louisiana History* 21 (1980): 159–60.

22. Gerald David Jaynes, *Branches Without Roots: Genesis of the Black Working Class in the American South, 1862–1882* (New York, 1986), 64; Hannah Rosen, *Terror in the Heart of Freedom: Citizenship, Sexual Violence, and the Meaning of Race in the Postemancipation South* (Chapel Hill, 2008), 50; Noralee Frankel, *Freedom's Women: Black Women and Families in Civil War Mississippi* (Bloomington, IN, 1999), 32–33; Carol Faulkner, *Women's Radical Reconstruction: The Freedmen's Aid Movement* (Philadelphia, 2003), 118; Janette Thomas Greenwood, *First Fruits of Freedom: The Migration of Former Slaves and Their Search for Equality in Worcester, Massachusetts, 1862–1900* (Chapel Hill, 2010), 54.

23. Reid, *Freedom for Themselves*, 215–16; Testimony by the Superintendent of Contrabands, May 9, 1863, in Berlin, ed., *Freedom: Series 1*, 1: 88; Trial of Private Calvin Smith, January 20, 1865, in Compiled Military Service Records of Volunteer Union Soldiers, 41st U.S. Colored Infantry, Record Group 94, NA.

24. Kevin R. Hardwick, "'Your Old Father Abe Lincoln is Dead and Damned': Black Soldiers and the Memphis Race Riot of 1866," *Journal of Social History* 27 (1993): 113; Frankel, *Freedom's Women*, 22–23; David Goldfield, *America Aflame: How the Civil War Created a Nation* (New York, 2011), 282.

25. John Boston to Elizabeth Boston, January 12, 1862, in Berlin, ed., *Freedom: Series 1*, 1: 357; Meunomennie L. Maimi to T. A. Maimi, March 1863, in Ripley, ed., *Black Abolitionist Papers*, 5: 189–90.

26. Geoffrey Perret, *Lincoln's War: The Untold Story of America's Greatest President as Commander in Chief* (New York, 2004), 298; Jim Downs, *Sick from Freedom: African-American Illness and Suffering During the Civil War and Reconstruction* (New York, 2012), 46–47; Ulysses S. Grant to Abraham Lincoln, June 11, 1863, in Lincoln Papers, LC; Schwalm, *Emancipation's Diaspora*, 60–61; William T. Sherman to Lorenzo Thomas, June 26, 1864, in *Sherman's Civil War: Selected Correspondence of William T. Sherman, 1860–1865*, ed. Brooks Simpson (Chapel Hill, 1999), 657–58; Lorenzo Thomas, Special Order No. 45, August 13, 1863, in Berlin, ed., *Freedom: Series 1*, 3: 719–20.

27. Reidy, "Coming from the Shadow of the Past," 404, 411; Steven Hahn, *A Nation Under Our Feet: Black Political Struggles in the Rural South from Slavery to the Great Migration* (Cambridge, 2003), 82; Oliver O. Howard, General Order, December 4, 1865, in Register of Letters Received by the Commissioners, Freedmen's Bureau Papers, Reel 23, NA.

28. R. I. Cromwell to B. F. Flanders, November 17, 1864, in Berlin, ed., *Freedom: Series I*, 3: 558–59; *Morning Oregonian* (Portland, February 28, 1866; Eric Foner, ed., *Freedom's Lawmakers: A Directory of Black Officeholders During Reconstruction*, 2nd ed. (Baton Rouge, 1996), 53–54.

29. W. F. Nelson to Oliver O. Howard, April 9, 1864, and November 22, 1864, in Register of Letters Received by the Commissioners, Freedmen's Bureau Papers, Reel 23, NA; Saville, *Work of Reconstruction*, 37–38; Schwalm, "Sweet Dreams of Freedom," 14.

30. *New Orleans Tribune*, January 7, 1865; Litwack, *Been in the Storm So Long*, 240; Amy Dru Stanley, *From Bondage to Contract: Wage Labor, Marriage, and the Market in the Age of Slave Emancipation* (Cambridge, 1998), 44.

31. Catherine Clinton, "Reconstructing Freedwomen," in Clinton and Silber, eds., *Divided Houses: Gender and the Civil War* (New York, 1992), 307; Frankel, *Freedom's Women*, 82.

32. *New Orleans Tribune*, August 31, 1866, October 2, 1866; John Kimball to A. E. Hines, January 4, 1867, in Records of the Assistant Commissioner for the District of Columbia, Freedmen's Bureau Papers, Reel 3, NA.

33. Litwack, *Been in the Storm So Long*, 229; New Orleans *Black Republican*, April 29, 1865; *New Orleans Tribune*, January 7, 1865, and August 31, 1866.

34. *Flake's Bulletin* (Galveston, TX), March 6, 1869; Oliver O. Howard to R. G. Rutherford, February 18, 1867, in Records of the Assistant Commissioner for the District of Columbia, Freedmen's Bureau Papers, Reel 3, NA; Oliver O. Howard, Order, February 7, 1867, Ibid.

35. Hahn, *A Nation Under Our Feet*, 168–69; David Williams, July 19, 1866, in Register of Signatures in Branches of the Freedman's Savings and Trust Company, Reel 21, NA; Ann Jackson, February 2, 1871, Ibid., Reel 17; Margaret Haler, February 6, 1871, Ibid., Reel 17.

36. John Henry Neal, November 9, 1870, in Register of Signatures in Branches of the Freedman's Savings and Trust Company, Reel 17, NA; James Walker Rutledge, No-

vember 10, 1870, Ibid., Reel 17; Louisa Emily Trusty, November 13, 1870, Ibid., Reel 17.

37. Eric Foner, *Reconstruction: America's Unfinished Revolution, 1863–1877* (New York, 1988), 87; Frankel, *Freedom's Women*, 136.

38. Litwack, *Been in the Storm So Long*, 191; *Flake's Bulletin* (Galveston, TX), March 30, 1866; Alvan C. Gillem to Oliver O. Howard, January 20, 1867, in Register of Letters Received by the Commissioners, Freedmen's Bureau Papers, Reel 43, NA; Charles Riggs to Oliver O. Howard, January 28, 1867, Ibid., Reel 43; A. L. Lazar to Alvan C. Gillem, May 1, 1868, Ibid., Reel 24. As late as December 21, 1867, agent H. Metcalf reported from Mississippi that it was "useless to attempt to restore those Children to their Mother without a guard of Soldiers to enforce the Order." See his letter to Colonel Webster of that date, Reel 43, Ibid.

39. Alvan C. Gillem to Oliver O. Howard, February 15, 1867, in Register of Letters Received by the Commissioners, Freedmen's Bureau Papers, Reel 43, NA; *Cincinnati Daily Gazette*, June 1, 1867; Joseph Browne, "'To Bring Out the Intellect of the Race': An African American Freedmen's Bureau Agent in Maryland," *Maryland Historical Magazine*, 104 (2009): 388; George H. Hanks to Nathaniel P. Banks, April 8, 1863, in Berlin, ed., *Freedom: Series 1*, 3: 434–35; Richard Paul Fuke, "Hugh Lennox Bond and Radical Republican Ideology," *Journal of Southern History* (hereafter *JSH*) 45 (1979): 574; E. M. Gregory to Oliver O. Howard, December 31, 1866, in Register of Letters Received by the Commissioners, Freedmen's Bureau Papers, Reel 43, NA; Oliver O. Howard to O. S. Wall, February 13, 1867, in Records of the Assistant Commissioner for the District of Columbia, Freedmen's Bureau Papers, Reel 3, NA.

40. Charles Joyner, *Down By the Riverside: A South Carolina Slave Community* (Urbana, IL, 1984), 221; Allen C. Guelzo, *Lincoln's Emancipation Proclamation: The End of Slavery in America* (New York, 2004), 216; David Blake, May 11, 1862, in Company Descriptive Book, Compiled Military Service Records of Volunteer Union Soldiers, U.S. Colored Troops, 33rd Infantry, Record Group 94, NA.

41. John B. Boles, *Black Southerners, 1619–1869* (Lexington, 1983), 43; Litwack, *Been in the Storm So Long*, 249; Sinclair Cupit, March 16, 1866, Register of Signatures in Branches of the Freedman's Savings and Trust Company, Reel 4, NA; George Augustus, October 1863, Company Descriptive Book, in Compiled Military Service Records of Volunteer Union Soldiers, 1st Colored Infantry, Record Group 94, NA; Richard Reid, "USCT Veterans in Post–Civil War North Carolina," in John David Smith, ed., *Black Soldiers in Blue: African American Troops in the Civil War Era* (Chapel Hill, 2001), 397–98.

42. Berlin, *Generations of Captivity*, 260–61; Hannah Grant, October 18, 1869, in Register of Signatures in Branches of the Freedman's Savings and Trust Company, Reel 21, NA; Robert Mustafa Sr., October 7, 1869, Ibid.; Charles Francis Barager, November 9, 1870, Ibid.; Samuel Simmons, June 7, 1871, Ibid.

43. Andrew Jackson Free, April 4, 1867, in Register of Signatures in Branches of the Freedman's Savings and Trust Company, Reel 21, NA; Freeman Pew, June 2, 1866, Ibid.; Jim Cullen, "Gender and African American Men," in Clinton and Silber, eds.,

Divided Houses, 90; Stanley, *From Bondage to Contract*, 38–39; Elizabeth Regosin, *Freedom's Promise: Ex-Slave Families and Citizenship in the Age of Emancipation* (Charlottesville, 2002), 56.

44. Craig L. Symonds, *Stonewall of the West: Patrick Cleburne and the Civil War* (Lexington, 1998), 195; Boles, *Black Southerners*, 196–97; Robinson, *Bitter Fruits of Bondage*, 278–79; William C. Davis, *Jefferson Davis: The Man and His Hour* (New York, 1991), 557, 597.

45. McCurry, *Confederate Reckoning*, 338, 342; J. H. Stringfellow to Jefferson Davis, February 8, 1865, in Berlin, ed., *Freedom: Series II*, 292; Bruce Levine, *The Fall of the House of Dixie: How the Civil War Remade the American South* (New York, 2013), 256; Bruce Levine, *Confederate Emancipation: Southern Plans to Free and Arm Slaves During the Civil War* (New York, 2007), 158.

46. Anne Sarah Rubin, *A Shattered Nation: The Rise and Fall of the Confederacy, 1861–1868* (Chapel Hill, 2005), 106–7; *Charleston Mercury*, November 12, 1864; James L. Roark, *Masters Without Slaves: Southern Planters in the Civil War and Reconstruction* (New York, 1977), 102–3.

47. *New Orleans Tribune*, January 14, 1865, and April 6, 1865; Emory Thomas, *The Confederate Nation, 1861–1865* (New York, 1979), 290–93; Genovese, *Roll, Jordan, Roll*, 129–30.

48. Boles, *Black Southerners*, 197; General Orders, No. 14, March 23, 1865, and *Richmond Dispatch*, March 21, 1865, both in Durden, ed., *Grey and the Black*, 268–71; *Charleston Mercury*, January 13, 1865.

49. Ward, *The Slaves' War*, 242–43; Rembert W. Patrick, *The Fall of Richmond* (Baton Rouge, 1960), 68; Noah Andre Trudeau, "Proven Themselves in Every Respect to Be Men: Black Cavalry in the Civil War," in Smith, ed., *Black Soldiers in Blue*, 299; Nelson Lankford, *Richmond Burning: The Last Days of the Confederate Capital* (New York, 2002), 129–31; Ernest B. Furgurson, *Ashes of Glory: Richmond at War* (New York, 1996), 337.

50. Margaret Washington, *Sojourner Truth's America* (Urbana, IL, 2009), 314–15; William C. Harris, *With Charity for All: Lincoln and the Restoration of the Union* (Lexington, 1997), 183; Frederick Douglass, *Life and Times of Frederick Douglass* (New York, 1962 ed.), 289–90.

51. Donald, *Lincoln*, 584–85; Brooks D. Simpson, *The Reconstruction Presidents* (Lawrence, KS, 1998), 43; Ronald C. White Jr., *A. Lincoln: A Biography* (New York, 2009), 671; *New Orleans Tribune*, April 16, 1865; Salmon P. Chase to Abraham Lincoln, April 12, 1865, in Lincoln Papers, LC.

52. *New Orleans Tribune*, July 22, 1865; Marilyn Mayer Culpeper, *Trials and Triumphs: The Women of the American Civil War* (East Lansing, MI, 1991), 385 note; Patrick, *Fall of Richmond*, 124–25; Susan Warfield Diary, August 1, 1875, in Warfield Papers, Maryland Historical Society.

53. Jourdon Anderson to P. H. Anderson, August 7, 1865, in *The Freedmen's Book*, ed. Lydia Maria Child (Boston, 1865), 265–67. According to the federal census records of 1870 and 1880, Jourdon Anderson and his wife, Amanda, born in Tennessee in

1825 and 1829, respectively, were then living in Ohio. Their former master, Patrick Henry Anderson, was a merchant and farmer in Wilson County who had owned thirty-two slaves. See Montgomery County, Ohio, 1870 federal census, page 44, and Wilson County, Tennessee, 1860 federal census, page 133, NA.

54. Ward, *The Slaves' War*, 250–51; Martin R. Delany to black Americans, April 20, 1865, in *A Grand Army of Black Men: Letters from African-American Soldiers in the Union Army 1861–1865*, ed. Edwin S. Redkey (Cambridge, 1992), 221–22; Douglass, *Life and Times*, 294–95.

55. Boles, *Black Southerners*, 202–3; Goldfield, *America Aflame*, 411; David Brion Davis, *Inhuman Bondage: The Rise and Fall of Slavery in the New World* (New York, 2006), 322, regards Johnson as "surely one of the worst of our presidents" but doubts the "counterfactual" conclusion that Reconstruction would have been an easier process had Lincoln not died, given "the new conditions in the North as well as the defeated South's commitment to white supremacy." Although a sizeable minority of southern whites were indeed dedicated to maintaining their antebellum world, a majority of whites either were grudgingly willing to recognize that the victorious North could make whatever demands it wished, or actually felt betrayed by the planter class and welcomed some Republican reforms. The argument made here is that by turning his back on Lincoln's later policies, Johnson allowed the vocal, determined minority to regain power, and that a very small window of political opportunity was squandered by the new president.

Chapter Three: "All De Land Belongs to De Yankees Now"

1. Tunis Campbell, *Sufferings of the Rev. T. G. Campbell and His Family, in Georgia* (Washington, 1877), 1; Russell Duncan, *Freedom's Shore: Tunis Campbell and the Georgia Freedman* (Athens, GA, 1986), 13.

2. Campbell, *Sufferings*, 1; Duncan, *Freedom's Shore*, 14–15; Eric Foner, ed., *Freedom's Lawmakers: A Directory of Black Officeholders During Reconstruction*, 2nd ed. (Baton Rouge, 1996), 38. Campbell's guide was republished as late as 1973 under the title *Never Let People Be Kept Waiting: A Textbook on Hotel Management*.

3. Duncan, *Freedom's Shore*, 16–17; *Daily Macon Telegraph*, June 6, 1866; William S. McFeely, *Sapelo's People: A Long Walk into Freedom* (New York, 1994), 83.

4. Duncan, *Freedom's Shore*, 22–23; *Daily Macon Telegraph*, June 6, 1866.

5. Allison Dorsey, "'The Great Cry of Our People is Land!': Black Settlement and Community Development on Ossabaw Island, Georgia, 1865–1900," in *African American Life in the Georgia Lowcountry: The Atlantic World and the Gullah Geechee*, ed. Philip D. Morgan (Athens, GA, 2010), 240; Duncan, *Freedom's Shore*, 68; Steven Hahn, *A Nation Under Our Feet: Black Political Struggles in the Rural South from Slavery to the Great Migration* (Cambridge, 2003), 241; Paul A. Cimbala, "The Freedmen's Bureau, the Freedmen, and Sherman's Grant in Reconstruction Georgia, 1865–1867," *JSH* 55 (1989): 621.

6. Claude F. Oubre, *Forty Acres and a Mule: The Freedmen's Bureau and Black Land Ownership* (Baton Rouge, 1978), 11; William T. Sherman, General Order No. 9, February

6, 1862, in Berlin, ed., *Freedom: Series I*, 3: 153–54; William H. Reynolds to Salmon P. Chase, January 1, 1863, Ibid., 121–22; Keith P. Wilson, *Campfires of Freedom: The Camp Life of Black Soldiers During the Civil War* (Kent, 2002), 192–93.

7. Michael Les Benedict, *The Impeachment and Trial of Andrew Johnson* (New York, 1973), 36–37; *Congressional Globe*, 37th Cong., 2nd Sess., 271; Philip Shaw Paludan, *The Presidency of Abraham Lincoln* (Lexington, 1994), 145.

8. Eric Foner, *Reconstruction: America's Unfinished Revolution, 1863–1877* (New York, 1988), 59; William C. Davis, *Jefferson Davis: The Man and His Hour* (New York, 1991), 410; (author unknown), *The Results of Emancipation in the United States of America* (New York, 1867), 25; Janet Hermann, *The Pursuit of a Dream* (New York, 1981), 44–46; J. E. Thomas to Abraham Lincoln, January 1, 1865, in Lincoln Papers, LC.

9. Joel Williamson, *After Slavery: The Negro in South Carolina During Reconstruction, 1861–1877* (Chapel Hill, 1965), 56–57; "The Freedmen at Port Royal," *North American Review* 208 (1865): 24; Oliver Fraysée, *Lincoln, Land and Labor, 1809–60* (Urbana, IL, 1994), 182–83; Rufus Saxton to Edwin M. Stanton, December 7, 1862, in Berlin, ed., *Freedom: Series I*, 3: 220–21; John H. Major to Abraham Lincoln, March 1, 1864, Ibid., 297–98; Laura M. Towne, *Letters and Diary of Laura M. Towne, Written from the Sea Islands of South Carolina* (Cambridge, 1912), 9; Edward S. Philbrick to Albert G. Browne, March 25, 1864, in Lincoln Papers, LC.

10. Paludan, *Presidency of Lincoln*, 263; *Congressional Globe*, 38th Cong., 2nd Sess., 94; Mansfield French to Salmon P. Chase, January 6, 1863, in Lincoln Papers, LC.

11. Washington *Daily National Intelligencer*, February 5, 1866; *Lowell Daily Citizen and News*, February 5, 1866; Philadelphia *Daily Age*, February 7, 1866; Mitchell Snay, *Fenians, Freedmen, and Southern Whites: Race and Nationality in the Era of Reconstruction* (Baton Rouge, 2007), 90.

12. Eric Foner, *The Fiery Trial: Abraham Lincoln and American Slavery* (New York, 2010), 320–21; David Goldfield, *America Aflame: How the Civil War Created a Nation* (New York, 2011), 411; Philadelphia *Daily Age*, February 7, 1866; *Morning Oregonian* (Portland, OR), February 28, 1866; William T. Sherman to Edwin M. Stanton, January 19, 1865, in *Sherman's Civil War: Selected Correspondence of William T. Sherman, 1860–1865*, ed. Brooks Simpson (Chapel Hill, 1999), 801–02; Cimbala, "The Freedmen's Bureau, Freedmen and Sherman's Grant," 599.

13. Philip Dray, *Capitol Men: The Epic Story of Reconstruction Through the Lives of the First Black Congressmen* (New York, 2010), 51; Foner, *Reconstruction*, 158–59; Kenneth M. Stampp, *The Era of Reconstruction, 1865–1877* (New York, 1966), 131–32; William S. McFeely, *Yankee Stepfather: General O. O. Howard and the Freedmen* (New Haven, 1968), 23; Annette Gordon-Reed, *Andrew Johnson* (New York, 2011), 115; Willie Lee Rose, *Rehearsal for Reconstruction: The Port Royal Experiment* (New York, 1964), 337–38. LaWanda Cox, "The Promise of Land for the Freedmen," *Mississippi Valley Historical Review* 45 (1958): 413–40, remains the best account of the bill's creation and emphasizes the connection between the final act and Sherman's Order.

14. Benedict, *Impeachment and Trial of Johnson*, 38; D. Richards to Lyman Trumbull,

June 7, 1866, in Trumbull Papers, LC; Noralee Frankel, *Freedom's Women: Black Women and Families in Civil War Mississippi* (Bloomington, IN, 1999), 53.

15. Amy Dru Stanley, *From Bondage to Contract: Wage Labor, Marriage, and the Market in the Age of Slave Emancipation* (Cambridge, 1998), 123; Henry Wilson, Speech of April 1865, in Child, ed., *Freedmen's Book*, 260; Oubre, *Forty Acres and a Mule*, 14–15; Foner, *Reconstruction*, 143; *New Orleans Tribune*, March 1, 1863. A number of historians emphasize the "war on dependency" waged by white agents, particularly against black women. See especially Mary J. Farmer, "'Because They Are Women': Gender and the Virginia Freedmen's Bureau's War on Dependency," in Cimbala and Miller, eds., *Freedmen's Bureau*, 162–63 and 176–77, and Laura F. Edwards, *Scarlett Doesn't Live Here Anymore: Southern Women in the Civil War Era* (Urbana, IL, 2000), 137. Although true, the critique of "female loaferism" was less commonly heard from black agents, and regardless of race, most Bureau agents supported black efforts to obtain their own land, which is the focus of this chapter.

16. *New Orleans Tribune*, March 1, 1865; Dray, *Capitol Men*, 258–259; Carl R. Osthaus, *Freedmen, Philanthropy, and Fraud: A History of the Freedman's Savings Bank* (Urbana, IL, 1976), 1–2; William S. McFeely, *Frederick Douglass* (New York, 1991), 281.

17. Andrew Johnson, Speech of March 22, 1862, in Graf, ed., *Papers of Johnson*, 5: 230–31; Hans L. Trefousse, *Andrew Johnson: A Biography* (New York, 1989), 45, 89, 226–27; Hahn, *A Nation Under Our Feet*, 130.

18. Elizabeth D. Leonard, *Lincoln's Avengers: Justice, Revenge, and Reunion After the Civil War* (New York, 2004), 182–83; James L. Roark, *Masters Without Slaves: Southern Planters in the Civil War and Reconstruction* (New York, 1977), 182–83; James M. Morrison to Thaddeus Stevens, January 16, 1866, in *The Papers of Thaddeus Stevens*, ed. Beverly Wilson Palmer (Pittsburgh, 1998), 2: 63; Thomas Chapman, *False Reconstruction; Or, The Slavery That Is Not Abolished* (Saxonville, 1876), 15; *Charleston Advocate*, May 11, 1867; John M. Forbes to Charles Sumner, December 27, 1862, copy in Lincoln Papers, LC; *Albany Journal*, March 29, 1866.

19. Thaddeus Stevens, Speech of September 6, 1865, in Palmer, ed., *Papers of Stevens*, 2: 22–23; Trefousse, *Stevens*, 168, 172; Thaddeus Stevens, *Reconstruction Speech of the Hon. Thaddeus Stevens* (Lancaster, PA, 1865), 5.

20. Justin D. Fulton, *Radicalism: A Sermon Preached in Tremont Temple, on Fast-Day* (Boston, 1865), 37; (author unknown), *Nationality Vs. Sectionalism: An Appeal to the Laboring Men of the South* (Washington, 1868), 5; Nathaniel P. Banks, *Emancipated Labor in Louisiana* (Boston, 1864), 3; Charles Delery, *Black Ghost of Radicalism in the United States* (New Orleans, 1868), 27–28

21. J. M. Brinckerhoff to Rufus Saxton, August 3, 1865, in Records of the Assistant Commissioner for the State of South Carolina, Freedmen's Bureau Papers, Reel 19, NA; McFeely, *Yankee Stepfather*, 96, 104–5; Oubre, *Forty Acres and a Mule*, 40–41; Rose, *Rehearsal for Reconstruction*, 351–52.

22. Oubre, *Forty Acres and a Mule*, 24–25; Leonard, *Lincoln's Avengers*, 184; McFeely, *Yankee Stepfather*, 126–27, 134–35.

23. Eric Foner, *Nothing But Freedom: Emancipation and Its Legacy* (Baton Rouge, 1983), 55–56; Leon Litwack, *Been in the Storm So Long: The Aftermath of Slavery* (New York, 1979), 388–89; Martin Delany, Speech of July 23, 1865, in Ripley, ed., *Black Abolitionist Papers*, 5: 350–51.

24. Michael W. Fitzgerald, *The Union League Movement in the Deep South: Politics and Agricultural Change During Reconstruction* (Baton Rouge, 1989), 139–40; Snay, *Fenians, Freedmen, and Southern Whites*, 97; Lewis Douglass to Frederick Douglass, June 9, 1865, in Douglass Collection, Howard University; Leslie A. Schwalm, "Sweet Dreams of Freedom: Freedwomen's Reconstruction of Life and Labor in Lowcountry South Carolina," *Journal of Women's History* 9 (1997): 15; Rembert W. Patrick, *The Fall of Richmond* (Baton Rouge, 1960), 125.

25. Foner, *Nothing But Freedom*, 82–83; Reid, *Freedom for Themselves*, 278; Saville, *Work of Reconstruction*, 16–17; *Boston Journal*, January 29, 1866.

26. Martin Abbott, "Free Land, Free Labor, and the Freedmen's Bureau," *Agricultural History* 30 (1956): 152; Edwards, *Scarlett Doesn't Live Here Anymore*, 132; Concord *New-Hampshire Patriot*, February 28, 1866; *Cincinnati Daily Enquirer*, February 16, 1866.

27. Foner, *Reconstruction*, 105; Schwalm, "Sweet Dreams of Freedom," 20; Freedmen of Edisto Island to Oliver O. Howard, October 28, 1865, in Register of Letters Received by the Commissioners, Freedmen's Bureau Papers, Reel 23, NA.

28. Eugene D. Genovese, *Roll, Jordan, Roll: The World the Slaves Made* (New York, 1974), 313; Julie Saville, *The Work of Reconstruction: From Slave to Wage Laborer in South Carolina 1860–1870* (Cambridge, 1994), 68–69; Schwalm, "Sweet Dreams of Freedom," 24; Louisa Rebecca Hayne McCord, Recollections, South Caroliniana Library, Columbia.

29. Michael W. Fitzgerald, *Splendid Failure: Postwar Reconstruction in the American South* (Chicago, 2008), 62; *Memphis Daily Avalanche*, February 3, 1866; *New Orleans Tribune*, November 21, 1865.

30. Carl Schurz to Andrew Johnson, August 13, 1865, in *Advice After Appomattox: Letters to Andrew Johnson, 1865–1866*, eds. Brooks D. Simpson and Leroy P. Graf (Knoxville, 1987), 94–95; Saville, *The Work of Reconstruction*, 145–46; Janette Thomas Greenwood, *First Fruits of Freedom: The Migration of Former Slaves and Their Search for Equality in Worcester, Massachusetts, 1862–1900* (Chapel Hill, 2010), 84; *New Orleans Tribune*, September 30, 1865; Benjamin F. Perry to F. Marion Nye, May 25, 1867, in Perry Papers, Wilson Library, University of North Carolina.

31. Sanford W. Barber to Benjamin F. Perry, July 10, 1865, in Perry Papers, Alabama Department of Archives and History; John L. Manning to Benjamin F. Perry, November 27, 1865, Ibid.; John L. Manning, Sumter District, 1850 federal census, slave schedule, NA; Dan T. Carter, "The Anatomy of Fear: The Christmas Day Insurrection Scare of 1865," *JSH* 42 (1976): 345–64, influenced by Richard C. Wade's theories on southern paranoia, described white fears of black violence as "mass hysteria." Although he compiled considerable evidence that white concerns in late 1865 were based on previous worries of servile revolt, he did not discuss testimony by northern

Bureau agents that black veterans *were* preparing to fight to hold on to land promised them.

32. Thomas Wagstaff, "Call Your Old Master—Master: Southern Political Leaders and Black Labor During Presidential Reconstruction," *Labor History* 10 (1969): 341; Dan T. Carter, *When the War Was Over: The Failure of Self-Reconstruction in the South, 1865–1867* (Baton Rouge, 1985), 196–97; Harvey Watterson to Andrew Johnson, October 14, 1865, in Simpson, ed., *Advice After Appomattox*, 164–65; *Memphis Daily Avalanche*, January 13, 1866. The idea that black soldiers were spreading this rumor was not limited to southern whites. After a fall tour of the Southeast, even Ulysses S. Grant blamed Bureau agents and "colored troops" for telling freedmen "that the property of his late master should by rights belong to him." See Hahn, *A Nation Under Our Feet*, 133, 135.

33. *New Orleans Tribune*, December 27, 1865; *Memphis Daily Avalanche*, January 1, 1865; *New-Hampshire Sentinel* (Keene, NH), January 4, 1866; *Dallas Herald*, January 13, 1866.

34. Philadelphia *Daily Age*, January 1, 1866; Washington *Daily National Intelligencer*, January 1, 1866; *Memphis Daily Avalanche*, January 1, 1865; *Albany Journal*, January 5, 1866.

35. *New Orleans Tribune*, December 27, 1865; Cimbala, "The Freedmen's Bureau, Freedmen and Sherman's Grant," 613; P. B. S. Pinchback, Speech, Montgomery, Alabama, 1865, in P. B. S. Pinchback Papers, Moorland-Springarn Research Center, Howard University; Scott French and Carol Sheriff, *A People at War: Civilians and Soldiers in America's Civil War*, 298; Foner, *Reconstruction*, 116.

36. *Boston Daily Journal*, January 29, 1866; Foner, *Reconstruction*, 166; Litwack, *Been in the Storm So Long*, 183.

37. Macon *Daily Telegraph*, June 6, 1866; Philadelphia *Daily Age*, January 1, 1866.

38. *New Orleans Tribune*, August 16, 1865; Jacqueline Jones, *Soldiers of Light and Love: Northern Teachers and Georgia Blacks, 1865–1873* (Chapel Hill, 1980), 56–57; Gavin Wright, *Old South, New South: Revolutions in the Southern Economy Since the Civil War* (New York, 1986), 84–85; Litwack, *Been in the Storm So Long*, 366–67.

39. Connor, "Reconstruction Rebels," 173; Stanley, *From Bondage to Contract*, 42–43; Barbara Jeanne Fields, *Slavery and Freedom on the Middle Ground: Maryland During the Nineteenth Century* (New Haven, 1985), 162–63.

40. John C. Rodrigue, "The Freedmen's Bureau and Wage Labor in the Louisiana Sugar Region," in Cimbala and Miller, eds., *Freedmen's Bureau*, 211; Roark, *Masters Without Slaves*, 136–37; *Loyal Georgian* (Augusta, GA), February 3, 1866; Gerald David Jaynes, *Branches Without Roots: Genesis of the Black Working Class in the American South, 1862–1882* (New York, 1986), 221; *New-York Tribune*, January 14, 1867.

41. Schwalm, "Sweet Dreams of Freedom," 16, 25; Fannie to Dearest Ma, January 12, 1864, in Berlin, ed., *Freedom: Series I*, 3: 490.

42. Mary J. Farmer-Kaiser, *Freedwomen and the Freedmen's Bureau: Race, Gender, and Public Policy in the Age of Emancipation* (New York, 2010), 20–21; Osthaus, *Freedmen, Philanthropy, and Fraud*, 33–34; Franklin, *Reconstruction*, 36; John M. Cormick

to Alvan C. Gillem, April 15, 1868, in Records of the Assistant Commissioner for the State of Mississippi, Freedmen's Bureau Papers, Reel 24, NA; Sidney Andrews, *The South Since the War* (Boston, 1866), 26.

43. Alvan C. Gillem to Oliver O. Howard, February 15, 1867, in Records of the Assistant Commissioner for the State of Mississippi, Freedmen's Bureau Papers, Reel 43, NA; D. W. McRae to Alvan C. Gillem, February 28, 1868, Ibid., Reel 24; Barry A. Crouch, "A Spirit of Lawlessness: White Violence, Texas Blacks, 1865–1868," *Journal of Social History* 18 (Winter 1984): 223; Schwalm, "Sweet Dreams of Freedom," 19.

44. C. R. Williams to S. C. Greene, June 23, 1868, in Records of the Assistant Commissioner for the State of Mississippi, Freedmen's Bureau Papers, Reel 24, NA; M. Sathrop to S. C. Greene, May 26, 1868, Ibid., Reel 24; *New-Hampshire Sentinel* (Keene, NH), March 15, 1866.

45. Leslie A. Schwalm, *Emancipation's Diaspora: Race and Reconstruction in the Upper Midwest* (Chapel Hill, 2009), 138–39; Carol Faulkner, *Women's Radical Reconstruction: The Freedmen's Aid Movement* (Philadelphia, 2003), 84, 122; Unsigned letter, January 24, 1867, Records of the Assistant Commissioner for the District of Columbia, Freedmen's Bureau Papers, Reel 3, NA; Order of Oliver O. Howard, January 19, 1867, Ibid., Reel 3; Oliver O. Howard to J. E. Guitterlin, February 19, 1867, Ibid., Reel 3.

46. Charles Stearns, *The Black Man of the South and the Rebels* (Boston, 1872), 109; Litwack, *Been in the Storm So Long*, 406; Jaynes, *Branches Without Roots*, 73; Memorandum of Charles Whittlesey, November 1865, in Register of Letters Received by the Commissioners, Freedmen's Bureau Papers, Reel 23, NA; William R. Nevins to William H. Seward, April 10, 1866, in William H. Seward Papers, University of Rochester (hereafter UR).

47. *New-Hampshire Patriot* (Concord, NH), March 4, 1868; LaWanda Cox and John H. Cox, *Politics, Principle, and Prejudice, 1865–1866: Dilemma of Reconstruction America* (New York, 1963), 92–93; *Albany Journal*, March 12, 1866; Macon *Daily Telegraph*, April 9, 1866; *Cincinnati Daily Gazette*, June 1, 1867. Historians estimate the federal government spent forty thousand dollars in 1854 to return a single bondman, Anthony Burns, to slavery. See Gordon S. Barker, *Imperfect Revolution: Anthony Burns and the Landscape of Race in Antebellum America* (Kent, 2011).

48. Mary Farmer-Kaiser, "'With a Weight of Circumstances like Millstones About Their Necks': Freedwomen, Federal Relief, and the Benevolent Guardianship of the Freedmen's Bureau," *Virginia Magazine of History and Biography* 115 (2007): 417, 421; C. E. Lippincott to Lyman Trumbull, January 25, 1866, in Lyman Trumbull Papers, LC. The refusal of whites to assist freed people on the state level was widespread. One Montgomery newspaper emphasized that state efforts were "in behalf of the destitute *white* population." See Howard N. Rabinowitz, *Race Relations in the Urban South, 1865–1890* (New York, 1978), 129.

49. *Flake's Bulletin* (Galveston, TX), February 7, 1866; Philadelphia *Daily Age*, January 1, 1866; Rose, *Rehearsal for Reconstruction*, 356–57; *Albany Journal*, January 5, 1866; Du Bois, *Black Reconstruction*, 227.

50. *Congressional Globe*, 39th Cong., 1st Sess., 102, 143; Macon *Daily Telegraph*, January 27, 1866, March 4, 1866.

51. *Morning Oregonian* (Portland, OR), February 28, 1866; Foner, *Reconstruction*, 247; David Donald, *The Politics of Reconstruction, 1863–1867* (Cambridge, 1965), 24–25. The idea that the Republicans might drop Johnson from the ticket in 1868 was not as far-fetched as it sounds today, when parties never abandon incumbents. In 1852, the Whigs passed over President Millard Fillmore, who, like Johnson, had become president upon the death of his predecessor but, unlike the Tennessee Democrat, was a regular member of his party. No Democrat seriously considered nominating the aged and unpopular James Buchanan in 1860, and some progressive Republicans even considered finding a candidate to replace Abraham Lincoln in 1864.

52. Andrew Johnson, Freedmen's Bureau Veto Message, February 19, 1866, in Bergeron, ed., *Papers of Johnson*, 10: 120–27; Brooks D. Simpson, *The Reconstruction Presidents* (Lawrence, KS, 1998), 94–95; Albert E. Castel, *The Presidency of Andrew Johnson* (Lawrence, KS, 1979), 66–67; Bowen, *Johnson and the Negro*, 136–37. John H. Cox and LaWanda Cox, "Andrew Johnson and His Ghost Writers: An Analysis of the Freedmen's Bureau and Civil Rights Veto Messages," *Mississippi Valley Historical Review* 48 (1961): 460–79, is a thoughtful and persuasive analysis of the role Johnson's advisors played in crafting the message. But see also John Niven, *Gideon Welles: Lincoln's Secretary of the Navy* (New York, 1973), 523–24.

53. Trefousse, *Johnson*, 243, 253; David O. Stewart, *Impeached: The Trial of President Andrew Johnson and the Fight for Lincoln's Legacy* (New York, 2010), 51; Castel, *Presidency of Andrew Johnson*, 68, 75; Benedict, *Impeachment and Trial of Johnson*, 42–43, 90.

54. Duncan, *Freedom's Shore*, 30–31; Tunis Campbell, *Sufferings of the Rev. T. G. Campbell and His Family, in Georgia* (Washington, 1877), 8; Ann Short Chirhart, *Torches of Light: Georgia Teachers and the Coming of the Modern South* (Athens, GA, 2005), 146–147; Foner, ed., *Freedom's Lawmakers*.

55. Osthaus, *Freedmen, Philanthropy, and Fraud*, 10; Frederick Douglass, *Life and Times of Frederick Douglass* (New York, 1962 ed.), 400–1; Marion B. Lucas, *History of Blacks in Kentucky: From Slavery to Segregation, 1760–1891* (Lexington, 2001), 282–83; Foner, *Reconstruction*, 531–32.

56. Solomon Brown, August 31, 1865, in Register of Signatures in Branches of the Freedman's Savings and Trust Company, Reel 4, NA; Catherine Smith, October 18, 1867, Ibid., Reel 4; Edward King, September 5, 1867, Ibid., Reel 4; 114th USCT, October 12 to November 1, 1865, Ibid., Reel 4.

57. *Charleston Advocate*, May 11, 1867; John. W. Alvord, *Letters from the South, Relating to the Condition of the Freedmen* (Washington, 1870), 9; George S. Holmes, December 19, 1865, in Register of Signatures in Branches of the Freedman's Savings and Trust Company, Reel 21, NA; Martin R. Delany, November 28, 1871, Ibid., Reel 23; John Cook, July 25, 1871, Ibid., Reel 23; Robert A. Vesey, August 30, 1871, Ibid., Reel 23; William B. Penceel, June 10, 1869, Ibid., Reel 21; Charleston Home Association, September 28, 1869, Ibid., Reel 21; Malcolm M. Brown, no date, Ibid., Reel 23; Charles Nesbitt, July 19, 1869, Ibid., Reel 21.

58. Independent Sons and Daughters of Richard Allen, January 25, 1871, in Register of
Signatures in Branches of the Freedman's Savings and Trust Company, Reel 19, NA;
Thaddeus Stevens Lodge No 24, Ibid., Reel 19; Annie Louisa Broadfoot, November
5, 1870, Ibid., Reel 17; Christopher Bradley, November 4, 1870, Ibid., Reel 17; Joseph Taylor, March 31, 1871, Ibid.

59. Osthaus, *Freedmen, Philanthropy, and Fraud*, 25, 183; Dray, *Capitol Men*, 260–61;
(author unknown), *The Results of Emancipation in the United States of America*, 34;
McFeely, *Yankee Stepfather*, 323; McFeely, *Douglass*, 282–86; Frederick Douglass to
Nathan Sprague, May 30, 1874, in Douglass Papers, LC.

60. Roger L. Ransom and Richard Sutch, *One Kind of Freedom: The Economic Conse-
quences of Emancipation* (Cambridge, 2001), 95, 98; Foner, *Reconstruction*, 405; John
B. Boles, *Black Southerners, 1619–1869* (Lexington, 1983), 208–9; Albion W. Tourgée, *A Fool's Errand, By One of the Fools* (New York, 1879), 91.

61. Alvord, *Letters from the South*, 19; Dray, *Capitol Men*, 369–70; Sharon Ann Holt,
Making Freedom Pay: North Carolina Freedpeople Working for Themselves, 1865–1900
(Athens, GA, 2000), 54; McPherson, *Lincoln and the Second American Revolution*, 18–
19; Macon *Daily Telegraph*, February 10, 1874.

Chapter Four: "The Lord Has Sent Us Books and Teachers"

1. Richard Paul Fuke, "Hugh Lennox Bond and Radical Republican Ideology," *Journal
of Southern History* (hereafter *JSH*) 45 (1979): 571; Jean Baker, *The Politics of Continu-
ity: Maryland Political Parties from 1858 to 1870* (Baltimore, 1973), 183; Hugh L. Bond
to Henry Winter Davis, February 4, 1856, in Bond-McCulloch Family Papers, Maryland Historical Society.

2. Charles Lane, *The Day Freedom Died: The Colfax Massacre, the Supreme Court, and
the Betrayal of Reconstruction* (New York, 2008), 116; Hugh L. Bond to Boston Minis-
terial Education, November 10, 1866, in Bond-McCulloch Family Papers, Maryland
Historical Society; Charles Lowe to Hugh L. Bond, February 15, 1866, Ibid.; Charles
E. Adams to Hugh L. Bond, April 26, 1866, Ibid.

3. Fuke, "Hugh Lennox Bond," 580; *New-Orleans Times*, September 10, 1866; *Baltimore
Sun*, September 6, 1867.

4. *Albany Journal*, November 9, 1866; Curtis to Hugh L. Bond, November 1866, in
Bond-McCulloch Family Papers, Maryland Historical Society; Thomas Russell to
Hugh L. Bond, November 8, 1866, Ibid.

5. *Baltimore Sun*, October 12, 1866; *Boston Daily Journal*, November 14, 1866.

6. David Goldfield, *America Aflame: How the Civil War Created a Nation* (New York,
2011), 412; *Flake's Bulletin* (Galveston, TX), May 23, 1867. The image of carpetbaggers as greedy scoundrels determined to "destroy the spirit of the [white] Southern
people so that they would conform to Northern standards" lives on in the modern
racist, neo-Confederate writings of Walter Kennedy and James Kennedy, *The South
Was Right!* (Gretna, 1994), 20, and Thomas DiLorenzo, *The Real Lincoln: A New
Look at Abraham Lincoln, His Agenda, and an Unnecessary War* (Seattle, 2002), 7, who
argue that the purpose of Reconstruction was to "plunder" the region. The most thor-

ough debunking of this view is Richard N. Current, *Those Terrible Carpetbaggers: A Reinterpretation* (New York, 1988).

7. Joseph Browne, "'To Bring Out the Intellect of the Race': An African American Freedmen's Bureau Agent in Maryland," *Maryland Historical Magazine*, 104 (2009): 380–81; Cynthia Everett to Dear Brother and Sister, Christmas 1869, in Everett Papers, Newberry Library, Chicago; William A. Hord, January 15, 1872, in Register of Signatures in Branches of the Freedman's Savings and Trust Company, Reel 23, NA.

8. Martha Augusta Washington, November 7, 1870, in Register of Signatures in Branches of the Freedman's Savings and Trust Company, Reel 17, NA; Charlotte Ann Clarke, April 4, 1871, Ibid., Reel 17; Stephen Green, November 5, 1870, Ibid., Reel 17.

9. Davis Laws, November 5, 1870, in Register of Signatures in Branches of the Freedman's Savings and Trust Company, Reel 17, NA; Alexander Bridgeford, February 24, 1871, Ibid., Reel 17; Charles Friday Roberson, October 25, 1870, Ibid., Reel 17; Cornelius Fletcher, November 2, 1870, Ibid., Reel 17.

10. "The Freedmen at Port Royal," *North American Review* 208 (1865): 9; Steven Hahn, *A Nation Under Our Feet: Black Political Struggles in the Rural South from Slavery to the Great Migration* (Cambridge, 2003), 45; Howard N. Rabinowitz, *Race Relations in the Urban South, 1865–1890* (New York, 1978), 198–99.

11. Claude H. Nolen, *African American Southerners in Slavery, Civil War, and Reconstruction* (Jefferson, 2001), 174; Rabinowitz, *Race Relations in the Urban South*, 204; Leon Litwack, *Been in the Storm So Long: The Aftermath of Slavery* (New York, 1979), 468; Nicholas Lemann, *Redemption: The Last Battle of the Civil War* (New York, 2006), 56–57.

12. Rabinowitz, *Race Relations in the Urban South*, 204–5; *Georgia Weekly Telegraph* (Macon, GA), August 6, 1869; Powers, *Black Charlestonians*, 206; Moses Brown, May 25, 1871, in Register of Signatures in Branches of the Freedman's Savings and Trust Company, Reel 17, NA. Brown signed his account with "his mark" rather than a signature.

13. Carla L. Peterson, *Black Gotham: A Family History of African Americans in Nineteenth-Century New York City* (New Haven, 2011), 65; Janette Thomas Greenwood, *First Fruits of Freedom: The Migration of Former Slaves and Their Search for Equality in Worcester, Massachusetts, 1862–1900* (Chapel Hill, 2010), 142; Leslie A. Schwalm, *Emancipation's Diaspora: Race and Reconstruction in the Upper Midwest* (Chapel Hill, 2009), 146–47; John J. Johnson, October 27, 1870, in Register of Signatures in Branches of the Freedman's Savings and Trust Company, Reel 17, NA.

14. Benjamin M. Bond to unknown, July 22, 1865, in *A Grand Army of Black Men: Letters from African-American Soldiers in the Union Army 1861–1865*, ed. Edwin S. Redkey (Cambridge, 1992), 183–84; Laura M. Towne, *Letters and Diary of Laura M. Towne, Written from the Sea Islands of South Carolina* (Cambridge, 1912), 20; Peter Kolchin, *First Freedom: The Responses of Alabama's Blacks to Emancipation and Reconstruction* (Greenwood, 1972), 112–13; Edmund L. Drago, *Black Politicians and Reconstruction in Georgia: A Splendid Failure* (Baton Rouge, 1982), 18–19.

15. Noralee Frankel, *Freedom's Women: Black Women and Families in Civil War Mississippi*

(Bloomington, IN, 1999), 84–85; "The Freedmen at Port Royal," *North American Review* 208 (1856): 25

16. Joel Williamson, *After Slavery: The Negro in South Carolina During Reconstruction, 1861–1877* (Chapel Hill, 1965), 204; Vernon Burton, "Race and Reconstruction: Edgefield County, South Carolina," *Journal of Social History* 12 (1978): 33; *Georgia Weekly Telegraph* (Macon, GA), June 18, 1866; John C. Rodrigue, "Black Agency After Slavery," in *Reconstructions: New Perspectives on Postbellum America*, ed. Thomas J. Brown (New York, 2006), 57; Sally G. McMillen, *To Raise Up the South: Sunday Schools in Black and White Churches, 1865–1915* (Baton Rouge, 2001), 18–19.

17. Eric Foner, *Reconstruction: America's Unfinished Revolution, 1863–1877* (New York, 1988), 93; Hahn, *A Nation Under Our Feet*, 233; Thomas Holt, *Black over White: Negro Political Leadership in South Carolina During Reconstruction* (Urbana, IL,1977), 90–91; Eric Foner, ed., *Freedom's Lawmakers: A Directory of Black Officeholders During Reconstruction*, 2nd ed. (Baton Rouge, 1996), xx–xxi, 168.

18. Barbara Jeanne Fields, *Slavery and Freedom on the Middle Ground: Maryland During the Nineteenth Century* (New Haven, 1985), 144–45; William Mallet to Thaddeus Stevens, May 28, 1866, in *Papers of Stevens*, 2: 152.

19. Robert C. Morris, *Reading, 'riting, and Reconstruction: The Education of Freedmen in the South, 1861–1870* (Chicago, 1981), 67; interview with Sylvia Cannon, August 4, 1937, in George Rawick, ed., *American Slave: South Carolina Narratives* (Westport, 1972), 192; Richard L. Hume and Jerry B. Gough, *Blacks, Carpetbaggers, and Scalawags: The Constitutional Conventions of Radical Reconstruction* (Baton Rouge, 2008), 250; Michael W. Fitzgerald, *Splendid Failure: Postwar Reconstruction in the American South* (Chicago, 2008), 151; Rabinowitz, *Race Relations in the Urban South*, 152.

20. John B. Reid, "'A Career to Build, a People to Serve, a Purpose to Accomplish': Race, Class, Gender, and Detroit's First Black Women Teachers, 1865–1916," *Michigan Historical Review* 18 (1992): 11–12; Ira V. Brown, "Pennsylvania and the Rights of the Negro, 1865–1887," *Pennsylvania History* 28 (1961): 46; James C. Mohr, *Radical Republicans and Reform in New York* (Ithaca, 1973), 186–87; Philip S. Foner and George E. Walker, eds., *Proceedings of the Black National and State Conventions, 1865–1900* (Philadelphia, 1986), 211.

21. *Freedmen: The American Missionary Association* (Boston, 1864), 2; Walter B. Edgar, *South Carolina: A History* (Columbia, SC, 1998), 366; Philip Dray, *Capitol Men: The Epic Story of Reconstruction Through the Lives of the First Black Congressmen* (New York, 2010), 6; Henry Rowntree to Esteemed Friends, April 14, 1864, in Berlin, ed., *Freedom: Series I*, 3: 822; Janet Hermann, *The Pursuit of a Dream* (New York, 1981), 56; Greenwood, *First Fruits of Freedom*, 40; Drago, *Black Politicians and Reconstruction*, 27; Jones, *Soldiers of Light and Love*, 73.

22. *Freedmen: The American Missionary Association*, 1; *Minutes of the Convention of Freedmen's Commissions, Held at Indianapolis* (Cincinnati, 1864), 25; Foner, *Reconstruction*, 97; Current, *Those Terrible Carpetbaggers*, 26–27; Ronald Butchart, *Schooling the Freed People: Teaching, Learning, and the Struggle for Black Freedom, 1861–1876* (Chapel Hill, 2010), 96.

23. Marjorie H. Parker, "Some Educational Activities in the Freedmen's Bureau," *Journal of Negro Education* 23 (1954): 10–11; Morris, *Reading, 'riting, and Reconstruction*, 32–33; Span, *From Cotton Field to Schoolhouse*, 50–51; Browne, " 'To Bring Out the Intellect,' " 374–75.

24. Peggy Lamson, *The Glorious Failure: Black Congressman Robert Brown Elliott and the Reconstruction in South Carolina* (New York, 1973), 56; Russell Duncan, *Freedom's Shore: Tunis Campbell and the Georgia Freedman* (Athens, GA, 1986), 48–49; Alvan C. Gillem to Oliver O. Howard, January 20, 1867, in Register of Letters Received by the Commissioners, Freedmen's Bureau Papers, Reel 43, NA.

25. Kenneth M. Stampp, *The Era of Reconstruction, 1865–1877* (New York, 1966), 165–66; Michael Perman, *The Road to Redemption: Southern Politics, 1869–1879* (Chapel Hill, 1984), 105; Laura Wakefield, " 'Set a Light in a Dark Place': Teachers of Freedmen in Florida, 1864–1874," *Florida Historical Quarterly* 81 (2003): 406.

26. Carol Faulkner, *Women's Radical Reconstruction: The Freedmen's Aid Movement* (Philadelphia, 2003), 111; Cynthia Everett to My Darling, February 26, 1870, in Everett Papers, Newberry Library, Chicago; "Freedmen at Port Royal," *North American Review* 208 (1865): 4; Richard Paul Fuke, "The Freedmen's Bureau, Education, and the Black Community in Post-Emancipation Maryland," in *The Freedmen's Bureau and Reconstruction*, eds. Paul A. Cimbala and Randall M. Miller (New York, 1999), 294–94; Christopher M. Span, *From Cotton Field to Schoolhouse: African American Education in Mississippi, 1862–1875* (Chapel Hill, 2009), 28–29; *Boston Daily Advertiser*, December 10, 1866; *New-York Tribune*, February 3, 1866.

27. Holt, *Making Freedom Pay*, 114; *New-York Tribune*, January 26, 1871; San Antonio *Express*, August 24, 1867; Historical Library Association, November 3, 1869, in Register of Signatures in Branches of the Freedman's Savings and Trust Company, Reel 21, NA; Harriet Beecher Stowe, "The Education of Freedmen," *North American Review* 128 (1879): 615.

28. Span, *From Cotton Field to Schoolhouse*, 30–31; Kolchin, *First Freedom*, 84–85; Little Rock *Morning Republican*, April 16, 1870; Cynthia Everett to Dear Brother, Christmas 1869, in Everett Papers, Newberry Library, Chicago; *Boston Daily Journal*, August 13, 1867; John W. Alvord, *Semi-Annual School Reports* (Washington, 1869), 8; Litwack, *Been in the Storm So Long*, 485.

29. Although generally admiring of these teachers, among the scholars who emphasize their bourgeois attitudes is Sandra E. Small, "The Yankee Schoolmarm in Freedmen's Schools: An Analysis of Attitudes," *JSH* (1970): 392; Mary Evans to Cynthia Everett, April 6, 1870, in Everett Papers, Newberry Library, Chicago; Cynthia Everett to Dear Sister, April 12, 1870, Ibid.; Towne, *Letters and Diary*, 146.

30. Cynthia Everett to Robbie Everett, December 30, 1870, in Everett Papers, Newberry Library, Chicago; Albion W. Tourgée, *A Fool's Errand, By One of the Fools* (New York, 1879), 104; Robert C. Morris, "Educational Reconstruction," in *The Facts of Reconstruction: Essays in Honor of John Hope Franklin*, eds. Eric Anderson and Alfred A. Moss Jr. (Baton Rouge, 1991) 145; Austin Love, March 20, 1871, in Register of Signatures in Branches of the Freedman's Savings and Trust Company, Reel 23, NA;

Butchart, *Schooling the Freed People*, 80–81; *Cincinnati Daily Gazette*, September 30, 1869; Cynthia Everett to Robbie Everett, December 30, 1870, in Everett Papers, Newberry Library, Chicago. As the Reverend Fulton put it: "Radicalism grows from the gospel." See his *Radicalism: A Sermon Preached in Tremont Temple, on Fast-Day* (Boston, 1865), 42.

31. Carol Lasser, "Enacting Emancipation: African American Women Abolitionists at Oberlin College and the Quest for Empowerment, Equality, and Respectability," in *Women's Rights and Transatlantic Antislavery in the Era of Emancipation*, eds. Kathryn Kish Sklar and James B. Stewart (New Haven, 2007), 327; Morris, *Reading, 'riting, and Reconstruction*, 70–71; Howard N. Rabinowitz, "'Half a Loaf': The Shift from White to Black Teachers in the Negro Schools of the Urban South 1865–1890," *JSH* 40 (1974): 568.

32. R. D. Harper to O. L. Shepherd, May 9, 1868, in Records of the Assistant Commissioner for the State of Alabama, Freedmen's Bureau Papers, Reel 14, NA; Jones, *Soldiers of Light and Love*, 121; *New-Hampshire Sentinel* (Keene, NH), May 31, 1866; Duncan, *Freedom's Shore*, 63.

33. *New-Hampshire Sentinel* (Keene, NH), January 4, 1866; (author unknown), *The Results of Emancipation in the United States of America*, 29; Cynthia Everett to Dear Sister, April 12, 1870, in Everett Papers, Newberry Library, Chicago; *Flake's Bulletin* (Galveston, TX), March 6, 1869.

34. A. C. Elder to unknown, September 25, 1869, in Records of the Assistant Commissioner for the State of South Carolina, Freedmen's Bureau Papers, Reel 19, NA; *Boston Daily Advertiser*, November 5, 1866; Cynthia Everett to Jennie Everett, November 22, 1869, in Everett Papers, Newberry Library, Chicago.

35. Macon *Daily Telegraph*, March 15, 1867; *New-York Tribune*, August 9, 1867; Litwack, *Been in the Storm So Long*, 486; Jacob R. Shepherd to Andrew Johnson, October 14, 1865, in Register of Letters Received by the Commissioners, Freedmen's Bureau Papers, Reel 43, NA; Alvan Gillem to Oliver O. Howard, January 20, 1867, Ibid., Reel 43; R. D. Harper to Edwin Beecher, October 19, 1868, in Records of the Assistant Commissioner for the State of South Carolina, Freedmen's Bureau Papers, Reel 14, NA.

36. Charles Stearns, *The Black Man of the South and the Rebels* (Boston, 1872), 132; Maria Waterbury, *Seven Years Among the Freedmen* (Chicago, 1890), 14; *New-York Tribune*, February 3, 1866, May 15, 1866; John B. Myers, "The Education of Alabama Freedmen During Presidential Reconstruction, 1865–1867," *Journal of Negro Education* 40 (1971): 169; Wakefield, "Set a Light in a Dark Place," 409.

37. Browne, "'To Bring Out the Intellect,'" 377, 383; *San Antonio Express*, May 22, 1869; *New-York Tribune*, May 15, 1866; John Russell Bartlett, *Memoirs of Rhode Island Officers Who Were Engaged in the Service of Their Country* (Providence, 1867), 437; *New Orleans Tribune*, August 31, 1866.

38. Duncan, *Freedom's Shore*, 25; Cynthia Everett to Sarah Everett, December 4, 1869, in Everett Papers, Newberry Library, Chicago; Henrietta Burtlett to Cynthia Everett, April 11, 1870, Ibid.; Paul Mishow to Cynthia Everett, February 13, 1871, Ibid.; Wal-

ter J. Fraser, *Charleston! Charleston! The History of a Southern City* (Columbia, SC, 1990), 274.

39. Cynthia Everett to Jennie Everett, December 3, 1870, in Everett Papers, Newberry Library, Chicago; John L. Dart to Cynthia Everett, August 14, 1870, Ibid.; Cynthia Everett to Mary Everett, no date, Ibid. The Charleston Workhouse was destabilized by the 1886 earthquake—as was the tower on the city jail—and eventually razed.

40. Butchart, *Schooling the Freed People*, 134–35; Cornelius to Cynthia Everett, February 22, 1870, in Everett Papers, Newberry Library, Chicago; Elizabeth Gregorie to Cynthia Everett, February 7, 1871, Ibid.; A. G. Townshend to Cynthia Everett, May 25, 1871, Ibid.

41. F. A. Fiske to Oliver O. Howard, November 28, 1865, in Register of Letters Received by the Commissioners, Freedmen's Bureau Papers, Reel 23, NA; *Lowell Daily Citizen and News*, October 8, 1866; Washington *Reconstructionist*, March 24, 1866; *Flake's Bulletin* (Galveston, TX), February 14, 1866; Macon *Daily Telegraph*, June 18, 1866.

42. *Cincinnati Daily Gazette*, June 1, 1867, September 26, 1867; *Daily Columbus Enquirer*, April 21, 1867; *Charleston Advocate*, May 11, 1867; Edward Coke Billings, *Struggle Between the Civilization of Slavery and That of Freedom, Recently and Now Going on in Louisiana* (Northampton, 1873), 25; E. M. Gregory to A. P. Ketcham, April 11, 1867, in Register of Letters Received by the Commissioners, Freedmen's Bureau Papers, Reel 43, NA; *Flake's Bulletin* (Galveston, TX), November 2, 1867; *New-Hampshire Sentinel* (Keene, NH), October 3, 1867; Martin Abbott, "The Freedmen's Bureau and Negro Schooling in South Carolina," *SCHM* 57 (1956): 72; *Columbus Daily Enquirer*, April 21, 1867.

43. Morris, "Educational Reconstruction," 152; Rabinowitz, "Half a Loaf," 566; Butchart, *Schooling the Freed People*, 19; *Daily Columbus Enquirer*, April 21, 1867; *Cincinnati Daily Gazette*, June 1, 1867, Cynthia Everett to Jennie Everett, January 1, 1870, in Everett Papers, Newberry Library, Chicago.

44. Morris, *Reading, 'riting, and Reconstruction*, 90–91; Nolen, *African American Southerners*, 170; Thomas L. Webber, *Deep Like the Rivers: Education in the Slave Quarter Community, 1831–1865* (New York, 1978), 248–49; Rabinowitz, "Half a Loaf," 578; "Father" Hill to Blanche K. Bruce, May 22, 1880, in Bruce Papers, Howard University; Foner, ed., *Freedom's Lawmakers*, xxi.

45. Williamson, *After Slavery*, 216–17; William Lee Trenholm, *Local Reform in South Carolina* (Charleston, 1872), 8; Morris, "Educational Reconstruction," 157.

46. Om Langhorne to Blanche K. Bruce, December 16, 1879, in Bruce Papers, Howard University; Waterbury, *Seven Years Among the Freedmen*, 123.

47. William C. Harris, *Day of the Carpetbagger: Republican Reconstruction in Mississippi* (Baton Rouge, 1979), 150; Franklin, *Reconstruction*, 110–11; Alfred H. Kelly, "Congressional Controversy over School Segregation," *American Historical Review* (hereafter *AHR*) 64 (1959): 540; Dray, *Capitol Men*, 46–47.

48. Mohr, *Radical Republicans and Reform in New York*, 197; San Francisco *Elevator*, February 28, 1874; Nancy Bertaux and Michael Washington, "The 'Colored Schools' of

Cincinnati and African American Community in Nineteenth-Century Cincinnati, 1849–1890," *Journal of Negro Education* 74 (2005), 45.

49. T. J. Mackey to Oliver O. Howard, May 17, 1867, in Register of Letters Received by the Commissioners, Freedmen's Bureau Papers, Reel 43, NA; Bradford Lecly to James Gillette, June 13, 1868, in Records of the Assistant Commissioner for the State of Alabama, Freedmen's Bureau Papers, Reel 14, NA; Edward F. Sweat, "Establishment of South Carolina Schools," *Phylon* 22 (1961): 163; *New Orleans Tribune*, October 29, 1867.

50. Alvord, *Semi-Annual School Reports*, 6; Rabinowitz, *Race Relations in the Urban South*, 153; *Vermont Journal* (Windsor, VT), June 2, 1866.

51. Chicago *Inter-Ocean*, December 4, 1877; *New-York Tribune*, July 7, 1866.

52. Michael Goldhaber, "A Mission Unfilled: Freedmen's Education in North Carolina, 1865–1870," *JNH* 77 (1992): 200; Alvan C. Gillem to Oliver O. Howard, February 18, 1867, in Register of Letters Received by the Commissioners, Freedmen's Bureau Papers, Reel 43, NA; Thayer Swayne to Jacob R. Shipherd, September 30, 1865, Ibid., Reel 23; Myers, "Education of Alabama Freedmen," 170; Chicago *Inter-Ocean*, December 4, 1877; Little Rock *Morning Republican*, April 16, 1870.

53. Lemann, *Redemption*, 98; Cynthia Everett to Anna Everett, January 30, 1870, in Everett Papers, Newberry Library, Chicago; Edwin L. Dawes to Oliver O. Howard, July 21, 1869, in Records of the Assistant Commissioner for the State of Alabama, Freedmen's Bureau Papers, Reel 19, NA.

54. Nashville *Colored Tennessean*, March 24, 1866; Joe M. Richardson, "Francis L. Cardozo," *Journal of Negro Education* 48 (1979): 77; Goldfield, *America Aflame*, 411–12.

55. *Baltimore Sun*, October 15, 1867; *Lowell Daily Citizen and News*, November 11, 1869; Alvord, *Semi-Annual School Reports*, 3–4; Du Bois, *Black Reconstruction*, 648–49; Philadelphia *Public Ledger*, November 21, 1868.

56. Holt, *Making Freedom Pay*, 122; Fitzgerald, *Splendid Failure*, 152; McPherson, *Lincoln and the Second American Revolution*, 16–17, rightly describes this success as "revolutionary."

Chapter Five: "We Will Remember Our Friends, and Will Not Forget Our Enemies"

1. *New National Era*, reprinted in New Orleans *Weekly Louisianian*, October 22, 1871. One year earlier, on September 1, 1870, Frederick Douglass bought a fifty-percent share in the paper. See William S. McFeely, *Frederick Douglass* (New York, 1991), 273.

2. Harry C. Silcox, "Nineteenth Century Philadelphia Black Militant: Octavius V. Catto," *Pennsylvania History* 44 (1977): 53–57.

3. Silcox, "Nineteenth Century Philadelphia Black Militant," 59–61; Frederick M. Binder, "Pennsylvania Negro Regiments in the Civil War," *JNH* 37 (1952): 386–87; Daniel R. Biddle and Murray Dubin, *Tasting Freedom: Octavius Catto and the Battle for Equality in Civil War America* (Philadelphia, 2010), 321.

4. Hugh Davis, *"We Will Be Satisfied with Nothing Less": The African American Struggle for Equal Rights in the North During Reconstruction* (Ithaca, NY, 2011), 27; *New York Times*, May 18, 1865.

5. Silcox, "Nineteenth Century Philadelphia Black Militant," 65–66; Ira V. Brown, "Pennsylvania and the Rights of the Negro, 1865–1887," *Pennsylvania History* 28 (1961): 48; Carol Faulkner, *Lucretia Mott's Heresy: Abolition and Women's Rights in Nineteenth-Century America* (Philadelphia, 2011), 192–93; Foner, "Discrimination on Philadelphia Streetcars," 281; Biddle and Dubin, *Tasting Freedom*, 340.

6. New Orleans *Weekly Louisianian*, November 9, 1871; Biddle and Dubin, *Tasting Freedom*, 428–29.

7. New Orleans *Weekly Louisianian*, October 22, 1871, and October 29, 1871; W. E. B. Du Bois, *The Philadelphia Negro* (Philadelphia, 1899), 40.

8. New Orleans *Weekly Louisianian*, November 9, 1871.

9. Elizabeth D. Leonard, *Lincoln's Avengers: Justice, Revenge, and Reunion After the Civil War* (New York, 2004), 179–80; Stephen Budiansky, *The Bloody Shirt: Terror After Appomattox* (New York, 2008), 21–22; Philip Dray, *Capitol Men: The Epic Story of Reconstruction Through the Lives of the First Black Congressmen* (New York, 2010), 24–25; Goose Creek Parish, South Carolina, 1850 federal census, slave schedules, page 48, NA. Benjamin F. Perry raised eyebrows in the North by publishing a letter in which he asserted that the Confederacy's "great unpardonable crime" had been to adhere to "that sacred principle set forth in the Declaration of Independence," to "peaceably secede." See (author unknown), *Is the South Ready for Restoration?* (no publication data, 1866), 7.

10. Annette Gordon-Reed, *Andrew Johnson* (New York, 2011), 110; Kenneth M. Stampp, *The Era of Reconstruction, 1865–1877* (New York, 1966), 56–57; LaWanda Cox and John H. Cox, *Politics, Principle, and Prejudice, 1865–1866: Dilemma of Reconstruction America* (New York, 1969), 152–53; Du Bois, *Black Reconstruction*, 244–45.

11. Thomas Wagstaff, "Call Your Old Master—Master: Southern Political Leaders and Black Labor During Presidential Reconstruction," *Labor History* 10 (1969): 323; Harris, *With Charity for All*, 270; Eric Foner, *Reconstruction: America's Unfinished Revolution, 1863–1877* (New York, 1988), 189–90; Martha Hodes, *White Women, Black Men: Illicit Sex in the Nineteenth-Century South* (New Haven, 1997), 156; Budiansky, *Bloody Shirt*, 21–22.

12. George C. Rable, *But There Was No Peace: The Role of Violence in the Politics of Reconstruction* (Athens, GA, 1984), 4–5; *Salt Lake City Telegraph*, March 6, 1866; Wagstaff, "Call Your Old Master—Master," 336; Carter, *When the War Was Over*, 261; Brooks D. Simpson, *The Reconstruction Presidents* (Lawrence, KS, 1998), 80–81.

13. John Gardiner to Lyman Trumbull, January 26, 1866, in Trumbull Papers, LC; Samuel Parks to Lyman Trumbull, January 30, 1866, Ibid.; Charles Palmer to William H. Seward, February 9, 1866, in Seward Papers, UR. Palmer was typical of those who had voted for Constitutional Unionist candidate John Bell in 1860 and deplored secession that spring. In 1860, his Pennsylvania-born father, William Palmer, was a Richmond-based "Agricultural Machinist." See Richmond, 2nd Ward, Virginia, 1860 federal census, page 112, NA.

14. The term "Confederate Reconstruction" was first coined by John Hope Franklin in his book *Reconstruction After the Civil War*, published in 1961 (see 44–45). See also

Augusta *Colored American*, January 6, 1866; Washington *Reconstructionist*, March 24, 1866.

15. Michael Vorenberg, *Final Freedom: The Civil War, the Abolition of Slavery, and the Thirteenth Amendment* (Cambridge, 2001), 228; Barry Crouch, "To Enslave the Rising Generation," in *The Freedmen's Bureau and Reconstruction*, eds. Paul A. Cimbala and Randall M. Miller (New York, 1999), 262; Walter B. Edgar, *South Carolina: A History* (Columbia, SC, 1998), 383; Sidney Andrews, *The South Since the War* (Boston, 1866), 285; D. J. Baldwin to William H. Seward, January 25, 1866, in Seward Papers, UR; C. E. Lippincott to Lyman Trumbull, August 29, 1865, in Trumbull Papers, LC. Notification of Mississippi's ratification was not received by the National Archivist until February 7, 2013, and thus was not official until then.

16. Hans L. Trefousse, *Andrew Johnson: A Biography* (New York, 1989), 230; *New-York Tribune*, March 22, 1866; Michael W. Fitzgerald, *Splendid Failure: Postwar Reconstruction in the American South* (Chicago, 2008), 34–35; Simpson, *Reconstruction Presidents*, 82–83; W. W. Holden, *Union Meeting in Raleigh* (Raleigh, 1866), 11; *Hartford Daily Courant*, March 29, 1866; *Springfield Republican* (Springfield, MA), April 21, 1866.

17. Sandford W. Barber to Benjamin F. Perry, July 10, 1865, in Perry Papers, Alabama Department of Archives and History; Barry Crouch, "'All the Vile Passions': The Texas Black Code of 1866," *Southwestern Historical Quarterly* 97 (1993): 21, 24; *New York Herald*, March 15, 1866.

18. Christopher Waldrep, *Roots of Disorder: Race and Criminal Justice in the American South, 1817–80* (Urbana, 1998), 106; Carter, *When the War Was Over*, 219; Augusta *Colored American*, January 6, 1866; J. W. C. Pennington to *Weekly Anglo-African*, November 29, 1865, in *The Black Abolitionist Papers, Vol. V: The United States, 1859 to 1865*, eds. C. Peter Ripley and Michael Hembree (Chapel Hill, 1992), 5: 394–95.

19. Amy Dru Stanley, *From Bondage to Contract: Wage Labor, Marriage, and the Market in the Age of Slave Emancipation* (Cambridge, 1998), 126; C. E. Lippincott to Lyman Trumbull, August 29, 1865, in Trumbull Papers, LC; (author unknown), *The Results of Emancipation in the United States of America* (New York, 1867), 10; Eric Foner, *Nothing But Freedom: Emancipation and Its Legacy* (Baton Rouge, 1983), 49–50; Michael W. Fitzgerald, *The Union League Movement in the Deep South: Politics and Agricultural Change During Reconstruction* (Baton Rouge, 1989), 29–30; Crouch, "To Enslave the Rising Generation," 275.

20. Morgan, *Yazoo*, 205; Laura F. Edwards, *Scarlett Doesn't Live Here Anymore: Southern Women in the Civil War Era* (Urbana, IL, 2000), 127; Hodes, *White Women, Black Men*, 149.

21. Wagstaff, "Call Your Old Master—Master," 337; Albion W. Tourgée, *A Fool's Errand, By One of the Fools* (New York, 1879), 119; Christopher M. Span, *From Cotton Field to Schoolhouse: African American Education in Mississippi, 1862–1875* (Chapel Hill, 2009), 93–94; Nashville *Colored Tennessean*, March 31, 1866.

22. *New-York Tribune*, February 21, 1866; "Kentucky blacks" to Andrew Johnson, June 1865, in Berlin, ed., *Freedom, Series I*, 1: 624–25; Wagstaff, "Call Your Old Master—Master," 325; Cincinnati *Colored Citizen*, May 19, 1866.

23. Edward Coke Billings, *Struggle Between the Civilization of Slavery and That of Freedom, Recently and Now Going on in Louisiana* (Northampton, 1873), 8; A. S. Wallace to William H. Seward, May 5, 1866, in Seward Papers, UR; Thomas Holt, *Black over White: Negro Political Leadership in South Carolina During Reconstruction* (Urbana, IL,1977), 23; Hyman Rubin, *South Carolina Scalawags* (Columbia, SC, 2006), 6; Thomas Keneally, *American Scoundrel: The Life of the Notorious Civil War General Dan Sickles* (New York, 2003), 321.

24. Cincinnati *Colored Citizen*, May 19, 1866; Augusta *Loyal Georgian*, February 17, 1866.

25. David Donald, *Charles Sumner and the Rights of Man* (New York, 1970), 241; Span, *Cotton Field to Schoolhouse*, 98–99; James Embry to Andrew Johnson, February 9, 1866, in Bergeron, ed., *Papers of Johnson*, 10: 62–63.

26. William Warner testimony, in *Testimony Taken By the Joint Select Committee to Inquire into the Conditions of Affairs in the Late Insurrectionary States: Alabama* (Washington, D.C., 1872), 1: 357; P. J. Staudenraus, *The African Colonization Movement, 1816–1865* (New York, 1961), 248–49, 251; Reid, "USCT Veterans in Post–Civil War North Carolina," 403; Peter Mountain, Company Descriptive Book, May 1863, Compiled Military Service Records of Volunteer Union Soldiers, U.S. Colored Troops, 35th Infantry, Reel 77, NA.

27. William F. Bryan to Blanche K. Bruce, March 27, 1879, in Bruce Papers, Howard University; Washington Chavis to Blanche K. Bruce, February 6, 1879, Ibid.; Margaret Washington, *Sojourner Truth's America* (Urbana, IL, 2009), 328.

28. James Gillette to Assistant Commissioner, April 20, 1868, in Records of the Assistant Commissioner for the State of Alabama, Freedmen's Bureau Papers, Reel 14, NA; L. W. Ballard to Blanche K. Bruce, February 17, 1876, in Bruce Papers, Howard University; D. D. Bell to Blanche K. Bruce, January 19, 1878, Ibid.; Thomas H. Brown to Blanche K. Bruce, April 13, 1878, Ibid.

29. Benjamin Quarles, *The Negro in the Civil War* (Boston, 1953), 189; "Manifesto of the Colored Citizens of the State of New York," July 16, 1863, in Ripley, ed., *Black Abolitionists Papers*, 5: 224–25. On the antebellum black conventions, see Howard H. Bell, "The Negro Emigration Movement, 1849–1854: A Phase of Negro Nationalism," *Phylon* 20 (1959): 132–42.

30. Vincent Harding, *There Is a River: The Black Struggle for Freedom in America* (New York, 1981), 244–46; William Cheek and Aimee Lee Cheek, *John Mercer Langston and the Fight for Black Freedom, 1829–1865* (Urbana, IL, 1989), 425; Davis, *"We Will Be Satisfied with Nothing Less,"* 17–18, 22; Carla L. Peterson, *Black Gotham: A Family History of African Americans in Nineteenth-Century New York City* (New Haven, 2011), 273; Steven Hahn, *A Nation Under Our Feet: Black Political Struggles in the Rural South from Slavery to the Great Migration* (Cambridge, 2003), 106. The Syracuse Wesleyan Methodist Church still stands but today houses the Mission restaurant.

31. *Proceedings of the National Convention of Colored Men, Held in the City of Syracuse, N.Y.* (Boston, 1864), 36–40; Foner, *Reconstruction*, 27; John Rock, Speech of October 6, 1864, in Ripley, ed., *Black Abolitionist Papers*, 5: 304–5; *New Orleans Tribune*, October 25, 1864.

32. *New Orleans Tribune*, May 12, 1866.

33. "Constitution of the Colored Men's Equal Rights League of Richmond," May 9, 1865, in Ripley, ed., *Black Abolitionist Papers*, 5: 324–25; Philip S. Foner and George E. Walker, eds., *Proceedings of the Black National and State Conventions, 1865–1900* (Philadelphia, 1986), 80–84. On other postwar references to the Crater by black veterans, see Kevin M. Levin, *Remembering the Battle of the Crater: War as Murder* (Lexington, 2012), 79.

34. San Francisco *Elevator*, February 14, 1868; Foner, *Reconstruction*, 64; Leon Litwack, *Been in the Storm So Long: The Aftermath of Slavery* (New York, 1979), 508–9; Eric Foner, *The Fiery Trial: Abraham Lincoln and American Slavery* (New York, 2010), 318; Foner and Walker, eds., *Proceedings of the Black National and State Conventions*, 78–79.

35. Foner and Walker, eds., *Proceedings of the Black National and State Conventions*, 112–13, 115–16; Loren Schweninger, *James T. Rapier and Reconstruction* (Chicago, 1978), 38–39; John Cimprich, "The Beginnings of the Black Suffrage Movement in Tennessee, 1864–1865," *JNH* 65 (1980): 190.

36. San Francisco *Elevator*, June 16, 1865; Foner and Walker, eds., *Proceedings of the Black National and State Conventions*, 40–41, 44–45, 133–34; Brown, "Pennsylvania and the Rights of the Negro," 50; Biddle and Dubin, *Tasting Freedom*, 340–41. David W. Ruggles was evidently no relation to the New York–based activist of the same name. According to the June 1880 federal census, San Francisco, Schedule 1, page 20, NA, Ruggles was born in 1830 in Virginia to Virginia-born parents.

37. Fields, *Slavery and Freedom*, 132–33; Lewis H. Douglass to Amelia Loguen, January 7, 1866, in Evans Collection, Savannah.

38. Peter Kolchin, *First Freedom: The Responses of Alabama's Blacks to Emancipation and Reconstruction* (Greenwood, 1972), 152–53; *Circular, Call for a Convention, 1865*, in P. B. S. Pinchback Papers, Moorland-Springarn Research Center, Howard University; Charles Sumner to Andrew Johnson, June 30, 1865, in *The Selected Letters of Charles Sumner*, ed. Beverly Wilson Palmer (Boston, 1990), 2: 312; *New Orleans Tribune*, May 8, 1865; Augusta *Loyal Georgian*, February 17, 1866; Du Bois, *Black Reconstruction*, 232–33.

39. Foner and Walker, eds., *Proceedings of the Black National and State Conventions*, 246; McFeely, *Douglass*, 247. For Downing's wartime service, see Commonwealth of Massachusetts, Special Order 281, March 7, 1864, and War Department, Pass, April 21, 1864, both in George T. Downing Papers, Moorland-Springarn Research Center, Howard University.

40. Foner and Walker, eds., *Proceedings of the Black National and State Conventions*, 214–215; Benjamin Quarles, *Frederick Douglass* (New York, 1967 ed.), 226–27.

41. McFeely, *Douglass*, 247–48; Oakes, *The Radical and the Republican*, 250; Albert E. Castel, *The Presidency of Andrew Johnson* (Lawrence, KS, 1979), 64.

42. "Interview with Delegation of Blacks," February 7, 1866, in Bergeron, ed., *Papers of Johnson*, 41–43.

43. Quarles, *Douglass*, 227–28; Gordon-Reed, *Johnson*, 125–26; Trefousse, *Johnson*,

241–42. Paul H. Bergeron, in *Andrew Johnson's Civil War and Reconstruction* (Knoxville, 2011), 104, admits that the president's words reflected his "racist attitude" but suggests that "the absolute reliability of the quotation can be questioned."

44. *Boston Daily Journal*, April 4, 1866; New Orleans *Daily Picayune*, March 31, 1866; *Salt Lake Daily Telegraph*, March 31, 1866; Philadelphia *Daily Age*, March 30, 1866; *Albany Evening Journal*, March 31, 1866.

45. *New Orleans Tribune*, November 9, 1866; Macon *Daily Telegraph*, March 27, 1866; *Memphis Daily Avalanche*, January 2, 1866; *New Hampshire Patriot and Gazette* (Concord, NH), February 21, 1866.

46. Macon *Daily Telegraph*, September 14, 1866 and October 4, 1866; *Memphis Daily Avalanche*, September 11, 1866; Frederick Douglass, *Life and Times of Frederick Douglass* (New York, 1962 ed.), 386–87.

47. *Cincinnati Enquirer*, September 18, 1866; New Orleans *Daily Picayune*, September 16, 1866.

48. Trefousse, *Stevens*, 138; *Reconstruction Speech of the Hon. Thaddeus Stevens* (Lancaster, PA, 1865), 4.

49. Samuel Shellabarger, *Disfranchisement of the Rebels* (Washington, D.C., 1866), 1; Charles G. Loring, *Reconstruction* (Boston, 1866), 62, 106; *Philadelphia Inquirer*, March 9, 1866.

50. Carter, *When the War Was Over*, 234–35; *Boston Journal*, April 4, 1866; *New Hampshire Patriot and Gazette* (Concord, NH), March 14, 1866; *Albany Journal*, January 1, 1866 and March 21, 1866; *Vermont Journal* (Windsor, VT), March 17, 1866.

51. *Congressional Globe*, 39th Cong., 1st Sess., 92–93; L. P. Brockett, *Men of Our Day: Biographical Sketches of Patriots, Orators, Statesmen, Generals, Reformers, Financiers and Merchants, Now on the State of Action* (Philadelphia, 1872), 501; Donald, *Sumner*, 281; Washington *Daily Constitutional Union*, January 3, 1866 and January 13, 1866; Macon *Daily Telegraph*, January 27, 1866; Philadelphia *Daily Age*, April 23, 1866; *Lowell Daily Citizen and News*, March 6, 1866.

52. *Congressional Globe*, 39th Cong., 1st Sess., 1–3; Windsor *Vermont Journal*, March 31, 1866; *New-York Tribune*, January 12, 1866; *Wooster Republican*, March 29, 1866; Nashville *Colored Tennessean*, March 31, 1866.

53. New Orleans *Daily Picayune*, March 31, 1866; Macon *Daily Telegraph*, April 23, 1866; *Albany Journal*, April 7, 1866; *Boston Daily Advertiser*, March 9, 1866; *Charleston Advocate*, May 11, 1867; *Baltimore Sun*, July 31, 1866.

54. Macon *Daily Telegraph*, March 5, 1866; *Baltimore Sun*, March 31, 1866; Washington *Reconstructionist*, March 24, 1866; *Albany Journal*, March 19, 1866; Philadelphia *Daily Age*, March 15, 1866; "Maryland blacks" to Andrew Johnson, March 17, 1866, in Bergeron, ed., *Papers of Johnson*, 10: 265–66.

55. New Orleans *Daily Picayune*, March 31, 1866; Macon *Daily Telegraph*, April 1, 1866 and April 9, 1866; Little Rock *Arkansas State Gazette*, March 10, 1866.

56. *Albany Journal*, March 30, 1866; *New-Hampshire Sentinel* (Keene, NH), April 5, 1866; *Boston Cultivator*, April 7, 1866; *New-York Tribune*, April 5, 1866; Bowen, *Johnson and the Negro*, 138; Nashville *Colored Tennessean*, March 31, 1866. Johnson's vetoes even

cost Secretary Seward among his "friends in Europe," who were forced to conclude "that the absolute abandonment, and if need be, the immolation of the negro race are the implicit condition for the reestablishment, at any price, of the Union." See Agénor Étienne to William H. Seward, April 30, 1866, in Seward Papers, UR.

57. Leonard, *Lincoln's Avengers*, 208; Stampp, *Era of Reconstruction*, 111; Richard Zuczek, *State of Rebellion: Reconstruction in South Carolina* (Columbia, SC, 1996), 32.

58. Philadelphia *Daily Age*, April 5, 1866; *Boston Daily Advertiser*, March 9, 1866; *New-York Tribune*, April 9, 1866; *Philadelphia Inquirer*, April 9, 1866; *Albany Journal*, April 6, 1866.

59. *Baltimore Sun*, April 10, 1866; *Philadelphia Inquirer*, March 10, 1866; Cincinnati *Daily Gazette*, August 7, 1871; Amherst *Farmers' Cabinet*, March 12, 1866.

60. Matt Talbott to Lyman Trumbull, July 16, 1866, in Trumbull Papers, LC; *Albany Journal*, April 7, 1866; *Philadelphia Inquirer*, April 4, 1866; Salt Lake City *Telegraph*, April 12, 1866; Des Moines *Iowa State Daily Register*, April 8, 1866.

61. *New Orleans Tribune*, July 7, 1867; Macon *Daily Telegraph*, March 23, 1866.

62. New Orleans *Daily Picayune*, September 14, 1866; Harrisburg *Weekly Patriot and Union*, October 4, 1866.

63. Fred Miller to Oliver O. Howard, January 4, 1867, in Register of Letters Received by the Commissioners, Freedmen's Bureau Papers, Reel 43, NA; Alvan C. Gillem to Oliver O. Howard, March 15, 1867, Ibid., Reel 43; Charles Whittlesey to Oliver O. Howard, February 18, 1866, Ibid., Reel 23; David Goldfield, *America Aflame: How the Civil War Created a Nation* (New York, 2011), 424; *New-York Tribune*, February 6, 1866.

64. B. S. Whittin to William H. Seward, April 13, 1866, in Seward Papers, UR; Clinton, "Reconstructing Freedwomen," 316–17; *New Orleans Tribune*, September 8, 1866, August 16, 1865; Lewis H. Douglass to Amelia Loguen, February 10, 1868, in Evans Collection, Savannah; N. H. Hunter to Office of Assistant Superintendent of Education, August 16, 1868, in Records of the Assistant Commissioner for the State of Alabama, Freedmen's Bureau Papers, Reel 14, NA.

65. Fields, *Slavery and Freedom*, 143; Washington *National Intelligencer*, October 22, 1866; New Orleans *Daily Picayune*, October 30, 1866; *New-York Tribune*, October 27, 1866; Albany *Evening Journal*, November 5, 1866.

66. Gordon-Reed, *Johnson*, 117–18; Richard H. Abbott, *For Free Press and Equal Rights: Republican Newspapers in the Reconstruction South* (Athens, GA, 2004), 130; *Baltimore Sun*, April 5, 1866; *Memphis Daily Avalanche*, January 16, 1866; Melinda Hennessey, "Racial Violence During Reconstruction," *SCHM* 86 (1985): 102; *New-York Tribune*, March 3, 1866; Robert J. Zalimas Jr., "A Disturbance in the City," in John David Smith, ed., *Black Soldiers in Blue: African American Troops in the Civil War Era* (Chapel Hill, 2001), 376.

67. Franklin, *Reconstruction*, 62–63; James Gilbert Ryan, "The Memphis Riots of 1866: Terror in a Black Community During Reconstruction," *JNH* 62 (1977): 243–49; Trefousse, *Stevens*, 187; Litwack, *Been in the Storm So Long*, 281; Hardwick, "Your Old Father Abe Lincoln is Dead," 109–120; Rosen, *Terror in the Heart of Freedom*, 64;

Altina L. Waller, "Community, Class and Race in the Memphis Riot of 1866," *Journal of Social History* 18 (1984): 238; Edwards, *Scarlett Doesn't Live Here Anymore*, 131.

68. Hogue, *Uncivil War*, 42–43; Charles Lane, *The Day Freedom Died: The Colfax Massacre, the Supreme Court, and the Betrayal of Reconstruction* (New York, 2008), 18; James G. Hollandsworth, *An Absolute Massacre: The New Orleans Race Riot of July 30, 1866* (Baton Rouge, 2001), 29; Michael Perman, *Reunion Without Compromise: The South and Reconstruction, 1865–1868* (Cambridge, 1973), 230–31; Dennis C. Rousey, *Policing the Southern City: New Orleans, 1805–1889* (Baton Rouge, 1997), 116–17; *New Orleans Tribune*, September 2, 1866, May 23, 1867, and July 30, 1867; Dray, *Capitol Men*, 30, places the death toll at forty-six, but he evidently confused the number killed in New Orleans with that in Memphis.

69. *New-York Tribune*, October 5, 1866 and January 14, 1867; *New Orleans Times*, January 11, 1867 and January 15, 1867; Trenton *Daily State Gazette*, January 10, 1867; *New Orleans Tribune*, August 31, 1866 and, September 1, 1866; Rable, *But There Was No Peace*, 56–57; Biddle and Dubin, *Tasting Freedom*, 382.

70. Trefousse, *Johnson*, 265; Augusta *Colored American*, January 6, 1866; *New Orleans Tribune*, September 20, 1866; Loring, *Reconstruction*, 85; Sally E. Hadden, *Slave Patrols: Law and Violence in Virginia and the Carolinas* (Cambridge, 2001), 205.

Chapter 6: "Andrew Johnson Is But One Man"

1. Fawn M. Brodie, *Thaddeus Stevens: Scourge of the South* (New York, 1959), 86–87; Cleveland *Plain Dealer*, August 26, 1868.

2. Brodie, *Stevens*, 88–89; *Albany Argus*, August 24, 1868; *Richmond Whig*, August 21, 1868.

3. Brodie, *Stevens*, 90–91; Cleveland *Plain Dealer*, August 26, 1868; Kenneth M. Stampp, *The Era of Reconstruction, 1865–1877* (New York, 1966), 103. Hans L. Trefousse, in *Thaddeus Stevens: Nineteenth-Century Egalitarian* (Chapel Hill, 1997), 46, argues that scholars should not attribute his "antislavery beliefs" to his relationship with Smith. Although it is undoubtedly true that he was an abolitionist before 1848, most white abolitionists were less vocal in their support for black social equality, and Stevens's support for equal rights may well have been influenced by Smith.

4. Jacob Hoke, *Reminiscences of the War, or, Incidents Which Transpired In and About Chambersburg During the War of the Rebellion* (Chambersburg, 1884), 53; No name to Thaddeus Stevens, Christmas, in *The Papers of Thaddeus Stevens*, ed. Beverly Wilson Palmer (Pittsburgh, 1998), 2: 338–39; No name to Thaddeus Stevens, March 10, 1868, Ibid., 2: 371–72.

5. Brodie, *Stevens*, 92; Trefousse, *Stevens*, 242; *New Orleans Tribune*, July 18, 1867.

6. *Philadelphia Inquirer*, August 19, 1868; Washington *National Intelligencer*, August 20, 1868; *Cincinnati Daily Gazette*, August 21, 1868.

7. St. Louis *Missouri Democrat*, June 18, 1867; *New Orleans Tribune*, September 11, 1866.

8. Elizabeth D. Leonard, *Lincoln's Avengers: Justice, Revenge, and Reunion After the Civil War* (New York, 2004), 216; Cincinnati *Colored Citizen*, May 19, 1866; Charleston *South Carolina Leader*, May 12, 1866.

9. David Goldfield, *America Aflame: How the Civil War Created a Nation* (New York, 2011), 427; Annette Gordon-Reed, *Andrew Johnson* (New York, 2011), 129; Walter B. Edgar, *South Carolina: A History* (Columbia, SC, 1998), 385; Eric Foner, *Reconstruction: America's Unfinished Revolution, 1863–1877* (New York, 1988), 270; Garrett Epps, *Democracy Reborn: The Fourteenth Amendment and the Fight for Equal Rights in Post–Civil War America* (New York, 2006), 246; James L. Roark, *Masters Without Slaves: Southern Planters in the Civil War and Reconstruction* (New York, 1977), 186–87; *New Orleans Tribune*, September 19, 1866.

10. *New Orleans Tribune*, May 22, 1867; Gregg Cantrell, "Racial Violence and Reconstruction Politics in Texas," *Southwestern Historical Quarterly* 93 (1990): 344; Undated newspaper clipping, in George T. Downing Papers, Moorland-Springarn Research Center, Howard University; *Congressional Globe*, 39th Cong., 2nd Sess., 76; J. W. Alvord to Oliver O. Howard, January 29, 1867 in Register of Letters Received by the Commissioners, Freedmen's Bureau Papers, Reel 67, NA; E. M. Gregory to A. P. Ketcham, January 29, 1867, Ibid., Reel 43.

11. *Flake's Bulletin* (Galveston, TX), January 5, 1867; *Boston Daily Advertiser*, January 5, 1867; Trefousse, *Stevens*, 205; *Lowell Daily Citizen and News*, March 6, 1866; William B. Downey to Thaddeus Stevens, January 7, 1867, in Palmer, ed., *Papers of Stevens*, 2: 237.

12. Blue, *Sumner*, 172–73; Foner, *Reconstruction*, 238; Richardson, *Death of Reconstruction*, 42–43; Gordon-Reed, *Johnson*, 101–2, persuasively argues that the president's constitutional inconsistencies are explained only by his belief in "white supremacy." Although he pointed to Article IV, Section 4 of the Constitution when arguing against Congressional exclusion of southern delegates, he was less inclined to adopt that clause, which guaranteed every state "a republican form of government" when it came to South Carolina's determination to deny the franchise to the state's black majority.

13. Christian G. Samito, *Becoming American Under Fire: Irish Americans, African Americans, and the Politics of Citizenship during the Civil War* (Ithaca, NY, 2009), 165; Xi, *The Trial of Democracy: Black Suffrage and Northern Republicans, 1860–1910* (Athens, GA, 1997), 38–39; Benjamin Gratz Brown, *Universal Suffrage* (St. Louis, 1865), 16; Ohio *Wooster Republican*, September 6, 1866; *Annapolis Gazette*, September 6, 1866; Eva Phyllis Field, *The Politics of Race in New York: The Struggle for Black Suffrage in the Civil War Era* (Ithaca, NY, 1982), 176–77.

14. Franklin E. Felton, *The Purification and Reconstruction of the American Union* (San Francisco, 1867), 17; John H. Reagan, *Memoirs, With Special Reference to Secession and the Civil War* (New York, 1906), 234; Cleveland *Plain Dealer*, October 31, 1867.

15. *New-York Tribune*, March 22, 1867, and March 24, 1867; *New York Herald*, March 22, 1867.

16. Cox and Cox, *Politics, Principle, and Prejudice*, 162; *Albany Journal*, February 23, 1867; James Mullins to Thaddeus Stevens, March 10, 1867, in Palmer, ed., *Papers of Stevens*, 2: 270.

17. Donald, *Politics of Reconstruction*, 36–37; Hans L. Trefousse, *Andrew Johnson: A Bi-

ography (New York, 1989), 278; *Cincinnati Daily Gazette*, February 11, 1867; Perman, *Reunion Without Compromise*, 270–71; *Baltimore Sun*, February 8, 1867.

18. Michael Les Benedict, *The Impeachment and Trial of Andrew Johnson* (New York, 1973), 16–17; Stampp, *Era of Reconstruction*, 147; Brooks D. Simpson, *The Reconstruction Presidents* (Lawrence, KS, 1998), 13; *Albany Journal*, March 25, 1867; *Philadelphia Inquirer*, March 26, 1867.

19. *New York Herald*, March 16, 1868; *Albany Journal*, February 23, March 21, and March 25, 1867; Glyndon Van Deusen, *William Henry Seward* (New York, 1967), 476; *New Orleans Tribune*, April 9, 1867.

20. W. W. Holden, *Union Meeting in Raleigh* (Raleigh, 1866), 7; *Cincinnati Daily Enquirer*, February 18, 1867; *Springfield* (Massachusetts) *Republican*, March 23, 1867; *Albany Journal*, March 21, 1867.

21. *Springfield* (Massachusetts) *Republican*, March 23, 1867; J. G. Wilson to Lyman Trumbull, January 21, 1866, in Trumbull Papers, LC; Charles Sumner to John Bright, May 27, 1867, in *The Selected Letters of Charles Sumner*, ed. Beverly Wilson Palmer (Boston, 1990), 2: 398; Holden, *Union Meeting in Raleigh*, 10; John Quincy Adams, ed., *Massachusetts and South Carolina. Correspondence Between John Quincy Adams and Wade Hampton and Others of South Carolina* (Boston, 1868), 5, 18; Alvan C. Gillem to Oliver O. Howard, April 11, 1867, in Register of Letters Received by the Commissioners, Freedmen's Bureau Papers, Reel 43, NA.

22. Perman, *Reunion Without Compromise*, 272–73; *Oregon State Journal* (Eugene, OR), November 14, 1867; *Albany Journal*, March 25, 1867; *New Orleans Tribune*, April 28, 1867; *Lowell Daily Citizen and News*, February 15, 1867; Macon *Weekly Telegraph*, February 15, 1867.

23. Richardson, *Death of Reconstruction*, 54–55; Edmund L. Drago, *Black Politicians and Reconstruction in Georgia: A Splendid Failure* (Baton Rouge, 1982), 30–31; *New Orleans Tribune*, June 12, 1867 and June 25, 1867.

24. *New Orleans Tribune*, April 23, 1867; *New-York Tribune*, April 6, 1867; Augusta *Loyal Georgian*, May 16, 1867.

25. *Albany Journal*, March 27, 1867; *Boston Daily Journal*, March 27, 1867; *New-York Tribune*, March 27, 1867; *New Orleans Tribune*, July 26, 1867; San Francisco *Elevator*, January 3, 1868.

26. *Baltimore Sun*, July 20, 24, 1866; *Albany Journal*, October 18, 1866; Macon *Weekly Telegraph*, October 22, 1866; New Orleans *Daily Picayune*, October 30, 1866; *Dallas Herald*, January 27, 1866.

27. *Baltimore Sun*, November 6, 1866; *New-Orleans Times*, October 15, 1867; Macon *Weekly Telegraph*, November 4, 1866; *Cincinnati Enquirer*, November 4, 1866; Herbert [no surname] to Hugh L. Bond, November 4, 1866, in Bond-McCulloch Family Papers, Maryland Historical Society; William H. Brown to Hugh L. Bond, July 20, 1867, Ibid.; L. Abbott to Hugh L. Bond, November 8, 1866, Ibid.; *Annapolis Gazette*, September 6, 1866.

28. Dennis C. Rousey, *Policing the Southern City: New Orleans, 1805–1889* (Baton Rouge, 1997), 122–23; L. P. Brockett, *Men of Our Day: Biographical Sketches of Patriots,*

Orators, Statesmen, Generals, Reformers, Financiers and Merchants, Now on the State of Action (Philadelphia, 1872), 502; Michael Fitzgerald, *Urban Emancipation: Popular Politics in Reconstruction Mobile, 1860–1890* (Baton Rouge, 2002), 96–97; *New Orleans Tribune*, May 16, 1867 and May 23, 1867; *Boston Daily Journal*, May 5, 1867; Christopher Waldrep, *Roots of Disorder: Race and Criminal Justice in the American South, 1817–80* (Urbana, 1998), 121; Harris, *Day of the Carpetbagger*, 18–19.

29. San Francisco *Elevator*, September 27, 1867; John Niven, *Salmon P. Chase: A Biography* (New York, 1995), 418; Gordon-Reed, *Johnson*, 134; Paul A. Hutton, *Phil Sheridan and His Army* (Lincoln, 1985), 24; *New Orleans Tribune*, June 27, 1867 and December 15, 1867; Cantrell, "Racial Violence and Reconstruction Politics," 347; *New Hampshire Patriot* (Concord, NH), March 25, 1868.

30. *Albany Journal*, April 3, 1866; *Cincinnati Enquirer*, January 25, 1866; Dr. H. Schroeder to Lyman Trumbull, December 23, 1865, in Trumbull Papers, LC; J. F. Alexander to Lyman Trumbull, June 22, 1866, Ibid.

31. Albert E. Castel, *The Presidency of Andrew Johnson* (Lawrence, 1979), 135; Philadelphia *Public Ledger*, January 9, 1868; *Boston Daily Journal*, January 16, 1868; Benedict, *Impeachment and Trial of Andrew Johnson*, 58–59.

32. William S. McFeely, *Grant: A Biography* (New York, 1981), 266; David O. Stewart, *Impeached: The Trial of President Andrew Johnson and the Fight for Lincoln's Legacy* (New York, 2010), 120; *Cincinnati Daily Gazette*, November 27, 1867; *New York Herald*, December 6, 1867; San Antonio *Express*, December 5, 1867.

33. Benedict, *Impeachment and Trial of Andrew Johnson*, 92; *Baltimore Sun*, January 16, 1868; *Cincinnati Daily Gazette*, February 4, 1868; *New Hampshire Patriot* (Concord, NH), March 25, 1868; *New York Herald*, March 12, 1868.

34. *New Orleans Tribune*, November 9, 1867; San Francisco *Elevator*, November 22, 1867, November 29, 1867, and December 13, 1867; Augusta *Loyal Georgian*, February 15, 1867; Charleston *Free Press*, April 5, 1867.

35. Michael W. Fitzgerald, *Splendid Failure: Postwar Reconstruction in the American South* (Chicago, 2008), 89; Josiah Bunting, *Ulysses S. Grant* (New York, 2004), 80–81; Castel, *Presidency of Johnson*, 158; *Cincinnati Daily Gazette*, February 24, 1868, February 27, 1868; *Flake's Bulletin* (Galveston, TX), February 23, 1868; San Francisco *Elevator*, March 13, 1867.

36. Washington *National Intelligencer*, February 11, 1868 and February 24, 1868; San Francisco *Evening Bulletin*, March 4, 1867; *Cincinnati Daily Gazette*, February 2, 1868; Trefousse, *Stevens*, 225; L. P. Brockett, *Men of Our Day*, 502.

37. *New York Herald*, March 17, 1868; New Orleans *Daily Picayune*, Trefousse, *Stevens*, 236; Stewart, *Impeached*, 166; *New Orleans Tribune*, December 9, 1866.

38. Robert J. Cook, *Civil War Senator: William Pitt Fessenden and the Fight to Save the American Republic* (Baton Rouge, 2011), 230–31; Frederick Allen to Charles Sumner, May 1868, in Palmer, ed., *Selected Letters of Sumner*, 2: 435 note 2; San Francisco *Elevator*, May 15, 1868.

39. Jean Edward Smith, *Grant* (New York, 2001), 455; San Francisco *Elevator*, April 4, 1868 and May 22, 1868.

40. Leonard, *Lincoln's Avengers*, 185–86; Mark E. Neely, *Lincoln and the Triumph of the Nation: Constitutional Conflict in the American Civil War* (Chapel Hill, 2011), 158; *Leavenworth Evening Bulletin*, March 11, 1868; William E. Parrish, *Frank Blair: Lincoln's Conservative* (Columbia, MO, 1998), 254–60; Washington *National Intelligencer*, July 4, 1868; New Orleans *Daily Picayune*, July 7, 1868; San Francisco *Elevator*, October 30, 1868.

41. Mark W. Summers, *A Dangerous Stir: Fear, Paranoia, and the Making of Reconstruction* (Chapel Hill, 2009), 230; San Francisco *Elevator*, October 23, 1868; George C. Rable, *But There Was No Peace: The Role of Violence in the Politics of Reconstruction* (Athens, GA, 1984), 108; Edward Coke Billings, *Struggle Between the Civilization of Slavery and That of Freedom, Recently and Now Going on in Louisiana* (Northampton, 1873), 16; Howell C. Flournoy to C. C. Sibley, October 5, 1868, in Records of the Assistant Commissioner for the State of Georgia, Freedmen's Bureau Papers, Reel 23, NA.

42. Morgan, *Yazoo*, 206–7; R. Blair to Edwin Beecher, November 15, 1868, in Records of the Assistant Commissioner for the State of Alabama, Freedmen's Bureau Papers, Reel 14, NA; R. Blair to Edwin Beecher, September 14, 1868, Ibid., Reel 14.

43. *New York Times*, October 19, 1868; San Francisco *Elevator*, December 4, 1868; Eric Foner, ed., *Freedom's Lawmakers: A Directory of Black Officeholders During Reconstruction*, 2nd ed. (Baton Rouge, 1996), 175–76; Richard H. Cain to Robert K. Scott, October 24, 1868, in Governor's Correspondence, South Carolina Department of Archives and History. I am grateful to Professor Brian Kelly for sharing this letter with me.

44. Deposition of James Roberts, October 6, 1868, in Records of the Assistant Commissioner for the State of Georgia, Freedmen's Bureau Papers, Reel 23, NA; Augusta *Loyal Georgian*, May 9, 1867; Morgan, *Yazoo*, 231–32.

45. San Francisco *Elevator*, December 11, 1868; William L. Black to J. R. Lewis, October 21, 1868, in Records of the Assistant Commissioner for the State of Georgia, Freedmen's Bureau Papers, Reel 23, NA; Ibid., Reel 23; Charles Rauschenberg to Frank Gallagher, October 15, 1868, Ibid., Reel 23.

46. R. G. Anthony to J. R. Lewis, November 2, 1868, in Records of the Assistant Commissioner for the State of Georgia, Freedmen's Bureau Papers, Reel 23, NA; Charles Rauschenberg to Frank Gallagher, September 20, 1868, Ibid., Reel 23; H. Carley to Frank Gallagher, November 1, 1868, Ibid; Galveston *Free Man's Press*, October 24, 1868.

47. S. H. Carter to Oliver O. Howard, September 29, 1868, in Records of the Assistant Commissioner for the State of Georgia, Freedmen's Bureau Papers, Reel 23, NA; Deposition of Albert Jones, September 30, 1868, Ibid., Reel 23; Charles Rauschenberg to Frank Gallagher, October 6, 1868, Ibid., Reel 23.

48. A. Pokorny to H. F. Brownson, November 3, 1868, in Records of the Assistant Commissioner for the State of Georgia, Freedmen's Bureau Papers, Reel 23, NA; San Francisco *Elevator*, October 23, 1868 and November 6, 1868; Charleston *Free Press*, April 5, 1868; Charles Lane, *The Day Freedom Died: The Colfax Massacre, the Supreme Court, and the Betrayal of Reconstruction* (New York, 2008), 24.

49. San Francisco *Elevator*, December 4, 1868 and December, 6, 1868; Michael Perman,

The Road to Redemption: Southern Politics, 1869–1879 (Chapel Hill, 1984), 4–5; Foner, *Reconstruction*, 343; Joan Waugh, *U.S. Grant: American Hero, American Myth* (Chapel Hill, 2009), 122; R. Blair to Edwin Beecher, December 22, 1868, in Records of the Assistant Commissioner for the State of Alabama, Freedmen's Bureau Papers, Reel 14, NA.

50. Trefousse, *Stevens*, 240; Du Bois, *Black Reconstruction*, 344; *Cincinnati Daily Gazette*, August 12, 1868; New York *Commercial Advertiser*, August 12, 1868; *Lowell Daily Citizen and News*, August 12, 1868.

51. New York *Commercial Advertiser*, August 12, 1868; Trefousse, *Stevens*, 241–43; *Philadelphia Inquirer*, August 15, 1868; *St. Paul Daily Press*, August 15, 1868.

52. San Francisco *Elevator*, January 1, 1869; Augusta *Daily Constitutionalist*, August 30, 1868; *Cincinnati Daily Gazette*, August 21, 1868.

53. Charles Sumner to John Bright, August 13, 1868, in Palmer, ed., *Selected Letters of Sumner*, 2: 439; San Francisco *Elevator*, April 29, 1868.

Chapter Seven: "We Knows That Much Better Than You Do"

1. David Donald, *Lincoln* (New York, 1995), 584–85; Concord *New-Hampshire Patriot*, March 10, 1875; Lawrence O. Graham, *The Senator and the Socialite: The True Story of America's First Black Dynasty* (New York, 2006), 1; *Memphis Planet*, in New Orleans *Weekly Louisianian*, December 25, 1875. Bruce would have been the third black senator, as P. B. S. Pinchback was elected by the Louisiana assembly as senator for the term beginning in March 1873, but his election was successfully contested. See P. B. S. Pinchback to Francis Nichols, December 8, 1877, in P. B. S. Pinchback Papers, Moorland-Springarn Research Center, Howard University.

2. Edward E. Leslie, *The Devil Knows How to Ride: The True Story of William Clarke Quantrill and His Confederate Raiders* (New York, 1996), 237; Philip Dray, *Capitol Men: The Epic Story of Reconstruction Through the Lives of the First Black Congressmen* (New York, 2010), 206.

3. Graham, *The Senator and the Socialite*, 34–54; *Cincinnati Daily Gazette*, March 11, 1875; Dray, *Capitol Men*, 207; John Hope Franklin, *Race and History: Selected Essays, 1938–1988* (Baton Rouge, 1989), 255; Charleston *Free Press*, April 5, 1875; Middletown *Daily Constitution*, March 11, 1875.

4. New Orleans *Weekly Louisianian*, April 3, May 1, 1875; E. D. Russell to Blanche K. Bruce, May 7, 1879, in Bruce Papers, Moorland-Springarn Research Center, Howard University.

5. Richard Bailey, *Neither Carpetbaggers Nor Scalawags: Black Officeholders During the Reconstruction of Alabama, 1867–1878* (Montgomery, 1991), 41–42; Francis Lewis Cardozo, *Address Before the Grand Council of the Union Leagues at Their Annual Meeting* (Columbia, SC, 1870), 4; Melinda Lawson, *Patriot Fires: Forging a New American Nationalism in the Civil War North* (Lawrence, KS, 2002), 88; Mitchell Snay, *Fenians, Freedmen, and Southern Whites: Race and Nationality in the Era of Reconstruction* (Baton Rouge, 2007), 58. The three oldest Union League clubs and buildings still exist and remain private clubs; a fourth, in New Haven, Connecticut, is now a restaurant.

6. Bailey, *Neither Carpetbaggers Nor Scalawags*, 50; Janet Hermann, *The Pursuit of a Dream* (New York, 1981), 184; Steven Hahn, *A Nation Under Our Feet: Black Political Struggles in the Rural South from Slavery to the Great Migration* (Cambridge, 2003), 180, 184; Thomas Holt, *Black over White: Negro Political Leadership in South Carolina During Reconstruction* (Urbana, IL,1977), 30–31; Augusta *Loyal Georgian*, February 3, 1866 and March 10, 1866; Charleston *South Carolina Leader*, March 31, 1866; Andrew Johnson, ironically, was an honorary member of the Nashville chapter, although that did not stop him from publicly denouncing the League while in Philadelphia. See *New Orleans Tribune*, September 5, 1866.

7. Michael W. Fitzgerald, *The Union League Movement in the Deep South: Politics and Agricultural Change During Reconstruction* (Baton Rouge, 1989), 52–53; James A. Baggett, *The Scalawags: Southern Dissenters in the Civil War and Reconstruction* (Baton Rouge, 2003), 223; Sandusky (Ohio) *Daily Commercial Register*, March 20, 1867; *New Orleans Tribune*, September 15, 1866 and May 5, 1867.

8. *New Orleans Tribune*, May 7, 1967 and July 26, 1867; P. B. S. Pinchback, Speech, Montgomery, Alabama, 1865, in P. B. S. Pinchback Papers, Moorland-Springarn Research Center, Howard University; Fitzgerald, *Union League Movement*, 4–5, 124–25; Cardozo, *Address Before the Grand Council of the Union Leagues*, 15; Snay, *Fenians, Freedmen, and Southern Whites*, 84.

9. *New Orleans Tribune*, June 13, 1867; Fitzgerald, *Union League Movement*, 12–13, 22–23, 96–97; Harris, *Day of the Carpetbagger*, 102–3.

10. Eric Foner, *Reconstruction: America's Unfinished Revolution, 1863–1877* (New York, 1988), 305–6; Richard L. Hume and Jerry B. Gough, *Blacks, Carpetbaggers, and Scalawags: The Constitutional Conventions of Radical Reconstruction* (Baton Rouge, 2008), 160; *New Orleans Tribune*, April 18, 1867 and April 25, 1867; Baggett, *Scalawags*, 216.

11. Nicholas Lemann, *Redemption: The Last Battle of the Civil War* (New York, 2006), 152; Peter Cozzens, *General John Pope: A Life for the Nation* (Urbana, IL, 2000), 286; Russell Duncan, *Freedom's Shore: Tunis Campbell and the Georgia Freedman* (Athens, GA, 1986), 43–44, 81; Anne Sarah Rubin, *A Shattered Nation: The Rise and Fall of the Confederacy, 1861–1868* (Chapel Hill, 2005), 161.

12. Hahn, *A Nation Under Our Feet*, 224; William Lee Trenholm, *Local Reform in South Carolina* (Charleston, 1872), 3; (author unknown), *Speech of Hon. Frank Arnim, Republican Senator From Edgefield County* (Columbia, SC, 1870), 2; *Cincinnati Daily Gazette*, September 26, 1867; Christopher Waldrep, *Roots of Disorder: Race and Criminal Justice in the American South, 1817–80* (Urbana, IL, 1998), 124–25; *New Orleans Tribune*, October 31, 1867; Franklin, *Reconstruction*, 86–87. Both Stringer and Johnson won seats to the state constitutional convention, and then both lost in contests for the state assembly. Stringer remained active in the black convention movement; see San Francisco *Elevator*, February 12, 1869.

13. Baggett, *Scalawags*, 196–97; P. B. S. Pinchback, Speech, June 19, 1867, in P. B. S. Pinchback Papers, Moorland-Springarn Research Center, Howard University; Eric Foner, ed., *Freedom's Lawmakers: A Directory of Black Officeholders During Reconstruction*, 2nd ed. (Baton Rouge, 1996), 53; San Francisco *Elevator*, January 3, 1868; *New*

Orleans Tribune, November 30, 1867, December 7, 1867; Salt Lake City *Telegraph*, December 9, 1867.

14. Little Rock *Arkansas State Gazette*, January 7, 1868; Schweninger, *Rapier*, 56–57; San Francisco *Elevator*, October 25, 1867.

15. Macon *Daily Telegraph*, December 27, 1867, February 19, 1868; Augusta *Loyal Georgian*, July 6, 1867; *Baltimore Sun*, February 1, 1868.

16. Dray, *Capitol Men*, 42–44; Hume and Gough, *Blacks, Carpetbaggers, and Scalawags*, 168; Peggy Lamson, *The Glorious Failure: Black Congressman Robert Brown Elliott and the Reconstruction in South Carolina* (New York, 1973), 48; Cardozo, *Address Before the Grand Council of the Union Leagues*, 7; *Troy Weekly Times*, April 4, 1868; Charleston *Free Press*, April 5, 1868.

17. Hahn, *A Nation Under Our Feet*, 207–8; Foner, *Reconstruction*, 318; Michael W. Fitzgerald, *Splendid Failure: Postwar Reconstruction in the American South* (Chicago, 2008), 78; Hume and Gough, *Blacks, Carpetbaggers, and Scalawags*, 13; Holt, *Black over White*, 17.

18. Slap, *Doom of Reconstruction*, 84; Alexandria *Gazette*, May 12, 1868; *New Orleans Tribune*, May 15, 1867; Richard H. Abbott, *For Free Press and Equal Rights: Republican Newspapers in the Reconstruction South* (Athens, GA, 2004), 30–31.

19. Cleveland *Plain Dealer*, October 31, 1867; Hume and Gough, *Blacks, Carpetbaggers, and Scalawags*, 253; Fitzgerald, *Splendid Failure*, 122; Lamson, *Glorious Failure*, 56; Barry Crouch, "Self-Determination and Local Black Leaders in Texas," *Phylon* 39 (1978): 348; *Proceedings of the Constitutional Convention of the State of South Carolina: Debates and Proceedings* (Charleston, 1868), 68.

20. *Charleston Mercury* quoted in *Boston Daily Journal*, April 3, 1868; Hume and Gough, *Blacks, Carpetbaggers, and Scalawags*, 2; *Norwich Aurora* (Norwich, CT), May 19, 1869; Fitzgerald, *Splendid Failure*, 80.

21. David Donald, *Charles Sumner and the Rights of Man* (New York, 1970) 2: 420; W. H. Bartholomew to S. C. Greene, June 23, 1868, in Records of the Assistant Commissioner for the State of Mississippi, Freedmen's Bureau Papers, Reel 24, NA; Jared Moore to S. C. Greene, June 23, 1868, Ibid., Reel 24; J. Hawser to unknown, December 23, 1867, Ibid., Reel 24.

22. Interview with Andy Brice, in Rawick, ed., *American Slave: South Carolina Narratives*, 78; Charles Grogin to Oliver O. Howard, February 18, 1867, in Register of Letters Received by the Commissioners, Freedmen's Bureau Papers, Reel 43, NA; James Gillette to Assistant Commissioner, February 26, 1868, in Records of the Assistant Commissioner for the State of Alabama, Freedmen's Bureau Papers, Reel 14, NA; W. G. Sprague to John Tyler, July 2, 1868, in Records of the Assistant Commissioner for the State of Mississippi, Freedmen's Bureau Papers, Reel 24, NA.

23. *New-York Tribune*, July 4, 1868; Affidavit of Will Henderson, July 3, 1868, in Records of the Assistant Commissioner for the State of Mississippi, Freedmen's Bureau Papers, Reel 24, NA; J. S. Roberts to Irvin McDowell, July 2, 1868, Ibid., Reel 24; Alfred Hulberg to Acting Assistant Adjutant General, March 24, 1868, in Records of the Assistant Commissioner for the State of Alabama, Freedmen's Bureau Papers,

Reel 14, NA. On Kellis's Confederate service, see National Park Service, Civil War Soldiers and Sailors System, http://www.itd.nps.gov/cwss.

24. Samuel Gardiner to George Shorkley, July 13, 1868, in Records of the Assistant Commissioner for the State of Alabama, Freedmen's Bureau Papers, Reel 14, NA; Samuel Gardiner to G. K. Sanderson, May 21, 1868, Ibid., Reel 14. On Cunningham's Confederate record, see Muster Rolls of Alabama Civil War Units, Alabama Department of Archives and History, www.archives.state.al.us.

25. Affidavit of Martha Tipton, July 23, 1868, in Records of the Assistant Commissioner for the State of Mississippi, Freedmen's Bureau Papers, Reel 24, NA; Crouch, "Self-Determination and Local Black Leaders in Texas," 351; William M. Dickson, *Absolute Equality of All Men Before the Law*, 15; Perry Downs to Frederick Douglass, February 21, 1867, in Douglass Collection, Howard University.

26. Emmanuel Hardy to Alvan C. Gillem, July 5, 1868, in Records of the Assistant Commissioner for the State of Mississippi, Freedmen's Bureau Papers, Reel 24, NA; John L. Churchill to Alvan C. Gillem, July 28, 1868, Ibid., Reel 24; Perman, *Reunion Without Compromise*, 314–15; Rubin, *A Shattered Nation*, 241.

27. *Flake's Bulletin* (Galveston, TX), December 11, 1869; Harris, *Day of the Carpetbagger*, 76–77.

28. Biddle and Dubin, *Tasting Freedom*, 378–79; Charles Delery, *Black Ghost of Radicalism in the United States* (New Orleans, 1868), 39; Davis, *"We Will Be Satisfied with Nothing Less,"* 29, 45, 51.

29. Davis, *"We Will Be Satisfied with Nothing Less,"* 29; Eugene Berwanger, "Reconstruction on the Frontier: The Equal Rights Struggle in Colorado, 1865–1867," *Pacific Historical Review* 44 (1975): 322; *New Orleans Tribune*, December 18, 1866; Salt Lake City *Telegraph*, March 31, 1866.

30. Mohr, *Radical Republicans and Reform in New York*, 208–9, 213–14, 224–25; Xi Wang, *The Trial of Democracy: Black Suffrage and Northern Republicans, 1860–1910* (Athens, GA, 1997), 5–6.

31. Browne, " 'To Bring out the Intellect,' " 392; Richard Paul Fuke, "Hugh Lennox Bond and Radical Republican Ideology," *Journal of Southern History* (hereafter *JSH*) 45 (1979): 572; Slap, *Doom of Reconstruction*, 10–11.

32. Ira V. Brown, "Pennsylvania and the Rights of the Negro, 1865–1887," *Pennsylvania History* 28 (1961): 52; Justin D. Fulton, *Radicalism: A Sermon Preached in Tremont Temple, on Fast-Day* (Boston, 1865), 36; Albert E. Castel, *Presidency of Andrew Johnson* (Lawrence, 1979), 208–9; Sally G. McMillen, *Seneca Falls and the Origins of the Women's Rights Movement* (New York, 2008), 173; Davis, *"We Will Be Satisfied with Nothing Less,"* 70; Patrick Riddleberger, *George Washington Julian, Radical Republican: A Study in Nineteenth Century Politics and Reform* (Bloomington, IN, 1966), 214–15; *New Orleans Tribune*, February 16, 1869.

33. John Mercer Langston, *Equality Before the Law: Oration Delivered by Prof. J. M. Langston of Howard University* (Oberlin, OH, 1874), 4–5; Christian G. Samito, *Becoming American Under Fire: Irish Americans, African Americans, and the Politics of Citizenship during the Civil War* (Ithaca, NY, 2009), 166; San Francisco *Elevator*, March 19, 1869;

Frederick Douglass, *Life and Times of Frederick Douglass* (New York, 1962 ed.), 378–79; Joan Waugh, *U.S. Grant: American Hero, American Myth* (Chapel Hill, 2009), 139.

34. Field, *Politics of Race in New York*, 182–83; Richardson, *Death of Reconstruction*, 80–81; Thomas Spellman to Adelbert Ames, April 26, 1879, in Ames Family Papers, Smith College Library; San Francisco *Elevator*, April 22, 1870.

35. John B. Boles, *Black Southerners, 1619–1869* (Lexington, KY., 1983), 204–5; Union Progressive Club Minutes, June 20, 1870, in P. B. S. Pinchback Papers, Moorland-Springarn Research Center, Howard University; Foner, *Reconstruction*, 355; Foner, ed., *Freedom's Lawmakers*, xiv-xv.

36. Fitzgerald, *Splendid Failure*, 168; Hahn, *A Nation Under Our Feet*, 219; Foner, ed., *Freedom's Lawmakers*, xvii–xviii.

37. Charleston *Free Press*, April 5, 1868; Reid, "U.S.C.T. Veterans in Post–Civil War North Carolina," 406; Holt, *Black over White*, 77–78; Walter J. Fraser, *Charleston! Charleston! The History of a Southern City* (Columbia, SC, 1990), 276; Foner, ed., *Freedom's Lawmakers*, 24, 226.

38. Walter B. Edgar, *South Carolina: A History* (Columbia, SC, 1998), 388; Trenton *Daily State Gazette*, May 9, 1870; Richard N. Current, *Those Terrible Carpetbaggers: A Reinterpretation* (New York, 1988), 142–43; Holt, *Black over White*, 68–69; Leigh Fought, *Southern Womanhood & Slavery: A Biography of Louisa S. McCord, 1810–1879* (Columbia, MO, 2003), 180; Du Bois, *Black Reconstruction*, 402–3; Michael Perman, *The Road to Redemption: Southern Politics, 1869–1879* (Chapel Hill, 1984), 40–41.

39. Charles Lane, *The Day Freedom Died: The Colfax Massacre, the Supreme Court, and the Betrayal of Reconstruction* (New York, 2008), 38; San Francisco *Elevator*, October 30, 1868; Richard Follett, "Legacies of Enslavement: Plantation Identities and the Problem of Freedom," in *Slavery's Ghost: The Problem of Freedom in the Age of Emancipation*, eds. Richard Follett, Eric Foner, and Walter Johnson (Baltimore, 2011), 63, observes that Warmoth "proved relatively conciliatory to the white upper classes." Fitzgerald, *Splendid Failure*, 129–30, incorrectly identifies Dunn as an "ex-slave."

40. Macon *Daily Telegraph*, January 18, 1870; Edmund L. Drago, *Black Politicians and Reconstruction in Georgia: A Splendid Failure* (Baton Rouge, 1982), 36–37, 68–69, 88.

41. Foner, *Reconstruction*, 364–65; Fitzgerald, *Splendid Failure*, 83–84; Crouch, "Self-Determination and Local Black Leaders in Texas," 346; *New-York Tribune*, March 27, 1867; *Charleston Advocate*, May 11, 1867.

42. Lane, *The Day Freedom Died*, 114; Joel Williamson, *After Slavery: The Negro in South Carolina During Reconstruction, 1861–1877* (Chapel Hill, 1965), 358–59; Langston, *Equality Before the Law*, 5.

43. Harris, *Day of the Carpetbagger*, 56; Delery, *Black Ghost of Radicalism*, 48–49; *New Orleans Tribune*, April 28, 1867; Macon *Daily Telegraph*, August 6, 1869.

44. Waldrep, *Roots of Disorder*, 114; New Orleans *Daily Picayune*, May 16, 1871.

45. *Cincinnati Commercial Tribune*, May 28, 1871; *Baltimore Sun*, July 27, 1871; *St. Albans Daily Messenger* (St. Albans, VT), July 21, 1871; New Orleans *Weekly Louisianian*, May 11, 1871.

46. Howard N. Rabinowitz, *Race Relations in the Urban South, 1865–1890* (New York, 1978), 182–83; Roger A. Fischer, "A Pioneer Protest: The New Orleans Streetcar Controversy of 1867," *JNH* 53 (1968): 220; Leon Litwack, *Been in the Storm So Long: The Aftermath of Slavery* (New York, 1979), 262; *Thirty-Third Annual Report of the Philadelphia Female Anti-Slavery Society* (Philadelphia, 1867), 25–26; Ira Berlin, *Generations of Captivity: A History of African-American Slaves* (New York, 2004), 267.

47. *New Orleans Tribune*, July 7, 1867 and October 29, 1867; P. B. S. Pinchback, Speech, January 4, 1869, in P. B. S. Pinchback Papers, Moorland-Springarn Research Center, Howard University; Langston, *Equality Before the Law*, 6; San Francisco *Elevator*, May 18, 1872; New Orleans *Weekly Louisianian*, March 21, 1868.

48. New York *World*, November 16, 1890, and Chillicothe *Scioto Gazette*, August 26, 1885, both in John Mercer Langston Collection, Moorland-Springarn Research Center, Howard University.

49. *New Orleans Tribune*, April 30, 1867 and May 1, 1867; Fischer, "New Orleans Streetcar Controversy," 223; Dray, *Capitol Men*, 105.

50. James M. McPherson, "Abolitionists and the Civil Rights Act of 1875," *Journal of American History* 52 (1965): 495; Davis, *"We Will Be Satisfied with Nothing Less,"* 15; Foner, *Reconstruction*, 471; Carla L. Peterson, *Black Gotham: A Family History of African Americans in Nineteenth-Century New York City* (New Haven, 2011), 191; Macon *Daily Telegraph*, May 23, 1871.

51. Rabinowitz, *Race Relations in the Urban South*, 184; Michael W. Fitzgerald, *The Union League Movement in the Deep South: Politics and Agricultural Change During Reconstruction* (Baton Rouge, 1989), 182–83; Dray, *Capitol Men*, 18–19; *New Orleans Tribune*, July 7, 1867; Washington Chavis to Blanche K. Bruce, February 6, 1879, in Bruce Papers, Moorland-Springarn Research Center, Howard University.

52. Masur, *An Example for All the Land*, 108; *Memphis Daily Avalanche*, January 2, 1866; New Orleans *Weekly Louisianian*, November 16, 1871; *Hartford Daily Courant*, January 1, 1866.

53. Leslie A. Schwalm, *Emancipation's Diaspora: Race and Reconstruction in the Upper Midwest* (Chapel Hill, 2009), 204–5; Kate Masur, "Patronage and Protest in Kate Brown's Washington," *Journal of American History* 99 (2013): 1061–64; New Orleans *Weekly Louisianian*, July 9, 1871; *Baltimore Sun*, May 19, 1871; *Cincinnati Enquirer*, May 25, 1871; Foner, ed., *Freedom's Lawmakers*, 42.

54. Hume and Gough, *Blacks, Carpetbaggers, and Scalawags*, 158; Du Bois, *Black Reconstruction*, 403; New Haven *Columbian Register*, October 29, 1879; *Galveston Tri-Weekly News*, October 31, 1870; *Cincinnati Daily Gazette*, November 18, 1870; New York *Commercial Advertiser*, December 5, 1870.

55. Cleveland *Plain Dealer*, December 14, 1870; Lamson, *Glorious Failure*, 176; Richard M. Valelly, *The Two Reconstructions: The Struggle for Black Enfranchisement* (Chicago, 2004), 78.

56. Dray, *Capitol Men*, 60–61; Donald, *Sumner*, 427; Washington *Critic-Record*, January 21, 1870; *New-Orleans Times*, January 21, 1870; *Cincinnati Daily Gazette*, March 17, 1875; *New-York Tribune*, February 26, 1870; *Philadelphia Inquirer*, November 30, 1870.

57. *Albany Journal*, February 17, 1871; *Alexandria Gazette*, January 31, 1870; *Leavenworth Bulletin*, July 26, 1870; O. H. Crandall to Adelbert Ames, April 2, 1870, in Ames Family Papers, Smith College Library; *Flake's Bulletin* (Galveston, TX), September 24, 1870.

58. Mitchell Snay, *Horace Greeley and the Politics of Reform in Nineteenth-Century America* (Lanham, MD, 2011), 176–77; Perman, *Road to Redemption*, 38–39; *Circular, Headquarters Sub-Executive Committee, Regular Republican Party of Louisiana, July, 1872*, in P. B. S. Pinchback Papers, Moorland-Springarn Research Center, Howard University; A. J. Jones to Adelbert Ames, March 21, 1872, in Ames Family Papers, Smith College Library; A. S. Morgan to Adelbert Ames, April 13, 1872, Ibid.; *Cincinnati Enquirer*, January 27, 1871.

59. McFeely, *Grant*, 382–83; Edward Billings, *The Struggle Between the Civilization of Slavery and That of Freedom, Recently and Now Going on in Louisiana* (Northampton, 1873), 21; *Boston Journal*, July 9, 1872; New Orleans *Daily Picayune*, July 17, 1872; (author unknown), *Grant or Greeley—Which? Facts and Arguments for the Consideration of Colored Citizens of the United States* (Harrisburg, 1872), 4–5.

60. P. B. S. Pinchback to U.S. Senate, 1875, in P. B. S. Pinchback Papers, Moorland-Springarn Research Center, Howard University; P. B. S. Pinchback, "The Great Rail Road Race," September, 1872, Ibid.; *New York Globe*, January 21, 1882; Unidentified Petersburg, Virginia, newspaper, December 18, 1874, in John Mercer Langston Collection, Moorland-Springarn Research Center, Howard University; *New York Times*, August 17, 1876.

61. (Author unknown), *Grant or Greeley*, 6; San Francisco *Elevator*, October 18, 1871; Litwack, *Been in the Storm So Long*, 534.

62. F. W. Kornman to Blanche K. Bruce, February 11, 1876, in Bruce Papers, Moorland-Springarn Research Center, Howard University.

Chapter Eight: "An Absolute Massacre"

1. William Dennis, Company Descriptive Book, July 11, 1864, Compiled Military Service Records of Volunteer Union Soldiers, U.S. Colored Troops, 45th USCT, Reel 77, NA; Adams County, Mississippi, 1870 federal census, page 181A, NA.

2. *Albany Evening Journal*, March 17, 1871; William Clopton, Company Descriptive Book, February 29, 1864, Compiled Military Service Records of Volunteer Union Soldiers, U.S. Colored Troops, 55th USCT, Reel 1657, NA; *New York Herald*, March 12, 1871.

3. *Albany Evening Journal*, March 17, 1871; *New York Herald*, March 12, 1871.

4. *Albany Evening Journal*, March 17, 1871; *New-Hampshire Patriot* (Concord, NH), March 15, 1871; *New York Herald*, March 12, 1871; Macon *Daily Telegraph*, March 14, 1871; Middletown *Daily Constitution* (CT), March 15, 1871; *Houston Daily Union*, March 16, 1871.

5. Camden County, New Jersey, 1870 federal census, Reel M593, page 272B, NA; *New York Herald*, February 4, 1871 and February 5, 1871; Trenton *Daily State Gazette*, January 18, February 3, and February 20, 1871, January 10, 1872.

6. LeeAnna Keith, *The Colfax Massacre: The Untold Story of Black Power, White Terror, and the Death of Reconstruction* (New York, 2008), 69; Philip Dray, *Capitol Men: The Epic Story of Reconstruction Through the Lives of the First Black Congressmen* (New York, 2010), 340; Paul Ortiz, *Emancipation Betrayed: The Hidden History of Black Organizing and White Violence in Florida from Reconstruction to the Bloody Election of 1920* (Berkeley, 2005), 24.

7. Franklin, *Reconstruction*, 154–55; Dray, *Capitol Men*, 80; Benjamin Butler, *The Negro in Politics: Review of Recent Legislation for His Protection* (Lowell, MA, 1871), 9.

8. Interview with Frances Andrews, in George Rawick, ed., *American Slave: South Carolina Narratives* (Westport, CT, 1972), 17; Claude H. Nolen, *African American Southerners in Slavery, Civil War, and Reconstruction* (Jefferson, 2001), 164; Mitchell Snay, *Fenians, Freedmen, and Southern Whites: Race and Nationality in the Era of Reconstruction* (Baton Rouge, 2007), 67–68; Sally E. Hadden, *Slave Patrols: Law and Violence in Virginia and the Carolinas* (Cambridge, 2001), 212–13; Horatio Ballard to Adelbert Ames, April 30, 1870, in Ames Family Papers, Smith College Library.

9. J. C. A. Stagg, "The Problem of Klan Violence: The South Carolina Up-Country, 1868–1871," *Journal of American Studies* 8 (1974): 306–7; *Wooster Republican* (Wooster, OH), December 8, 1870; Snay, *Feniens, Freedmen, and Southern Whites*, 60. George C. Rable, *But There Was No Peace: The Role of Violence in the Politics of Reconstruction* (Athens, GA, 1984), 68–69, argues that white violence itself did not end Reconstruction, which was already being abandoned by white Unionists. Although generally true, the elimination of hundreds of black registrars, poll workers, and black Republican candidates effectively ended progressive reform in pockets of the South.

10. Perman, "Counter Reconstruction: The Rise of Violence," in *The Facts of Reconstruction: Essays in Honor of John Hope Franklin*, eds. Eric Anderson and Alfred A. Moss Jr. (Baton Rouge, 1991), 132–33; *Wooster Republican* (Wooster, OH), December 8, 1870; E. J. Jacobson to Adelbert Ames, August 7, 1871, in Ames Family Papers, Smith College Library.

11. Dray, *Capitol Men*, 84–85; Charles Lane, *The Day Freedom Died: The Colfax Massacre, the Supreme Court, and the Betrayal of Reconstruction* (New York, 2008), 3; John. W. Alvord, *Letters from the South, Relating to the Condition of the Freedmen* (Washington, 1870), 22; Tunis Campbell, *Sufferings of the Rev. T. G. Campbell and His Family, in Georgia* (Washington, 1877), 11.

12. William Warner testimony, in *Testimony Taken By the Joint Select Committee to Inquire Into the Conditions of Affairs in the Late Insurrectionary States: Alabama*, 1: 26; Charles Stearns, *The Black Man of the South and the Rebels* (Boston, 1872), 219; W. B. Cunningham to Adelbert Ames, April 7, 1870, in Ames Family Papers, Smith College Library; William Atwood to Adelbert Ames, April 8, 1870, Ibid.; J. H. Morton to Adelbert Ames, April 21, 1870, Ibid.

13. *Boston Journal*, November 3, 1870; *Albany Evening Journal*, November 3, 1870; *New-York Tribune*, November 3, 1870; *Cincinnati Daily Gazette*, November 3, 1870; *Cincinnati Commercial Tribune*, November 3, 1870 and November 17, 1870; *Quincy Whig* (Quincy, IL), November 3, 1870.

14. Richard N. Current, *Those Terrible Carpetbaggers: A Reinterpretation* (New York, 1988), 228–29; Nelson, *Iron Confederates*, 126; Michael W. Fitzgerald, *The Union League Movement in the Deep South: Politics and Agricultural Change During Reconstruction* (Baton Rouge, 1989), 244.

15. Butler, *Negro in Politics*, 13; Steven Hahn, *A Nation Under Our Feet: Black Political Struggles in the Rural South from Slavery to the Great Migration* (Cambridge, 2003), 273, 276; Lane, *The Day Freedom Died*, 225; Maria Waterbury, *Seven Years Among the Freedmen* (Chicago, 1890), 24.

16. Alvord, *Letters From the South*, 35–36; Michael W. Fitzgerald, *Splendid Failure: Postwar Reconstruction in the American South* (Chicago, 2008), 69; Burton, "Race and Reconstruction," 37.

17. Martha Hodes, *White Women, Black Men: Illicit Sex in the Nineteenth-Century South* (New Haven, 1997), 154–55; Hyman Rubin, *South Carolina Scalawags* (Columbia, SC, 2006), 42–43; Scott French and Carol Sheriff, *A People at War: Civilians and Soldiers in America's Civil War*, 306–7; Gregg Cantrell, "Racial Violence and Reconstruction Politics in Texas," *Southwestern Historical Quarterly* 93 (1990): 350.

18. Rable, *But There Was No Peace*, 72–73; *Morning Oregonian* (Portland, OR), January 14, 1871; *Lowell Daily Citizen and News*, October 30, 1868; *St. Paul Daily Press*, October 29, 1868.

19. Albion W. Tourgée, *A Fool's Errand, By One of the Fools* (New York, 1879), 166; *Hartford Daily Courant*, May 8, 1871; New York *Morning Telegraph*, March 5, 1871; Deposition of Dike Michee, October 7, 1868, in Records of the Assistant Commissioner for the State of Mississippi, Freedmen's Bureau Papers, Reel 64, NA.

20. Eric Foner, *Reconstruction: America's Unfinished Revolution, 1863–1877* (New York, 1988), 442; Trenton *Daily State Gazette*, July 15, 1872; Fitzgerald, *Splendid Failure*, 94; McPherson, "Redemption or Counterrevolution," 549.

21. Richard H. Abbott, *For Free Press and Equal Rights: Republican Newspapers in the Reconstruction South* (Athens, GA, 2004), 146; Burton, "Race and Reconstruction," 41; interview with Brawley Gilmore, in Rawick, ed., *American Slave: South Carolina Narratives*, 121; Richard Zuczek, *State of Rebellion: Reconstruction in South Carolina* (Columbia, SC, 1996), 58–59.

22. Macon *Daily Telegraph*, June 21, 1870; San Francisco *Daily Evening Bulletin*, September 9, 1870; *Daily Columbus Enquirer*, March 14, 1871; Barry Crouch, "Self-Determination and Local Black Leaders in Texas," *Phylon* 39 (1978): 350.

23. Elaine Frantz Parsons, "Klan Skepticism and Denial in Reconstruction-Era Public Discourse," *JSH* 77 (2011): 58; William M. Barney, *Battleground for the Union: The Era of the Civil War and Reconstruction, 1848–1977* (New York, 1989), 291; Michael Perman, *The Road to Redemption: Southern Politics, 1869–1879* (Chapel Hill, 1984), 34–35, 64; San Francisco *Daily Evening Bulletin*, January 18, 1871.

24. Xi Wang, *The Trial of Democracy: Black Suffrage and Northern Republicans, 1860–1910* (Athens, GA, 1997), 57–58; Joan Waugh, *U.S. Grant: American Hero, American Myth* (Chapel Hill, 2009), 141; McFeely, *Grant*, 368–69; *Congressional Globe*, 41st Cong., 2nd

Sess., H.R. 1293; Parsons, "Klan Skepticism and Denial," 56–57; New York *Commercial Advertiser*, September 27, 1870.

25. New Orleans *Daily Picayune*, November 23, 1871; *Weekly Eastern Argus* (Portland, ME), June 29, 1871; Schweninger, *Rapier*, 104–5; *Cincinnati Enquirer*, May 10, 1871.

26. Campbell, *Sufferings*, 13; Christian G. Samito, *Becoming American Under Fire: Irish Americans, African Americans, and the Politics of Citizenship during the Civil War* (Ithaca, NY, 2009), Brooks D. Simpson, *The Reconstruction Presidents* (Lawrence, KS, 1998), 155; *Cincinnati Daily Gazette*, August 7, 1871.

27. McFeely, *Grant*, 367; Wang, *Trial of Democracy*, 96–97; Dray, *Capitol Men*, 98–99.

28. E. J. Jacobson to Adelbert Ames, July 25, 1871, in Ames Family Papers, Smith College Library; G. Wiley to Adelbert Ames, April 9, 1872, Ibid.; Lane, *The Day Freedom Died*, 4–5; *Address, the Convention of Colored People of the Southern States, Columbia, South Carolina, October 18, 1871*, in P. B. S. Pinchback Papers, Moorland-Springarn Research Center, Howard University; Everette Swinney, "Enforcing the Fifteenth Amendment, 1870–1877," *JSH* 28 (1962): 211.

29. Perman, "Counter Reconstruction," 130–31; Dray, *Capitol Men*, 215; San Francisco *Elevator*, October 31, 1874.

30. Macon *Daily Telegraph*, May 18, 1875, September 5, 1875; Russell Duncan, *Freedom's Shore: Tunis Campbell and the Georgia Freedman* (Athens, GA, 1986), 89–90, 99–101.

31. Duncan, *Freedom's Shore*, 91; Macon *Daily Telegraph*, August 22, 1871 and January 19, 1875.

32. Duncan, *Freedom's Shore*, 108–9; Campbell, *Sufferings*, 17, 23–25; Macon *Daily Telegraph*, September 1, 1875 and August 1, 1876.

33. Nicholas Lemann, *Redemption: The Last Battle of the Civil War* (New York, 2006), 24. Two modern accounts of the bloodbath are LeeAnna Keith, *The Colfax Massacre: The Untold Story of Black Power, White Terror, and the Death of Reconstruction* (New York, 2008), and Lane, *The Day Freedom Died*.

34. Lemann, *Redemption*, 25, 77–78; David Goldfield, *America Aflame: How the Civil War Created a Nation* (New York, 2011), 491; New York *Commercial Advertiser*, September 15, 1874; Melinda Meek Hennessey, "Racial Violence During Reconstruction: The 1876 Riots in Charleston and Cainhoy," *SCHM* 86 (1985): 100.

35. Rable, *But There Was No Peace*, 134–35; Hahn, *A Nation Under Our Feet*, 305; Lawrence O. Graham, *The Senator and the Socialite: The True Story of America's First Black Dynasty* (New York, 2006), 82; John Mercer Langston, *The Other Phase of Reconstruction* (Washington, 1877), 5.

36. Graham, *The Senator and the Socialite*, 68–69; Lemann, *Redemption*, 71–72, 144; Stephen Budiansky, *The Bloody Shirt: Terror After Appomattox* (New York, 2008), 192–93.

37. Hogue, *Uncivil War*, 152–53; Fitzgerald, *Splendid Failure*, 132, 179; Waugh, *Grant*, 150; Richardson, *Death of Reconstruction*, 100; Simpson, *Reconstruction Presidents*, 160; James A. Rawley, "The General Amnesty Act of 1872: A Note," *Mississippi Valley Historical Review* 47 (1960): 482.

38. McPherson, "Redemption or Counterrevolution?," 547; Barney, *Battleground for the*

Union, 321; Harris, *Day of the Carpetbagger*, 682–83; Bauman Morris to Blanche K. Bruce, February 14, 1876, in Bruce Papers, Moorland-Springarn Research Center, Howard University.

39. John Heart to Cynthia Everett, June 23, 1870, in Everett Papers, Newberry Library; Thomas Holt, *Black over White: Negro Political Leadership in South Carolina During Reconstruction* (Urbana, IL,1977), 203–4.

40. Ronald B. Jager, "Charles Sumner, the Constitution, and the Civil Rights Act," *New England Quarterly* 42 (1969): 362; David Donald, *Charles Sumner and the Rights of Man* (New York, 1970) 529–30; Washington *Critic-Record*, January 21, 1871; *New York Globe*, January 21, 1882; Dray, *Capitol Men*, 151–52.

41. Donald, *Sumner*, 517–18; Dray, *Capitol Men*, 154–55; Bertram Wyatt-Brown, "The Civil Rights Act of 1875," *Western Political Quarterly* 18 (1965): 763; Alfred H. Kelly, "Congressional Controversy Over School Segregation," *AHR* 64 (1959): 539.

42. *Circular, Convention of Colored Newspaper Men*, August 1875, in P. B. S. Pinchback Papers, Moorland-Springarn Research Center, Howard University; James McPherson, "Abolitionists and the Civil Rights Act of 1875," *JAH* 52 (1965): 496; New Orleans *Weekly Louisianian*, March 21, 1872; Petition to Adelbert Ames, April 21, 1872, in Ames Family Papers, Smith College Library; John A. Bryson to Blanche K. Bruce, February 17, 1876, in Bruce Papers, Moorland-Springarn Research Center, Howard University.

43. Lexington *American Citizen*, July 24, 1875; Perman, *Road to Redemption*, 140.

44. Alfred H. Kelly, "Congressional Controversy Over School Segregation," *AHR* 64 (1959): 552; *Congressional Record*, 43rd Cong., 1st Sess., 378–79, 407–8.

45. McPherson, "Abolitionists and the Civil Rights Act," 506; Stewart, *Phillips*, 306; Donald, *Sumner*, 586–87; Carla L. Peterson, *Black Gotham: A Family History of African Americans in Nineteenth-Century New York City* (New Haven, 2011), 279.

46. McPherson, "Abolitionists and the Civil Rights Act," 508; unidentified Petersburg, Virginia, newspaper clipping, December 19, 1874, in John Mercer Langston Collection, Moorland-Springarn Research Center, Howard University; P. B. S. Pinchback, Speech, June, 1874, in P. B. S. Pinchback Papers, Moorland-Springarn Research Center, Howard University; Circular, Convention of Colored Newspaper Men, August, 1875, Ibid.

47. Macon *Daily Telegraph*, March 9, 1875; McPherson, "Abolitionists and the Civil Rights Act," 509; McFeely, *Grant*, 418–19; Wyatt-Brown, "Civil Rights Act of 1875," 774.

48. Michael F. Holt, *By One Vote: The Disputed Presidential Election of 1876* (Lawrence, KS, 2008), 13; Ari Hoogenboom, *Rutherford B. Hayes: Warrior and President* (Lawrence, KS, 1995), 266; G. M. Buchanan to Blanche K. Bruce, February 14, 1876, in Bruce Papers, Moorland-Springarn Research Center, Howard University;

49. Rable, *But There Was No Peace*, 109; Hoogenboom, *Hayes*, 271; Dray, *Capitol Men*, 240–41; Macon *Daily Telegraph*, March 9, 1875.

50. Holt, *Black over White*, 199–200; Fitzgerald, *Splendid Failure*, 201–2; Dray, *Capitol Men*, 249–50.

51. Hoogenboom, *Hayes*, 270; Jefferson L. Edmonds to Blanche K. Bruce, July 18, 1876,

in Bruce Papers, Moorland-Springarn Research Center, Howard University; William M. Hancock to Blanche K. Bruce, August 6, 1876 and August 8,1876, Ibid.

52. S. G. Hubert to Blanche K. Bruce, April 5, 1876, in Bruce Papers, Moorland-Springarn Research Center, Howard University; W. H. Kennon to Blanche K. Bruce, October 7, 1877, Ibid.; J. G. Embry to Blanche K. Bruce, February 21, 1876, Ibid.

53. Hennessey, "Racial Violence During Reconstruction," 111; Mark M. Smith, "'All Is Not Quiet in Our Hellish Country': Facts, Fiction, Politics, and Race: The Ellenton Riot of 1876," *SCHM* 95 (1994): 151; Henry J. Hunt, Report, November 27, 1876, Department of the South and South Carolina, Part 5, Letters Sent, NA (I am grateful to Brian Kelly of Queen's University for sharing this document); Budiansky, *Bloody Shirt*, 248; Benjamin Leas to Blanche K. Bruce, September 1, 1877, in Bruce Papers, Moorland-Springarn Research Center, Howard University.

54. Hoogenboom, *Hayes*, 288; Roy Morris Jr., *Fraud of the Century: Rutherford B. Hayes, Samuel Tilden, and the Stolen Election of 1876* (New York, 2003), 72–73; Holt, *By One Vote*, 84.

55. William S. McFeely, *Frederick Douglass* (New York, 1991), 289; *Charleston Free Press*, April 5, 1875; *Knoxville Daily Journal*, November 1, 1888; Omaha *Morning World-Herald*, August 27, 1900; *New York Herald*, June 21, 1892; *Duluth Daily News*, March 2, 1888.

56. Richard M. Valelly, *The Two Reconstructions: The Struggle for Black Enfranchisement* (Chicago, 2004), 83; *Indianapolis News*, September 3, 1891.

57. James E. Bruce to Blanche K. Bruce, June 8, 1879, in Bruce Papers, Moorland-Springarn Research Center, Howard University; John Mercer Langston, *From the Virginia Plantation to the National Capitol* (Hartford, 1894), 351; *Newport Daily Observer*, September 24, 1891; *Circular, The President's Southern Policy: Letter of Hon. O.P. Morton*, in Pinchback Papers, Moorland-Springarn Research Center, Howard University; P. B. S. Pinchack to Doctor [no name], November 25, 1884, Ibid.

58. Frederick Douglass to George T. Downing, January 9, 1892, in Downing Papers, Moorland-Springarn Research Center, Howard University; Executive Committee to National Conference, February 22, 1879, in P. B. S. Pinchback Papers, Ibid.; P. B. S. Pinchback to Members of the National Executive of the American Citizen's Rights Association, February 24, 1890, Ibid.; P. B. S. Pinchback, An Appeal to the Governors, Legislators, and Judicial Officers of the Southern States, 1899, Ibid.

59. Dray, *Capitol Men*, 346–47; Benjamin R. Justesen, *George Henry White: An Even Chance in the Race of Life* (Baton Rouge, 2001), 270; unidentified Petersburg, Virginia, newspaper, January 24, 1891, in John Mercer Langston Collection, Moorland-Springarn Research Center, Howard University; unidentified Galesburg, Illinois, newspaper, June 21, 1892, Ibid.; *Indianapolis Sentinel*, September 4, 1891; Washington *Colored American*, July 22, 1893.

60. Graham, *The Senator and the Socialite*, 157–59; *Chicago Daily Tribune*, August 26, 1900; P. B. S. Pinchback, Speech, 1901, in P. B. S. Pinchback Papers, Moorland-Springarn Research Center, Howard University; Colored Citizens League, Resolutions, February 26, 1901, Ibid.

61. Graham, *The Senator and the Socialite*, 203; David Levering Lewis, *W.E.B. Du Bois: Biography of a Race* (New York, 1993), 262–63.

Chapter Nine: "We Shall Be Recognized As Men"

1. David Levering Lewis, *W.E.B. Du Bois: Biography of a Race* (New York, 1993), 11–22; on Jack Burghardt and Elizabeth Freeman, see my *Death or Liberty: African Americans and Revolutionary America* (New York, 2009), 170–74.
2. Manning Marable, *W.E.B. Du Bois: Black Radical Democrat* (Boston, 1986), 8–11.
3. W. E. B. Du Bois to Harvard University secretary, October 29, 1887, in *The Correspondence of W.E.B. Du Bois*, ed. Herbert Aptheker (Amherst, 1973), 1: 6; Marable, *Du Bois*, 17–22.
4. W. E. B. Du Bois to Booker T. Washington, July 27, 1894, in Aptheker, ed., *Correspondence of Du Bois*, 38; Lewis, *Du Bois: Biography of a Race*, 151, 226.
5. Lewis, *Du Bois: Biography of a Race*, 260; Booker T. Washington, *Up from Slavery: An Autobiography* (New York, 1901), 80; Booker T. Washington to W. E. B. Du Bois, July 15, 1902, in Aptheker, ed., *Correspondence of Du Bois*, 45; Benjamin R. Tillman to W. E. B. Du Bois, July 23, 1914, Ibid.; Kansas City *American Citizen*, November 17, 1905; Indianapolis *Freeman*, July 18, 1903; *Cleveland Gazette*, May 16, 1903.
6. Lewis, *Du Bois: Biography of a Race*, 316–17; Chicago *Broad Axe*, August 5, 1905; W. E. B. Du Bois to Archibald Grimké, August 13, 1905, in Aptheker, ed., *Correspondence of Du Bois*, 112–13; Du Bois initially planned to write a biography of Douglass, but the contract was instead offered to Washington. Aside from Brown, he also considered writing on Blanche K. Bruce. See W. E. B. Du Bois to Ellis Oberholter, January 30, 1904, Ibid.
7. Bowman, *At the Precipice*, 49–50; William C. Davis, *Jefferson Davis: The Man and His Hour* (New York, 1991), 676–79; Edward A. Pollard, *The Lost Cause: A New Southern History of the War of the Confederates* (New York, 1867), 49; Alexander H. Stephens, *A Constitutional View of the Late War Between the States* (Philadelphia, 1868).
8. Gaines M. Foster, *Ghosts of the Confederacy: Defeat, the Lost Cause, and the Emergence of the New South, 1865–1913* (New York, 1987), 116–17; Thomas J. Brown, "Civil War Remembrance as Reconstruction," in Brown, ed., *Reconstructions*, 212–13; Stephen Budiansky, *The Bloody Shirt: Terror After Appomattox* (New York, 2008), 269–70; Barbara Gannon, *The Won Cause: Black and White Comradeship in the Grand Army of the Republic* (Chapel Hill, 2011), 148; Janette Thomas Greenwood, *First Fruits of Freedom: The Migration of Former Slaves and Their Search for Equality in Worcester, Massachusetts, 1862–1900* (Chapel Hill, 2010), 146.
9. William A. Dunning, *Reconstruction, Political and Economic, 1865–1877* (New York, 1907), xv; John R. Lynch, "Some Historical Errors of James Ford Rhodes," *JNH* 2 (1917): 353; Franklin, *Race and History*, 265; Kennedy, *After Appomattox*, 9.
10. David Goldfield, *Still Fighting the Civil War: The American South and Southern History* (Baton Rouge, 2002), 21; James Battle Avirett, *The Old Plantation: How We Lived in Great House and Cabin Before the War* (New York, 1901), 193–94; David W. Blight, *Race and Reunion: The Civil War in American Memory* (Cambridge, MA, 2001), 112;

Bruce E. Baker, *What Reconstruction Meant: Historical Memory in the American South* (Charlottesville, 2007), 52–53.

11. Anthony Slide, *American Racist: The Life and Films of Thomas Dixon Jr.* (Lexington, 2004), 52; Maxwell Bloomfield, "Dixon's *The Leopard's Spots*: A Study in Popular Racism," *American Quarterly* 16 (1964): 387–88; Nina Silber, *The Romance of Reunion: Northerners and the South, 1865–1900* (Chapel Hill, 1993), 185–86; Merrill D. Peterson, *Lincoln in American Memory* (New York, 1994), 168–69; Blight, *Race and Reunion*, 111.

12. Bloomfield, "Dixon's *The Leopard's Spots*," 394–96; Nicholas Lemann, *Redemption: The Last Battle of the Civil War* (New York, 2006), 189–90; Thomas Dixon Jr., *The Clansman: An Historical Romance* (New York, 1905), 289, 322, 330, 334; Walter H. Page to W. E. B. Du Bois, November 27, 1905, in Aptheker, ed., *Correspondence of Du Bois*, 114.

13. John Roy Lynch, *The Facts of Reconstruction* (New York, 1913), 14; David Goldfield, *America Aflame: How the Civil War Created a Nation* (New York, 2011), 529; Lewis, *Du Bois: Biography of a Race*, 384–85; W. E. B. Du Bois, "Reconstruction and Its Benefits," *AHR* 15 (1910): 781–99.

14. Gary W. Gallagher, *Causes Won, Lost, and Forgotten: How Hollywood and Popular Art Shape What We Know About the Civil War* (Chapel Hill, 2008), 42–43; Kennedy, *After Appomattox*, 9; Blight, *Race and Reunion*, 395; Melvyn Stokes, *D.W. Griffith's The Birth of a Nation: A History of the Most Controversial Motion Picture of All Time* (New York, 2008), 23, 49, 150.

15. Arthur S. Link, *Wilson: The New Freedom* (Princeton, 1956), 252–53 and note 40; Peterson, *Lincoln in American Memory*, 170; Woodrow Wilson, *A History of the American People* (New York, 1903), 5: 46; Indianapolis *Freeman*, March 20, 1915; Chicago *Broad Axe*, June 5, 1915.

16. Lewis, *Du Bois: Biography of a Race*, 506–7; Franklin, *Race and History*, 17; St. Paul *Appeal*, May 8, 1915; Oakland *Western Outlook*, March 20, 1915.

17. Indianapolis *Freeman*, April 17, 1915; Cleveland *Gazette*, April 10, 1915 and April 24, 1915.

18. Cleveland *Gazette*, April 10, 1915 and June 5, 1915.

19. Lewis, *Du Bois: Biography of a Race*, 509; St. Paul *Appeal*, July 3, 1920; Chicago *Broad Axe*, January 17, 1920.

20. Foner, "Reconstruction Revisited," 82; Bernard A. Weisberger, "The Dark and Bloody Ground of Reconstruction Historiography," *JSH* 25 (1959): 428; Bowen, *Andrew Jackson and the Negro*, 157–58; Peter Sehlinger and Holman Hamilton, *Spokesman for Democracy: Claude G. Bowers, 1878–1958* (Indianapolis, 2000), 120; Anna Julia Cooper to W. E. B. Du Bois, December 31, 1929, in Aptheker, ed., *Correspondence of Du Bois*, 411.

21. David Levering Lewis, *W.E.B. Du Bois: The Fight for Equality and the American Century, 1919-1963* (New York, 2000), 359; W. E. B. Du Bois to Franklin Hooper, February 14, 1929, in Aptheker, ed., *Correspondence of Du Bois*, 390–91; Franklin Hooper to W. E. B. Du Bois, February 19, 1929, Ibid., 393; W. E. B. Du Bois to Franklin Hooper, March 4, 1829, Ibid., 399.

22. Albert Evander Coleman, *The Romantic Adventures of Rosy, the Octoroon: With Some Account of the Persecution of the Southern Negroes During the Reconstruction Period* (New York, 1929); Kansas City *Plaindealer*, May 8, 1931; Howard W. Odum, *Cold Blue Moon, Black Ulysses Afar Off* (New York, 1931); Kansas City *Wyandotte Echo*, July 3, 1931.

23. Baker, *What Reconstruction Meant*, 114; Kansas City *Plaindealer*, September 7, 1934 and July 19, 1935; Chicago *Spokesman*, March 4, 1933; *Our Colored Missions* (New York), May 1, 1930.

24. George Fort Milton, *The Age of Hate: Andrew Johnson and the Radicals* (New York, 1930), 262–64; Alfred Harcourt to W. E. B. Du Bois, September 11, 1931, in Aptheker, ed., *Correspondence of Du Bois*, 442–43; W. E. B. Du Bois to Alfred Harcourt, September 23, 1931, Ibid., 443; Baker, *What Reconstruction Meant*, 125.

25. W. E. B. Du Bois, *Black Reconstruction, 1860–1880* (New York, 1999 ed.), 717–27.

26. Lewis, *Du Bois: Fight for Equality*, 365–66; Marable, *Du Bois*, 146–47.

27. Marable, *Du Bois*, 147; Wichita *Negro Star*, February 21, 1936; Kansas City *Plaindealer*, June 7 and July 5, 1935.

28. Goldfield, *Still Fighting the Civil War*, 26; Darden Asbury Pyron, *Southern Daughter: The Life of Margaret Mitchell* (New York, 1991), 85; Kenneth M. Stampp, *The Era of Reconstruction, 1865–1877* (New York, 1966), 156–57; Kansas City *Plaindealer*, May 15, 1937.

29. Pyron, *Southern Daughter*, 311; Kansas City *Plaindealer*, March 5, 1937.

30. *Cleveland Gazette*, May 29, 1837; Elizabeth Young, "Here Comes the Bride: Wedding, Gender, and Race," in *The Horror Reader*, ed. Ken Gelder (New York, 2000), 138; Gallagher, *Causes Won, Lost, and Forgotten*, 29; Wichita *Negro Star*, February 23, 1940.

31. Steven Watts, *The Magic Kingdom: Walt Disney and the American Way of Life* (Boston, 1997), 279; Wichita *Negro Star*, December 6, 1946 and January 24, 1947; Little Rock *Arkansas State Gazette*, January 17, 1947.

32. Thomas Cripps, *Making Movies Black: The Hollywood Message Movie from World War II to the Civil Rights Era* (New York, 1993), 166; Little Rock *Arkansas State Gazette*, March 14, 1947; Kansas City *Plaindealer*, July 23, 1948.

33. Fred A. Bailey, "E. Merton Coulter," in *Reading Southern History: Essays on Interpreters and Interpretations*, ed. Glenn Feldman (Tuscaloosa, 2001), 32–33; E. Merton Coulter, *The South During Reconstruction, 1861–1877* (Baton Rouge, 1947), xi, 147; Weisberger, "Dark and Bloody Ground," 434–36; John Hope Franklin, "Whither Reconstruction Historiography," *Journal of Negro Education* 17 (1948): 446–61; Thomas A. Bailey, *The American Pageant: A History of the Republic* (Boston, 1956), 467–74.

34. Lemann, *Redemption*, 206–7; John F. Kennedy, *Profiles in Courage* (New York, 1956), 161; Herbert S. Parmet, *Jack: The Struggles of John F. Kennedy* (New York, 1980), 298.

35. Franklin, *Race and History*, 290; Franklin, *Reconstruction*, 93–94, 59, 236.

36. Reviews by Hans L. Trefousse, *AHR* 67 (1962): 745–46; Alan Conway, *English Historical Review* 78 (1962): 811–12; Edgar A. Toppin, *JNH* 47 (1962): 57–59; and Avery Craven, *JSH* 28 (1926): 255–56.

37. Lewis, *Du Bois: Fight for Equality*, 559; Stephen B. Oates, *Let the Trumpet Sound: The Life of Martin Luther King Jr.* (New York, 1982), 263.

38. *New York Times*, June 22, 1976.

Epilogue: The Spirit of Freedom Monument

1. Francis Lewis Cardozo, *Address Before the Grand Council of the Union Leagues at Their Annual Meeting* (Columbia, SC, 1870), 10–11.

2. *Circular, The President's Southern Policy: Letter of Hon. O.P. Morton*, in Pinchback Papers, Moorland-Springarn Research Center, Howard University.

3. "North Carolina City Confronts Its Past in Report on White Vigilantes," *New York Times*, December 19, 2005.

4. Gary W. Gallagher makes this point about Longstreet's fictional dialogue in *Causes Won, Lost, and Forgotten: How Hollywood and Popular Art Shape What We Know about the Civil War* (Chapel Hill, 2008), 57.

5. "'Day Lincoln Was Shot' Is Simply Assassinine," *New York Daily News*, April 10, 1998; "Foster, Gere Put Heart into Summersby," *Orlando Sentinel*, February 5, 1993. Respected Lincoln scholar Harold Holzer, "What's True and False in 'Lincoln' Movie," *The Daily Beast*, November 22, 2012, praised Spielberg's depiction of Stevens as accurate but also referred to Lydia Smith as the congressman's "African American mistress." Under Pennsylvania law, of course, Smith and Stevens could not legally marry.

6. Reviews on Amazon.com by John Blangero, September 5, 2010; G. F. Gori, August 7, 2004; Joaquin Hawkins, May 3, 2012; Gregory M. Kay, July 29, 2009.

7. Review on Amazon.com by William H. Losch, April 22, 2011; Thomas DiLorenzo, *The Real Lincoln: A New Look at Abraham Lincoln, His Agenda, and an Unnecessary War* (Seattle, 2002), 118; "McDonnell's Confederate History Month Proclamation Irks Civil Rights Leaders," *Washington Post*, April 7, 2010; "Virginia 4th-grade Textbook Criticized Over Claims on Black Confederate Soldiers," *Washington Post*, October 20, 2010.

8. "Bust of Civil War General Stirs Anger in Alabama," *New York Times*, August 24, 2012; Billy E. Price to editor, *Birmingham News*, August 28, 2012; (author unknown), *Is the South Ready for Restoration*, 20. A similar fight ensued in Memphis in 2013 when the city council voted to rename Forrest Park, a move that led to staged protests by the Ku Klux Klan and the Sons of Confederate Veterans. See Kevin M. Levin, "The Ku Klux Klan Protests as Memphis Renames City Park," *The Atlantic*, February 28, 2013.

9. "Former S.C. Slave's Legacy Disputed," *USA Today*, November 20, 2007; Blain Roberts and Ethan J. Kytle, "Looking the Thing in the Face: Slavery, Race, and the Commemorative Landscape in Charleston, South Carolina, 1865–2010," *JSH* 78 (2012): 680.

10. Roberts and Kytle, "Looking the Thing in the Face," 680; C. Gail Jarvis to editor, Charleston *Post and Courier*, July 1, 2000; Charleston *City Paper*, April 26, 2006.

11. Roberts and Kytle, "Looking the Thing in the Face," 677–78; Charleston *Post and Courier*, January 30, 2010 and February 2, 2010.

12. Michael Trouche to editor, Charleston *Post and Courier*, February 24, 2004; "Vesey Evokes Honor, Horror," Ibid., March 8, 2010.

13. Michael Trouche to editor, Charleston *Post and Courier*, February 19, 2010; Postings online at www.postandcourier.com, February 15, 2010.

14. Roberts and Kytle, "Looking the Thing in the Face," 681 and note 170; "Civil War Is Nothing to Celebrate," Charleston *Post and Courier*, April 25, 2011.

15. For Vesey's decision not to emigrate, see my *He Shall Go Out Free*, 121–22.

Douglas R. Egerton is a professor of history at Le Moyne College. He is the author of six books, including *Year of Meteors: Stephen Douglas, Abraham Lincoln, and the Election That Brought on the Civil War, He Shall Go Out Free: The Lives of Denmark Vesey, Gabriel's Rebellion: The Virginia Slave Conspiracies of 1800 and 1802,* and *Death or Liberty: African Americans and Revolutionary America.* He has also written numerous essays and reviews regarding race in early America, some of which have appeared in the *Boston Sunday Globe* and the *Nation,* and he also appeared on the PBS series *Africans in America* (1998) and *This Far by Faith* (2002). He lives near Syracuse, New York.